Los ROMEROS

MUSIC IN AMERICAN LIFE

A list of books in the series appears at the end of this book.

Los Romeros

Royal Family of the Spanish Guitar

Walter Aaron Clark

UNIVERSITY OF
ILLINOIS PRESS
Urbana, Chicago, and Springfield

Publication of this book is supported by the Donna Cardamone Jackson Endowment of the American Musicological Society, funded in part by the National Endowment for the Humanities and the Andrew W. Mellon Foundation, and by the University of California, Riverside.

© 2018 by the Board of Trustees
of the University of Illinois
All rights reserved
Manufactured in the United States of America
1 2 3 4 5 C P 5 4 3 2 1
♾ This book is printed on acid-free paper.

Library of Congress Cataloging-in-Publication Data
Names: Clark, Walter Aaron, author.
Title: Los Romeros : royal family of the Spanish guitar / Walter Aaron Clark.
Description: Urbana : University of Illinois Press, 2018. | Series: Music in American life | Includes bibliographical references and index.
Identifiers: LCCN 2018007558 | ISBN 9780252041907 (hardcover : alk. paper) | ISBN 9780252083563 (pbk. : alk. paper)
Subjects: LCSH: Romeros. | Romero, Celedonio. | Romero, Pepe. | Romero, Celín. | Romero, Angel. | Guitarists—United States—Biography.
Classification: LCC ML421.R65 C53 2018 | DDC 787.87092/246 [b]—dc23
LC record available at https://lccn.loc.gov/2018007558

Frontispiece: The Romero family in Santa Barbara in 1963, six years after their arrival in the United States (from left to right in front, Celedonio, Celin, and Angelita; from left to right behind, Angel and Pepe)

*Dedicated to the memory of Manolito Pinazo
and all innocent victims of political
and religious violence*

Be like the nightingale, which looks not at the ground from the green branch where it sings.
[Sé como el ruiseñor, que no mira a la tierra desde la rama verde donde canta.]

—Ramón del Valle-Inclán, *La lámpara maravillosa*

CONTENTS

Foreword by Jesús López Cobos, Sir Neville Marriner, Federico Moreno-Torroba Larregla, and Cecilia Rodrigo   xi

Introduction   1

PART 1. SOUTHERN SPAIN

Chapter 1   From Málaga's Mountains   13

Chapter 2   Cuba, qué linda es Cuba   21

Chapter 3   The City of Paradise, Regained   27

Chapter 4   Seville and Adiós   58

PART 2. SOUTHERN CALIFORNIA

Chapter 5   Santa Barbara   73

Chapter 6   Hollywood   94

Chapter 7   Del Mar   115

Chapter 8   The World   121

Intermission: Photo Gallery   128

PART 3. PROFILES

Chapter 9   Celedonio and Angelita, the Poet and His Muse   153

Chapter 10   Celin, the Romantic   163

Chapter 11   Pepe, the Philosopher   168

Chapter 12   Angel, the Proteus   176

PART 4. LEGACY

Chapter 13   The Romero Technique   193

Chapter 14   The Romero Repertoire   215

Chapter 15   Breakin' Up Is Hard to Do   248

Chapter 16   The Next Generations   256

Encore   271

Appendixes

1. Chronology   275
2. Romero Genealogy   278
3. List of Albums   285
4. Sources and Publications   297

Notes   301

Glossary of Names and Terms   323

Selected Bibliography   329

Index   333

FOREWORD

Celedonio Romero and his family belong to a generation that, in the years following the Spanish Civil War, fled the cultural desert of the Franco regime, especially in regards to music. Along with the many other expatriates among whom I found myself, we had to open roads distant from Spain, but thanks also to this exile we could carry our art to the world and collaborate in creating an image of Spain that did not consist solely of bullfights and flamenco. Like Segovia before them, the Romeros rescued the guitar from the ghetto of flamenco in order to internationalize it and make it one of the most beloved instruments in the world.

I met the Romeros during my first trip to California in the 1970s, and since that time I have continued to collaborate with them, both as a quartet (the original quartet and, after the father's death, in its present configuration) and also on numerous occasions with Pepe and Angel.

I always admire their flawless technique, their marvelous sense of color, and also their quest to enlarge the repertoire of their instrument by commissioning works from composers such as Leonardo Balada, Lorenzo Palomo, and others. Above all, I have been deeply impressed by their love for the guitar. To see Los Romeros play is to witness them making love to

FOREWORD

an instrument that, in their hands, is transformed into the most beautiful human voice.

Jesús López Cobos
Lausanne, Switzerland

II

Perhaps one of the careful considerations before working with an artist one admires is the possibility of a common taste in repertoire. Before I met Pepe Romero in 1970, my acquaintance with the guitar was minimal—soon to be challenged by his extraordinary talent and enthusiasm for the instrument and its history.

After my introduction to the works of Giuliani and Rodrigo, I was introduced to the rest of the Romero family, Angel, Celedonio, and Celin, and to Torroba, Villa-Lobos, Castelnuovo-Tedesco, Carulli, Molino, and composers of ensemble works for this immensely gifted family.

For the protraction of my musical education and the great pleasure of their company, I am truly grateful to the family Romero.

Sir Neville Marriner
London

III

It brings me great satisfaction to contribute a portrait of the Romeros, given the affection, love, and close friendship I share with them, and because of the important role they have played in the life of the Torroba family.

In the late 1960s, my father and I frequently visited the unforgettable Andrés Segovia, a lifelong friend. During one such visit, Segovia told my father that he should get in touch with a family of Andalusian guitarists living in California. They were called Los Romeros and had formed a quartet consisting of the father and his three sons. As soon as our visit ended, we began to think how we could contact the Romeros, but that proved unnecessary because the Romeros contacted us! I'm not sure now, but I think it was Celedonio who wrote to my father, requesting a large-scale work for guitar quartet and orchestra. This was the birth of the *Concierto ibérico*.

FOREWORD

In the event, my father soon became fully aware of what Segovia had described so perfectly about the Romeros, and he then traveled to the United States to meet them and attend one of their concerts. They were authentic virtuosos. Over time, our relationship with the Romeros ripened into something more than a friendship; they became family. Although we are talking about the Romero guitarists, I do not want to fail to mention Angelita Romero, Celedonio's wife, who loved to play the castanets and who greatly enjoyed performing with the quartet.

I could say so much more about Los Romeros, in terms of our professional collaborations as well as our friendship. We have been together for many years and shared many pleasant times, which I can never forget.

Federico Moreno-Torroba Larregla
Santesteban, Navarra

IV

The relationship between Joaquín Rodrigo and the Romeros began on June 30, 1966, when the composer received a letter from Celedonio Romero telling of the guitar quartet he had founded with his three sons and of their brilliant international career as soloists. The letter finished with the request that had prompted it, saying: "Great orchestras of international stature are asking us to play a Spanish concerto, and there is no one better than you, Sr. Rodrigo, to write this concerto, for you are the summit and glory of the world."[1] That letter did not leave the composer indifferent. The Romeros premiered *Concierto andaluz* on November 18, 1967.

Thus began a relationship between the composer and the Romeros, which I would qualify as unique since it has enriched the universal guitar repertoire. This repertoire, magnificently performed by the Romeros, contributed to the triumphant entry of the guitar to the world's greatest concert halls. I underline that of the five concertos my father wrote for the guitar as solo instrument, three were premiered in the United States by the Romeros.

Over a period of forty years, our two families maintained a close personal friendship, bringing me to feel part of the Romero family. Outstanding moments in Joaquín Rodrigo's life were related to the Romeros. Considered by my parents as a highlight was the honorary doctorate degree that my father received from the University of Southern California, for which Pepe

FOREWORD

nominated him. Another was the premiere of *Concierto madrigal*, at the Hollywood Bowl in 1970, by Pepe and Angel, with Rafael Frühbeck de Burgos as conductor.

In my own personal and professional life, certain events are engraved in my memory, such as the premiere of *Concierto para una fiesta* in Fort Worth, by Pepe, at the McKay family's concert party; the premiere in Los Angeles of *Serenata al alba del día*, by Pepe and my husband, violinist Agustín León Ara; the presentation of *Concierto andaluz* in the framework of the World Expo 1992 in Seville with a long-lasting ovation on flamenco beats. Also the various concerts in which the violin *Concierto de estío*, performed by Agustín, was programmed with a concerto performed by one or more of the Romeros, in particular the Rodrigo Festival in 1986 in London, which my parents attended as well.

The filming of the documentary *Shadows and Light: Joaquín Rodrigo at 90*, featuring Pepe, is unforgettable. But the most moving was Pepe's visit to our home in Brussels in June 1983 to rehearse *Concierto para una fiesta* prior to the first recording, in the presence of the composer, who was recovering with us from a serious illness. To Pepe's complaints about the technical difficulties of the work, the maestro exclaimed, "Pepe, I wrote it for you. You just have to work on it." After Pepe's brilliant performance, with my father repeatedly cheering him on with "Olé," he gave him a big hug, saying, "Bravo, Pepe, it went really well!"[2]

It is a special coincidence that between 1996 and 1999 our parents passed away. Pepe attended the burial of my father at the cemetery of Aranjuez. On the professional side, all the Rodrigo recordings by the Romeros are considered landmarks. The guitar publications by Ediciones Joaquín Rodrigo are revised and have fingerings by either Pepe or Angel.

It is indeed a pleasure to recall forty years of close friendship and artistic collaboration with the Romeros. They are unparalleled in the world as they constitute a saga of great guitarists, now into the third generation.

Bravo for Los Romeros!

Cecilia Rodrigo
Madrid

Los Romeros

INTRODUCTION

> When I laugh, it laughs.
> When I cry, it cries.
> And that is because its words
> Are like those of love
> And reach the soul.
> [Cuando yo río, ríe.
> Cuando yo lloro, llora.
> Y es que sus palabras
> Son como de amores
> Y llegan al alma.]
> —Celedonio Romero, from "La guitarra es mi vida"

As I enter his living room, Pepe Romero is sitting in a large leather easy chair, intent on the sounds he elicits from an exquisitely crafted guitar made especially for him by his son, Pepe Jr., affectionately known as "Little" Pepe. Afternoon sunlight streams across the glistening expanse of the Pacific Ocean and through a large window next to where Pepe is seated, casting his face in a dramatic play of light and shade. This chiaroscuro seems to mimic the tones he draws out of the instrument, contrasting dusky bass notes with brilliant shafts of melodic luminescence in the upper register. Nearby photographic portraits of his late father and mother, Celedonio and Angelita, overlook the scene with beaming approbation.

In mid-phrase Pepe's cell phone rings, a frequent occurrence at this Romero home in Del Mar, a northern seaside suburb of San Diego in

INTRODUCTION

Southern California. Indeed, ring tones jangle, and family, friends, and students arrive and depart in a steady rhythm throughout the day. His intense concentration can readily shut out such distractions, but this time Pepe suspends his musical rapture to take the call. Reluctant to set the guitar aside, he instead tilts it upright on his right leg, so that he can support it with his right hand while holding the phone in his left. (Though naturally left-handed, he plays the guitar in the traditional manner, plucking the strings with the fingers of his right hand.) Despite being engrossed in an animated conversation, he continues to move his thumb in a circular motion across the bass strings, unconsciously but with obvious sensitivity to the volume and texture of each string. Repeating movements he has made literally millions of times, he caresses each string with sure-footed awareness, with an agility and precision that are hallmarks of the Romero style.

In that brief moment, one perceives Pepe's continuous absorption not just in the guitar but also in musical sound itself, activated by neurological processes connecting the heart and mind to the strings of the guitar through the medium of the arms, hands, and fingers. A passage from Walt Whitman's stirring poem *Song of Myself* springs to mind, in which the poet declares that "the narrowest hinge in my hand puts to scorn all machinery." Though indeed complex beyond normal human comprehension, this manual "machinery" is nonetheless mastered through visualization and aural memory, appearing entirely natural, even effortless, when Pepe plays. Only those who have attempted to replicate what he does truly understand how much effort is required to achieve such apparent effortlessness.[1]

Strewn across the domestic landscape of the Romero abode are numerous classical and flamenco guitars, all of them acoustic instruments with six strings made of nylon and metal thread. Each is a valuable creation by a celebrated builder; indeed, some of them are antiques, though most are less than half a century old. Little Pepe's instruments are well represented here and enjoy pride of place on the couches, chairs, tabletops, and other open spaces that will accommodate a guitar. Competing for this real estate is music, some of it printed and much of it in manuscript. To the casual observer, this may seem a fairly chaotic way to organize one's musical affairs, but there is a method to the madness.

For instance, here is a guitar part from a work by the American composer Morton Gould written specifically for the Romero Quartet. That will be

INTRODUCTION

rehearsed later and will remain right where it is and belongs. Over there is Federico Moreno Torroba's *Sonatina*, a warhorse in the solo-guitar repertoire and a specialty of the Romeros, who were close friends of the Spanish composer. Pepe's eldest brother, Celin, will be performing that at an upcoming concert, and as if on cue, he now saunters into a nearby room, picks up the guitar lying alongside the music, and begins carefully negotiating its many tricky passages, with a deliberate focus on contrapuntal detail. He has played this piece for decades, but he knows that the *Sonatina* is a demanding taskmaster and requires regular attention. Neglecting it now would produce calamitous consequences on stage later, regardless of their long acquaintance.[2]

Celin shares this abode with Pepe, but his relaxed, right-at-home demeanor is deceptive and barely conceals a strong will harnessed to an appetite for hard work; indeed, his systematic preparation is another Romero hallmark. For all the inspiration in the world will avail even a great guitarist little if the mind and the mechanism have not been adequately prepared for the rigors of performing in front of hundreds or thousands of people or on television before millions. The psychophysiology of successful performance is refined through disciplined training, repeated experience, and one-pointed concentration on the task at hand. It is the secret of the Romeros' success, something Celin learned from his father, who then delegated him to pass it on to his brothers.

Doors remain open to facilitate communication, but this also facilitates a certain cacophony as the *Sonatina* competes with Pepe's flamenco outpourings, on this occasion a spirited *guajira* composed by Celedonio. After an hour or so of solo practice, Celin's son Celino and brother Angel's son Lito show up to rehearse the quartet's repertoire. Their fingers move with the same relaxed celerity and precision that characterized their grandfather's playing, producing the same mellifluous tones.

After two hours, the rehearsal is finally over. Just as Celino and Lito are about to return home to their waiting families, from the doorway downstairs comes a booming tenor voice that resounds like the "Hallelujah Chorus," and everyone knows it's Angel, whose boundless energy and charisma fill up any space he occupies. After ascending the stairs, he proceeds to regale everyone with tales of his latest triumphs and impending exploits, not only as a guitarist but also as an arranger, composer, and conductor.

INTRODUCTION

The three brothers are now joined by their respective life companions, Nefy (Angel), Claudia (Celin), and Carissa (Pepe). It is no exaggeration to assert that these three are the glue that holds the Romero family together. They provide the considerable domestic and logistical support three demanding concert careers require. In addition, however, each has her own particular artistic and professional identity: Nefy is a talented soprano and mother to Angel's appropriately named daughter Bella; Claudia is a gifted guitarist as well as a college music professor with a doctorate in administration; Carissa has a degree in health sciences and is both a skillful guitarist and a captivating flamenco dancer. Thus they easily hold their own when the discussion inevitably lapses into guitar talk, for example, the ideal neck length (what works best for a particular hand) and wood (Celin prefers spruce because of it clarity). The women begin to lose interest only when the subject of soccer comes up, as invariably it does. At any rate, the Romero residence is a sort of Tower of Babel where conversations move in and out of American English, Andalusian Spanish, and even *Hochdeutsch* (Claudia is from northern Germany).

Spotting a new guitar made by Pepe's grandson Bernardo, Angel uses it to demonstrate his recent transcription of *Rumores de La Caleta*, a *malagueña* by piano composer Isaac Albéniz, for whose music Angel exhibits a special affinity. The ensuing rendition demonstrates not only technical mastery but also a remarkable subtlety and nuance in phrasing and tone production. Especially admirable is his scrupulous attention to the composer's original intentions in terms of rhythm and harmony. Angel is a perfectionist and doesn't perform a work until it is firmly lodged in his fingers, as this piece now clearly is. Though one understands intellectually how difficult a feat this is, for Angel it is as natural a thing to do as, well, smoking a cigar, which the Romero brothers proceed to do on the adjacent patio.

This pleasant locale overlooks the Pacific and offers a commanding view of now wine-dark waters, as well as majestic palm trees silhouetted against a turquoise and tangerine sunset—just the sort of thing one gets used to in Southern California beach communities but tries never to take for granted. Indeed, life could be a lot worse than this, and lurking in the Romeros' collective memory is the realization that it once was. Much worse.

* * *

INTRODUCTION

This book explores in depth the Romero family's singular devotion to and particular genius for making music. Rising from poverty and obscurity in Málaga during the 1930s and 1940s, Celedonio and his three sons, Celin, Pepe, and Angel, came to prominence in the world of classical guitar in the latter half of the 1900s. Through their concert appearances, recordings, compositions, arrangements, revivals, commissioning of new music, and especially their teaching, they have played a major role in shaping the history of their instrument. Theirs is a living legacy of Spanish music.

This is my fourth biography of Spanish musicians, each volume representing the first such study in the English language. It rounds out a survey of 150 years of Spanish music, from the birth of Albéniz in 1860 (d. 1909) to the year 2010, in which work on this book began in earnest. This survey spans not only time but also space, from the northern to southern extents of Spanish music making. Albéniz, of Basque and Catalan descent, spent most of his adult life outside Spain, first in London and then Paris. Enrique Granados (1867–1916) was ethnically Castilian but was born and raised in Catalonia, and he spent his entire career in Barcelona. Moreno Torroba (1891–1982) was a *madrileño* through and through, and though he enjoyed spending time in Navarra, his life and music primarily reflected the culture of Madrid, where he was born and died. Now, at last, I have reached the southern extremity of the geographical arc, as the subjects of this book are Andalusian to their core. (I am currently researching a final biography, on Joaquín Rodrigo, which takes me to the delightful region of Valencia.)

This commitment of over a quarter century to researching and writing about Spanish musicians constitutes an affirmation of my growing conviction that the best way to comprehend this history is to examine in depth the lives of those who made it. Of course, the story I am about to tell is unique among those cited above because it presents not only a history of Spain's music but also that of the United States. In fact, the Romeros have woven the threads of their Spanish musical heritage very deeply into America's cultural tapestry. That reality is one of the main reasons for my early exposure and lifelong dedication to studying Spanish music.

Already in 1966, at age fourteen, I was smitten with the stirring sounds of flamenco guitar and undertook formal study of it, as well as of the classical repertoire. My studies followed a circuitous route but eventually led me to take my first lesson with Pepe in January 1976, just after completing a bachelor's

INTRODUCTION

degree in guitar performance at the University of North Carolina's School of the Performing Arts, where I performed in a master class with Andrés Segovia. In 1982, I enrolled in the master's program at the University of California, San Diego (UCSD), to study with both Pepe and Celin, and received my degree two years later. A Fulbright grant in West Germany to study early music with lutenist Jürgen Hübscher and then doctoral studies in musicology with the legendary Hispanist Robert Stevenson at UCLA led me down a new career path. I subsequently taught at the University of Kansas for a decade, before taking up a position at the University of California, Riverside (UCR), in 2003. Throughout all of this, I remained in touch with the Romeros, who live only an hour from my home in Murrieta. Ready access to their family archive (see appendix 4) and a deepening of our friendship, founded on a mutual love of Spanish music and culture, inspired me to undertake this project.

It gradually dawned on me during the course of this research that my first exposure to Spanish guitar was the Romeros' appearance on popular television programs of the 1960s, such as the *Tonight Show* and *Ed Sullivan*. They were part of a larger wave of Spanish music that inundated the United States during the 1960s and 1970s and included Carlos Montoya, Sabicas, and Andrés Segovia, among many others. And this Hispanophilia was part of a long-standing "Latin tinge" in American culture, exemplified by a persistent fascination with songs and dances like the tango, samba, mambo, bolero, and bossa nova, as well as by the artistry of musicians like Xavier Cugat, Antonio Carlos Jobim, and Tito Puente.[3] The Romeros' stirring renditions of *malagueñas* and *sevillanas*, along with the Spanish classics, was of a piece with this trend, insofar as Spanish music has often been subsumed under the "Latin" rubric.

The present volume is different from the others I have authored in one important respect: most of the subjects are still alive and active. In many ways it is easier to write about someone who is no longer among the living; it is certainly easier to write about one person and not an entire family. Albéniz and Granados both died just short of their forty-ninth birthdays. Torroba lived and remained productive to the ripe old age of ninety-one. But the history of the Romeros extends over a century and involves a whole cast of characters. I hasten to add, however, that this is not an "authorized" biography, as the Romeros have neither supervised nor attempted to monitor the preparation of my manuscript or to exert editorial control in any

INTRODUCTION

way. In fact, they early on said they did not need to see it before it went to press. I did show it to them just the same, in order to catch any mistakes or fill in any lacunae, but this book presents my personal assessment of their importance in the musical and cultural history of the past several decades. The book's subtitle was also the title of their first quartet album, in 1963. Fifty-five years later, it is still a valid summary of their achievements.

A few editorial notes are in order. The rules of stress in Spanish require acute accents in names like Ángel and Celín. However, the Romeros have become every bit as much American as they are Spanish, and over many years it has been standard editorial practice to write their names sans accents, that is, Angel and Celin (though one pronounces these names in a Spanish fashion, i.e., AHN-hel and say-LEEN). I adhere to that practice throughout this book. Toponyms pose similar problems. Should one write Sevilla or Seville, Andalucía or Andalusia? My policy has always been to use the English spellings for commonly known places (hence, Seville and Andalusia) and Spanish spellings for cities and regions that may not be as immediately familiar to foreigners (hence, Málaga and Cádiz), especially when correct pronunciation depends on the inclusion of accents.

Along these same lines, the word *Gypsy* has become increasingly problematic, as the time has come to recognize that it has often been wielded as an ethnic slur. I have always capitalized it, but my preference now is simply to avoid it as much as possible. Instead, *Roma* seems to me the most appropriate substitute, though I retain *Gypsy* when it appears in quoted material.

Finally, in regard to the citation of sources, some of the hundreds of clippings in the family archive do not include crucial information, for example, the name of the periodical, the title of the article, the author, or the page number. In all cases, I provide as much identifying information as possible. In fact, unless otherwise indicated, nearly all the primary documentation consulted for this book is now located in the Special Collections of the University Libraries at UCR. For information about the contents of the family archive (henceforth referred to as the Romero archive, RA), see appendix 4, which also includes the website where anyone can consult the RA online catalog. (The RA was acquired and cataloged by Special Collections only after I had finished working with it, so my citations do not include specific information about the current location of materials within the RA at UCR.)

INTRODUCTION

* * *

The introductions here must not fail to include those individuals and organizations that have made this book possible, through their generous sharing of insights and materials, as well as their moral and material support.

First and foremost, I wish to convey heartfelt thanks to the Romero family, in particular Celin, Claudia, Pepe, Carissa, Angel, and Nefy, for their many exertions in making the family archive available for my consultation and for donating it to Special Collections at UCR, where it will be available to scholars long after we are all gone. Without their unstinting collaboration in organizing and making accessible these materials, this book would have been in no way conceivable. I am also indebted to Little Pepe, Bernardo, Lito, and Celino for their patience in answering my many questions, and to the spouses and children of all the quartet's members for their support.

Of all the Romeros, however, I reserve highest praise for Celedonio and Angelita, the late pater and mater familias, for their conscientious preservation of correspondence, official documents, press clippings, programs, photographs, and memorabilia over eight decades. Without their constant dedication to compiling and maintaining a tangible record of the family's history, neither I nor any other writer could hope to compose a saga as epic as this one.

Of course, I am deeply grateful to the late Sir Neville Marriner as well as to Jesús López Cobos, Federico Moreno-Torroba Larregla, and Cecilia Rodrigo for their eloquent contributions to the foreword. Their collective testimony is proof of the high esteem in which the Romeros have consistently been held by leading musicians of the twentieth century. Cecilia merits further thanks for making materials in the archive of the Fundación Victoria y Joaquín Rodrigo in Madrid available for my consultation and for inviting me to write a biography of her father, a task in which I am now absorbed with my coauthor, Javier Suárez-Pajares.

A number of Spaniards closely connected with the family, professionally and personally, have provided invaluable assistance as well as logistical support. Dr. José Manuel Gil de Gálvez and his wife, Marina, are talented violinists and members of Concerto Málaga, which José Manuel conducts. They have given me numerous valuable insights into Málaga's history and culture, as well as the Romeros' relationship to them. They also graciously

INTRODUCTION

provided a place for me to stay while in Málaga, as well as transportation to remote locales associated with the family's early history. Rosa María Álvarez Campos, the daughter of Col. Antonio Álvarez González, and her grandson, Pedro Ángel González Mazone Álvarez, are proud residents of Seville who shared their love of the city with me. They also have a close historical connection to the Romero family, which they patiently explained. Sonsoles González is Pepe's Spanish agent, and she and her husband, Antonio, very kindly provided me with transportation and friendship as we traced the Romero family's history through various Andalusian capitals. I remain grateful to them for their effervescent amiability. Vicente and Manuel Coves continue the tradition of family music making in Spain, as guitarist Vicente is a Pepe pupil and a celebrated concert and recording artist who often collaborates with his brother Manuel, one of Spain's leading conductors today. Both honored me with support and encouragement, as well as sincere friendship. Ana Benavides is a leading musicologist and pianist in Spain, as well as a proud *malagueña*. Her generous gifts of books about Málaga and the many historical insights she has shared with me about her native city are greatly appreciated.

The Archivo Militar in Guadalajara yet again came to my rescue, this time by helping me to excavate the records of military service for Celedonio and his three brothers. The archivo staff's professional competence is exceeded only by its unfailing courtesy. Thanks go to Miguel Torres and the staff at the Archivo Municipal in Málaga for allowing me to consult photographs and newspapers in their priceless and well-organized collection. María Luz Paz at the Sociedad General de Autores y Editores yet again merits thanks for her research support, as does director Elena Magallanes Latas and her capable staff in the library of the Real Conservatorio Superior de Madrid, who provided their customary expert assistance to me as I consulted documentation in their valuable archive. For over twenty-seven years, I have benefited from the expertise and courtesy of the staff of the Biblioteca Nacional in Madrid and more recently from the Archivo General de la Administración in Alcalá de Henares. Sincere thanks go to them as well.

In the United States, I am indebted to my longtime friend and colleague Bill Krause, who has provided so much to me in the way of encouragement, inspiration, and research support. Laurel Ornish is a Dallas-based media celebrity and fervent devotee of the Romeros. I thank her sincerely for

INTRODUCTION

sharing with me her valuable collection of photographs, newspaper clippings, and other publications, as well as recordings of her radio interviews with the Romeros. The eminent guitar scholar Thomas Heck provided invaluable editorial suggestions, for which I am also grateful.

My research was generously supported by my own university through an Academic Senate COR Research Fellowship (2013), an Academic Senate Research and Travel Award (2014), and a grant for international research from the Office of Research and Economic Development (2014). I am especially grateful to Eric Milenkiewicz and his staff in Special Collections at UCR for their indispensable assistance in acquiring and organizing the Romero archive, a resource that will surely be of great value and interest to future researchers in this area. Leilani Dade and Eric Johns, both of them my doctoral students in musicology at UCR, have played a central role in cataloging these materials; Daniel Castro, another doctoral student at UCR, provided vital assistance in compiling the list of albums in appendix 3.

I am inexpressibly grateful to editor Laurie Matheson at the University of Illinois Press for her enthusiastic support of this book project and her editorial team's careful attention to its production. There is no doubt that the Music in American Life series is the perfect home for the Romero saga.

As always, I appreciate the patient forbearance of my wife, Nancy, and our late son, Robert (1996–2017), during the seemingly endless process of researching and writing a book such as this. Finally, I wish to express loving gratitude to my parents, Ernest Linwood Clark (1906–83) and Beatrice Faith Clark (née Smith, 1910–82), whose passionate love of beauty and unfailing encouragement of my road-less-traveled enthusiasms have made all the difference in this life.

And now, ¡Los Romeros!

Murrieta, California, 2017

PART 1

SOUTHERN SPAIN

I am the brother of the wind, of the stars; I have love affairs with the morning star, with the moon, the mountains, the oceans; my friends the sound waves take me flying through the entire universe.

[Soy hermano del viento, de las estrellas, tengo amores con los luceros, con la luna, los montes, los mares; mis amigas las ondas sonoras, me llevan volando por todo el universo.]

—Celedonio Romero, from "Pensamiento" (Madrid, January 1973)

CHAPTER 1

FROM MÁLAGA'S MOUNTAINS

Standing alone on the mountainside, I quietly contemplate a lulling sensory counterpoint. Soon a favorite line from Clemens Brentano's poetry begins to echo in my consciousness, becoming a sort of mantra in this moment: "Silence, silence, let us listen intently!"[1] All about me, bees hum in a unison drone while wood-pecking *carpintero* birds hammer out insistent rhythms on bark drums; a steady breeze stirs pine needles into undulations yielding both scent and sound; shimmering white clouds traverse the azure savannah overhead with a majestic gait, *andante maestoso*; great crescendos of warm North African air, laced with the vivifying fragrance and moisture of the Mediterranean, engulf the verdant earth; sea and sky blend seamlessly into a monochromatic canvas of blue, articulated in staccato fashion by brown, haze-shrouded islets off the Andalusian coast.

A hundred meters or so away, a chaotic chorus of bleating heralds the arrival of a herd of goats gamboling up the slopes of a dry wash and then threading its way through the local luxuriance of *palo*, pepper, pine, and palm trees, scrub oak, aloe, cactus, chaparral, wild grasses, yucca, oleander, as well as pomegranate, eucalyptus, mulberry, and olive trees. Here and there about me grow delicately fulsome rosemary plants, shyly adorned with pale-blue blossoms. Their celestial hue has made rosemary a popular emblem of religious devotees over the centuries, and the plant's Spanish

PART 1. SOUTHERN SPAIN

name has thus become the same as that for a pilgrim, *romero*, or a pilgrimage, *romería*. I pluck a tender shoot to savor its pungent perfume.

Yet despite this Edenic nirvana, my mind wanders again and again to the place whence I have come this day and commands my eyes to trace the long, tortuous road that runs like a serpentine scar across the face of the mountain, to trace it down and away to the distant seaport of Málaga. Málaga, with its Roman amphitheater, its Moorish fortress, its cavernous cathedral, its tree-lined boulevards, and its timeless flamenco songs. Málaga, birthplace of Pablo Picasso and the twentieth-century surrealist poet and Nobel laureate Vicente Aleixandre, who dubbed it the "City of Paradise." But my restless thoughts remain unsatisfied with Málaga's paradisial enchantments and set sail ever farther, *plus ultra*, through the Pillars of Hercules and across the Atlantic to the margent of another world, to another ocean, other cities to discover, and other mountains to ascend.

This poetic scenario is both the beginning and the end of our saga. It is the saga itself, as we shall see. My companions on this outing include Pepe and Celin Romero, who are visiting their ancestral ground for the first time. Clambering over the tumbledown remains of a church that once formed the nucleus of a small farming village called Jotrón, they marvel at this place, hallowed by the memory of an earlier generation of Romeros and the first Spanish locale ever inhabited by their father, Celedonio. Spanish poet Antonio Machado seemed almost to have been speaking to them when, over a century earlier, he wrote, "Muy cerca está, romero, la tierra verde y santa y florecida de tus sueños" (Very close, pilgrim, is the green, sacred, and flowering land of your dreams).[2] Indeed, it was from these extremely humble beginnings that their family's against-all-odds ascent to global fame (and relative fortune) began. Here it was that *romero* first became Romero.

Yet we would not even have known of this place without the remarkable memoirs of José Romero (henceforth Uncle Pepe, to distinguish him from Celedonio's renowned son, Pepe Romero), Celedonio's eldest brother, who recalled in photographic detail the early history of his family. The following account of Celedonio's ancestry and early life is greatly indebted to Uncle Pepe's recollections, which he expressed in lapidary Spanish prose. Indeed, a flair for language is just one of many talents that have characterized several generations of Romeros, as his grandson, José Francisco Romero, is a published poet.[3]

1. FROM MÁLAGA'S MOUNTAINS

MALAK

There are actually two Málagas: the city itself and the province of which it is the capital. Phoenicians colonized the area around the harbor already in the eighth century BCE and named it after their goddess of beauty, Malak. This commercially and militarily strategic locale changed hands over the ensuing centuries, yielding to Greeks, Carthaginians, Romans, Vandals, Visigoths, Moors, and Arabs, in addition to welcoming many other groups of people, including Jews and Roma, as well as French and Italian settlers. Christian *malagueños* enthusiastically embraced the Blessed Virgin Mary, making the Virgen de la Victoria their patron saint, in honor of her undoubted succor in liberating the city from Muslim rule in 1487. But the city itself retained the name of that previous goddess, one whose images and places of worship had long since fallen to pieces. The entire region around the port city adopted this name as well and became one of fifty provinces in modern Spain.[4]

Although Málaga's initial attraction was as a trading center along the southern coast of the Iberian Peninsula, conveniently situated near the Strait of Gibraltar and the North African coast, the historic mainstay of the region's economy has been fishing and agriculture, especially the cultivation of grains, grapes, citrus, and olives. The mountainsides to the north of the city and throughout the province have yielded a cornucopia of profitable produce ever since those ancient times, and certainly in the 1800s, when our story begins.

Yet the City of Paradise has not always been as hospitable as it might seem to the casual observer today. It has proven lamentably prone to floods, droughts, earthquakes, epidemics of plague, cholera, and typhus, as well as to naval and aerial bombardments, invasions, and economic ups and downs. It has experienced its fair share of political upheaval, too. Miserable conditions for workers prompted the rise of unionism and socialism in the 1880s and 1890s, and this laid the groundwork for continued unrest in the 1900s, especially leading up to the civil war of 1936–39, as communists and anarchists joined the fray.

Historically, illiteracy was a major problem throughout Spain, particularly Andalusia. In 1910 illiteracy in Málaga stood at 80 percent of the population, compared to a national rate of 60 percent (today 98.1 percent of Spaniards are literate).[5] Upward mobility was thus difficult, and someone born into a

PART 1. SOUTHERN SPAIN

lower caste was likely—though not destined—to remain there, as were his or her offspring. This problem seemed resistant to the municipal government's attempts to establish schools and to educate children. And life in the provincial countryside was even harder than in the capital city.[6]

DE LOS MONTES

Celedonio Romero's maternal great-great-grandparents were prosperous landowners who were born and settled near Jotrón in the northern *montes*. They owned a beautiful house and much property, which produced an abundance of fruit, grains, and vegetables of various kinds, depending on the amount of rain the usually fertile soil received. They grew enough to sustain themselves and sold any surplus in Málaga. The rugged, stony pathways into town could hardly be called roads, as they were steep, narrow, winding, and infested with bandits. The family's goods were transported on mules or donkeys and guarded by men hired to protect them, called *escopeteros*, whose mission it was to repulse the daring *bandoleros*! They always traveled on Saturdays so that their harvest would be in markets for the beginning of the week.

When these distant ancestors died, they left behind a fortune, but it was siphoned off by others, and Celedonio's maternal great-grandparents never saw a *centavo* of it. Thus they were reduced to working the land their family once owned. Little else is known about them or about the paternal lineage during this time except for an uncle of Celedonio's grandfather who was a day laborer in Totalán, a small village on another mountainside north of the city. This charming locale boasts the lovely sixteenth-century Iglesia de Santa Ana and is replete with the squat, whitewashed dwellings and their old red-tile roofs so characteristic of the region. It makes a pleasant destination for a day outing. But in the 1800s, it was a place one could readily weary of as a *jornalero*, or field hand. This anonymous uncle tired of backbreaking labor that was poorly paid, in a place that was scorching hot in the summer and bitter cold in the winter. So he moved to Málaga in search of work and education; like the majority of Spaniards at that time, he was illiterate. With the assistance of a generous patron, though, he found lodging, employment, and was enrolled in a school. He completed his education in only two years

1. FROM MÁLAGA'S MOUNTAINS

and set his sights on becoming an engineer of canals, ports, and roads, which required moving to Madrid.

Once in the Spanish capital, he worked during the day and studied in the evening. He proudly reported the following in a letter to his parents: "The rich kids showed up in their finery and elegant coaches, while I was in my dusty shoes. Everyone thought I was a goner. But I got the highest score on the exam!"[7] He went on to occupy the position of superintendent in the Ministry of Public Works and began writing poetry in his spare time. We may never learn his name, but the pattern of his life runs like a thread through the Romero family history, an example of superior intelligence, self-application, and boundless ambition, as well as a knack for understanding how mechanical things work. The United States would one day beckon a group of smart, diligent, and supremely ambitious Romeros and give them ample opportunity to realize their dreams, an opportunity that Spain has throughout its history often been unable to offer some of its most talented sons and daughters, resulting in recurrent brain drain.[8]

After this frustrating anonymity, it's refreshing to start encountering actual names in these memoirs (see the genealogical chart in appendix 2). Celedonio's paternal grandfather was José Romero Falcón, a man of short stature, though strong and clever, who was also born in Totalán and worked as a day laborer there. He, too, eventually tired of Totalán and removed to another mountainside agricultural settlement, Moclinejo, which was somewhat larger and more prosperous. Here it was that he met and married María López González, by whom he had four children: José, María, Enriqueta, and Antonio.

It is now that we encounter for the first time the bewildering family penchant for recycling names from one generation to the next, giving rise to a small army of men named José (or Pepe, the nickname for José) and women named Josefa. Celedonio's maternal grandparents were José Pinazo Gutiérrez and Josefa Gutiérrez Ternero, who were born in the vicinity of Jotrón, where they worked in the fields. They lived in a house they inherited from their great-great-grandparents, and in their skillful care, the land yielded olives, grains, legumes, almonds, and grapevines, which gave them oil, bread, and wine to eat throughout the year and which they could sell in Málaga. The maternal grandfather was of slight stature and not very strong, but he was nonetheless nice looking and somewhat rustic. His wife was tall, strong, and attractive, though not especially clever. Together they had four offspring: Josefa, Dolores, Rafael, and Isabel.

On the paternal side, the oldest of Celedonio's grandparents' children was José Romero López, who was born in Moclinejo on April 15, 1866. He worked as a *jornalero* there but grew weary of arduous stoop labor and in 1880 made his way to Málaga, where he became an apprentice in the construction trade and demonstrated real talent for that work, though he was only fourteen years old. (He thus followed the same general course as the anonymous *tío-abuelo* mentioned above.) He was short like his father but with a darker complexion and uncommon intelligence.

While working on a convent for monks, Las Morillas, in Málaga's Camino de Casabermeja, he noticed a fetching young woman pass by one day and fell in love with her at first sight. He made inquiries and learned that she was from the Jotrón area and was spending a few days with some friends in a house near the convent. He made every effort to find and court her. In fact, she was Josefa Pinazo Gutiérrez and was born in Jotrón on August 28, 1871, making her five years younger than José. They became steadies, or *novios*, though she had to return for a time to Jotrón. But they stayed in touch. After finishing work on the convent, he was offered a job as a foreman at Noirot and Company, a responsible position that involved maintaining the roads from Bobadilla to Algeciras. This assignment would greatly complicate their courtship, so they simply married.

His work required him to move frequently, and after Bobadilla they moved to Campillos, Canete la Real, and other places in Málaga province until landing in Ronda, where their first child to survive infancy was born, Josefa, around 1898. According to family tradition, three offspring before Josefa died at birth or shortly thereafter. From Ronda they moved to Algeciras and then from village to village, ever closer to Gibraltar. An English company was building some docks (*diques*) in the harbor, and they hired him, so he left his job with Noirot.

Being highly competent, José was soon promoted to first superintendent. He and Josefa lived in nearby Línea de la Concepción in a house on the Calle Reina Cristina, where he also opened a grocery store called El Rincón (The Corner), managed by his resourceful wife. In between Ronda and Línea, at least three other children had been born but also died shortly after birth.

1. FROM MÁLAGA'S MOUNTAINS

The rate of infant mortality in Spain at this time was high; about 20 percent died within the first year, so the demise of a baby was to be expected. The loss of so many children, however, was devastating. Still, they kept trying, even though they were thirty-nine and thirty-four years old, respectively—rather advanced in years for having children. Finally, in La Línea, a son was born, Uncle Pepe, on March 25, 1905. Of course, their chief concern was that he survive infancy and not follow his previous siblings to an early grave. Their spirits sank as he developed double pneumonia a few days after birth, but he soon recovered, something they attributed to divine intervention. (Why such intervention had not been forthcoming on the previous occasions was a question that could not be answered and which they were probably disinclined to ask.) The parents wanted to name him José but were a little leery of doing so because one of the deceased children had been given that name. Still, he was born only a few days after the feast day of Saint Joseph, the family patron, so they tempted fate and named him José. He would lead a long and eventful life.

Given that Papá José had a new mouth to feed, it was a good thing that the wages paid in Gibraltar were better than those in Spain, which is why so many Spanish workers wanted to relocate there. In fact, Papá was able to get jobs for his brother Antonio and his brother-in-law Rafael. Another incentive was the lower prices that workers paid there for tobacco products and food. The area also attracted lots of tourists, which was good for local businesses. But the British did not want their colony overrun with unemployed Spaniards, so though Spanish workers could live in Gibraltar while working there, once their employment was up, they had to leave the next day.

Papá José's father, tired of working in Moclinejo for low wages, heard about how much money people in Cuba were making, so he decided to move there to make his fortune. He took his family with him except for his son Antonio, who kept working in Gibraltar with his brother. Papá José made good money with the English company, but he began to have dreams of Cuba, too, and decided to join his father there. In 1908, he quit his job, closed the grocery, and left for Havana. "Go west, young man, go west," was the clarion call he resolved to heed. He would not be alone in this. There was a conspicuous outflow of population from Spain during this period precisely because of the many problems the country faced, particularly in places like

PART 1. SOUTHERN SPAIN

Málaga, whose economy was very depressed in the early 1900s and which suffered through a smallpox epidemic in 1903–4 and a devastating drought in 1905.

* * *

In 1887, the city of Málaga boasted a population of 139,788; by 1900, there were 136,193 residents.[9] Most of the decrease was the result of emigration to Argentina, Brazil—and Cuba. Though this island nation had gained its nominal independence from Spain in 1898, as a result of Spain's war with the United States, it remained a popular destination for Spaniards seeking an opportunity to improve their lot in life. Not for the last time would Romeros now cross an ocean in search of just such an opportunity.

CHAPTER 2
CUBA, QUÉ LINDA ES CUBA

The lyrics of a popular *chachachá* by Ernesto Saborit rejoice in "Cuba, how lovely is Cuba." That was the sentiment that now persuaded the family to board the steamer *König Albert*, which plied Atlantic waters between Gibraltar and Havana, as well as other Latin American ports. On this voyage, it stopped first in New York, where Uncle Pepe was hugely impressed by the Statue of Liberty. He also remembered a perpetual storm of noise caused by all the traffic in the city, something to which he was obviously not accustomed. After docking in Havana, they immediately entrained for Cienfuegos, a seaport on the southern coast of the island, about one hundred miles to the southeast of Havana. Grandpa José had already found work in Cienfuegos and settled in. They rented a small abode in the Calle La Lealtad, and Papá soon found work helping to build a park called Villuendas.

Cuba was at a crucial juncture in its history. The Spanish-American War of 1898 had given the new nation nominal independence, but in fact the United States had seized control of the island and its political and economic life. By the time the Romeros arrived in 1909, American troops had just departed after a lengthy military occupation, and they would return whenever U.S. business interests were threatened. The economy was doing well, as U.S. corporations developed the country's infrastructure and invested resources in the agricultural sector, especially sugarcane. Though the burgeoning economy beckoned poor Andalusians like the Romeros, racism was still widespread on the island, and discrimination against blacks and mulattoes was common.

Despite these realities, Uncle Pepe thought that Cuba was nothing less than a tropical paradise, and his remarkable memory recalled a sort of Garden of Eden offering an abundance of fruits and vegetables, of flora and fauna. It also possessed considerable mineral wealth. The climate was benign in winter and hot in summer, though the heat was moderated by marine breezes; however, the electrical and tropical storms were horrific and on occasion terrifying in their intensity and destructive force. Of special interest to a boy like Uncle Pepe were the local girls, whom he found very attractive, especially light-skinned *mulatas*.

Cienfuegos was a thriving metropolis of about twenty thousand inhabitants, most of whom lived in houses made of brick and mortar. The city boasted some large stores, like La Borla and El Palo Gordo; theaters, like the Terry; and two cinemas, El Prado and Niza. He was able to locate his father, who was both pleased and surprised to see him. (Finding him was not too difficult insofar as his letters to Spain bore his return address in Cienfuegos.)

On August 11, 1909, only a few months after the family's arrival in Cuba, Uncle Pepe's brother Maximino was born. It was about this time that they moved to a country house called Muñoz, a large edifice with lots of acreage covered with trees, some fruit, and a brick-and-cement pond that retained rainwater and was their source of water for everything. The entire estate was surrounded by barbed wire. He also remembers the roosters waking him up, but at least those sounds had a rational explanation. The family occasionally heard other, more mysterious and very loud sounds, which the locals explained as follows. The country estate (*finca*) on which they were living had been used as a camp for prisoners during the war between Cuba and Spain, and many prisoners had been shot and buried there. The noises were believed to be those of the restless spirits leaving their graves and disturbing the locals.

Despite supernatural interference, only a few months after the birth of Maximino, sister Josefita was married there. And on January 17, 1911, Uncle Pepe's new brother was born, Adolfo. Three months later, Josefita gave birth to a daughter named Celedonia. This is an uncommon name and one I have not previously encountered in the family's annals; indeed, it is one rarely encountered in Spain today. Even Spaniards find it unusual, the general explanation for this being that it is old-fashioned. I will have more to say about its colorful origins later.

Mamá got tired of the poltergeists at Muñoz and the work required to keep such a large home clean, so she and the kids moved to a smaller house, in a neighborhood of Cienfuegos called La Juanita. Other residents of this area included a cow, whose milk they used to nourish little Adolfo. Of course, most everyone enjoys milk in some form, and though Uncle Pepe's studies at a local school (*colegio*) afforded him little practical knowledge, he nonetheless savored the sugared milk that the students were served every day.

Uncle Pepe retained distinct memories of the sinking of the *Titanic* in April 1912, with its horrific loss of life; however, some eleven months later, on March 2, 1913, his mother brought new life into the world with one more child, whom she named Celedonio. Curiously, Celedonio's passport gives a birthdate of April 2, but this discrepancy was due to the fact that his birth was not recorded for a month after it happened. So many infants died during that first crucial month that it made sense to record only the births of children who survived their first few weeks on earth. Though Celedonio clearly survived, his arrival was attended by one significant and ironic medical complication: a slightly defective hand, which was corrected later.

The choice of his name stimulates further speculation. Clearly this has become a favorite with the family, though trying to spell it would bedevil many a reviewer in later years, even in Spanish-speaking areas. Celedonio was named after Saint Celedonius, a Roman soldier in Spain who was decapitated for his faith around 300 CE. He is the patron saint of Santander and other cities in the Cantabria region of the north. (His feast day is August 30, so there was no connection with Celedonio's birth date.)

During the time the Romeros lived there, the Cuban government was secular, and religion wasn't taught in the schools. Therefore, Uncle Pepe was enrolled in a Jesuit school and learned Catholicism there. Despite this, the Romeros would always occupy a somewhat ambiguous religious space somewhere in that vast theological expanse between orthodoxy and secularism. They were neither observant nor faithless, though when push came to shove, during the civil war, they would side with the secularists.

PART 1. SOUTHERN SPAIN

Of course, there was nothing in Catholic dogma that forbade the enjoyment of alcoholic beverages. Uncle Pepe's dad had been a great drinker of wine, cognac, and gin in Spain, but when he first arrived in Cuba, he gave up drinking. Now, however, he started again, adding rum to his menu, and he would not heed his wife's entreaties to stop. There is no clear pattern of alcoholism or drug abuse in the Romero family, but Papá nonetheless had a serious drinking problem. He also liked to smoke, which only made matters worse. In addition to these vices, he was an avid cardplayer, but since he was not prone to losing much money that way, he never felt compelled to give it up. He *did* try to give up drinking and smoking, but old habits died hard. One day, after ostensibly getting back on the wagon, he sent Uncle Pepe on an errand to buy tobacco and rum, claiming that it was for his workers, though Uncle Pepe knew it was really for his dad. This saddened him because these dependencies were clearly ruining his father's health.

Still, Papá was uncommonly good at what he did, and his drinking and smoking don't seem to have interfered with his livelihood. While employed by a local contractor named Calzadilla, he developed a reputation for doing excellent work on time and within budget. And he was not only dependable but also honest. As his renown spread, so did employment opportunities with other firms. One day, a certain Pepe Iriza came by the house and declared that Papá was the best builder (*maestro de obras*) in Cienfuegos and that he wanted to hire him for a job; unfortunately, Papá wasn't available, but this was one of many such offers. Indeed, he eventually built the Liceo in Cienfuegos, a concert hall still in use today and a local landmark.

Of course, he could build nothing by himself and depended on the services of many laborers. He employed all sorts of people, but he said the best workers were the *gallegos*, from Galicia in northwest Spain, because they always did what they were told without complaint and executed their tasks well. But one day an Andalusian from Almería showed up, and he was the best worker ever. It was necessary to do work that was delicate and had to be done fast, and this fellow never made a mistake. This led Papá to proudly declare that "when Andalusians want to work, they have no equal."

Papá obviously inherited his talent for designing and building things from his own father, who once gave the family a wooden statue of a mountaineer he had carved that was a genuine work of art. He was very talented, and this gift for woodworking has been passed on to his descendants Little Pepe and

2. CUBA, QUÉ LINDA ES CUBA

Bernardo. Mamá was not much of a woodworker but rather an avid reader of novels, and the house was full of books. The Romeros' love of literature was already evident at this early stage in their history.

The Angel of Death once again paid the Romero family an unwelcome visit when sister Josefita had a miscarriage and died. She was a talented singer whose specialty was *granadinas*, a type of fandango associated with Granada. She was only twenty years old when she passed away, and she left behind her four still-young brothers. As was their wont, especially after such a tragedy, the family moved again, this time to the Calle San Fernando between Gloria and Luis Armada. This new house was made of wood and designed to withstand the hurricanes that lashed the island. Relatively palatial, it had five bedrooms; a covered terrace; long, narrow hallways between rooms; a kitchen; an indoor bathroom; and a patio with a tree in the middle. There was also a lagoon nearby where they could swim, and a train station was not far away.

These affluent circumstances notwithstanding, however, Mamá knew that poverty was just a missed paycheck away, so she was a careful manager of household finances and a thrifty shopper. Prosperity also reinforced her awareness of the hardships and misfortunes many people around them were experiencing. Rather than trying to insulate herself and her family from the harsh realities of life, she nurtured a charitable streak and continued to give money to the poor. This impulse is characteristic of the family in general, and years later Celedonio and his sons would give many benefit concerts to aid the less fortunate.

Uncle Pepe and his brothers loved to play baseball, and they didn't hesitate to include black children in their games. In fact, the Romeros very much sympathized with them because of their second-class status. The Romeros obviously made an impression on their black neighbors. Many decades later, during a visit to Cienfuegos, Pepe met an old mulatto in the Plaza de Mercado, near where the family had lived, and the man actually recalled playing baseball with Celedonio when he was a child. He even remembered that Celedonio's father was an architect.

This close proximity to blacks had additional benefits. Once, during a torrential downpour, water started pouring into the Romero's house. A black man named Pancho risked his own life in helping the family escape to dry ground. Thus there was every good reason to feel sympathy for the marginalized and downtrodden blacks in Cuba, whose socioeconomic status resembled that of the Spanish Roma. The Romeros had known hard times and would know them again. They knew what life was like on the bottom rung, and this would later inspire Celedonio's brothers to fight on the side of the republic. It continues to inform the family's left-leaning politics.

Uncle Pepe paid close attention to developments in the First World War, noting that those who sided with the Germans were on a black list, as Cuba favored the Allies and had declared war on Imperial Germany only a day after the United States, on April 7, 1917. But disease was no respecter of political affiliations, and one of the transnational consequences of the war was an epidemic of flu, called Spanish flu because it began there in 1918, eventually claiming two hundred thousand lives in Spain, as well as millions worldwide. Cuba was directly in the bacteriological line of fire, and Papá fell ill with the dreaded disease. He was treated with a mixture of oregano with white honey and aspirin, and he recovered, though one suspects he did so in spite rather than because of this improbable cure.

His own father was not a victim of the flu, but he died at age eighty, four years after his retirement. He had always had gainful employment and worked for important people in Cienfuegos, including a general and the mayor. His passing was too much for Mamá to bear, as she was still grieving for her late daughter and grandbaby. In fact, she was battling depression, and her doctor prescribed a return to Spain, to the mountains of Málaga and her family there. Papá would have to stay behind for a while in order to make the money to support this plan, so Mamá and her four boys returned home without him.

* * *

Celedonio had spent a very formative first six years of his life in Cuba, and he always retained a sentimental attachment to the island. Still prominently displayed on one of the walls in his Del Mar home is a small Cuban flag, a treasured souvenir. His signature piece was a *guajira*, a type of flamenco song and dance imported from Cuba that he immortalized in his own *Fantasía* for solo guitar, the instrument with which he was soon to become acquainted in a land at once distant and near.

CHAPTER 3

THE CITY OF PARADISE, REGAINED

In September 1919, the family departed from Havana on the steamship *Barcelona*, a vessel that displaced 10,500 tons, roughly a fourth the size of the RMS *Titanic*. Most of those on board were from the Canary Islands heading home after helping harvest the Cuban sugar crop, but the Romeros were bound for the Atlantic port of Cádiz, in Andalusia. The four brothers looked over the railing to catch a last glimpse of the country where Uncle Pepe had spent eleven years of his life, and his young brother, Celedonio, his first six. It was a melancholy vista because they were leaving behind their grandpa and sister, who had died in Cuba.

They arrived in Santa Cruz de Tenerife, then went to Las Palmas, where the islanders improvised a little ditty in honor of Uncle Pepe's youngest brother: "Celedonio, Celedonio, who is almost to Cádiz." These islanders knew whereof they sang, because a short time later the family reached their destination. For breakfast, the boys enjoyed their first-ever taste of Spanish *churros*, a pastry of fried dough but without the dusting of sugar that connoisseurs of the Mexican variety expect. This fortified them for the long train trip to Málaga, which began early in the morning and terminated late at night. The tedium and discomfort of the trip were ameliorated somewhat by impressive scenery along the way, which offered stunning tableaux of expansive plains dotted with lime and orange groves, all framed by majestic mountains in the distance.

PART 1. SOUTHERN SPAIN

A RUSTIC INTERLUDE

The family's uncles showed up with the customary and reliable mules to take them to Jotrón, their ultimate destination. The roads weren't any better than in the old days: narrow, twisting, and riddled with stones. After several hours on the dusty trail, and having crossed the Guadalmedina River at various points, they finally arrived. Their initial impression of the place was not good: it was a motley cluster of hovels made of stone and mud, without whitewash, and without any "architectonic order," as Uncle Pepe put it. Their own high-quality modern clothes contrasted with the rustic garb of the locals.

Of course, they were in no position to be too particular. Their only income was the 500 pesetas that Papá would send home every month from Cuba. There were always life's little pleasures, however, as they all liked to drink brandy and consume *churros* with their coffee (still a repast favored by the Romeros). Bread, wine, and various kinds of dessert also helped to relieve the monotony and tedium of rural life. During the March festival of San José, it was the local custom to dine on fried eggs and rice, a local specialty. Playing cards was also a favorite pastime, and there was music as well. When it came time to harvest the wheat, local *jornaleros* lustily sang their special work songs called *trilleras*. The major local song and dance, however, was the *verdiales*, a type of fandango native to this mountainous region. The snapping of castanets, energetic strumming of guitars, full-throated singing, and athletic movements of the dancers no doubt lightened many an otherwise heavy heart. A characteristic verse goes like this: "I like wine and lemonade, but most of all I like your face!" (Me gusta vino y limonada pero tu cara, pero tu cara me gusta más.) *Verdiales* festivals are still popular today, especially in late fall.

One thinks of a characteristic poem by Antonio Machado that no doubt describes the denizens of this district:

> And everywhere I've seen
> people who dance and play,
> when they can, and work
> their few feet of land. . . .
> They are good folks who live,
> Labor, pass by and dream,

3. THE CITY OF PARADISE, REGAINED

And on a day like all the others,
They relax below the earth.[1]

Still, domestic life gave these Romeros relatively little to sing about. The house in which they lived in Jotrón was owned by Mamá's sister Isabel. It was small and cramped, with just two rooms to accommodate four boys and at least two adults. Needless to say, there was a distressing lack of privacy. True, Jotrón offered a splendid view of the surrounding region, as noted in an earlier chapter, but in terms of creature comforts and convenience, it nonetheless formed a stark contrast with Cienfuegos, or even Málaga. Thus, according to Uncle Pepe, they did not remain there for very long, though exactly when they relocated to the capital city for good is not known.

EARLY YEARS IN MÁLAGA

What goes up must come down, and the Romeros went down with their belongings in the same fashion they had brought them up: on the backs of *mulas*. They soon moved into a small dwelling in Málaga that nevertheless seemed palatial compared to Aunt Isabel's rustic hut. What's more, they did not have to say good-bye to the *verdiales*, as a friend of the family named Antonio Ternero provided memorable renditions of it on the violin.

The period during which the Romeros relocated to Spain was one of turmoil. Though the Spanish economy had prospered during the First World War, a result of Spanish neutrality and a demand for its raw materials and industrial goods, once the war ended, hard times returned. Because so much unrest emanated from the lower-class workers who lacked employment or living wages, the period from 1918 to 1920 came to be called the "three years of bolshevism," with repeated strikes and protests by leftist labor organizations. However, the economy gradually improved during the 1920s, and Málaga's population growth reflected this, increasing from about 136,000 in 1900 to 188,000 by 1930 (with a population now approaching 600,000, it is the sixth largest city in Spain today, after Madrid, Barcelona, Valencia, Seville, and Zaragoza).[2]

It was during this relatively halcyon epoch that Papá returned from Cuba and located a new residence for his family, in the Calle Dos Aceras. He initially had a hard time finding work but gradually got back into construction

PART 1. SOUTHERN SPAIN

and found jobs building and renovating structures. He clearly benefited from the economic revitalization of the 1920s. Ever concerned for their education, he also enrolled his children in a local *colegio*, San José de Calasans. In addition, Uncle Pepe seems to have developed an interest in the guitar at this point, and his mother secured the services of a guitar instructor who could teach him flamenco. Moving is something the Romeros have perfected through much practice, and Papá soon found a new dwelling, at Calle Parras 27.

Life in Málaga may have been *easier* than in Jotrón, but it was not *easy*. Still, as a booming urban center, it had its charms. On Sundays and festivals, the family enjoyed going to theaters, movies, and bullfights and embarking on little excursions. Carnival and Holy Week were also memorable occasions, with parties, processions, music, and refreshments. They also took in performances by the legendary dancer Antonia Mercé (La Argentina), actress Pastora Imperio, flamenco *cantaora* Niña de los Peines, violinist Juan Manén, and zarzuela baritone Emilio Sagi-Barba.[3] In fact, in the 1920s and early 1930s, zarzuela (Spanish operetta) had not yet lost major ground to cinema and remained an immensely popular form of entertainment, in both Madrid and the provinces. At Málaga's Novedades theater, the Romero family attended such hits as *Gigantes y cabezudos*, *La verbena de la Paloma*, *La reina mora*, *Bohemios*, *Doña Francisquita*, *Luisa Fernanda*, *La revoltosa*, *Los gavilanes*, and *El huesped del sevillano*. These titles will mean little to English-speaking readers of this book, but in the world of the Spanish musical, I just rattled off a list of works comparable to *Showboat*, *Oklahoma*, and *South Pacific* in their renown and enduring popularity. No wonder that Uncle Pepe developed a mania to collect posters of popular singers known as *cupletistas*, the theatrical singers of *cuplés* (slightly risqué songs of a very accessible character).

The Romeros and many thousands of their fellow *malagueños* saw no sharp distinction between urban folklore, popular culture, and classical music. Just as, on many days, the blue ocean merged seamlessly into a cloudless sky, so these various forms of entertainment had very permeable boundaries and flowed one into the other. Our family of guitarists would embrace and reflect this laissez-faire attitude, as they would always program their native *malagueñas* and fandangos side by side with hoary masterworks by Bach and Vivaldi. After all, a classical piece for piano by Albéniz might sound remarkably similar to a *bulerías* performed at a local tavern, which in turn

3. THE CITY OF PARADISE, REGAINED

might use techniques borrowed from the classical-guitar repertoire. That same *bulerías* might well form the foundation of a song-and-dance number in a zarzuela. It was all Spanish and fair game for enterprising guitarists. This cultural milieu probably inspired Pepe to remark many years later that "to play Bach well it is necessary to know how to play *bulerías*"![4]

By the early twentieth century, the city had some firmly rooted cultural institutions of high quality, including the Sociedad Filarmónica de Málaga (1869), Real Conservatorio de Música María Cristina (1886), and the Teatro Miguel de Cervantes (1870). Newspaper readers had several publications to choose from, including the *Diario de Málaga*, *El Cronista*, *La Unión Mercantil*, *El Popular*, and the very leftist *Sur*. Most important, of course, was the city's musical life. Though these names will, again, have little meaning to many readers, they are prominent in the annals of Spanish music of the twentieth century, both classical and especially flamenco: El Planeta, Antonio Chacón, Niño de Cabra, Antonio Mairena, Juan Breva, Tomatito, and Fosforito. Málaga was also an important center for guitar making, and some of the leading builders included Francisco Domínguez, Antonio de Lorca Ramírez (active in Málaga 1909–29), and Juan Galán (active in Málaga 1900–1920). Some of these fine instruments are now on display in the Peña Juan Breva museum in Málaga.

Celedonio also came to enjoy a time-honored Spanish institution called the *tertulia*. This was an informal gathering of like-minded individuals at a café or restaurant where they could discuss history, literature, politics, music, or art—whatever interests they might have in common. Celedonio enjoyed *tertulias* at the elegant Café Madrid in the heart of Málaga. This venerable establishment, which had opened its doors in 1892, attracted just the sort of people—poets, painters, and musicians—whose company Celedonio found congenial. It is true that a young man like Celedonio probably had a good deal less formal schooling than most students today, but studies and education are not necessarily the same thing, and taking classes in literature and art wasn't the only way to become educated in such matters. Celedonio's socializing with artists and writers gave him an education that no school at the time would have provided.

Reading was also a leisure activity central to the Romero way of life, and Mamá loved books. As noted previously, she amassed a very large library in Cienfuegos, which included volumes by Spanish authors such as Calderón,

PART 1. SOUTHERN SPAIN

Espronceda, Valera, Bécquer, Valle-Inclán, Blasco-Ibáñez, and Baroja, as well as translations of foreign authors Sophocles, Virgil, Dante, Shakespeare, Dumas, and Tolstoy. Though this collection had to be sold before their departure, a love of literature had been implanted in the Romero boys and would soon manifest itself in various ways.

Of course, the family also enjoyed less intellectual pastimes. Strolls down the tree-lined *alameda*, or boulevard, in the center of the city were always pleasant. In later years, Celedonio would take his family for a hike up Monte Coronado, a mountain in Málaga about two hundred meters high whose name derives from the fact that the rocky mesa at the summit resembles a crown (*corona*). His purpose in leading these outings was not only to enjoy a picnic in scenic surroundings but also to watch soccer matches (for free) in the stadium at the base of the mountain. He would always bring along a pair of binoculars to enhance his ability to follow the game. Not surprisingly, the Romeros remain soccer (*fútbol*) fanatics to this day and continue to follow the progress (or lack thereof) of Málaga's team.

Celedonio wasn't the only guitarist in the family, just the only one to make a career of it. Tío Pepe participated as a guitarist in the music group Juventud Artística (Artistic Youth), which would sometimes play in the flamenco style. It was directed by Virgilio Roman and included *bandurrias*, a type of mandolin, and violins. They would stroll the streets during carnival playing *pasodobles* (two-step) and popular songs. They wore distinctive black suits and hats in the manner of *las tunas universitarias*, a type of strolling musical group made up of students (hence the other name for such groups, *estudiantinas*).

No one knows for sure when Celedonio acquired his first guitar. Uncle Pepe seems to think that it was around this time, after the family was settled in Málaga. Celedonio himself told his sons that he began playing the guitar in Jotrón. One thing everyone agrees on is that Celedonio and his mother were walking down the street in Málaga one day (whether near their home or on an excursion from Jotrón) and passed a music store in the Calle Compañía that was displaying a guitar in the window. Pepe says of this epiphany: "Just the shape of the instrument, the way it looks, captivated him and he fell completely in love with it. His attraction to it was immediate, and he begged her to buy him the guitar," which she did.[5] In any case, once in Málaga, Mamá arranged for him to take lessons with a local teacher

3. THE CITY OF PARADISE, REGAINED

named Juanito Martínez. Juanito was the first in a line of intermittent instructors, but in truth Celedonio basically taught himself how to play the instrument.

Certainly he heard and carefully observed many accomplished guitarists in his vicinity, and his mother bought him recordings of Andrés Segovia to listen to and study. According to Uncle Pepe, he took some lessons with a blind man named Juan Belmar. But he never became a full-fledged disciple of any of them or of any "school" of playing. He picked up bits and pieces from every guitarist he encountered and then assembled these into a style and technique that were very much his own. For instance, his approach owes something to the flamenco-guitar technique to which he was exposed, just as it does to the method of virtuoso and pedagogue Francisco Tárrega (1852–1909), as transmitted to him by Tárrega's disciple Daniel Fortea (1878–1953) and others who were active in Málaga during this period. But Celedonio was by no means a clone of any of these artists. As Pepe would later explain, "These other players influenced him and guided him without really giving him lessons."[6] He blended these various approaches and created something unique.

All of this caused Celedonio to remark later, "Perhaps I was a guitarist in some earlier existence. Because, when I picked up the guitar as a very young child, I simply began to play, almost without difficulty, as if my fingers had already been trained previously. I dreamed of the instrument. It dominated me. The piano is very lovely, but a bit cold; just the position from which you must play the instrument tells you that. When you play the guitar, you embrace it. It gives you its heat."[7] (The sexual nature of such an observation requires no elaboration here.) At fourteen, he played for Miquel Llobet (1878–1938), Tárrega's greatest disciple, who was incredulous and asked, "With whom did you study?" "Well, actually, I taught myself everything," was the young man's response. Llobet exclaimed, "But you have exactly the same technique as Don Francisco!"[8]

Although he clearly did not teach himself *everything*, he was by any definition a remarkable prodigy. Yet despite his abundant natural gifts, Celedonio felt the need for formal musical study, and in his late teens he enrolled at the Málaga Conservatory. By this point, however, he was very advanced in his guitar studies, and the guitar professor there, José Navas, refused to accept him because he declared Celedonio's abilities superior to his own!

Thus Celedonio enrolled to study solfège and harmony with Leandro Rivera Pons during the years 1932–34.[9]

Although Uncle Pepe claimed that Celedonio gave his first public recital in 1931, already in 1928 the local paper *Vida Gráfica* was praising the fifteen-year-old's "agility and exquisite art" in a program that he gave for the Unión Cristiana de Jóvenes. Celedonio also saved a 1929 clipping from the Málaga press in which Ortiz Barili praised him as "the insuperable guitarist, the young artist who harvests triumphs in bulk, had the gentility to entertain us with his admirable renditions. . . . He knows how to touch the soul with the unexpected cadences of his lyre."[10] Now, to be sure, this sort of fustian was standard fare in reviews of the time. One could be tempted to dismiss this review as nothing more than the cooings of some provincial hack who was either a friend of the Romero family or simply interested in showing how much he could "appreciate" something as refined as the classical guitar, but that isn't really the case. These same critics could just as readily use their colorful prose to skewer performers they didn't like. And they were not afraid to do so. The truth remains that Celedonio made this sort of impression on critics and the public throughout his career. They couldn't all have been mistaken or misled. This teenager had a special gift and was poised to make his way through the guitar ranks with remarkable alacrity.

Perhaps his real coming-out recital was the one he gave at Málaga's main concert venue, the Teatro Cervantes, on February 10, 1933. Shortly after Franklin Delano Roosevelt's inauguration as president of the United States, and shortly before Hitler became the German chancellor, young Celedonio ascended the stage to perform in a recital of music and poetry in which Agustín Alarcón read selections from the poems of Manuel Machado, Luis de Góngora, Enrique López Alarcón, and Juan Antonio Cavestany. Then Celedonio launched into his renditions of Tárrega's *Recuerdos de la Alhambra*, Albéniz's "Granada (Serenata)," and Torroba's *Sonatina*. A student chorus from Cádiz, La Tuna Normalista Gaditana, concluded the program.

This was the sort of variety show that *malagueños* patronized at the Cervantes, and it speaks to the taste not only of the concert-going public but also of the guitarist who chose to appear in such a format. As we'll see, poetry was a lifelong passion of Celedonio's, as a reader and a writer, and he didn't confine his collaboration to Alarcón. Already in Granada on May

3. THE CITY OF PARADISE, REGAINED

15, 1929, when he was only sixteen, Celedonio appeared with poet Andrés Molina Moles. Critics praised the reader's emotive rendition of his and others' poems.[11] They also extolled the refinement and clarity of Celedonio's execution. In October 1931, Celedonio made an important appearance in a public concert at the Casa del Pueblo, and an *ilusionista* (magician) also performed in this same concert. This pairing is not as improbable as it might at first seem. When he was still very young, Celedonio loved to do magic tricks and acrobatics; not surprisingly, he had a knack for prestidigitation. However, one day he almost killed himself performing tricks on a bicycle, so he abandoned that career path. The guitar was not only a more appealing performance medium but also much safer!

Despite all this aesthetic refinement, though, some critics were apparently suspicious of too much musical erudition. Thus a reviewer said of his recital in Seville at the Teatro Lope de Vega: "The figure of Celedonio Romero captured our attention. He does not put on the airs of a conservatory professor. He is small, nervous, and has a gaze both passionate and melancholy."[12] Some of the highest praise he received during this period came from fellow guitarists such as Fortea, who wrote from Madrid in May 1936 to congratulate him on his recent success: "I am always grateful to receive news from you, and I congratulate you on your brilliant concerts. I wish you continued superlative success." On another occasion, he offered the following encomium, "The guitar in your hands is as a seduced woman unable to resist and full of art."[13] The eminent composer Joaquín Turina also acknowledged the young guitarist's great talent, proclaiming him a "magnificent artist in the difficult art of playing the guitar. He transports us like no one else to a higher plane. I am certain of great success for him."[14]

Regarding this early period, Pepe recalls: "I was just recently reading a letter [from one pupil of Tárrega to another] saying, 'I thought that the memories of the maestro'—referring to Tárrega—'were never to be lived again. But this young boy plays like the maestro used to play. And listening to him has renewed my memories of those unforgettable days of the past.'"[15] Young Celedonio's talents would prove a revelation to concert audiences and critics throughout Spain for the next quarter century.

Of course, life wasn't all fun and fandangos. Somebody had to make money to support the family, and these concert appearances were neither frequent nor remunerative enough for that purpose. Fortunately, Papá found another job, this one at a mining company called Los Guindos, one of the largest and most prominent industrial concerns in Málaga at that time. Thus the family's finances improved, especially after his job there became a permanent appointment and he was made head of the section of *albañilería* (masonry, brickwork). He was soon able to get Uncle Pepe a job there as well, in the same line of work. Young Celedonio did occasionally do regular work, which was necessary to supplement his father's income; for instance, at age fifteen he got a job making rubber soles for sandals.

These difficult economic realities compel us to survey the historical context of which they were a part. The increasing importance of industry to Málaga's economy, beginning in the nineteenth century, had resulted in the formation of labor unions and the growing prominence of socialist, communist, and even anarchist groups there. By the early 1900s, Málaga had become a hotbed of republicanism. For instance, in the summer of 1923, troops were embarking from Málaga for Melilla in Spanish Morocco, and one of them, a corporal, refused to go. He wanted nothing to do with the army's ongoing conflict with local tribesmen there in order to maintain the last vestige of Spain's once-vast empire. He was court-martialed and sentenced to death, but the *malagueños* rose up en masse to protest this, and his sentence was changed to life in prison.

Also in 1923 Captain General Miguel Primo de Rivera (1870–1930) staged a coup and became dictator, reducing the monarch, Alfonso XIII, to a mere figurehead. True, Primo restricted press freedoms and moved against the unions, but the country had been in such chaos that many business leaders and intellectuals welcomed his rule, as they hoped it would restore order and some measure of prosperity.

Uncle Pepe may have had leftist sympathies, but he basically approved of Primo's programs to build roads and dams, improve municipal services, and bring peace to Spanish Morocco. Indeed, there was still plenty of enthusiasm for the old order, and on February 10, 1926, King Alfonso XIII and his wife visited Málaga and were fêted at the conservatory where Celedonio would one day study.[16] Though there was still a large reservoir of sympathy for the royal family, by the late 1920s Primo and his autocratic ways were beginning to wear out their welcome.

In any case, the Romeros themselves were hardly insurrectionaries. Uncle Pepe was drafted in 1926 (at age twenty-one, per the 1912 conscription law) and was destined for the Batallón Cazadores de Africa No. 5, stationed in

3. THE CITY OF PARADISE, REGAINED

Tetuán, Morocco. After nine months, he was promoted to corporal and granted a month's leave to go home. Despite this service to his country and the burdens it imposed, he and his brothers Maxi and Celedonio found time to indulge their passion for collecting stamps, a hobby Celedonio never abandoned.

However, Uncle Pepe lost interest in the guitar after his period of active-duty service ended in 1929, and he soon decided to settle down and raise a family. Instead of returning to Los Guindos, he opened a family business selling shoes, and a short time later, he married his sweetheart, Lola. The nuptials took place on May 7, 1931, when he was twenty-six and she seventeen. Celedonio worked for a time as a sales clerk in his brother's shoe store, and though this might seem far less glamorous than performing in concert halls, it had its exciting moments. On the morning of May 11, 1931, he reported to work only to find that the store had been broken into and several items stolen. The police soon determined that some escaped convicts were responsible for the burglary. But far worse crises awaited. In 1932 Lola's pregnancy ended with a stillborn baby girl. Papá Romero was so distressed by this loss that he died only four days later, on September 7, 1932, from a heart attack and a stroke. He was buried at San Miguel cemetery, though the grave is no longer there and the whereabouts of his remains are unknown.

Now a widow in rather desperate straits, Mamá received financial assistance from the Caja de Beneficencia (a sort of public life insurance), and she used it to start a business in the Calle Cruz Verde selling shoes, sandals, and other sorts of footwear. Celedonio worked behind the counter at this new store and developed a very good rapport with the customers. In fact, he demonstrated a real knack for salesmanship, on one memorable occasion selling hundreds of pairs of popular white beach sandals in a single day. This capacity for moving product would stand him in good stead years later while promoting the very novel idea of a guitar quartet. Still, despite this commercial success, Celedonio didn't have extensive resources, and Uncle Pepe helped him with medical expenses and clothing.

Again, however, the realities of the world beyond Málaga impinged on the Romeros' domestic life, with its various triumphs and tragedies. For one thing, the 1930s were the decade in which all the Romero brothers would wear an army uniform, if not always in the same army. In 1930, upon turning twenty-one, Maximino reported for compulsory military service, and the following year, the reign of Alfonso XIII came to an end and the Second Republic was proclaimed, on April 14, 1931. There was widespread public support for this transformation, and the Republicans handily won national elections in June of that year. Málaga itself was increasingly controlled by powerful labor unions, and though the leftists did not prevail in national balloting two years later, the city sent the first-ever communist to the national congress in 1933. In that same year, it was Adolfo's turn to serve his country, and he wound up in Uncle Pepe's old unit, stationed in Granada. A leftist revolt in the north in 1934 presaged the coming civil war, and the Romero brothers' military background would literally put them in the front lines of that conflict, as we shall see.

In the meantime, however, the peripatetic Romeros decamped from Calle Parras 27 in 1933 and found a new home nearby, at Calle Parras 8. Mamá had her hands full as a widow with four boys, and as had always been her custom, she hired some domestic help. However, the maid soon stole some of her precious jewelry and never reappeared. This maid's replacement created a different sort of dilemma. Her name was Teresa, and her pheromones called in an irresistible way to young Celedonio. Mamá forbade their association and fired Teresa, but Celedonio continued to see her on the sly. Uncle Pepe was given the assignment of keeping an eye on them. Here is yet another juncture where our story might have taken a drastically different turn, because if Celedonio had married Teresa, the Romeros as we know them would never have existed. As luck would have it, the dalliance with Teresa lost steam as Celedonio rediscovered his first love, the guitar, in preparation for the concert at the Teatro Cervantes in 1933. And there were other distractions.

"HELLO, I AM CELEDONIO ROMERO"

During the early 1930s, Celedonio met and courted Inez de los Ángeles (Angelita) Gallego Molina. Born January 4, 1910, she was over three years older than her suitor. She lived with her parents, sister, and grandmother at Calle Carretería 70, in a nice part of town, centrally located. The conservatory and the Teatro Cervantes were within easy walking distance, and an electric streetcar ran directly in front of their home. Her father was a carpenter, but his upwardly mobile wife pushed him to become a successful

3. THE CITY OF PARADISE, REGAINED

businessman by turning their residence into a furniture store, behind which they maintained their living quarters.

The first meeting of Celedonio and Angelita was memorable, which explains why today's Romeros relish retelling the story. Her sister, Dolores (Loli), a student of piano and Spanish dance at the conservatory, wanted to take guitar lessons and had secured the tutorial services of a young student there. He showed up for the first lesson and announced in his dignified way, "Hello, I am Celedonio Romero." He was dressed in a black suit with a new hat, in order to make himself look important; however, his extremely youthful appearance and diminutive stature did not inspire confidence in the Gallego sisters. Undeterred by their incredulous reaction, he assured them that he would one day play at Carnegie Hall in "Nueva York." Whether that was actual clairvoyance or youthful braggadocio we cannot say. It was probably a bit of both, but in any case it had the desired effect of getting his foot in the door—literally—and stimulating some interest.

Of course, what mattered most was not his hat but rather his guitar playing, and this clearly passed muster. The first piece he ever played for his future bride was the passionate and spirited *Serenata española* by piano virtuoso Joaquim Malats (1872–1912), a work for piano that Celedonio had transcribed.[17] This animated serenade is still a Romero family favorite and regularly appears on their concert programs. But the young guitarist aspired to compose as well as arrange. While courting Angelita, Celedonio once attempted to steal a kiss. Angelita resisted, leading the lovesick Celedonio to compose the "Tango Angelita," whose plaintive lyrics assert, "All I wanted was a kiss."[18] In the end, as muse and matriarch, Angelita would give him all the kisses he wanted, and a great deal more.

Angelita's house was a popular meeting place for talented young *malagueños*. Celedonio's musical friends would now come by to visit, including pianist Miguel Dochado Díaz (1917–2000), who later went on to become a notable interpreter of Albéniz's music and composed a spirited piano piece titled *Málaga*. Angelita was no passive observer of the arts, however. She was herself a student at the conservatory, studying drama and dance, and she was an outstanding singer. She premiered some of Leandro Rivera Pons's songs on Radio Nacional de España (Málaga), accompanied on the piano by Don Leandro himself (recall that he was Celedonio's harmony and solfège teacher). She also had a philosophical bent very congenial to Celedonio's, and in later years considered that all their early poverty and hardships were a valuable learning experience. This was a good thing, because at this point, their problems were just beginning.

Several decades later, Pepe's daughter Angelina had to write about a family member as a school assignment. She chose to write about her grandmother, and it's fortunate for us that she did, because her short vignette sheds fascinating light on this period in Angelita's early history, about her family's generosity to the poor, and the difficult times during which they lived. I quote it here as it was written by a young Angelina:

> When Angelita Romero was about 3 years old she lived in the back of a furniture store. She didn't have any sisters so a lot of times she would talk to the people who came to buy furniture. One day a very poor girl came very quiet to the door, she was very dirty and had bugs in her hair and was very skinny because she was very hungry. Angelita's mommy [Encarnación, or Encarma for short] asked her what she wanted, she said she wanted to have a piece of bread so Angelita's mother got her a piece of bread and left.[19] But the next day she came again and Angelita said what do you want? And the girl wanted another piece of bread so she got it and she went. Etc. But then for a few days she didn't come any more. Maybe she was sick. Angelita's mom's name was Encarma, who asked the girl why she didn't come for a long time. The girl said that the police put her in jail. Then Encarma asked the girl her name, her name was Rosa [Rosario]. "Don't you have a mommy?" asked Encarma. "Yes," said Rosa, "but I don't have a daddy, he died and my mommy got married to another man and he doesn't like me he has another little girl about 6 years old." "Tell your mommy that I want to have a talk with her," said Encarma. "OK," said Rosa. So Rosa got her mommy and she came. Encarma said, "Why don't you want her? Don't you like her?" Rosa's mother said, "no." Encarma said she would take her and that was okay. She washed Rosa and while doing her hair bugs crawled on to Encarma's arms. She cut off all her hair and put medicine on it to kill lice. Rosa and Angelita became like sisters. She lived with them for many years. Rosa's mother never returned.

In 1933 Adolfo returned from military service and began working for Los Guindos, his father's old firm, in the masonry section. At this time, Loli Gallego finished her dance studies and started to perform in theaters, earning good reviews from the critics. The really big news from this period, however, was the nuptials of Celedonio and Angelita, which took place on November

3. THE CITY OF PARADISE, REGAINED

29, 1934. The newlyweds took up residence in Celedonio's mother's house at Calle Hinestrosa 3, a flat with five small rooms and a kitchen. In fact, they were married in the *piso* (flat) just below theirs, where a woman named Justa lived. Unfortunately, shortly after his wedding, Celedonio was inducted into the military and sent to Granada in the same regiment in which his brothers had served.

In January 1935 Angelita received a letter from Celedonio saying he was laid up in the military hospital due to a strong attack of rheumatism, in this case chest pains suggesting a weak heart. Angelita, Adolfo, Lola, and Uncle Pepe immediately boarded a train to go visit him. Though they were relieved to find that Celedonio was already getting better, Uncle Pepe was able to use his connections to have him declared unfit for duty by a medical tribunal, and he was subsequently sent home.

After Celedonio recovered, he was featured on Radio Nacional de España in Málaga, where he gave a concert every Wednesday; although the pay wasn't generous, it was regular. Celedonio was now able to resume his studies at the conservatory, taking harmony with Pedro Megias in 1935. However, Celedonio also had an insatiable curiosity about music history, and clippings in the family archive bear witness to his efforts to enlarge his understanding of it. For instance, in its January 19, 1936, issue, the newspaper *El Debate* published a big spread under the headline "The First Spanish Guitar Book Was Published in Valencia in 1536" ("El primer libro español de guitarra data de 1536 y se imprimió en Valencia"). Celedonio devoured such information, and he cut out the article to save for future consultation. There are many such clippings in the family archive, mostly about Renaissance music and composers but also some about contemporary performers, especially Regino Sainz de la Maza and Segovia. Celedonio was acutely aware of Segovia's success and had already determined to match or surpass it. He would have to clear many hurdles before that could happen, and some of them posed a threat not only to his career but also to his very life.

CIVIL WAR

The challenges that Celedonio had faced thus far paled in comparison to the storm that was about to break over the entire country and, soon enough, the world. National elections were again held on February 16, 1936, and these were to be the last free elections in Spain for four decades. The leftists regained power, and a coalition of fascists, monarchists, militarists, landowners, and the Catholic Church rose up to overthrow the government and replace it with one more to their liking. Thus almost a half year after this fateful election, the Spanish Civil War began in Morocco on Friday, July 17, 1936, and spread to the peninsula the following day. Ironically, Celedonio was scheduled to give a concert at the conservatory that very Saturday evening, at 10:00 p.m.; needless to say, it was canceled. However, this turn of events did not mean the end of concert life in Málaga, as concerts became one of the principal means by which the local Republican forces could raise money, and Celedonio was very active on this front.

Throughout their careers, the Romeros have participated in benefit concerts for worthy causes. One of the first we know much about took place at the Teatro Cervantes on October 9, 1936, at 4:00 p.m., organized by the Professional Group of Journalists of the Spanish Graphics Federation, to help blood banks.[20] A genuine potpourri, it offered some symphonic works, a dramatic comedy, a recital of poetry, and then José Navas and Celedonio playing guitar. It closed with some numbers featuring tenor Aurelio Anglada. Celedonio had already played at one of these variety shows at the Cervantes on July 23, at 6:00 p.m., this one featuring the flamenco singer Manolete and the Banda Municipal, which played the Republican "Himno de Riego" (Hymn of Riego) and—lest anyone doubt the political orientation of these events—the "Internationale," the communist hymn.

The "Internationale" was a favorite in the Romero family, and Celin says that Uncle Adolfo taught him and his brothers this catchy tune during the Franco era. More recently, Pepe even made a guitar arrangement of it to serve as a ringtone for a friend of his. This says more about Pepe's sense of humor than his political leanings, which are liberal but hardly communist. In fact, Pepe believes that if he had asked Torroba or Rodrigo, both of whom were reliably conservative, to arrange the "Internationale" for string quartet, they would have done it. They weren't that ideologically hidebound and always appreciated a good melody.

Adolfo exhibited the anticlerical fervor of the Spanish left, and during the Franco period he not only taught Celedonio's boys the "Internationale" but also gave them lectures about the evils of the church. He *was* a communist, though he saw only the romantic side of the revolution; the real-

3. THE CITY OF PARADISE, REGAINED

ity of gulags, purges, and collectivization were evidently unknown to him. Nonetheless, his sermonettes had their intended effect on impressionable young minds. Celin recalls hearing the very right-wing Cardinal Pedro Segura y Saénz (1880–1957) speaking in church years after the war. Celin was repelled by the opulence of his surroundings and the power of someone like Segura, when the ordinary people were suffering so much, and he felt a sort of murderous rage toward Segura welling up inside him. To be sure, Celin is not a violent person, but this revelation makes clear the intensity of passions on all sides of the war, passions that lingered well after it was over. It was a conflict in which it became increasingly difficult to remain an innocent or passive bystander. People were forced to take sides, and the Romeros would not need much coaxing.

When war broke out, the local garrison was at first indecisive but then resolved to support the republic. Young workers formed a battalion of militias and named Adolfo their lieutenant instructor. He and his siblings Maximino and Pepe would remain loyal to the Republican government and fight on its side. Though Sevilla and Granada fell to Franco's forces right away and without much of a struggle, Málaga was a bastion of Republican fervor and determined to hold out. It would pay a steep price for its loyalty.

Franco's air force started bombing the city of Málaga in August 1936, only a month after the war began and about the same time that his thugs murdered Federico García Lorca in Granada. It is rarely noted but nonetheless tragically true that Málaga was one of the first cities in modern history to be subjected to aerial bombardment, for no other purpose than to terrorize the civilian population into submission. Picasso immortalized the May 1937 bombing of the Basque city of Guernica with his monumental black, white, and gray canvas of that name, but there is some irony in the fact that the city of his birth had started receiving the Nationalist terror treatment almost a year earlier, sans protest painting. This treatment hit close to the Romero family. A cousin of Celedonio's, Manolito Pinazo, was killed during one of these raids. He was only a teenager at the time and had gone with his aunt to buy some bread. On their way home, a bomb fell near him and ended his short life.

Church bells were used to warn of an impending attack, and there was a bomb shelter near where Celedonio and Angelita lived, at Calle Hinestrosa 3. But those defenses did little good if a woman was at home and in labor.

PART 1. SOUTHERN SPAIN

On the evening of November 23, 1936, that woman was Angelita Romero, giving birth to Celin (he was actually named Celedonio, after his father, but he is universally known by the nickname Celin, to distinguish between the two of them). This evening is remembered locally as the "Noche de Nueve Aviones" (Night of the Nine Planes). These aircraft appeared over the city and began to bomb and strafe at random. Fortunately for the Romero family, Hinestrosa was a narrow street and thus harder to attack with any precision. There was still plenty of rubble in the wake of the *bombardeo*, however, and Celedonio could not get to the Cruz Verde (Green Cross) station to report the birth for several days afterward. Thus Celin's official birthday is the twenty-eighth, though he was actually born five days earlier. Despite Franco's best efforts, the building in which Celin was born is still standing, though in serious disrepair and vacant. Years later, while Celin was visiting his birthplace, an elderly woman who had lived on Hinestrosa since the 1930s recognized him as the boy born during that terrible evening.

This horrific experience was but a rude initiation into the many tribulations that the civil war would visit on the Romeros. Angelita insisted on nursing her little Celin throughout the war, but because normal food was in short supply, she ate soup prepared from grass and various nuts to supplement her diet. After all, cows ate grass and produced the milk she would otherwise have given him. She figured that she could do the job herself, though having a bovine stomach, with four compartments instead of just one, would clearly have helped. Of course, milk was one thing, water another. Celin's parents recalled babies dying everywhere because the drinking water was tainted.[21]

This hardship was only one of the family's wartime ordeals, however. Celedonio had no concerts to give and no income, so they had to sell much of the family's furniture and other possessions just to survive. Worse, the republic was well aware of his earlier stint in the army and now sought to call him up. The records of his military service show that he was able to parry these thrusts by reminding them of his medical problems and also the fact that he was born not in Spain but rather in Cuba.[22] Cuba was an independent nation and would object to one of its citizens being pressed into service. Celedonio was nonetheless mobilized and sent to the front, but he was placed in the infirmary of his battalion and spent most of his time there. He was then declared unfit and sent home.

3. THE CITY OF PARADISE, REGAINED

All of this became moot as Franco advanced through Andalusia. The Nationalist army quickly triumphed not only in Granada and Sevilla but also in Cádiz and Córdoba. Almería, Jaén, Huelva, and Málaga, however, held out against the fascists as long as they could. But whereas the French and the English remained on the sidelines (and U.S. firms like Texaco, Ford Motor Company, General Motors, and Firestone Tire and Rubber Company did business with Franco), the Germans and the Italians were in the thick of the fighting by now, and Mussolini's Black Shirts played an important role in the conquest of Málaga, a campaign that was directed by the notorious General Gonzalo Queipo de Llano y Sierra (1875–1951). Queipo de Llano was a ruthless killer, and even to this day, when Pepe and Celin utter his name, they do so with intonations of loathing and dread.

Of course, ruthlessness in wartime can pay handsome dividends, and on February 6, 1937, the 12,000 lightly armed and poorly trained Republican militiamen of the Confederación Nacional del Trabajo (National Confederation of Labor) bowed to the inevitable and evacuated the city. Along with them fled 150,000 *malagueños*, heading north along the coast toward Motril, Almería, Alicante, Valencia, and even Barcelona. These refugees included Uncle Pepe and his brothers, but Celedonio and Angelita did not want to subject little Celin to such rigors and stayed put in Málaga. That was a potentially fatal decision.

On February 8, 1937, the Nationalists entered a Málaga in ruins, and as had happened elsewhere, reprisals by paramilitary groups commenced immediately. Thousands of people were imprisoned or executed after summary trials. Celedonio and the guitarist Navas were soon detained and taken to the patio of the *comisaría*, or precinct station, where they were forced to stand for hours with numerous other detainees. For many of these people, this would be their final stop before facing a firing squad. Fortunately, some reliably rightist friends showed up to attest to the guitarists' innocence, and they were released. But Celedonio's trial by fire was far from over, and he would now have to accommodate himself to a whole new order of things.

In the first place, Celedonio had to join the fascist workers union, Central Obrera Nacional-Sindicalista (Nationalist Syndicalist Workers Central), and his surviving membership card shows that he did so in March 1937, shortly after Málaga's capitulation. This union was founded in 1934 by the Falange (Phalanx), the Spanish fascist movement inspired by Mussolini and Hitler and directed by José Antonio Primo de Rivera, son of the late military dictator Antonio Primo de Rivera. This union, whose acronym is CONS, was brought under the umbrella of Franco's official union, the Organización Sindical Española, in 1940. From now on, if Celedonio wanted to give a concert, he would have to collaborate with the Falange, and he would do so often.

But at this precise moment, other compromises with the regime posed even greater dangers. In a classic case of double jeopardy, Celedonio was now drafted into the *Nationalist* army and faced the very real prospect of being sent north to fight his own brothers. Local medics in Franco's army declared him fit for service, and he was soon on a train to the front. However, he had no intention of going along with this plan and instead got off the train in Seville to seek the assistance of acquaintances there. He made his way to the home of Baldomero Romero Escacena, who he knew was a lover of the guitar and who had apparently already heard complimentary reports about Celedonio from no less a celebrity than Segovia.[23]

Romero Escacena received our guitarist sympathetically and took him to the head of the army medical corps in Seville, also a devotee of music. Col. Antonio Álvarez González (1899–1978) had studied medicine, then entered the military in 1927, and subsequently spent several years in the North African Spanish colony of Ceuta.[24] A specialist in dermatology, he was serious, formal, educated, cultured, and *very* Catholic. He went to Mass every morning and often to prayers and vespers. He knew Franco personally and was a *Franquista*. However, he was also a devotee of classical music, especially Bach, Beethoven, Schubert, and Schumann. Thus he and Celedonio had more in common than one might have imagined.

To his credit, Colonel Álvarez's love of music trumped his sense of military duty on this particular occasion, as he was also enamored of the guitar and saw no good reason why a talented artist like Celedonio should become cannon fodder. He wrote a letter stating that Celedonio had heart disease (which was true) and could not serve on active duty. Celedonio then returned to his family in Málaga and spent the rest of the war working in a hospital. A couple of lieutenants there doubted the authenticity of Álvarez's letter but were reprimanded for their insubordination and sent off to the front. Not for the last time had Celedonio succeeded in using his guitar to make a very influential friend.

3. THE CITY OF PARADISE, REGAINED

Though we are getting a little ahead of our story here, Celedonio and Colonel Álvarez became and remained mutual admirers. In fact, several years after the war, Álvarez sought him out for guitar instruction; eventually, Celedonio put a nine-year-old Pepe in charge of his lessons. Álvarez had a vexing technical problem, but the youthful prodigy quickly analyzed and solved it: The colonel was holding in his right-hand ring finger and then kicking it out rather than letting it return by itself. Once he let the finger return of its own accord, his technique improved. He was delighted with Pepe's tutelage, referred to the boy as "maestro," and addressed him with the formal *usted*, rather than the informal *tú*. Pepe also learned something in return. Álvarez played flamenco guitar, and the first flamenco piece Pepe ever learned he acquired from the colonel: a *tientos*, in which the chords D minor and C major figure prominently.[25]

While Celedonio was using guitar diplomacy to get back to his family in Málaga, Uncle Pepe and his family fled the city. Roads north were being bombarded by Nationalist naval vessels like the cruiser *Canarias*, which was soon joined by planes dropping incendiary bombs and strafing roads swollen with a growing tide of refugees, many of whom ended their journey in a heap of corpses. Uncle Pepe's little flock traveled by night and waited out the days, subsisting on coffee, sugar, and condensed milk, hitching rides on handcarts and any other sort of conveyance to put their little boy in. On February 10, they finally arrived in Almería, where they soon met up with Maximino and Adolfo, who were delayed in leaving Málaga and then had to make up for lost time.

Maximino left shortly thereafter for Crevillente under a safe conduct from the local Republican commander, who was forming battalions to send to the front. Adolfo was still of military age and went to Valencia to join the Republican army. He eventually wound up participating in the defense of Madrid, where he endured the rigors of combat: he was once buried under a pile of dirt from a bomb that exploded nearby, and on another occasion, a bullet just barely missed his head. He later took part in the battles of Brunete, Villanueva de la Cañada, and Quijorna. Meanwhile, Maximino remained with units stationed in Elche, near Alicante on the Mediterranean coast.

Uncle Pepe forged ahead to Valencia, where he found work in the local army offices. He became head of his particular administrative section and was given an assistant and two typists. While thus employed, he received a promotion to the rank of captain, with an increase in salary. Due to persistent physical ailments, he was declared unfit for frontline duty and spent the rest of the war in Valencia with his family. He was able to use his army connections to get Adolfo and Maximino out of harm's way, however, and Maximino spent the remainder of the war in Valencia and Adolfo in Barcelona. He had never wanted to join a political party, but during this time he was persuaded by some friends to become a member of the Socialist Party, though his membership would be brief.

As the war drew to its inevitable close, the brothers tried to flee the country, perhaps to Mexico or Nicaragua, but various logistical and bureaucratic obstacles made that plan impractical. So they would return to Málaga to face a very uncertain fate. On April 13, 1939, only a few days after Franco declared a formal end to the fighting, Uncle Pepe left Valencia for Málaga under safe conduct. At various points he lied to the Falange about his service and was able to get through, but Maximino and Adolfo were not so fortunate. Both wound up in concentration camps, Maximino in Albatera and Adolfo in Argelès-sur-Mer in France. To make matters worse, Uncle Pepe's brother-in-law was in a concentration camp in La Aurora. The prisoners all suffered from hunger and a lack of proper hygiene, but the Romero brothers survived and were able to return to Málaga, where they shared their stories with incredulous friends and relatives, who were both distressed and relieved by what they heard.

POSTWAR REALITIES

Meanwhile, times were tough in Málaga and would remain so for several years. Denunciations, accusations, vendettas, and the settling of old scores sent many hapless victims to Franco's killing fields. Celedonio recalled hearing the sound of guns as innocents were mercilessly slaughtered near his home and unceremoniously thrown into mass graves. But it wasn't just summary execution that kept people on edge. The year 1940 was called the Year of Hunger because even if one had money there was very little food to buy with it, especially fruits and vegetables. Uncle Pepe welcomed the arrival of a daughter during this time, but Lola's breasts no longer gave milk, so they fed the infant the condensed variety.

3. THE CITY OF PARADISE, REGAINED

Celin can still recall these troubled times in vivid detail: "The family had very little money. Once, when I was five [in 1942], we got to the point where we had no money at all, with nothing left to sell except for my bicycle. I went with my mother and father to sell my bicycle to a local shop, and we used the money to buy bread. But it was a very hard time for everybody, not just us."[26]

Epidemics were also a postwar scourge, especially typhus, which cut a swath of death through Málaga in the early 1940s because many homes lacked adequate sanitation. Although the epidemic was not responsible for taking her life, Celedonio's mother died May 30, 1942, adding to the family's already considerable distress. (Nonetheless, Celedonio gave a concert only five days later, on June 3, at the Centro de Estudios Andaluces Plaza de José Antonio.)

The disease did come calling for Celedonio and Angelita a few years later, though, and they almost died from intestinal bleeding and excruciating bedsores. Blood transfusions and visits from Celedonio's friend Dr. Atilano Cerezo saved them, though evening visits from the Hermanitas de la Cruz complemented the miracle of modern medicine with welcome spiritual support. Mamá appreciated the money these Little Sisters of the Cross would leave on the night table after departing in the morning.

Employment was hard to find as well, but Maximino was hired to work in a factory making hemp sandals, a trade that he would eventually convert into a very profitable business. Uncle Pepe was initially reduced to selling tickets for Celedonio's concerts, keeping a commission for himself. This was the first money he earned after returning to Málaga. He was eventually able to get back on his feet with loans from Celedonio, whose musical star was once again in the ascendant.

Indeed, despite all this hardship—or perhaps because of it—Celedonio wasted very little time rebooting his career. This is where things get politically a little murky. True, Celedonio was a man of decidedly Republican sentiments, from a family that had literally laid its life on the line for the republic. But the republic had lost, and Celedonio now did what was necessary to survive: he collaborated with the new regime, including giving many concerts for the Falange and its educational wing, the Delegación Provincial del Frente de Juventudes (Provincial Delegation of the Youth Front). He would give concerts under their auspices, and the press, now controlled by the Falange, would oblige with fulsome notices.

PART 1. SOUTHERN SPAIN

On June 13, 1939, the Falangist paper *Fe* (Faith) in Seville published a glowing review by E. Mariani of Celedonio's performance at the Ateneo two days earlier. It reported that the young virtuoso has performed in Barcelona, Valencia, Málaga, Granada, and elsewhere and made laudatory reference to his military service (he was technically still in the army and would not be discharged until July 1). On this occasion, Celedonio played his own Impromptu, two preludios, a *malagueña*, and a *jota*, in addition to canonic works in the guitar repertoire. *El Correo de Andalucía*, on June 11, 1939 (now officially referred to as the Year of Victory, or "Año de la Victoria"), also praised his performance, stating that with the completion of his military service he was again using his guitar "to delight the Spanish public."[27] On another occasion, he played for the Delegación Provincial de Sindicatos (Provincial Delegation of Unions), and in fact he would give many concerts for government-controlled labor unions (*sindicatos*) over the years. His long-delayed concert at the Málaga Conservatory finally took place on November 26, 1939, and featured poetry reciter Agustín Alarcón in an invitation-only program. He performed there again on December 6, 1941, only a day before Japan attacked the American naval base at Pearl Harbor and events in World War II suddenly took a dramatic turn for the worse for Franco's fascist friends in Italy and Germany.

The 1940s witnessed a gradual flowering of Celedonio's concert career. Always willing to perform benefit concerts, he appeared at Salamanca's Coliseum in an event organized by the Falange's Delegación Provincial de Educación Popular to combat infant mortality. Again he performed along with a reciter, this time Sandro Carreras reading passages from Rubén Darío and Julio de Hoyos. After an "homage" to the Falange Youth of Franco at the Gran Teatro Falla in Cádiz on September 9, 1942, the *Diario de Cádiz* reviewer heaped lavish praise on his tone and technique. The campaign against infant mortality continued for several years and was yet another indicator of the hardships Spain faced in the aftermath of a ruinous civil war. Celedonio returned to Cádiz two years later, and the September 6, 1944, issue of *Diario de Cádiz* reveals that he had been touring in the north of Spain, including in Bilbao at the Teatro Campos Eliseos as well as in Seville, an increasingly regular destination, as we shall see.

On one occasion, he performed at the Málaga Conservatory to benefit those who were sick and poor, in commemoration of the Festival of Saint

3. THE CITY OF PARADISE, REGAINED

James, the patron saint of Spain. Another group Celedonio collaborated with was the Asociación Mútuo Benefica del Colegio Oficial de Practicantes de Málaga y su Provincia (Beneficent Mutual Association of the Official School of Practitioners of Málaga and Its Province), which organized tours to, say, nearby Ronda. These excursions would often include a concert by Celedonio there.

In 1943 Celedonio gave another benefit concert for Málaga's Centro de Estudios Andaluces, located in an eighteenth-century building in Málaga. A local reviewer was reminded of the concerts of Padre Basilio, a monk-guitarist in the Palacete de la Moncloa in the court of Maria Luisa, wife of Carlos IV.[28] This evocation of the church and the ancien régime was entirely consistent with the cultural atmosphere of the reactionary Franco government. Interestingly, the reviewer described Celedonio himself as a "timid boy, sensitive and modest," though he went on to assert that even "famous guitarists" have something to learn from him. Celedonio's repertoire remained constant, however, regardless of locale, and included his arrangements of Bach, Schumann, and Malats, as well as his own original works and those by Matteo Carcassi, Fernando Sor, and Francisco Tárrega.

In fact, the dozens of extant reviews from the 1920s–1950s are consistently positive. Regardless of the political environment in which he was performing, he made the same favorable impression. There was something compelling, immediate, and deeply moving about his interpretations. And he showed good taste in his programming. One Seville critic lauded him for not making transcriptions of orchestral works.[29] Of course, he would later resort to just such a strategy in forging a completely new kind of repertoire, for quartet, though that was years in the future. But his choice of works by fellow Spaniards Tárrega, Malats, Albéniz, and Torroba could easily be construed by the Nationalists as an expression of patriotism. And the Germanophilic fascists had no objections to Bach and Schumann.[30] Of course, we can be certain he would have played the same pieces if the communists had prevailed.

As we know, the rightists had won, and only they could ensure both his survival and his professional success. Thus the most striking clipping of all in the Romero archive is untitled but dated January 26, 1944, stating that he had performed at the request of and before Franco himself in the Palacio de la Capitanía General de Barcelona![31] One hesitates to call this an honor, but it was a milestone in his career, an indication of just how far he had come. It is hard to believe that Celedonio was thus ever on any blacklist. It is much more likely that any subsequent difficulties he had in leaving the country resulted from the regime's desire to hold on to him. For now, at least, he would confine his moving to changes of residence in Spain rather than outside it.

WANDERLUST

The Romero family may have no actual Roma ancestry (see appendix 2 for a family genealogy), but during this period they changed addresses so often that one could be excused for suspecting a mark of wanderlust somewhere in the family tree. Celedonio was actually earning a good income now from concert performance, with a little help from the Falange. Around 1940 the family moved from Hinestrosa to a row house at Calle Rafaela 38, where Pepe would be born. About five years later, Celedonio hired Adolfo to build him a house at Calle Diego de Vergara 41, which is where Angel was born. They would soon sell this house, however, and move to Arroyo de los Ángeles, where they rented two rooms with access to a kitchen. An apartment on Teniente de Díaz Corpas would be their last residence in Málaga before they departed for Seville (and several other places of residence!).

These addresses may mean little to those unfamiliar with the city, but all the residences had one thing in common: they were fairly primitive by modern standards. At roughly five hundred square feet, they were anything but spacious, though they always included running water and indoor toilets, amenities many people at the time would have considered luxurious. For instance, the house at Calle Rafaela 38 offered two small bedrooms, a bathroom, a small living area, a kitchen, and a little enclosed patio.

José Luis Romero Gallego entered the world at this residence at 1:45 a.m. on March 8, 1944, though Papá waited until the eleventh to register the birth because a stubbornly high infant mortality rate made it very likely that his new baby would not survive. That same evening, Celedonio was giving a concert in Málaga, and though Angelita always attended his performances, on this particular evening she was clearly indisposed. So the local radio station broadcast the concert so that she could hear it. Pepe's introduction to the world thus featured auspicious accompaniment from his father's guitar.

3. THE CITY OF PARADISE, REGAINED

Two years later, on August 17, 1946, the final Romero child, Miguel Ángel Leonardo, was born at the Diego de Vergara address.[32] Although the house no longer stands, a walk through the neighborhood now reveals that it was one of the few new buildings in the area. Celin remembers that in those days there were still open fields and a blacksmith shoeing horses nearby. One would never guess that now, as the market occupying that real estate is in the middle of a bustling urban environment. This is a reminder of just how much Málaga has grown over the past century, and how much smaller and more intimate a city it was when the Romeros called it home.

LIKE FATHER, LIKE SONS

It was in these relatively humble abodes that first Celin, then Pepe and Angel would learn to play the guitar. They couldn't help learning something because Papá had no separate practice facilities, instead preferring the kitchen for this purpose. All the boys thus grew up with the sights and sounds of the guitar everyday. As Celin recalled:

> I started to play when I was about 3 years old. At a very early age, I loved music, the sounds that my father was producing. His melodic lines had such beauty. A guitar maker named Paco Domínguez lived close to us in Málaga, and every afternoon we went to see him. My parents bought me a little guitar from him, and while my father practiced, I would sit on his footstool and imitate what he did. During the winter it can get quite cold in Málaga, so we would keep warm in the kitchen while my mother was preparing food. Before I knew much of anything else, I was playing the guitar. I got more serious when I was eight or nine, and my father became stricter with me.[33]

As he explained in another interview, Celedonio was a "charismatic person, hard worker, one of the most refined musicians I have every heard. Also a loving father."[34]

When Pepe was three, he suffered a serious attack of what seemed to be polio, though luckily it wasn't. Anyway, he was confined to bed, where he listened to his father practicing. That was his first musical memory.[35] "It was completely a thing of free will," said Pepe. "I remember listening to my father and thinking it was wonderful, that it was beautiful. I could hear music very easily in my mind without an instrument. It was like having a radio in my head and I could not wait to learn how to play the guitar so that I could make that music come out."[36]

The brothers' guitar studies never involved any element of coercion, however. Celin explained Papá's motivational techniques: "Instead of stuffed animals, we had stuffed guitars. Our first toys were guitars made of cloth that we pretended to play. But my father would just give us guitars; he would never tell us to play them. And he didn't try to teach us. He just waited for us to pick them up by ourselves."[37]

It would not be too many years before Celin took over instructional responsibilities for his siblings and launched a performing career of his own. Like his father, Celin was very strict and did not tolerate inattention to detail. As Pepe much later recalled, "My father used to assign . . . Celin to teach me. He was only a few years older than I was and he used to start by slapping me. Then he would say, 'This is in case you don't play right.' I would respond by kicking him and we would always start out the lesson with a fight and then get down to business."[38] On some occasions, however, the fisticuffs were sufficiently acute that Papá's belt became the arbiter of justice, sparing neither son. Angel would hide under the bed, terrified of being implicated in the dispute.

Lest one be tempted to think that chaos reigned at the Romero home, these were exceptional outbursts. The image that emerges over and over from interviews and articles is of a lively household where poets, musicians, painters, and sculptors gathered. Of course, guitarists were frequent visitors, including renowned virtuoso Narciso Yepes (1927–97), whose friendship with the family endured even after the Romeros moved to California. Interestingly, the brothers recall avoiding political discussions with Yepes, who was much more conservative than the Romeros. This is a small example of a larger phenomenon in Spanish society during the postwar years, something called the Gran Olvido (Great Forgetting), in which people simply avoided dwelling on the war and politics, as these topics contained the seeds for future conflict, and no one wanted to plant such seeds ever again.

Art remained uncontroversial under Franco as long as it did not challenge the new order of things, politically or ecclesiastically. It is rather ironic that surrealist Salvador Dalí flourished under the Franco regime, in part because of his religiously themed paintings, which were in no way offensive to the faith, despite their avant-garde character. Pepe showed early art talent, and his parents thought it both safe and prudent to nurture it. Family friend Robin Price recalled a conversation with Mamá about a test Pepe had to take to get into an art school: "[During] Pepe's art exam . . . Mamá [is] waiting out in the hallway—a long time passes and he should be done by now, everyone telling her that Pepe has probably failed. Then when she is finally called inside, she sees that her little boy was just amusing himself with doing portraits of all the examiners, since he finished the test early."[39] Pepe proudly states that he later inherited some brushes and other materials from renowned Málaga artist José Nogales Sevilla (1860–1939), a close friend of the family.

For good reason, then, did Pepe observe that "although there was little money, there was a wealth of art." But if they tired of what was happening at home, there were enticements nearby. "We used to go to the Gypsy quarter to play our guitars," Pepe added. There was apparently a woman there named Mariana who assured them that if they ever got into trouble, they should tell their Roma friends, who would "swarm like bees to come to their aid."[40] Fortunately, no such aid was ever needed.

This little vignette speaks to a larger reality, however, insofar as the Roma in Spain at that time occupied the same lowest rung on the socioeconomic ladder as blacks did in the United States. The close physical, personal, and cultural proximity the Romeros maintained with the Roma was by no means common or acceptable among members of the middle class, even the petite bourgeoisie, to which the Romeros belonged at this time. Their lack of racial and class prejudice was part and parcel of their overall political outlook, which remained unchanged despite Celedonio's necessary collaboration with the Falange and Franco's "labor unions" and would persist over the decades.

This consistency is one thing that distinguished the Romeros from Segovia. The composer Federico Moreno Torroba knew Segovia very well, having collaborated with him since the 1920s. Torroba's son thus felt compelled to point out the following for this book: "Segovia was a great flamenco performer, but he never wanted to play it in public for fear of losing face. In those days, given the prejudices of certain critics, Segovia had good reason to avoid playing flamenco. But all of this disappeared with the Romeros, who had the honor of dignifying flamenco and including it in their concert programs, for example, after playing a concerto by Vivaldi, and the public reacted with great enthusiasm."[41]

Technically well-equipped and thoroughly steeped in the Euroclassical tradition of art music as well as Spanish folklore, Celedonio's boys were now ready to share with the world the education he had given them. Pepe's first performances were for the nuns of a nearby convent, Asilo de los Ángeles. He would play for the old nuns in the courtyard or on the patio, and then they would invite him to participate in an impromptu soccer match. The convent is still there, and on our visit to it in 2013, he recollected those early "concerts" with relish.

In 1951, Celin would follow in Papá's footsteps by appearing on Radio Nacional de España in Málaga.[42] He not only played several selections in his repertoire, mostly guitar works of Sor and Tárrega, but he was also interviewed at length. A typewritten transcript of the interview survives in the Romero archive, and his responses provide rare insights into the family's musical life at this time. He revealed that schoolwork was a priority and did not leave much time for music. The interviewer was somewhat surprised to learn that Celin practiced only a couple of hours a day, and that was when he was on vacation! Celedonio's daily regimen was three times that long because he had to maintain a repertoire of over three hundred works, explained Celin. Not surprisingly, he said that he liked his father's music and felt a special affinity with the works of Fernando Sor. His goal was to finish high school (*bachillerato*) and perfect his guitar playing so that he could perform with his father.

Angel made his debut in 1953, at age seven, on his father's long-running radio program. How many listeners did a program like this reach, at 10:30 p.m.? In the family archive is a notice about a radio broadcast of March 11, 1958, at 4:00 p.m. on Radio Sevilla that reached 1.5 million listeners. At a minimum, then, Celedonio and his boys were reaching tens of thousands of listeners through these appearances, and that was good publicity.

THE RISEN PHOENIX

In part due to his radio program, Celedonio himself was still very much in demand as a performer, and clippings in the archive provide evidence of concerts all over Spain, in Bilbao, Cádiz, Córdoba, Granada, Logroño, Madrid, Málaga, Salamanca, Sevilla, Valladolid, and Zaragoza. He played in a variety of venues, at various times of day. One of the more unusual appear-

3. THE CITY OF PARADISE, REGAINED

ances was at the Málaga Cinema for the Delegación Provincial de Sindicatos on September 28, 1952, at 11:30 a.m.[43] His standard program progressed chronologically through the centuries, from the Renaissance to Baroque, Classical, Romantic, and modern periods, from vihuelist Luis de Milán to Federico Moreno Torroba. And he never failed to include a few of his own creations. This kind of program had worked very well for Segovia, and it was paying off for Segovia's admirer, Celedonio. As a consequence of these numerous triumphs, in 1952 Celedonio was made an honorary member of Barcelona's Peña Guitarrística Tárrega and of the Barcelona Guitar Society.

Celedonio was now a phoenix who had arisen from the ashes of harrowing wartime dangers and postwar poverty. A welcome consequence of all these appearances was increasing income, which permitted him to indulge an understandable passion: guitars. The Romeros have always loved collecting guitars, and their brand preferences are international: Hauser from Germany, Rodríguez from Spain, and Giussani from Italy.[44]

Extant correspondence with various builders reveals some interesting things. One, the family was now doing pretty well financially, because these instruments were not cheap. In 1952, Celedonio ordered two guitars from Hauser, a Llobet model for 600 DM and a Segovia model for 800 DM. In 1955, Celedonio paid 11,770 pesetas to import a Hauser guitar.

In one letter, Hermann Hauser Jr. expresses regret that Celedonio's concert tour in Germany didn't work out, because he had wanted to meet him.[45] In fact, at this time Celedonio was attempting to arrange concert tours in Argentina, Cuba, Germany, France, and Italy, but the seeds he was sowing produced nothing but a crop of frustration.

* * *

Given his conspicuous success at the national level, it is not surprising that Celedonio wanted to share his talents on the international stage, even as Segovia was doing. This would prove much more difficult and eventually motivate him to move abroad for good. Málaga would not be the best platform for such a leap, however. By the early 1950s, Seville had become an increasingly important locale in the Romeros' life, and they would soon relocate there. But it was to be only a temporary way station on the road to much larger horizons.

CHAPTER 4
SEVILLE AND ADIÓS

Seville has been the dominant metropolis of Andalusia since the days of the Reconquest, so it was a natural destination for any *malagueño* like Celedonio seeking to "make it big." And it would be the gateway out of Spain, where his career had hit a sort of glass ceiling beyond which he could not ascend. Celedonio realized the necessity of leaving Spain but was still reluctant to take such a big step. Angelita felt no such inhibitions and was resolved to jump ship. They would do things her way.

To be sure, Celedonio had always hoped it might be possible to have an international career without leaving his homeland, and there were certainly possibilities. What one finds in the family archive, however, is documentation of repeated frustration in achieving the sort of global exposure he craved and deserved. Although one finds no direct proof of it, the available documents strongly suggest that the Franco regime was making it difficult for him to leave the country. He would need friends in high places to help him over this hurdle.

For instance, on July 12, 1949, he received an invitation from Charles Kiesgen, a concert agent in Paris, to perform at the Salle Chopin-Pleyel on November 10, 1949. A little over a month later, on August 17, 1949, Kiesgen sent him all the necessary papers and hoped there would be no problem.

4. SEVILLE AND ADIÓS

But there would be a problem. The Gestoría Administrativa (Administrative Agency) in Madrid wrote Celedonio saying that there were "defects" in the contract (for example, it did not specify the exact amount of remuneration). As a consequence, Celedonio never received the necessary permission to perform.

Sometimes, however, the people to whom Celedonio wrote were simply not interested. On September 28, 1949, Radiodiffusion et Télévision Françaises declined his offer to perform. A letter dated December 16, 1952, from Adrienne Fleuret in Paris expresses regret that she has been unable to line up any concerts for him, as he had requested. In a letter dated July 15, 1954, J. M. Pérez Peña in Havana claims that there was simply no market for classical guitar there. People preferred rumba, mambo, and other Afro-Cuban styles of music, he declared; apparently Sor and Tárrega were a bit too rarified for the popular taste.

The program for a concert in Seville on December 4, 1952, announced that Celedonio would be making a concert tour in America. (It also stated that he was born in 1918, five years later than his actual birth year.) This is something of a mystery, though a 1953 newspaper announcement of a concert in Granada stated that he would soon be going to South America as an "ambassador of Spanish art."[1] In a transcript of a radio interview from this same time, he confirmed that the former president of Peru had organized a tour for him there and that publicity was already circulating about it. But for whatever reason, it never happened. Other documents in the archive suggest the possibility of a concert in Buenos Aires, but that prospect went nowhere.

Celedonio did manage one appearance outside Spain, in Lisbon for an event organized by the Asociación de la Prensa. This was reported on by *ABC* in its March 3, 1954, issue and could have been his ticket to ride, as there were many foreign correspondents there, especially from France, and they expressed admiration for his art. But once again . . . *nada*. The Spanish Embassy in Rome set up some appearances for him there in early 1955, but this time Celedonio contracted colic nephritis, which delayed his preparations and caused the concerts to be canceled, much to the embassy's consternation. To add insult to injury, in 1954 the Radio Nacional de España in Málaga stiffed Celedonio for the back pay it owed him for weekly concerts he had performed from January 1942 to 1947, starting at 400 pesetas per month and increasing to 800. The radio service lamely claimed that a five-year statute of limitations prevented it from making good on its commitments.

These assorted frustrations, disappointments, and setbacks simply reinforced Angelita's argument that they needed to leave Spain. In 1954, a serendipitous encounter would make that departure possible and transform the Andalusian family's future. Farrington Stoddard and his wife, Evelyn, were a middle-aged couple from Santa Barbara, in Southern California.[2] He worked as a radio operator on ocean-going vessels, and she pursued her hobby of writing.[3] They were not wealthy, but they were well off enough that they could dream of spending an extended period in Spain, imbibing its music and other cultural offerings. They decided on Málaga as a locale where they could enjoy the sort of sun and surf they were accustomed to in California, as well as practice their Spanish.[4]

In 1954 they took up residence in Málaga. Fe (as Farrington was known) also had a hobby: guitar. One day he asked a friend, an American soldier, where he could find a good guitar teacher. As luck would have it, this person was the English tutor to a young man named Celin Romero. The Romeros were excellent teachers, he said, so Fe sought them out for instruction. Now, to be sure, there were alternative possibilities, as Málaga had no shortage of guitarists. One local star was Celedonio's old friend José Navas, who gave a recital that both Celin and Fe attended. However, Fe was unimpressed and reiterated his desire to study with the Romeros. He became Celin's first regular student, paying the young Spaniard the unheard of sum of one dollar per daily lesson. It seemed like a fortune to the up-and-coming virtuoso.

At this time, the Romeros were living on the second floor of the apartment building at Teniente Díaz Corpas 5. Like all of their past and future habitations in Spain, this one offered a few hundred square feet of living space and indoor plumbing. Fortunately, the neighbors never complained about the sounds of the guitar at all hours. Celin recalls that across the street from this building was a large open field used as an encampment by homeless *malagueños*, including Roma. During one particularly cruel inundation, these ramshackle abodes were swept away in a tsunami of raging rainwater, and survivors sought refuge in their building, refuge the Romeros were inclined to offer, especially if a stray Roma could play the guitar, sing, and/or dance.

4. SEVILLE AND ADIÓS

Fe and Evie both liked and respected the Romeros and wanted to help them realize their dreams of relocating abroad. But Fe also perceived the commercial potential of this family of ambitious and talented *malagueños*, and he began to dream dreams that coincided perfectly with Celedonio's desire to break out of the suffocating conditions limiting his career in Spain. Fe could become the Romeros' manager and transition to a line of work that wouldn't require so much strenuous travel. It would be a win-win situation. But Fe and Evie could not do this alone. They would need inside help, and that was already available—in Seville.

As we already know, the Romeros were no strangers to Seville. Celedonio had been giving concerts there for many years, and the family spent extended periods in the historic city. For instance, Pepe and Celin remember staying at the Pension Jovellanos in Seville, which was owned by a woman named Trini and her girlfriend.[5] She played the guitar, though not very well. Still, they were pleasant people, and Papá never uttered a disparaging word about their presumed sexual orientation. It was from this locale that Celedonio and his clever wife devised and put into a practice a scheme for increasing the attendance at Celedonio's concerts.

Mamá would call people at random, pretending to be from the Hermanitas de la Cruz (Little Sisters of the Cross) or the Frente de Juventudes (Youth Front), which was associated with the Falange. Using this assumed identity, she would then attempt to intimidate people into promising to buy tickets to a "benefit concert" that Celedonio would be giving for said organization. "Hello, I'm calling from the Hermanitas de la Cruz, and we are presenting a concert of the great Celedonio Romero to benefit our order. How many tickets do you want?" Any ambient noise in her vicinity she would explain as coming from the "office" from which she was calling. Celin's job was to copy the phone book so that Mamá would have the numbers she needed to call at any available phone.

Mamá's father would dress in a fake Falange outfit, putting on a blue shirt with a clutch-of-arrows design embroidered on it, and he would go to deliver the tickets and collect the money. The schemers never threatened reprisal for not buying a ticket, of course, but sometimes a person would smell something fishy and challenge them. Once they infelicitously phoned the cardinal of Seville, who immediately saw through the ruse. But they evaded serious trouble using a trademark mixture of Romero charm and diplomacy.

Of course, the concert wasn't really being organized by that group, but the strategy was first to sell the tickets and *then* go to the Hermanitas or Frente and convince the organization to sponsor the program, offering it a portion of the gate. The organization almost always went along because *dinero* was *dinero*, after all, and times were hard. This little arrangement went on for years and was quite successful. Virtually every benefit concert one comes across in the family archive from the 1940s and 1950s was organized in this fashion, which not only generated considerable income but also spread Celedonio's reputation far and wide.

Some events during these stays at the Jovellanos in Seville were anything but entertaining. Once Pepe became so ill that the doctor advised Papá to take him away from Mamá so that he wouldn't die in her arms. Desperate, Papá took his precious infant and immersed him in hot water, then cold water, back and forth. This wasn't a traditional family cure or any sort of systematic medicine, just purely intuitive guesswork. Soon Pepe started to vomit, then his fever broke, and not long thereafter he revived. This illness occurred before Pepe had been baptized, and though this didn't bother Papá, Mamá called a priest to come and baptize Pepe right away. The priest, however, was too busy and couldn't come. So Papá did the job himself, something anyone can do if he or she knows the proper method. After this close call with limbo, Mamá had all the boys formally baptized, just in case. As it turned out, her worst fears were never realized, and she predeceased them all.

During one of his stays in Seville in the early 1950s, Celedonio made the acquaintance of Gen. José Rodríguez Díaz de Lecea (1894–1967), the air force officer in charge of the base in that region, including the Strait of Gibraltar. Lecea was yet another military officer who loved music in general and the guitar in particular, and he became a genuine fan of Celedonio. Like our guitarist, he was also born in Cuba, though in Matanzas, not Cienfuegos. Despite numerous references to the Caudillo (Franco) in his letters to Celedonio, Lecea was not very ideological, even though he would go on to become minister of the air force and a close associate of "the Leader." Thus the Romero family's political past was of little importance to him.

4. SEVILLE AND ADIÓS

In fact, Lecea became a sort of Maecenas to Celedonio, giving him protection and arranging concerts for him. An undated newspaper clipping makes favorable reference to Celedonio's performance at a private function at the general's residence for his friends, who included the U.S. consul in Seville, Robert E. Wilson, along with other notables. This affair was no doubt arranged to assist Celedonio in his plans to move to the United States. Lecea valued his friendship with Celedonio and took an interest in the whole family. He facilitated Celedonio's purchase of Hauser guitars and their subsequent transport by air into Spain. Recognizing Pepe's remarkable artistic talent, he advised getting him into classes with a real art professor.[6] In fact, when Pepe auditioned for art school in Seville in 1956, the results were reported directly to Lecea. Not surprisingly, young Pepe was rated *sobresaliente* (outstanding).

Lecea also helped Celedonio establish contacts with the U.S. Foreign Service (USFS) in Seville. A letter from the USFS of December 2, 1953, indicates that he and Lecea had written it earlier about the possibility of giving concerts in the United States. The response suggested that they write to David Rubin at the USFS's New York office, as he might be able to arrange appearances at universities and conservatories around the country. The USFS wrote to Celedonio on August 6, 1954, thanking him for an autographed photo and hoping that he would be able to make his concert trip to the United States. None of this correspondence bore any fruit, however. At the urging of the Stoddards, and feeling that they had exhausted everything Málaga had to offer in the way of professional advancement, the Romeros decided to move closer to the likely source of their liberation, in Seville. The Stoddards and Lecea would make this possible.

SEVILLE OR BUST!

In 1954, the Romeros moved to Seville, a city with which Celedonio had long since been on familiar terms as a performing artist. The Stoddards encouraged the move because it would put them in close proximity not only to major concert venues but also to the American consulate, which would prove helpful in getting them to the United States, and to their benefactor Lecea. His assistance would prove invaluable in moving forward with what

Celedonio considered to be the "*engaño,*" the escape plot, or deception. It appears that Celedonio's manager also lived there, as one still finds in the family papers letterhead stationery of M. Fernández Mata, whose offices were at Calle Pureza 81.

However, in one last flirtation with a career in business, the family moved to Seville via Valencia. This circuitous approach speaks to the still somewhat nomadic nature of their existence. They moved from one opportunity to the next without having crystallized a long-term plan. So, when an opportunity presented itself in Valencia, off they went. The idea was to live with Celedonio's brother Maximino there. Entrepreneurially minded, Maximino's wife had started making headgear for donkeys, but the business went nowhere, so Maximino had the idea to make purses out of straw. These proved to be wildly popular, and the business really took off.

Recall that Celedonio had a head for business and was quite a good salesman, so the idea of his forming a partnership with his brother isn't quite so bizarre as it might seem. But Mamá was having none of it. She didn't like living there, especially because they had to cohabit with their in-laws. Most of all, she was afraid that Celedonio would be seduced by the business and leave music behind. When she gazed into her crystal ball (or consulted her tarot cards), she saw concerts, not purses. For these reasons, she quickly soured on Valencia and contacted her former maid, Juana, who had moved to Seville. Juana sent her a telegram claiming to have found just the right living quarters for the family and urging Mamá to bring her brood to Seville. Mamá didn't require much cajoling at this point, and they all left by train for their new home.

When they pulled into the train station in Seville, however, Juana was there to meet them—with bad news. Talking through copious tears, she confessed to having lied about locating living quarters for them. In reality, she had found nothing at all, so it was now late at night, and there was nowhere for them to stay. Celedonio called his friend Lecea, who sent his car and driver to help Celedonio look for lodging. Mamá and her three sons anxiously awaited his return to the station. He eventually succeeded in finding quarters for them—in a whorehouse! It was located in the Barrio de Santa Cruz, the historic Jewish quarter, in a little courtyard called the Plaza Santa Marta (the barrio and plaza are still there, but the brothel is not). They rented two rooms, one

4. SEVILLE AND ADIÓS

for Angel, Pepe, and Mamá and one for Celin and Papá. Pepe recalls that the women were attractively painted, friendly, and nice, though there was a lot of foot traffic in and out of the building. The next day, Lecea's driver returned to take Celedonio to look for more suitable accommodations. (He also advised Mamá not to stand in front of the brothel, since she was not for "rent.") It was difficult to find anything right away, so they spent one more evening with the "ladies." A dirty little secret of the ultrapuritanical Franco era was that poverty drove thousands of women into prostitution, which flourished during the otherwise theocratic regime.

Not far away was a place in another plaza in the Santa Cruz, this one named after Don Juan Tenorio, a historical figure who inspired the Don Juan epic of Gabriel Téllez (1579–1648), known to posterity as Tirso de Molina and a student of Lope de Vega. Molina used it as the basis for his play *El Burlador de Sevilla*, which later served as the inspiration for the Don Giovanni legend and Mozart's opera. In the play, Don Juan Tenorio falls in love with Doña Inés, and when the Don is confronted by her father, the Comendador de Calatrava, he kills him. Tradition holds that Doña Inés's house was right where the Romeros would now stay, though that building has since been replaced by the Hotel Boutique Doña Elvira.

This new residence was also next to a flamenco academy, where the Romeros met the great *cantaor* Manolo Caracol and many leading flamenco artists in Seville, among them Luisa Albéniz, Arturo and Tomás Pavón, La Niña de los Peines, and Niño Ricardo. Indeed, Seville is where Pepe truly fell in love with flamenco.

General Lecea finally found them a small house on a *cortijo*, or farm, on the outskirts of the city, near Tablada, a base used by the Spanish air force. (A big American air base was located in nearby Morón.) Pepe recalls that this Spanish base boasted a total of three planes at the time, all of them German (two Junkers and one Messerschmitt). There were three houses on the property: a big house that was deserted and two smaller structures, one occupied by the caretaker, his wife, and two daughters. The other, which the Romeros would live in, had a living room, a kitchen, and a bedroom. (All these buildings are still standing.) It was Spartan but a distinct improvement over the bordello. And they would only have to live there for a few months, until something else could be located.

PART 1. SOUTHERN SPAIN

Actually, Pepe remembers this as one of the most wonderful places he lived in Spain, and he was sad to leave it. He enjoyed living in the country and became quite attached to the two pet goats that Lecea gave him and Angel. Of course, they also had the customary chickens and dogs. True, they had to use a boat to cross the Guadalquivir River in order to go into town, but that was just the sort of Huck Finn adventure a boy his age craved.

Within a few weeks, Lecea found them an apartment near the center of Seville, at Claudio Boutelou 2.[7] This apartment offered the usual five hundred square feet with running water, but it was also on the second floor and featured a lovely balcony, perfect for practicing; in fact, Pepe practiced a lot on that balcony and says that it's where he acquired his technique. Another serendipitous coincidence was that a man named Antonio Pulpón lived there, and he was to become a very famous flamenco manager. Partly because of him, this particular address was a magnet for flamenco artists. Paco Avila became a close friend and would visit them with his girlfriend, a dancer. Paco would accompany her and at the same time teach Pepe how to accompany the *baile* (dance).

When Paco died in 2013, Pepe was deeply affected and grieved for his old friend, whom he respected and loved so much. In a moving testimonial posted on Facebook (November 29, 2013), Pepe wrote, "Paco taught me all the different flamenco forms with their intricate nuances and his own magnificent *rasgueados* [strumming patterns], which I have used in my own flamenco playing and to bring an extra dimension to all the Spanish repertoire for the guitar. . . . Our lessons were exuberant to say the least and one night our neighbor downstairs, Antonio Pulpón . . . came to our door to complain that the lamp on his ceiling had crashed to the floor from all the footwork upstairs!" Less obtrusive was the local mailman. He was a flamenco singer, and when he heard Pepe playing the guitar on the balcony, he would sing along. In this way, Pepe also learned how to accompany singers.

Other local attractions included the Teatro Lope de Vega, where Pepe had already appeared with his father in a concert at the tender age of seven; many years later, he gave the Andalusian premiere of Rodrigo's *Concierto para una fiesta* there. Right across the street from the Teatro Lope de Vega is the tobacco factory where Carmen supposedly worked. Another attraction in Seville was an ice cream parlor that Pepe loved to visit. It still operates

4. SEVILLE AND ADIÓS

today, and Pepe fondly points out the stool on which he would sit next to Papá as he ordered his favorite sundae. Most important, perhaps, was their new apartment's close proximity to the American consulate.

Of course, life in the big city was not inexpensive, and the family economized as best it could. Celin finished high school in Seville and continued his education there, in engineering. In an early extracurricular exercise, he conspired with a neighbor to rig their apartment building's electrical system so that the meter would register only a very minimal amount of use. This measure would save money without arousing suspicions, and it worked to perfection.

THE DECEPTION

The Romeros would spend a total of three years in Seville, most of that time dreaming of their escape to the United States. This would not be easy, but at least it seemed increasingly possible with the protection of Lecea, who smoothed the way, and the support of Fe, who provided the credentials, connections, and money they needed to go to the United States.

In his correspondence with the Romeros, Fe kept fanning the flames of this desire. He was dreaming now not only of managing Celedonio but also of establishing a "Casa de España" to serve as a sort of museum of Spanish things, as well as an "Academia Romero" where Celedonio and sons could teach. He would sometimes comment on Segovia's activities, noting that Segovia was featured on the BBC and stating that this was the sort of thing Celedonio should also be doing. Sabicas and Carlos Montoya were enjoying success in New York, so why not Celedonio?

By 1957, the plans for moving to America were reaching a critical mass: Fe would refer to this as "our great dream." His initial idea was for Celedonio to go alone and then bring the family over later. But the family was having none of that, especially since the Franco regime might have refused permission for them to leave, thus forcing Celedonio to return. No, it was better for them to leave together and for good.

The logistics and preparations for this move were complex and went through many changes. Suffice it to say here that Celin would be the point man. In the spring of 1957, he traveled to Lisbon to take care of a sick relative there. Lecea saw to it that his movement to Lisbon was not hindered. A notice from the Ministerio del Ejército (Army Ministry) dated February 9, 1957, regarding his application for a passport to go to Portugal gave him permission to remain there for five months. However, he was still required to present himself to the embassy in Lisbon. It becomes apparent from attached documentation that Lecea had prepared the way for this permission. It is also obvious that Celin needed permission because he would be required to serve in the army on his twenty-first birthday, per the old draft law. The board didn't want him skipping out and was determined to keep tabs on him. Five months from February would take him to July, just shortly before the family planned to flee from Portugal to the United States. Understandably, they wanted to avoid his being drafted if they were to go to America.

The family would later entrain for Lisbon, join Celin there, and then fly to the United States together. Before they could get a visa, however, they would have to prove that they or a sponsor had the financial resources to support them. This is where Fe played a crucial role. He took a job as radio officer on the steamship *Santa Mercedes* in order to earn the thousands of dollars this sponsorship would cost, in addition to travel expenses: airplane tickets from Lisbon to New York City to Los Angeles and finally to Santa Barbara cost $217.57 per person, a considerable sum at the time. This sum would be a loan to Celedonio, who could repay it later, after getting settled. Evie would rent a house in Santa Barbara big enough for both families.

Celin would have to appear at the Spanish Embassy in Lisbon to request an immigration visa to accompany his family to the United States, while the American consulate in Seville requested a *visto bueno* (clearance) from Madrid for all of them, which was then forwarded to the embassy in Portugal. This allowed the Romeros to leave directly from Lisbon. And they would have to have smallpox vaccinations in Lisbon before they could travel abroad.

Of course, the Romeros had few resources and were leaving most all their belongings behind, except for their guitars. The Stoddards stepped forward and supplied the necessary documentation attesting to their ability and intention to provide for the Romero family until they got on their feet in the United States. And their support of the Romeros was not just material but also moral. There are several missives in the family archive from

4. SEVILLE AND ADIÓS

the Stoddards giving their Spanish protégés plenty of advice about how to prepare for this transition.

In a letter of March 7, 1957, Evie told Angelita that a high-ranking naval officer (commander) with the Sixth Fleet would soon be visiting them with a package of "American things" for their use, as military personnel could purchase such items without paying duty. On July 18, 1957, Evie urged Celedonio to bring his "beautifully tailored" European clothes, explaining, "Here the public respects a well-groomed gentleman and you will make a very good impression with your European-cut clothes. For me you always looked so handsome in your grey and dark suits." It didn't hurt that Celedonio and his boys were handsome, period, regardless of the color of their suits. In another letter, dated June 9, 1957, Evie whetted Angelita's appetite for American life by telling her about refrigerators, "electric ice boxes" that keep food from spoiling. She could also look forward to gas and electric stoves, not wood!

Evie further prepared the family for its New World adventure by giving them a primer on the difference between East and West Coast lifestyles. On May 2, 1957, she wrote, "New York will be breathtaking, exciting and glamorous for a few days and then you will tire of the atmosphere as it is too fast for us all and you will want more out of living than what New York has to offer. Here in Santa Barbara you will find sunny warm skies and smiles on the people's faces. The weather in New York is either too hot or too cold and the humidity is unbearable."

The family entrained from Seville to Lisbon in order to meet Celin there. One of their neighbors in Seville was of a very liberal persuasion and worked on the train as a policeman. They made sure to be on his train so that he and not someone else would check their papers. Although in later years, as a publicity gesture, their departure was presented as a sort of Trapp family–style flight from dictatorship, sneaking over the Portuguese border to freedom, in fact, it required that every step of their way be carefully prepared in advance. Portugal was not Switzerland at this time, for it was in the grips of a right-wing dictatorship with close ties to the Franco regime. Even as the Romeros prepared to leave Lisbon, the Portuguese checked with the Spanish government to obtain final clearance. Fortunately, the Romeros had friends in places both high and low, and no impediments were placed in their way. The Andalusian family left Lisbon on August 11 at 9:30 p.m. aboard a TWA flight, final destination, Santa Barbara.

* * *

In reminiscing many years later about this relocation, Pepe shared the following observations with the press: "We left Spain with nothing. . . . But I knew that wherever we went, we would have music and the guitar."[8] "Celedonio was in search of political freedom and artistic freedom, in search of a dream he had—to take Spanish music to all the corners of the Earth."[9] The first corner would be Southern California.

PART 2

SOUTHERN CALIFORNIA

Completely free, free like the wind!
Like the sound waves of musical notes,
Like the birds and their warbling canticles.

[Completamente libre
¡libre como el viento!
Como las ondas sonoras
De las notas musicales
Como los pájaros y
Sus cantares de trinos.]
—Celedonio Romero, from "Libertad"

CHAPTER 5

SANTA BARBARA

The prime meridian traverses Aragón and Valencia in the eastern part of the Iberian Peninsula, making Spain one of only a few nations that lie in both hemispheres. First as *malagueños* and then as *sevillanos*, the Romeros had always resided in the Western Hemisphere, but only one of them had ever crossed the Atlantic Ocean. That person was, of course, Celedonio, though he did so on a steamer when he was only six years old. Now he was a middle-aged man of forty-four with a wife and three boys, headed in the opposite direction and to more terra incognita. Perhaps as he looked out the window of the airplane at the waters far below, his thoughts traveled back to that earlier voyage in 1919, one that enabled the seeds of his musical talent to take root and germinate in the cultural soil of Spain.

As Pepe would later observe, the art of the guitar "is very connected with Spain, and it's not something that you learn, it's something that you *are*."[1] In other words, Celedonio could not have become what he was anywhere other than in Spain; however, it is equally true that the Romeros would not have become what they are anywhere other than where they were now headed. The Atlantic would thus be the Romeros' Rubicon, and having crossed it, there would be no turning back.

PART 2. SOUTHERN CALIFORNIA

The TWA Lockheed L-188 Electra turboprop carrying the family westward was a comfortable aircraft, and Mamá later enthused in a letter to relatives back home that it was "the best plane in the world."[2] It no doubt seemed that way. At any rate, it was certainly the *only* plane she or any other Romero had ever traveled in. After refueling at Gander, on the island of Newfoundland in Canada, it made a safe landing in Boston at 6:00 a.m. on August 12. Here the family went through U.S. Customs before continuing on to New York. Pepe had had a reaction to the smallpox vaccine he received in Lisbon, and he was still recovering from the resultant fever. His first contact with American soil, however, was a favorable augur of things to come: he stepped on a silver dollar someone had dropped. That was one small step for a boy and one giant leap for the Romeros.

They next flew to New York, where they were greeted by a U.S. Navy commander and driven about in a "magnificent" car. Evie and Fe had thoughtfully provided several nice gifts for the naval officer to give them, since they themselves could not be on hand. The family spent one day sightseeing in New York, then continued their aerial voyage to Los Angeles, now aboard a TWA Lockheed Super Constellation.

Affectionately known as "Connies," these planes sported triple vertical stabilizers on the empennage, which one airline pilot found to be "fitting exclamation points to an unabashedly sinuous curvilinear fuselage."[3] Though they were also prop-driven aircraft and not jets, they were state-of-the-art flying machines at that time and would remain in service for another ten years. Interestingly, in 1957 TWA became the first airline to offer in-flight coffee service. No one recalls if the Romeros availed themselves of this luxury, but even if they did, one doubts that the beverage would have come up to the standard of the *cortados* (coffee mixed with milk) and *solos* (pure coffee) to which they were accustomed in Andalusia. Indeed, José Manuel Gil de Gálvez, one of Spain's leading musicians today, thinks of the *cortado* as a perfect metaphor for the Romeros themselves, insofar as they blend the *café* of classical music with the *leche* of flamenco. The result is delicious in either case, both figuratively and literally.

The Los Angeles airport was enveloped in a rare fog, but the redoubtable "Connie" and its doughty crew made a successful landing. This bit of excitement in the air was nothing compared to what awaited our guitarists on

5. SANTA BARBARA

the ground. Predictably, their arrival had generated considerable curiosity among local guitar aficionados. The Los Angeles Guitar Society turned out in force to greet the Romeros, along with other assorted well-wishers. However, a large group of Hollywood notables and fans was also waiting for some film stars to arrive on that same flight; basking in reflected adulation, the Romeros already felt like celebrities, even if vicarious ones. Paparazzi were snapping photos as the Romeros descended the stairway from the plane, but this had the unfortunate effect of making Mamá very self-conscious. She felt unkempt and even "ugly" after the long trip and later cried a bit about this untimely exposure. That crisis soon passed, however. They were to have flown from Los Angeles to Santa Barbara, but by this time Papá was tired of flying and refused to go any further by that means. A leading local guitarist, Theodore Norman, drove the family to their new home in his Chrysler. Fe was in Panama and could not be present to greet the Romeros, but Evie met them upon their arrival in Santa Barbara and took them to their new home, on East Gutierrez Street.

And what a home it was! Angelita saved her most ecstatic encomiums for the many conveniences they now enjoyed. Her "poor pen" could hardly describe such "grandeur." First and foremost, there was a large garden, verdant with stately magnolia and palm trees, as well as several varieties of roses. The interior of the house was nicely appointed with paintings by famous artists, elegant furnishings, and—wonder of wonders—a television. The bedrooms were all air-conditioned and featured very comfortable beds, which offered welcome relief after an arduous trip. The boys were all in one room, and she and Celedonio in another. Not surprisingly, she marveled at the automatic appliances in the kitchen, even as Evie had predicted she would. Evie later reflected on this new environment in which the Romeros now found themselves: "Everything was so different for them here," she said. "Department stores, supermarkets, the things we take for granted weren't to be found in Spain then." Of course, there was "never a dull moment with five Spaniards in the house. The family [was] so exuberant and full of joy."[4]

The appeal of Santa Barbara, as opposed to, say, New York City or Boston, was precisely because its clement Mediterranean climate reminded the Romeros of Málaga. It was on the coast, with open water on one side of the city and mountains on the other. The palm trees, cacti, chaparral, and other

PART 2. SOUTHERN CALIFORNIA

vegetation seemed to have come over on the Lockheed Electra with them. Most of the place-names in this area were in their native tongue, because it was originally a Spanish settlement centered around the mission established there in 1786 by Franciscan Padre Fermín Lasuén, on the feast day of Saint Barbara (December 4).

Santa Barbara was a locale that embraced and rejoiced in its Spanish heritage. Every summer it celebrated (and still celebrates) Old Spanish Days, and in 1957 this annual festival was held from August 7 to 11, ending just before the arrival of the new Spanish residents. The significance of this festival to Spain itself becomes clear in the copious diplomatic correspondence from the consulate in Los Angeles to the embassy in Washington, DC, and thence to Madrid, all of it now conveniently located in Spanish archives.[5]

In a letter of August 12, 1957, to the Spanish Embassy in DC, the Los Angeles consul, El Marqués de Alcántara, reported that he was invited to deliver opening remarks at the festival, followed by California governor Goodwin J. Knight, who spoke in fractured but well-intentioned Spanish; then the mayor of the city held forth in attempted Spanish. Spanish songs and dances soon followed, and a variety show of Spanish-flavored acts was presented at the Lobero Theatre that evening. Mass was sung at the mission on Sunday morning, and after a plenitude of earnest prayers and invocations, a banquet was served. (After all, man does not live by words alone.) There was then a two-hour parade honoring early California pageantry, with floats, palomino horses, and quasi bullfighters.

Reading between the lines, one detects a certain smugness in these reports, as the various festivities verged on, or crossed over into, kitsch. The spectacle of a chorus of seminarians singing love songs was a bit too much for the poor consul to bear. Such a thing would never be permitted in Spain, he snorted dismissively. Still, Spanish diplomats were very preoccupied with the way Spain was portrayed to American society in popular culture and mass media, as events like this could contribute greatly to (or detract from) the general rehabilitation of Spain's image in the United States, enhancing diplomatic and economic ties vital to Spain's recovery from the disastrous wars and isolation of the 1930s and 1940s. Tourism in particular would become increasingly important to the Spanish economy, and moneyed Americans were very welcome.

5. SANTA BARBARA

This situation helps to explain why another letter to the embassy expressed grave concerns about Stanley Kramer's 1957 film, *The Pride and the Passion*, which the consul warned was an unflattering and even insulting portrayal of Spain.[6] Although he made no mention of it, the previous year's film *Around the World in 80 Days* agreeably featured José Greco and his company performing a spirited flamenco number in a tavern after balloonists Phileas Fogg and his amanuensis Passepartout cross the Pyrenees and land in Spain. In retrospect, we can say that the consul likewise had nothing to fear from the *Zorro* television series, which featured a Spanish hero, Don Diego de la Vega, fighting corruption among local officials in colonial Los Angeles. This series premiered in October 1957, shortly after the Romeros arrived, and ran weekly for two years.[7] The movie *El Cid* (1961) would also burnish Spain's credentials as a land of heroic Christian knights in shining armor, fending off insidious infidels (even as now, under Franco, Christian capitalists were helping to fend off atheistic Bolsheviks). *The Man of La Mancha*, loosely based on Miguel de Cervantes's *Don Quijote*, was a runaway Broadway hit in 1965 and then a box-office success as a Hollywood musical in 1971. Even if these entertainments tended to reinforce stereotypes about Spaniards as being alternately dashing and daft, at least the caricatures were generally sympathetic and favorable, not menacing.

Musicians were helpful cultural ambassadors, and various names appear in these letters, including those of Hollywood celebrities José and Amparo Iturbi, cellist Pablo Casals, and guitarist Andrés Segovia. Curiously, however, nowhere in any of this diplomatic chatter from the 1950s and 1960s is there any mention of the Romeros. This absence does not mean that they were forgotten in Spain, however. Indeed, one Spanish newspaper reported on Celedonio's triumphs with genuine admiration.[8] Lecea had already written Celedonio on March 1, 1958, wishing him good luck in America; he wrote again on December 29, 1961, thanking Celedonio for the newspaper clippings he had sent, saying that they fulfilled his predictions of success. So the "*engaño*" was proceeding according to plans both official and private.

We must conclude from all of this that the Romeros' departure had ruffled no feathers in the Spanish government, as they were some of the most effective emissaries Spain could have asked for. They projected a consistently favorable image of Spain as a country of good-looking and talented people,

PART 2. SOUTHERN CALIFORNIA

skilled, energetic, and exhibiting admirable family values—long before those became buzzwords in the culture wars of 1980s and beyond. The fact that they were decidedly not white Anglo-Saxon Protestants but rather swarthy Hispanics of the Catholic faith (albeit a rather watery faith) did not matter now as much as it might have a few decades earlier, especially considering that the United States would soon elect an Irish American Catholic president.

A few years later, in the wake of Celin's wedding in 1966, Angelita observed the following about their new situation: "These Americans are so friendly that they love all of our things, and for this reason we feel very proud to be Spaniards."[9] (More will be said of the boys' wives and children in part 4.) There was definitely a deep reservoir of American goodwill towards Spain, Spaniards, and Spanish culture from which the Romeros would now draw professional success and personal satisfaction.

Part of the reason for this abundant goodwill was perhaps the realization that, in 1957, the United States needed all the Cold War allies it could get. On October 4 of that year, the Soviets launched Sputnik and threatened to seize the ultimate high ground, namely, outer space. Spain was a valuable friend to have, as it anchored southwest Europe and loomed over the entrance to the Mediterranean, which the United States was determined to retain as mare nostrum. It now also hosted U.S. military installations. Eisenhower's trip to Spain in 1959 would seal the relationship and pave the way for Spain's eventual admission to the North Atlantic Treaty Organization (NATO) and the European Union.

CONQUISTADORES

During the Romeros' early months in the United States, Fe was sometimes in Santa Barbara but usually elsewhere. Nonetheless, his thoughts rarely strayed far from his Andalusian friends. For instance, he wrote from Peru on September 25, 1957, of his relief that his charges were comfortable and happy in their new home. He offered hearty congratulations to Pepe on qualifying for eighth grade and on already making friends at school. Fe wrote a separate letter the same day to Angel, congratulating him on getting into sixth grade and being elected class president! The newly elected

5. SANTA BARBARA

líder was also going to give a guitar concert for his teachers and classmates, and he was making notable strides in acquiring English (Papá and Mamá were also taking English lessons at this same time).[10] Celin also received a personalized letter, encouraging him to enroll right away at a local college in Santa Barbara, in order to continue his progress toward eventually becoming an engineer. This advice is significant, because it becomes clear in this early correspondence that little thought was given to forming a quartet or marketing the whole family as a musical act. The guitar would be Celin's avocation and provide income while he pursued a career that promised remuneration, stability, and some prestige. As for Pepe and Angel, well, it was too early to tell what the future might hold, but their artistic talent could not be ignored.

Of course, the Romeros were now living in a car culture, and they would need a suitable conveyance. Hence, Fe instructed Evie to buy an automobile for Celin, since he would be the designated driver for the Romeros. Car-insurance papers in the family archive dated November 20, 1957, indicate that she bought a 1948 Pontiac two-door, four-cylinder sedan for ninety-nine dollars. It was hardly a luxury vehicle, but the price was right. In either case, his first goal was to obtain a driver's license, so he picked up a copy of the state driver's handbook and began studying while also taking driving lessons. A couple of weeks later, he received his license, passing the written exam without a single incorrect answer—a feat he never again duplicated. This achievement is all the more remarkable considering that he still didn't really understand English well and had never driven a car before.[11] A quick study, he was soon ferrying his family around Santa Barbara on four proud wheels.

As Málaga's *Sur* newspaper commented years later, "It was all a very risky adventure. Their ignorance of English, lack of money, and unfamiliarity with the country were compensated for by Celedonio's reserves of strength and dreams of triumph."[12] These sentiments were anticipated in the *San Francisco Chronicle*'s February 19, 1963, issue, in an article titled "The Romeros' Long Journey": "It takes boldness and a special kind of courage for a man to pull up stakes and strike out toward an uncertain future in a new land. . . . They left a country where they were already famous to come to a land where their chosen instrument is still regarded in some circles as a freak."

PART 2. SOUTHERN CALIFORNIA

This article appeared just before they were to give a concert in the Masonic Auditorium, on Washington's Birthday. And in conjunction with honoring America's most famous Freemason, they had made their formal application for American citizenship in Mayor George Christopher's office the day before. Citizenship was finally conferred on the Romeros in October 1967, ten years after their arrival; Ramsey Clark, U.S. attorney general, and the Los Angeles County Board of Supervisors sent Celedonio letters congratulating the family.

Providing all the amenities they now enjoyed required money, of course, and Fe informed everyone from New York on December 15, 1957, that he himself would have to earn another five or six thousand dollars in order to realize their ambitious dreams. That was a considerable amount of money at the time, and he could not carry the financial burden alone. Already in January 1958, it was obvious that they would have to economize in some areas, and he wrote from New York on the ninth that Celin should find a job right away so that he could add some income to the equation. Uncle Sam would not be slow in finding him gainful employment, though not of the kind anyone was seeking.

Indeed, money was not Fe's main concern. The main thing, he wrote, was to keep Celin out of the military. Having narrowly avoided service in the Spanish army, Celin now faced the very real prospect of being pressed into service with the U.S. Armed Forces. Another concern was the proper launching of Celedonio's global career. They were already discussing the possibility of him appearing in concert with one or two of the boys, but Fe initially disapproved the idea, fearing that the boys would distract attention from Celedonio and hamper his ascent. He needed to establish himself first, *then* bring them along, if necessary. As it turned out, that is more or less the way things evolved.

Others offering professional advice at this time included Ted Norman, who had written to Celedonio already on September 11, 1957, urging him to play only important concerts and to avoid performing for amateur groups, especially "guitar societies," because that would give him amateur standing. Celedonio would heed all this advice; he waited until June 1958 to give his breakout concert, at the leading venue in his new hometown, Santa Barbara's historic Lobero Theatre.

5. SANTA BARBARA

¡BRAVO!

This debut performance took place on Friday evening, June 13, and despite the seemingly inauspicious day and date, the concert was a stunning success. Celedonio presented his well-polished program of classical works from the Renaissance to the modern era, including his own pieces. The *Santa Barbara News-Press* reported the next day that "the audience would not go home so he had to add more encores."[13] He tossed in one of his own delightful numbers, then a bit of Chopin and Schumann. Finally the house lights came on, signaling the end of the concert, and the audience, still reluctant to go home, flocked back stage to meet the artist.

Fe was realizing his managerial dreams and had established the firm of Farrington F. Stoddard Artists & Management to handle Celedonio's career. On impressive letterhead, he sent out a press release reporting, "Applause is not the word for the storm of approval and wild enthusiasm raised by the audience. It was the greatest ovation this theatre has conferred in many years, with the audience on its feet, stamping the floor, clapping its hands, shouting Bravo! Bravo! until the building vibrated with a tempest of emotion. . . . I must confess to a greatly enlarged heart and a wet eye."

Another publicity blurb he prepared claimed, "[Celedonio's] triumph here reflects to the undying glory of Spain, a great country which continues as always to produce great men. His countrymen have good reason to be proud of him. Spain may well look forward in good time to a triumphant return of its honored son and once again to the enchantment of his guitar."[14]

Fe was not exaggerating when he claimed that Celedonio's conquest of the New World would delight his countrymen. Already in 1958, Málaga's *Sur* featured an interview with Celedonio, in which the guitarist sent his greetings to everyone and expressed his hopes to return soon. He also claimed to have concert dates lined up in Mexico and Cuba, though this *was* an exaggeration.[15] In any case, Fe's considerable investment in the Romeros already seemed to be paying handsome dividends, and the best was no doubt yet to come.

The overall strategy that the Stoddards mapped out for their Spanish protégés was always a bit sketchy, but it involved launching Celedonio's concert career, establishing some sort of guitar school, and perhaps creat-

PART 2. SOUTHERN CALIFORNIA

ing a museum where some of the Romeros' valuable instruments could be displayed. In fact, Fe began advertising shortly before the Lobero concert that the "Romero-Stoddard collection of rare guitars [would be] exhibited in a window display at Gammill's, Clothiers on State Street, from May 29th to the evening of Romero's concert." Based on the Romeros' reaction to their new life in California, Fe told his readers, "Malaguenians [sic] are the most friendly and gregarious people on earth. They admire us for our own friendliness, our sporty clothes and amazing gadgets, our bright optimisms and inexplicable but amusing energy."[16] Political freedom and relatively large incomes should have rated passing mention on this list.

Now, granted, this concert was a relatively small-scale affair. But it struck a nerve, and it demonstrated that this gamble was going to pay off. How big, no one could yet tell, but there was obviously a market for just the sort of thing Celedonio did and the way he did it. A little-known fact is that he was actually not the first Romero to perform in Santa Barbara. Pepe had already made appearances as a flamenco guitarist at El Paseo and at the armory for the Cinco de Mayo celebration. On August 13, 1958, he performed *siguiriyas* and *alegría por fiesta* for the Fiesta Pequeña at the Santa Barbara Mission.[17] On that very day, Celedonio and his family would also be celebrating the first anniversary of their arrival in the United States from Spain.

However, the Romeros weren't done with the Lobero yet, or it with them. Celedonio, Celin, and Pepe announced their plans to give a concert at the Lobero on November 28, 1959. It would include solos by Celedonio, then Celin, then some flamenco numbers by Pepe. But there would be a new twist: "The youngest of the Romeros, Angel, will play 'Plegaria' by Guillermo Gómez and a Sonata by Scarlatti."[18] His picture does not appear with the others' in this announcement, but this occasion was nonetheless his concert debut not only at the Lobero but also in the United States.

Recording companies quickly recognized the potential of a guitar quartet of photogenic Andalusians. As early as 1958, RCA executives were expressing interest in the Romeros, not as soloists but as a group playing arrangements of the more familiar and popular Spanish semiclassical music, along with integrated renditions of flamenco, on the first side of an LP record; on the flip side would be some original arrangements and compositions by Celedonio. The LP would retail for $3.98, and the family would receive 5 percent of the list price. The actual recording would be done

5. SANTA BARBARA

in Hollywood, and an initial run would be for twenty thousand covers and five thousand records. Such a flamenco record was eventually made, as we shall see, but not until 1967 (the family declined this initial offer on the advice of José Iturbi). At this point, the idea of a Romero guitar quartet was still very nebulous and would require some sort of catalyst for it to coalesce. That catalyst would soon come from a most unlikely source—the U.S. Army.

THE PARADISE OF THE WORLD

In the following year, 1959, the other major development was Celin's conscription into the U.S. Army. It is ironic that, having just barely evaded service in the Spanish armed forces two years earlier, he was now on his way to six months of basic training in the United States. The Romeros felt a sense of patriotism and gratitude to their adoptive country, and no thought was given to somehow evading this obligation. Then again, the Romeros had arrived at just the right time, in between the Korean and the Vietnam Wars. Had they fled Spain five years earlier, Celin might well have wound up in Korea, or five years later, in Vietnam. Avoiding combat in the rice paddies was a challenge that both of Celin's younger siblings would later face and overcome.

After Francis Gary Powers's U-2 plane was shot down by the Soviet Union on May 1, 1960, the Romeros did have reason to hold their collective breath—along with the rest of the world—fearing that any resultant conflict between the United States and the Soviet Union would inevitably involve Celin. In his letters home, Celin discountenanced such speculation, and as it turned out, both sides stepped back from the brink. In reality, the greatest danger Celin would confront in the army was the colder climate of the Bay Area, as he would undergo basic training at Fort Ord in Monterey (now the campus of California State University, Monterey Bay). Celin inherited the 1948 Pontiac and drove it north to Ft. Ord, though he later upgraded to a late-model Cadillac convertible, a car he considered beautiful.[19]

An undated letter from Major General Carl F. Fritzsche, commanding officer at Fort Ord, to the families of men in basic training made clear the purpose of this ordeal: "The discipline which we strive to inculcate is simply that cheerful obedience to properly constituted authority which is so essential in a military organization and so characteristic of the American soldier."[20] Vietnam would put all of this to the test.

Indeed, if there is one maxim to which Celin unreservedly subscribes, it is, "Make love, not war." During basic training, he didn't mind shooting at targets, but when it came to practicing close combat, where he had to stab and shoot a dummy in the heart, he refused. As he himself explained to me, life is precious, and he wouldn't want to kill someone, even if it simply involved *pretending* to do so with a straw man. Normally such insubordination would be a serious offense, and it might even have landed him in the brig. His officers were understanding, however, and after basic, they found him a job more compatible with his temperament—as a typist.

As it turned out, making love instead of war posed its own unique hazards. Celin went to interview with the Catholic chaplain, Father Sullivan, to be his assistant and typist. Even though Celin admitted to not being a practicing Catholic, he and Father Sullivan hit it off. This was fortunate, because Father was also a smoker, and at one point he asked Celin for a light. Celin reached into his breast pocket for what he thought was a packet of matches, but what he withdrew instead was a similarly shaped package of condoms, which he inattentively handed to the good father. Unfazed, the priest calmly returned the prophylactics to Celin and asked again for matches, which the chagrined Spaniard was only too happy to supply.

Father Sullivan hired Celin, but several other soldiers became envious of his comfortable job, and they tried to turn the priest against him by pointing out his sexual license. Father defended Celin by saying that at least he was not a hypocrite. Celin had other things going for him, too. Father Sullivan was a Jesuit, well educated, and a lover of classical music, a passion he could not readily share with most of his army associates but one that needed no explaining to Private Romero, who serenaded him on the guitar and gave him invaluable advice on building his record collection. Not everyone was quite so receptive to the sound of music. One day, during basic training, Celin and others were in their "underwear doing push-ups for four hours on the patio," when an officer arrived with a package. Celin recalled, "The drill sergeant looked at me and screamed 'Romero! What is this [expletive] banjo?' My father had the great idea of sending me a guitar, so you can imagine how that went over."[21] The drill sergeant gave Romero grief but told him to go to talk to the captain. More mild-mannered and with admirable

5. SANTA BARBARA

curiosity regarding the case's contents, the captain was impressed with the beautiful instrument. He even asked Celin to play for him, and soon thereafter, for the rest of the soldiers.

Army life was still hard on Celin, and his letters to the family leave no doubt that he grew weary of it. While in basic training, he wrote home complaining that all they did was "march and run." Somewhat later he told them that he was not getting enough sleep because the "stupid new recruits make so much noise in the corridor."[22] He needed ten hours every night but wasn't getting it because they would wake him up early. At other times, his plangent epistles told of a Northern California that was cold and cloudy much of the time. He much preferred Santa Barbara to Monterey. And to make matters worse, his room was green and didn't have windows, so it felt like a prison cell.

On the bright side, he became a member of the Club de Católicos, and they would go swimming and sunbathing in Carmel. Of course, the chief attraction in the club was some cute *muchachas católicas*. A fast worker, he had already gotten a date with one of them, who also happened to be the club president. On balance, Celin really loved California; he wrote home on May 10, 1960, that it was "the paradise of the world."[23]

Paradise or not, after Celin had spent many months in the army, his continued absence and distant remove up in Fort Ord were putting the brakes on the family's concert plans. So, Celedonio wrote to his son's commanding officer at Fort Ord on March 31, 1960, appealing for Celin to be stationed closer to home "because he [took] care of all the family business" (a friendly neighbor helped him write this letter). "Another problem that has arisen is due to the mental and physical condition of his mother. She is suffering from acute blood pressure and an acute nervous condition and is under medical care."[24] Captain Jennings had to deny the request, claiming that he had no control over such a transfer and that Celin would remain at Fort Ord for the next eight weeks.

Even though the appeal was unsuccessful, it wasn't because Celin had fallen out of favor with the authorities—far from it. By the end of his active-duty obligation in spring of 1960, Celin had become something of a local celebrity, and the post newspaper hailed his mastery of the classics but reserved special praise for his arrangement of the song "Stormy Weather," which was one of his favorites. The day after the article appeared, Celin

PART 2. SOUTHERN CALIFORNIA

proudly sent this clipping to his family, and from it they learned that he was rated a marksman with an M-1 rifle.[25] Fortunately, he never had to demonstrate his aim on a living target. He was soon released into the reserves and became an occasional "weekend warrior."

The most important thing that happened as a result of this stint in the army had nothing to do with condoms, weather, or rifles. Rather, it resulted in the formation of the Romero Quartet and its acquisition of a manager who could get it bookings throughout the country, in Chicago, Boston, and New York, not just Southern California. This turn of events resulted from the sort of serendipitous happenstance we have already come to expect in this saga.

If Celin couldn't go home, then home would have to come to him. A letter of February 17, 1960, from the base commander invited families to an open house on March 12 from 9:00 a.m. to 1:00 p.m. This event was where the quartet was launched, for reasons that Celin explained it to me in this way:

> A fellow soldier and I were at the PX, and he asked to see the guitar; so, I played it for him. His name was Jim Lucas, and he was a great lover of music. He was also a law student who wanted to start a music-management business in New York when he was finished with the army. He came from a well-to-do family, his Czech father having done a lot of welding for the Liberty ships during World War Two. Jim met my family at an open house that the army held for the soldiers and their relatives at the end of basic training. The army asked me to play for it, and I was joined by my father and brothers. We never travel anywhere, even on vacation, without our guitars, so they brought their guitars and performed with me. The four of us played together, and that was the birth of the quartet. We played a composition of my father's, a *malagueña*, and the soldiers loved it. So when Jim and I got out of the army, he became a manager, and I convinced him that the guitar quartet would be a success. He was a little reluctant, but I persuaded him to line up some concerts: Orchestra Hall in Chicago, Jordan Hall in Boston, Town Hall in New York, and the Opera House in San Francisco. And that was the professional beginning of the quartet.[26]

Ever an astute observer of his surroundings and the business opportunities they presented, Celin already had his finger on the pulse of larger trends in American popular culture, especially in relation to music and the guitar. Lucas may have required convincing, but proof of Celin's sagacity was soon at hand.

5. SANTA BARBARA

GUITAR RULES

Once again, timing was key to the Romeros' success. They had arrived at just the right historical moment to launch their unique career because the acoustic guitar itself was a selling point in a way that it might not have been just ten or twenty years earlier. Music critic and editor Shirley Fleming wrote an insightful essay in 1966 on the guitar's burgeoning popularity in the 1950s and 1960s, an article that included interview material with Celin and Celedonio. She puts it best:

> The rage for electric guitars among the young today owes much, of course, to the appearance on television and recordings of some extremely adept practitioners. Tony Mottola [a former student of Pepe] might qualify as one of the best all-around athletes in this respect. "You have to be able to use them all," he says, "just to cover the business." Chuck Wayne says, "When I started playing in '39 there were relatively few solo guitar players, and not much demand for them. So if the instrument had certain technical deficiencies, it didn't matter. Now the guitarist has to play faster and higher." After World War Two, in the words of one guitar dealer, "bowling and photography were grabbing the consumer dollar." Arthur Godfrey's television show in the early Fifties ignited a ukulele boom among an adult audience, which was then presumably prepared to go on to bigger things. Three paths were open—that is, three closely akin models of acoustic guitar beckoned to the potential player: [classical, folk, and flamenco]. In 1952, the Goya guitar distributors took a survey of their clientele and found that "a ridiculous number" of doctors were playing the classical guitar. "They played it because of snob appeal," says a representative. "Professional people took it up because it didn't have the reputation of being a stupid instrument." Peter Seeger and Joan Baez popularized folk guitar, which was easier to play. Sabicas and [Carlos] Montoya came along. Sabicas said, "Americans are more enthusiastic, accept more, than Europeans. They know about flamenco here. In Spain, there are very few concert guitarists." Montoya recalled an early US tour where he played in Fargo ND. He was astonished to find that the concert had been sold out before he ever reached town. College audiences are so anxious to penetrate the mysteries of flamenco style that they sometimes play his records at 16 rpm for a slow-motion look. [Finally, Celin says], "You have such beautiful schools of music here. So many students in this country are getting degrees in music. There is opportunity for a musician here; he knows almost for sure that he will be able to earn a living. It is different for a musician in Europe.

PART 2. SOUTHERN CALIFORNIA

In Spain, one's future is very difficult. Even though I studied guitar with my father from the time I was very young, my parents made me take a Bachelor of Science degree in case the guitar did not work out. My brother Pepe, also, studied mathematics." Celedonio broke in: "The US is the best country in the world for guitar."[27]

So the Romeros showed up in the right place at precisely the right time, with the advent of television and the skyrocketing popularity of the guitar, not only folk, rock, and jazz styles but also classical and flamenco. As reviewer Charles Passy would one day note of a Pepe appearance in West Palm Beach, the guitar "is . . . deeply entrenched in the everyday lives of everyday people."[28] And so it was, but critics did not always view the various styles of guitar playing as being of equal quality or value. It didn't take long for American reviewers to make invidious comparisons between what they deplored as the twang 'n' bang of rock 'n' roll, on the one hand, and the elegant and spirited arrangements of *café con leche* by the Romeros, on the other.

For instance, the *Corpus Christi Caller* featured an article about the Romeros written by Ralph Thibodeau, an associate professor of music at Del Mar College, who offered a colorfully erudite but highly opinionated assessment of the guitar's history and current stature:

The Spanish guitar—like its ancestors, the lute and the lyre, and the biblical and Grecian cithara—is a gentle instrument, capable of almost human expression. And, like the other classical stringed instruments, it is reminiscent of the Psalms of David and of the cult of Apollo, of man's higher nature. But in our day a transformation has taken place in the gentle guitar. It has been twelve-stringed and plugged in and amplified to the point where it is good only for tyros to vomit their obstreperous obscenities at decibel levels to destroy our hearing and to scare small children and sensible animals. So it is good occasionally to have one's sensibilities again in the authentic sound of the traditional guitar, to enjoy the lovely string sounds rather than suffer the shell-shock of the cannon shot. It is edifying, too, to hear a whole family of guitarists in a noble family profession, playing together, and taking us back in imagination to the days of the old musicians' guilds, when skills and performance traditions were passed, like precious heirlooms, from father to son.[29]

Lest one be tempted to think that such disdain for African American music was confined to the southern United States, the *Scrantonian* in Penn-

5. SANTA BARBARA

sylvania weighed in with its own critique of popular culture vis-à-vis the Romeros: "The 'guitar image' of a swivel-hipped youngster twanging a heavy beat through a laboratory of amplifiers was demolished. Instead we saw four serious musicians—three of them quite young—very carefully and lovingly recreating 200-year-old music. It took some getting used to, but it was worth the effort."[30]

In venerable old Boston, the *Christian Science Monitor* served up Nicolas Slonimsky's very condensed version of popular culture, heaving an almost audible sigh of relief at the advent of musicians like Segovia, patrician emissaries of high art from the Old World who would rescue civilized folk from the cultural corruption of the New World (and the African American influence that was clearly responsible for that corruption):

> Syncopated ragtime, Dixieland jazz, and cowboy ballads, meeting in an unholy synthesis, produced the mongrel genre of Rock 'n' Roll. The vociferation of the crooner, and the antiphonal responses from the youthful audience inflamed by the maddening monotony of the rhythmic beat, all but drowned out the six-stringed guitar; but, thanks to the achievements of modern technology, the sound of the guitar was electronically reinforced, a thousandfold when necessary. The electric guitar became the symbol of mass serenading, with the whirling Harlequin chained to the electric outlet by a cord and the portable microphone around his neck.
>
> But the guitar has not entirely dissipated its noble heritage. Making good music on the guitar is beginning to return. Serious composers have written concertos for guitar and orchestra. The Spanish guitar virtuoso Andrés Segovia has developed an amazing new technique on the instrument, and his concerts are artistic feasts to a musician.[31]

Comparisons with more popular and familiar styles of guitar playing were inevitable, and since reviewers of Romero concerts were already inclined toward the classics, a bias in their favor was predictable. A local reviewer reported on a Milwaukee concert in which "40 fingers and 24 strings worked their magic on the unamplified classical music of Vivaldi and Rodrigo, not today's deafening pop repertoire."[32] Nearly thirty years after the Romeros' arrival, the *Chicago Tribune* still found it necessary to draw the line between low and high art: "The most famous guitar group in the world works without an amp, never played a rock song and probably couldn't hum a Top 10 tune if its career depended on it. In fact, the members always perform in formalwear and prefer Bizet to Clapton by a mile. Except for Segovia, no classical guitarist has filled concert halls or sold records or appeared on TV quite so triumphantly as the Romeros."[33]

Of course, the technique of the classical guitar was a bit of a mystery to those habituated to seeing a pick used to pluck the strings. In 1972 the *Adrian (MI) Daily Telegram* published a Romero interview in its Women section that asserted the following: "These guitarists are of the old school. Since all the fingers are used it would not be possible to use a guitar pick. Yet there wasn't a trace of a callous on any Romero finger. 'We cannot have callouses,' Celin said, 'because it would make a buzz on the strings.'"[34]

Preferences in or knowledge about various styles of guitar playing does not seem to have been a matter of intelligence or education. Certainly the audience was among society's cognitive elite when the Romeros played in Beckman Auditorium at the California Institute of Technology in 1972. But the critic for the *California Tech* was still perplexed by the performance: "Most of us do not normally associate the guitar with classical music. It just does not seem to be a classical music instrument."[35]

It is true that the Romeros never dabbled in rock or played electric guitars. I distinctly remember an early lesson with Pepe during which his daughter Tina rushed into the room and pleaded with him to buy her an electric guitar. Pepe thought for a moment and then offered this Solomonic solution: "Learn any ten of the Carcassi etudes, and I will buy you the most electrified guitar there is." Tina never owned an electric guitar; instead, she married a highly accomplished guitarist, and her son is a talented builder. But the Romeros are rarely dismissive of any kind of music, and the truth is that some rock musicians incorporated classical-guitar music into their songs.

For instance, the Doors scored a hit in 1968 with "Spanish Caravan," which wove a guitar arrangement of Albéniz's "Leyenda" into an otherwise rock-style piece. And the following year, Jethro Tull based an entire song ("Bourée") on the Bourrée from Bach's Lute Suite no. 1 in E Minor, an evergreen favorite with classical guitarists. Rock guitar and its classical cousin thus did not exist in separate musical universes. Indeed, there was an obvious similarity between the Romero Quartet and many rock groups, because they had the same number of players. The *Fort Bragg (CA) Advocate-News* couldn't resist such a comparison in a 1964 issue: "And, after seeing and hearing the response of the many young people present at Cot-

5. SANTA BARBARA

ton Auditorium who can say that the Mendocino Coast needs the Beatles? We have had the Romeros!"[36] To be sure, the Waverly (Ohio) High School newspaper reassured its youthful readership in 1968, that "all the Romeros agreed that the Beatles were very good musicians and they enjoyed listening to the famous group."[37] There was a certain amount of diplomacy in such a remark, but it wasn't insincere.

Rock, however, wasn't the only kind of music that featured guitars and prompted comparisons with the Romeros. There was a whole lotta finger-pickin' goin' on in country-and-western music, too, and there were parallels and compatibilities here as well. In 1973, Iowa's *Clinton Herald* noted that "even the devotees of Chet Atkins, Roy Clark and Johnny Cash succumbed to the gentleness and refinement of the artists of the Royal Family of the Guitar."[38] A sort of crossover between classical and country was uniquely possible in the United States of that time and is not as surprising as one might expect. For instance, the Romeros appeared on the country-and-western variety show *Hootenanny*, in episode 28, on April 11, 1964, playing their standard repertoire, including Telemann. They were a big hit, as usual. And one of the best renditions of Ernesto Lecuona's *Malagueña* I've ever heard was performed by country guitarist Roy Clark.[39] Moreover, Atkins was a great admirer of the classical guitar and Segovia, and he eventually established the Chet Atkins International Guitar Competition.

Thus, though at the time it was natural for critics to distinguish in rather binary and disparaging terms between classical-guitar music and more popular styles, it was inappropriate in the case of the Romeros. As I have already established, in the context of their own culture, they were "crossover" artists who played both classical and vernacular repertoires, excelling at those kinds of classical music (e.g., Albéniz, Granados, Turina, Torroba) that were profoundly inspired by folk music. Precisely because they were *not* pretentious snobs and remained open to beauty in music regardless of its class and racial origins—urban or rural, white or Roma, patrician or plebeian—they were able to adapt very quickly to American culture without ever abandoning or misrepresenting their own Spanish roots, who and what they were. One hastens to add that jazz artists were especially smitten with Spanish music during this epoch. Miles Davis's 1960 album *Sketches of Spain* features his arrangement of the middle movement of Rodrigo's *Concierto de Aranjuez* for guitar and orchestra. This same

PART 2. SOUTHERN CALIFORNIA

work inspired arrangements by Chick Corea and the Modern Jazz Quartet, among others.

It was this very fealty to their native culture that gave the Romeros authenticity and helped them to correct numerous regressive stereotypes about Spain. As the *Kansas City Star* noted some years later in an interview with Pepe:

> Over the years, [Pepe] added, audiences have become more sophisticated about guitar music. It's not just about torchy, hand-clapping flamenco style any more, as the family's public initially expected. "Many of audiences had never heard the guitar before so they went thinking it was a flavor thing, something out of *Blood and Sand*, something they can put on a red scarf and a Spanish beret for and drink a glass of red wine and enjoy an evening of ethnic flavor, of bullfighting music. But they left the concert knowing that the guitar was something else . . . a very serious, very ancient traditional instrument."[40]

ADIÓS, AMIGOS

All of this would come about because of the national exposure made possible by a chance encounter between Jim Lucas and the Romero guitarists on an army base. Of course, this transition to Lucas's new agency would mean the end of Fe Stoddard's managerial dreams; as it turned out, Fe soon had health problems that nearly meant the end of his life. Evie wrote to the family in 1961 that he was in San Francisco "clinging to life," requiring the assistance of a tracheotomy to help him breathe. To make matters worse, he had developed arthritis in his hands and could no longer play the guitar. Two years later, Fe himself reported that he was "permanently disqualified for sea duty" because of his chronic illnesses. He decided to move down to Hollywood and gratefully accepted the Romeros' offer of a house they owned there to live in. Celin helped him and Evie with the move.

Sadly, Fe's condition never really improved. He wrote to Celedonio on May 23, 1967, pleading for financial assistance. He lamented, "After three years of personal sacrifices and effort devoted exclusively to the promotion of the Romeros I ended up with a severe cerebral hemorrhage and stone broke. Doctors declared me permanently unfit for further sea duty and I was forced to retire on a pension too small to live on in this country. When I went back to sea in 1959, I was not only completely broke but $6,000 in debt."

5. SANTA BARBARA

He claimed that those three years, from 1957 to 1960, had cost him $21,000, and that he had then paid a further $10,000 in cash on the Romeros' behalf. He then appealed to his old friend by reminding him of the success this investment had generated: "In more than five years of teaching, recording and concertizing you have grossed approximately a half a million dollars, you operate a fleet of cars, support a yacht in the yacht basin here and have purchased 4 city houses."[41]

No one knows how accurate his figures really were, but he now wanted $11,698 as reimbursement for his cash outlay. We know from extant bank statements that this amount was almost the total cash the Romeros had on hand at the time.[42] Still, Celedonio felt honor bound to assist Fe, considering all that the Stoddards had done to help the Romeros achieve the remarkable success they were now enjoying; in fact, he had already given him money on occasion. Moreover, Fe was a guest at the Romero home, where the family cared for him before he was hospitalized for the last time. The issue of compensation soon became moot, as Fe Stoddard died about two months after writing this letter, in July 1967, and only two months short of his sixty-fifth birthday. Evie outlived him by at least seventeen years.

* * *

The Stoddards are among the principal heroes in this story. As a direct result of their generous and visionary assistance, by 1960 the Romeros were on the verge of making it big in America, of realizing dreams Celedonio had harbored since the 1930s, when he promised Angelita that he would one day play in New York. Nearly thirty years later, that was a promise he was about to keep—from a new base of operations, in Hollywood.

CHAPTER 6

HOLLYWOOD

Although the biographical narrative in the previous chapter took us up to the early 1960s, after the Romeros had spent only a year or so in Santa Barbara, it was becoming increasingly clear to them that they needed to be closer to the center of cultural action in Southern California, and that was Hollywood. So they moved two hours south and took up residence in Tinseltown, where they would remain for over a decade, though at different addresses. They could no longer depend on the largesse of the Stoddards, however, and their concert appearances were not yet frequent or remunerative enough to support them. One thing they did excel at was dealing in guitars.[1] Unfortunately, the net income from buying and selling instruments was about zero, so they would teach. And teach and teach. And then they would teach some more.

On August 20, 1958, only a year after their arrival, they signed rental agreements for apartments at 711 and 715 North Wilton Place, for $100 and $80 a month respectively. One would be their living space, and the other would serve as a studio. They would eventually move their studio to more capacious quarters at 6320 1/2 Sunset Boulevard, which offered one thousand square feet for their expanding business. Canny investors in real estate, they would also buy houses on Maplewood Avenue and North Beachwood Drive (they still own these properties) during the 1960s.

6. HOLLYWOOD

Celedonio, Celin, and Pepe did almost all the teaching, and from the beginning they kept detailed records of names, lesson dates, and fees paid. Although I will have much more to say about the Romeros as teachers and about their leading students later on, among the names that jump out in these early notebooks are renowned classical guitarist Christopher Parkening, who began studying with Celedonio in 1958, as well as Tony Mottola and Tommy Tedesco, eminent studio guitarists who clearly felt they had much to learn from Celedonio and his sons. The front page of *Good Time Jazz & Contemporary Records News* for summer 1960 quotes drummer Shelly Manne as saying, "There's a fifteen year old boy [Pepe] who's teaching some of the top studio men, and they say he's great!"[2] Other names of interest here are Erna Rubinstein, a renowned violin virtuosa who had always wanted to learn the guitar; Frederick Noad, who would later become a leading teacher in his own right; José Oribe, renowned guitar maker; Kristine Eddy, Pepe's future wife; and Fe Stoddard, who continued to study. Celedonio gave on average four to six lessons a day and charged $7.50 per lesson.

Over the ensuing decades, the Romeros would turn Southern California into a mecca for those wanting to learn classical and flamenco guitar. To begin, however, the Romero Studio of Guitar was born at 711 North Wilton Place in Hollywood 38, phone number HO 4-3709. A brochure for the school states, "Mr. Romero, as a teacher, combines the indispensable methodic works of Aguado, of Sor, of Carcassi and of Tárrega and Pujol, with his own advanced technique of finger progression which produces the guitar magic for which he has been famous in Mediterranean countries for twenty years." Well, more than twenty, really, but that might have made him seem too old. And the only two Mediterranean countries to which this assertion was applicable were Spain and Portugal, not southern France, Italy, or Greece. We have already had occasion to note a tendency toward embellishment in Romero publicity materials and will do so again later. All that mattered now was that they were exceptional players and teachers, and word was getting out.

Talented, personable, and photogenic, the Romeros quickly adapted to Hollywood. In the fall of 1958, they made the acquaintance of Mel Ferrer and his wife, Audrey Hepburn. They would eventually count Desi Arnaz, Ricardo Montalban, Bob Hope, and numerous other luminaries among their friends. They also worked occasionally on film scores, though their recollections of these endeavors are a bit hazy now. Celin recalls appearing on screen in a western with Jane Wyman and Rory Calhoun, in a saloon scene during which two women fight over Celin. Alex North wanted to write something for the Romeros to play for a film score, but Celin didn't know who Alex North was and declined the offer! Decades later, Pepe played *Recuerdos de la Alhambra* on the soundtrack for an episode of the HBO hit series *The Sopranos*.

Angel in particular thrived in this environment, and I will have more to say about his Hollywood connections and activities in a later chapter. Pepe enrolled at Hollywood High School, while Angel attended Hollywood Professional School (HPS), whose curriculum was especially suitable for performing artists. Angel graduated from HPS, though by this time the Romeros were giving so many concerts (and making so much money) that finishing high school served no useful purpose. An interview that appeared in the *New York Times Magazine* reported, "Pepe says that most of Hollywood High probably thought he was 'a weirdo.'" Angel took the challenge of adolescent American society more seriously, immersing himself in sports, mostly the martial arts but also baseball. Because of his musical career, his grades suffered, but he was unconcerned. He was already a success in his chosen field, having appeared as a soloist at the Hollywood Bowl—the first classical guitarist to do so. "'I was always 10 going on 35,' Angel muses. 'Sometimes I wonder: Did I miss anything in my childhood?'"[3] Though Pepe never progressed beyond the eleventh grade, most of us would agree that he and his brothers have since earned the equivalent of several doctorates in music, and in Pepe's case, the University of Victoria and the San Francisco Conservatory of Music conferred honorary doctorates on him, in 1994 and 2011, respectively.

READY FOR PRIME TIME

The Romeros' first breakout concert took place not in San Francisco, Chicago, Boston, or New York but closer to home, in Los Angeles. They themselves arranged a concert at the Ebell-Wilshire Theater on Saturday, January 21, 1961, a day after the inauguration of John Fitzgerald Kennedy as the thirty-fifth president of the United States. It is interesting to look at the publicity Lucas prepared in advance of this performance. Celedonio had always demonstrated a willingness to stretch the truth here and there, es-

6. HOLLYWOOD

pecially about the year in which he was born, but Lucas took that approach to new heights (or depths) by claiming that Celin was a "piano prodigy at 10" and that Pepe was "the greatest flamenco guitarist in the world today," asserting, "Both critics and audiences agree that never before have they heard the flamenco guitar played with such subtlety and virtuosity."[4] Pepe was truly great, but even he would not have claimed (then or now) to be greater than Mario Escudero, Niño Ricardo, or Sabicas.

Nonetheless, the *Los Angeles Times* found the group "bewitching" and "spectacular."[5] The *Los Angeles Examiner* reported that the Romeros were "a handsome lot, poised and obviously experienced in concert manners." The reviewer noted, "I consider Celedonio second to no guitarist [an apparent reference to Segovia]. His personality is refreshingly warm, sincere and ingratiating. Angel gave evidence of what innate talent, hard work and good training can accomplish."[6] This estimation of the Romeros could well have served as the template for thousands of subsequent critiques. For this performance, they earned the princely sum of $2,300, after paying the theater's expenses.

The fact that they were handsome *was* important. John Kennedy had just proved how helpful good looks were in the television age. For reaching a mass audience in the 1960s, no mass medium was as effective as television. The Romeros were a natural for TV because of their attractive appearance and the visually stimulating nature of what they did: four suave Spaniards strumming and plucking their guitars with eye-popping dexterity and obviously total absorption, mentally and emotionally, in what they were doing. It was an act guaranteed to keep viewers from changing the channel.

In 1961 the quartet appeared on *The Jack Paar Show*. They also performed that fall on *PM East-West* and *CBS Calendar*. This exposure made the Romeros household words. Evie wrote them on November 10, 1961, to report that Pepe was building up quite a base of local fans who had seen him on television. "On Halloween night, when so many young people take the night to gad about, three nice-looking gals knocked on our door asking for Pepe."[7]

The family returned to the Lobero in Santa Barbara for a concert on April 8, 1961, this time as a quartet. Ironically, they played no actual quartet numbers but rather offered up a potpourri of solos and duets. And they appeared in the order of their age, Celedonio, Celin, Pepe, and Angel. Many of the numbers they played were now available to guitar lovers on two albums they had cut for Contemporary Records in 1960. ¡Flamenco fenómeno! featured Pepe playing flamenco standards with a flair and maturity far beyond his sixteen years. The other, *Spanish Guitar Music*, highlighted Celedonio and Celin playing a selection of classics from their homeland.

A few months later, they set out on their grand tour, starting in Chicago with a concert at Orchestra Hall on October 17. This program would feature something new—and risky. The chaconne is a variation form from the Baroque period. It was originally a rather lewd dance imported from Latin America that made its way from Spain to Italy and the rest of Europe. After it was adopted by the nobility, it became more formal and intricate. The most famous chaconne is from Bach's Second Violin Partita in D Minor and is justifiably considered one of the most challenging works, technically and interpretatively, in the repertoire. So when Angel decided at age fifteen to arrange and perform this piece, he met with understandable resistance from his oldest brother, who didn't feel he was mature enough for such a major work. When Angel played it at Orchestra Hall, however, he received an extended standing ovation, and his father was very moved.

However, the Romeros were also virtuosos at publicity and knew how to cater to local sensibilities to ensure that they would be invited back. The *Chicago Sun-Times* gleefully reported, "One aspect of the city Celin especially likes is the girls. They look like girls, he said. They are dressed, and they have faces here. According to Celin, in Los Angeles, the girls go around without shoes, and in shapeless dresses or pants, and are all of a color, either from the sun or because of the lack of it. Pepe and Angel said the city reminds them of Europe. Things are close enough together that you don't always have to ride in a car to get somewhere, like in Los Angeles."[8]

This gratuitous criticism of the region they preferred to call home was exactly the sort of thing earnest midwesterners wanted to read. Celin was a fast learner and knew this perfectly well, though he and his family were, in fact, still adapting to Southern California's car culture. The Romeros also helped themselves by giving a benefit concert for patients at the Rehabilitation Institute of Chicago, on the Tuesday night before their Sunday appearance, on October 15.[9]

They returned to the West Coast for a San Francisco debut at the Veterans' Auditorium on Saturday, October 28. The critic for the *News-Call Bulletin* actually complained about the aforementioned lack of ensemble numbers.[10] This criticism points up the fact that, at this early stage, there was absolutely no repertoire for guitar quartet other than what the Romeros transcribed or improvised. Their act was thus a sort of variety show featuring a kaleidoscopic assortment of solos, duets, and a few quartets. Someone expecting a plucked-and-strummed version of the Juilliard String Quartet might well be surprised and disappointed, though the vast majority of critics and audiences found this approach refreshingly different.

The *San Francisco Examiner*'s critic was faintly critical in finding Celedonio's solo repertoire in particular very reminiscent of Segovia's, which was no coincidence.[11] Celedonio had been tracking Segovia's career for decades and emulated what appeared to be a very successful approach to programming. However, there was one crucial difference: unlike Segovia, Celedonio never distanced himself from the Andalusian folklore with which he had grown up and that moved him so deeply. Every concert featured some flamenco numbers, played by Pepe or the quartet, or Celedonio playing his Cuban-inspired *guajira*, the *Fantasía*.

Reviewer Dean Wallace's piece in the *San Francisco Chronicle* offered unqualified praise of the program: "Many of us had heard the Romeros on television [Jack Paar]. . . . Celin is the lyricist of the family. Pepe is a something of a sleeper—behind his spectacles and studious air with the classics. . . . Angel played the Bach Cello Chaconne in C [*sic*; he was thinking of the Chaconne in D minor for Violin solo]. It was an impressive feat of memory, and an even more impressive display of prodigal technique—this 15-year-old is a genius at coloring the tone of his instrument."[12]

A few weeks later, it was on to Boston, for a concert at Jordan Hall on December 8. In a review the following day, the *Boston Globe* exclaimed that it was "one of the most extraordinary concerts this reviewer has enjoyed in three decades of his craft. . . . This instrument, sometimes denigrated as a mere strumming accompaniment to convivial song, is actually a remarkable source of music, lyrical, displayful and dramatic."[13] This program exemplified the sort of potpourri for which the quartet would become famous: Celedonio started it off by playing Luis de Milán, Robert de Visée, Bach, and Albéniz, and then Celin played some Heitor Villa-Lobos preludes and Albéniz's *Rumores de La Caleta*. After intermission, Angel played Gaspar Sanz, Bach, and Domenico

PART 2. SOUTHERN CALIFORNIA

Scarlatti, and Pepe served up a flamenco set of *soleares, fandango, granadinas, bulerías, alegrías*. Next came a Celedonio/Angel duet of some Baroque music and a Celin/Pepe duet of the Intermezzo from Granados's *Goyescas*. The concert concluded with the whole quartet playing *malagueñas*. And it worked!

All this commotion about the Romeros did not escape the notice of Sol Hurok, who wrote to Celedonio on November 30, 1961, expressing interest in managing them. However, those honors had already been claimed by James Lucas and would soon go to Columbia Artists Management, which began managing them the following year (Lucas remained on for a time as a "producer" with Columbia). They would soon part ways with Contemporary Records and sign a contract with Mercury, which would produce their landmark recordings of the 1960s, including of Rodrigo's *Concierto de Aranjuez* (with Angel as soloist) and *Concierto andaluz*, as well as a solo album featuring Celedonio.

These concerts were all excellent preparation for their most important date, in New York City at Town Hall on December 14. The *Herald Tribune* and the *Times* both extolled the group's stage presence, fleet-fingered virtuosity, and tasteful interpretations.[14] *World Telegram and Sun* critic Louis Biancolli declared, "In all my years of guitar listening, I never heard such fire and virtuosity."[15] Santa Barbara remained proud of its adopted Spaniards, and the local paper reported on January 7, 1962, that they had triumphed in their New York debut, citing these reviews as evidence of their success.[16] Such a hit had they been, they returned to Town Hall on April 10, 1962.[17] The Romeros finished their 1961–62 season with an appearance at the World's Fair in Seattle.

Ensuing programs in California during 1964 would take them from the Masonic Evergreen Lodge No. 2569 in Riverside to the Redondo Union High School Auditorium in Redondo Beach. One, two, or four Romeros were willing to play anywhere for any audience that wanted to hear them—and was willing to pay for the pleasure, unless it was a benefit of some kind. Community concert associations were particularly effective promoters of classical music in remote areas during this period, and the Romeros were perfectly suited for those kinds of appearances. Another thing that contributed to the Romeros' success was the way their particular act resonated with popular culture. This made them all the more approachable and attractive—even familiar, somehow.

6. HOLLYWOOD

MY THREE SONS

The root of the word *familiar* is, of course, *family*. What made the Romeros different from, say, the Juilliard String Quartet was that they were a family, a father and three sons. That configuration was highly unusual and very appealing, and it resonated on many levels of American culture at that time, especially the new cultural medium of television.

The same public that went to hear Celedonio and his three sons outgun all their competitors also thrilled to the adventures of the Cartwright family on *Bonanza*, which ran from 1959 to 1973 and weekly related the saga of a man and his three sons, Adam, Hoss, and Little Joe, in the Nevada of the Old West. This similarity was not lost on a reviewer for the *Houston Post*, who informed his readers that "Hoss never bailed out Little Joe as effectively as guitarist Pepe Romero filled in for his injured younger brother Angel at Friday's Society for the Performing ARTS concert in Jones Hall."[18] Of course, *The Sound of Music* popularized the exploits of the Trapp family singers, and the Romero family guitarists were more than a little reminiscent of their Austrian counterparts.

Those seeking a more contemporary dramatic setting chortled at fraternal capers on *My Three Sons*, starring Fred MacMurray as the beleaguered patriarch. *The Adventures of Ozzie and Harriet* featured a family of actual musicians, the Nelsons, and though there were only two sons, not three, the mother was part of the act, making them a group of four family musicians. In other words, there was something about the Romeros that vibrated in sympathy with popular culture, which they would turn to their advantage by appearing numerous times on network television.

In 1962, the *Santa Barbara News-Press* enthused about their recent concerts in New York, noting, "They are warmly remembered here, too, for their participation in Fiesta events and informal social gatherings."[19] Perhaps more than any other event, however, the glowing write-up they received in *Time* magazine in 1962 (and quoted extensively in the *News-Press* article) was proof positive of their now-national stature. This review then went on to summarize a piece in *Time* about the Romeros:

> At 6 o'clock every morning in the bungalow at No. 5152 Maplewood Ave. in Los Angeles, a man reaches beneath his bed and pulls out a $1,000 guitar. While still stretched out on his back, he plays Johann Sebastian Bach. He

seldom stops before 8, and when he does, it is the signal for his three sons, who sleep down the hall, to reach under their beds and grab their own guitars. The family plays together until 10. Then the father laces on some sneakers, and leads his sons in a run five times around the block. Just how the road work helps Celedonio and his sons play the guitar, no one in the family can explain. But it is all part of a pattern of dedicated practice that very clearly pays off.[20]

As it turned out, there *was* a wake-up piece, his version of reveille, which Celedonio would play in the morning, though it was the Gavotte from Bach's Lute Suite no. 4 in E Major. But by the sons' own admission, the story about running around the block was a fiction invented by someone—though they insist it was not a family member. Still, it made for great copy, and that helped sales.

In fact, Celedonio and his various agents consistently exhibited a tendency, not to mention a willingness, to resort to distortion and even fabrication if it would move product. The program for the concert at Chicago's Orchestra Hall in October 1961 stated that Celedonio's former "concert tours, starting in early youth, took him all over Europe," and that he married at age eighteen (i.e., in 1931). In the program for a Hollywood Bowl concert during the summer of 1968, the biography provides further howlers: Celedonio was "born into a prominent Malaga family in 1918. He graduated from the Madrid Conservatory and made his Madrid debut at age 18 [in 1936]. Soon thereafter, he married a young leading actress of Malaga's Teatro Cervantes." In an interview with a Spanish-language Seventh-Day Adventist magazine, Celedonio claimed that he had earned a doctorate in music from the Madrid Conservatory.[21]

As we know now, virtually every claim here is misleading. He had been in the habit since his Málaga days of shaving five years off his age, to make himself appear to have been even more of a prodigy than he clearly was. However, this would mean that his supposed Madrid premiere took place in 1936, during the civil war, when we know he was in Málaga. And, of course, he was born in Cuba, not Spain. During the Cold War, and given the recent emergence of Fidel Castro, it was probably not something he wanted to brag about. And we know that he married in 1934, before the civil war began, not when it was almost over! Angelita was very talented, to be sure, but she was

6. HOLLYWOOD

not a leading actress anywhere. And an exhaustive perusal of the records at the Madrid Conservatory from 1929 to 1945 has revealed no evidence of his studies there, though we know for certain that he studied at the Málaga Conservatory during the 1930s. That was not impressive enough, though, hence the claim of Madrid studies.[22]

Though the line between myth and reality may often have been indistinct in publicity about the Romeros, there was nothing fictional about the dangers of military service in the mid-1960s, and those dangers soon came knocking on the Romeros' door.

DON'T GET CAUGHT COLD IN THE DRAFT

The greatest hazard they now faced was that Pepe and Angel were coming of draft age. Angel's selective-service papers, dated July 3, 1967, indicate that his height was 5 feet 8¾ inches, his weight 130 pounds. Angel declared that he was paid $900 per concert and worked fifty hours a week teaching. However, the draft board advised him that he was *not* "required to report for Armed Forces Physical Examination on July 7, 1967." The reason given for this exemption was that he was deemed unsuited for military service, an opinion with which he wholeheartedly concurred.

Angel had first served in an artillery unit of the California Army National Guard. A record of Military Status of Registrant for Angel dated January 21, 1966, states tersely that Private Angel Romero had "ceased to serve satisfactorily," that is, "unsatisfactory participation due to failure to attend 90 percent of the scheduled drills and training periods held during current retirement year." Angel further explained to me that he had refused to do KP (kitchen duty) because he didn't want to damage his nails. He certainly wasn't going to scrub toilets in the latrine either. In a statement that he provided to the army in a letter dated February 1, 1966, Angel declared, "I should be released from military service for reasons . . . stated in the letter. I feel that these steps should be taken as soon as possible, since I do not wish to continue in a situation dangerous to my own health, and possibly to the safety of others." Angel was discharged from the National Guard and also exempted from army service. As it turned out, his platoon was deployed to Vietnam and suffered heavy casualties there.

PART 2. SOUTHERN CALIFORNIA

Pepe had already faced and survived his ordeal with the military. His excuse had less to do with his disposition than with his physical health. In the archive is a letter dated April 12, 1965, responding to Pepe's claim that he had a physical defect that disqualified him. He complained of nephritis, as well as "frequent severe pain in [his] back," arguing, "Since my specialty is the most attractive and requested feature of the quartet the ability of the other three to obtain engagements and maintain the support of my family would be seriously impaired by my absence." Pepe was declared 4-F and no longer eligible for military service.

A REALLY BIG SHOW

Instead of appearing on parade, Pepe and Angel, along with Celedonio and Celin, would return to television. Perhaps the most celebrated of the Romeros' TV appearances took place on *The Ed Sullivan Show*, during its nineteenth season, episode 25, which aired on February 26, 1967. This variety show featured a vaudeville-like succession of mime artists, jugglers, comedians, and musicians. Sullivan was often mimicked for the way he would say, "Tonight we have a really big SHEW!" This particular episode featured a conspicuously Latin twist that included not only the Romeros but also Xavier Cugat and his orchestra.

True to form, the Romeros made a big splash in the Sullivan pool, but it was almost a big bellyflop. For some reason, the time of the Romeros' scheduled appearance was moved up, but not everyone received the message. When Sullivan called on the quartet, only Pepe and his brother Celin were present. "Ed Sullivan announced us and he looked to us," Celin later recalled to me. "And there was only the two of us. You could see, in his face, that Sullivan was completely shocked." The brothers had asked Nancy Sinatra, also a guest, to locate the missing Romeros, and she soon did. Father and son strolled on stage in the nick of time, just as the camera rolled to them. Even though *The Ed Sullivan Show* was the most-watched variety program of its time, Pepe, then in his late teens, says that the potential debacle hadn't made him nervous. If the missing Romeros couldn't be found, he and his brother were prepared to perform as a duo. "You have to roll with things as they come," he assured me.

6. HOLLYWOOD

Pepe later expatiated on the significance of this event. "It was very exciting. Ed Sullivan was not really known for this particular type of music. And to bring the guitar to such a vast audience, it was an exciting and wonderful thought. It had some very funny things that happened because as it goes in live TV, everything changed."[23] Of course, they were already seasoned TV veterans, having performed on another much-watched program of that era, *The Tonight Show*, in January 1965.

THOSE FABULOUS FLYING ROMEROS

Critic Donal Henahan once wrote that "the four Romeros may sound like an aerial team."[24] That was a perspicacious observation. Reading and hearing about their life on the road during the 1960s, 1970s, and 1980s, one can easily imagine the Romeros as a sort of traveling circus act: The Fabulous Flying Romeros Perform Death-Defying Feats of Aerial Acrobatics, or something along those lines. They traveled the highways and byways of the United States and, despite their frequent appearances in the country's leading concert venues, never felt themselves too good or exalted to give a concert in any cow town or wide spot in the road that would have them. Like Liberace, they had found just the right formula for popularizing classical music and bringing it to ordinary Americans in the most ordinary of places. As Pepe later said, "You have to program music in a way that is like fishing. The idea is to give the audience something they will like if you want them to come to you."[25] For this very reason, a Columbus, Ohio, critic once noted, "What impresses one most about the Romeros is their realization that guitar playing can be as much enjoyed as endured."[26]

Celin recalled to me that those early days in the United States were just one "big adventure." He would receive an envelope from Jim Lucas with 125 concert contracts. He had never heard of most of these places, and since he was responsible for the driving, he bought a big map and put pins in it to mark their destinations. Still, nothing had prepared the Romeros for the vast distances and the drastic changes in climate.

They chose to drive across the United States because concerts were usually only two hundred to three hundred miles apart, and it was more practical to go by car than to fly. Also, thanks to the Eisenhower administration, they had a new interstate highway system at their disposal, so cross-country touring was easier than it would otherwise have been. One year Celin bought a GMC three-quarter-ton truck to transport them and their equipment around the country. A year later he traded that in on an early Suburban. This vehicle provided ample space for a new traveling companion, Melchor, a 121-lb. German shepherd (named after one of the three magi) that had been a Christmas present for Angelita. Melchor's job was to guard their luggage and guitars when they were not in the car. No would-be thief ever got past his vigilant eyes and nose—not to mention his teeth.

There was always a sort of carnival atmosphere when the Romero Quartet performed, and they would roll into town with their guitars and castanets to bring a bit of Andalusia to the high plains, southern bayous, or the Smokey Mountains. I distinctly recall attending one such performance in Burlington, Colorado, in 1976, and it was an experience never to be forgotten. They holed up in a local motel, nothing fancy, and prepared for their concert. It was a virtual certainty that the hardworking folk of this agricultural community in the eastern part of the state had never had to opportunity to see what they were about to witness, and the local auditorium was packed. Enter the Romeros, stage right, playing their standard repertoire of *pavanas* and preludes, *recuerdos* and *rumores*, sonatas and *soleares*. As always, a rousing *malagueña* finished off the program and brought the house down. I noticed that they brought the same intensity and infectious enthusiasm to this appearance that I have seen them bring to concerts in major venues. And they would repeat this carnival act in dozens of such communities all over the United States. Mamá saved postcards as souvenirs from every motel where they stayed, whether it was the Fiesta Motel in Pontiac, Illinois, the Showboat Motor Inn in Greenwich, Connecticut, a Holiday Inn in Gary, Indiana, or the Ramada Inn of Wichita, Kansas.

In the Romeros' case, however, it was not just a matter of breezing in and out of every "Burlington" that would have them. They were careful to cultivate good relations with the locals, to ensure a base of goodwill and the possibility of further invitations to perform. For instance, the *Billings (MT) Gazette* reported that after a Romero concert at the Billings Community Center, the visiting Spaniards were fêted at Earl Cranston's home, where they schmoozed with local guitarists and other fans.[27] This was just the sort of personal diplomacy at which they excelled, and it paid handsome

6. HOLLYWOOD

dividends over the years, in terms not only of concert appearances and attendance but also of sales of their recordings.

Still, most people would find this incessant driving and performing exhausting. The endorphins that performing produces do give one a sort of high that can be addictive, but after a concert the high is followed by a crash, and the performer has to rest. Pepe's wife, Carissa, says that the Romeros are ideally suited for their way of life. They are very tough, physically and mentally, and can endure the discomforts of touring. She thinks that this is typical of Andalusians, perhaps of an earlier generation that survived the civil war. There may be some truth to this hypothesis; as a *New York Times* critic observed: "There must be something about being born in Spain that gives artists a long-lasting vitality. Think of Pablo Casals, Pablo Picasso and Andrés Segovia—and of Carlos Montoya."[28] Or think of Celedonio Romero, who kept performing till age eighty-three, just before he died!

Appropriately enough, Carissa deploys an automotive metaphor to describe this condition, which is a sort of "sixth gear" that allows the Romeros to keep going when everyone else is collapsing from exhaustion. All that energy also gives a lot of joy to their listeners, especially when they have never seen anything like it before. Carissa has attended thousands of Romero performances, and she has noticed that the audience members generally walk out of the hall with a smile. She is not alone in noticing this: in 1968, Vancouver's *The Province* featured a review titled "Superb Romeros Made Music Fun."[29] That's about it.

Again, this principle applies regardless of venue. In Davenport-Bettendorf, Iowa, a critic asserted, "What people like most about the Romeros, I suspect, is their infectious good humor and charming rapport. And secretly, everyone must long to be able to pick up his own guitar like that and melt milady's heart."[30] A Seattle reviewer observed something similar: "The audience also obviously had fun—of the soul-cleansing, battery-charging kind. The audience applauded enthusiastically—with scattered shouts of Ole!"[31] Finally, a Philadelphia journalist noted the following about a concert at the Temple University Music Festival:

> [The Romeros] also are knowing entertainers. Their art is highly commercial, though it is still art. And one thing an entertainer must know is how to please an audience. This the Romeros do perfectly. They can get laughs merely by

announcing the next number. Last night they got quite a bit of mileage out of a broken footstool that had to be replaced with one just a shade too high. As each member of the family pushed the footstool along, the laughs grew louder, until the footstool was relegated to the background as the player simply crossed his legs to perform.[32]

Despite the rigors of concertizing, the family has been sustained to a large extent by the feeling that they are doing some good, not only as entertainers but also as cultural ambassadors. As Celin once remarked, "We knew that American people liked the guitar but we were surprised to discover that in many of the cities we have played, ours was the first guitar concert. Throughout our travels during our six years in the U.S. we have found the people very warm on and off stage."[33] And though their act is very entertaining, it never insults the intelligence of the audience by becoming coarse or tasteless. On the contrary, in the opinion of the *South China Morning Post*, the outstanding trait of the Romeros is "the unconditional dignity with which they treated their instrument and their music."[34] Dignity *can* be entertaining.

Jascha Heifetz understood all of this as well as any concert artist, and it led him to remark, "You always hear of the 'delicate, sensitive artist.' I assure you that it takes the nerves of a bullfighter, the digestion of a peasant, the vitality of a nightclub hostess, the tact of a diplomat, and the concentration of a Tibetan monk to lead the strenuous life of a virtuoso."[35] Though the life of a touring concert artist may seem glamorous and privileged, and though it may do a lot of good, it is full of mishaps, some comical and some life threatening.

ANYTHING THAT CAN GO WRONG MIGHT GO WRONG!

After reading through hundreds of reviews of Romero concerts and recording the family's reminiscences, I've been struck by just how many things can go wrong, even when there is a top-drawer management agency like Columbia Artists arranging logistical details.

People have accidents and get sick. That's a given. What matters is how a group like the Romeros responds to this inevitability. Thus the quartet occasionally became a trio on short notice: the *Anchorage Daily News* once

6. HOLLYWOOD

reported that "Celedonio Romero, the father of the other performers, became suddenly ill and was unable to perform. His three sons carried out a program showing great versatility."[36]

Given the millions of miles the Romeros have traveled, mostly by car and plane, one marvels that they are still alive and in one piece. Alas, the same could not always be said of their guitars. Angel reported, with a mixture of heartache and dismay, to *Hi-Fi News* that "his precious Miguel Rodríguez instrument, having just flown in to London from Amsterdam . . . was terribly cracked—it had been crushed." He said, "I gave the guitar first-aid with magic glue; I think the patient will live. . . . I always keep the glue with me, in case the instrument falls apart or my fingernails break."[37] A misplaced guitar was nearly as useless as a broken one. An Oregon newspaper gave its readers evidence of this in another review. Apparently the Romeros were called in at the last minute to substitute for an ailing José Carreras. "The switch had its complications. The Romeros, [engaged] less than 30 hours earlier, arrived in the early evening in Portland to find the airline had lost one of their guitars. Thirty minutes before curtain time it was found."[38]

In the early days, before seatbelts and other safety devices, Celin, who was the first to drive and remained in charge of motoring matters, made his passengers wear motorcycle helmets. He had seen the grisly aftermath of a car crash in which the passengers were thrown through the windshield and killed, and he thought the helmets a wise safety precaution. However, they would result in some misunderstanding and embarrassment. Once, after a concert in Hamilton, New York, they got lost driving back to their hotel in a heavy snowstorm—they went left when they should have gone right. As a result, they soon found themselves out in the middle of nowhere. They would need help, but there was no one around to give it. Then they noticed the lights of a house in the distance, so they decided to walk in that direction. The problem was that they had not worn anything but their tuxedos, as they didn't anticipate needing winter clothing. Mamá wanted everyone to keep at least their heads warm and made them wear their helmets.

They also did not want to leave anything in the car, so they trundled through the snow in their tuxes and helmets, carrying their guitars. They eventually arrived at a farmhouse and rang the doorbell. The poor old farmer could hardly believe his eyes: there on his doorstep were four men and a

PART 2. SOUTHERN CALIFORNIA

woman in formal dress and motorcycle helmets, covered in snow and carrying guitar cases. They must have looked somewhat like ET times five. The Romeros explained their predicament to him in accented English, and deciding they were harmless, the farmer let them in. He made eggs for them, and everyone got along famously. In fact, they became fast friends, and he stayed in touch with them over the years.

Sometimes motoring mishaps had more dire consequences. In South Carolina, on January 28, 1986, the same day that the space shuttle *Challenger* exploded, Pepe was on his way to the airport when he was rear-ended by a semitrailer, and his rental car flipped over twice into the median. He remembers seeing the horizon going around and around, and when he stopped, he felt great pain in his right arm. His next sensation was hearing someone outside asking if he was alive! He was alive but more worried about his ability to play. So he climbed out of the wreck, took out his guitar, and played the Villa-Lobos Étude no. 1 in E Minor, which demands great dexterity. His fingers still worked, so he knew he would be okay.

Everyone complains about the weather, but no one does anything about it. Though that remark is often attributed to Mark Twain, apparently its origin is somewhat obscure. Still, weather remains a phenomenon over which we have little control, and it often disrupted the best-laid concert plans of the Romeros. On July 16, 1966, Angel and Pepe performed at the Waikiki Shell. One would perhaps expect stormy weather in such a tropical locale but certainly not low temperatures. However, as the *Honolulu Star-Bulletin* reported, "It was so cold Angel Romero, one of the featured guitarists, had to stick his hands inside his tux to keep them warm during orchestral moments in the *Concierto de Aranjuez* by Rodrigo. Yet so hot when Pepe Romero took the spotlight alone for two Flamenco selections he appeared volcanic. That's because the Honolulu Symphony had retired backstage leaving Pepe alone as a white coat against red background lighting."[39]

Changes in temperature could also affect tuning. Though the *Green Bay Press-Gazette* had high praise for the Romeros' musicianship, it still found the concert "marred by long pauses while instruments were tuned and feet and shirt cuffs meticulously arranged." The reviewer observed, "Those things are necessary, but they still seem mildly insulting to an audience which has come to hear something other than the scales played."[40]

6. HOLLYWOOD

Tuning could apparently be insulting, but it wouldn't provoke a riot. Other violations of social norms could. Once, during the early 1960s, while on tour in the South, the quartet noticed that there were people sitting in the balcony while there were empty seats in front. Reminding the audience that the guitar was an intimate instrument, they called out for the folks in the balcony to come on down. But these particular folks were black, and they knew better than to accept the invitation. The Romeros understood nothing about segregation and were mystified by this hesitancy until someone later explained that what they did was dangerous and they could have gotten into serious trouble for it.

Also, where there is electricity, shocking things can happen. The *San Diego Union-Tribune* noted approvingly that "nothing seriously deterred these virtuosos. . . . Not even an electric short in a stage light, which prompted popping noises and cascading sparks during Pepe Romero's *Recuerdos de la Alhambra*. Such distractions made his sure-fingered professionalism particularly admirable."[41]

Then there are vexations that one can scarcely anticipate or mitigate. When the Romeros played at Cal Tech's Beckman Auditorium, the *California Tech*'s critic grumbled that "a woman with two small children was seated right next to [him] and proved quite a distraction to all those around her trying to quiet them down as they became bored. . . . It later turned out that the children were the offspring of one of the Romeros and the woman was their mother"![42]

Some disruptions were avian rather than human, proving even more intractable. Culpeper, Virginia's local paper reported on a 1971 Romero concert in the auditorium of the Culpeper County High School:

> A large bird had somehow gotten into the auditorium and was flying overhead, weaving and dipping his wings to the music, or so it seemed. The performers glanced overhead, but continued until they completed the opening number, "Quartet in A Major" by Antonio Vivaldi. Then they could ignore their competition no longer, and burst into chuckles themselves. Pepe remarked, "Vivaldi would be so pleased, he was very fond of birds." And to show his own appreciation of his feathered admirer, Pepe substituted two musical selections honoring Spanish birds instead of the Frescobaldi aria listed on the program. . . . The bird, perhaps feeling outclassed by such a variety of

sweet sounds, retired to a niche in the high ceiling, and apparently enjoyed the rest of the performance along with the enthusiastic audience.[43]

Performers take note: make the best of a bad situation, and remember that a little humor goes a long way.

Once again, the show must and will go on . . . most of the time. A Cleveland critic noted with some disapproval that "after playing a single flamenco encore (by Sabicas), [Pepe] Romero begged off from further duty because, he said, the nail on the index finger of his right hand was wearing down and 'I have to play tomorrow night in Cincinnati.' One hopes Romero's fingernail survives Cincinnati."[44] One *hoped*, and it *did*.

Other problems were less consequential than fingernails but just as vexing. Celedonio's name consistently gave journalists fits. All the variant spellings one encounters in periodicals cannot simply have been typographical errors. It's an unusual name, and writers weren't sure what to make of it. Even a Mexican newspaper once referred to him as *Macedonio*. Other choice misspellings have included Celendonio, Celedonia, Caledonio, Calodonio, Caledonia, Celestino, and Celadonio. Celin was a bit easier to spell but sometimes appeared as Celine. This is just the tip of an iceberg of incomprehension that the Romeros encountered as they crisscrossed North America, giving concerts under a variety of conditions and collaborating with a host of different performers.

On rare occasions, critics either didn't understand or simply didn't like what the Romeros had to offer. A Michigan critic counseled, "[A] Romeros concert requires patience. There were times one could grow impatient with the repetitive deliberateness of many of the guitar passages, particularly in the Rodrigo *Madrigal* [Concerto for Two Guitars and Orchestra]. . . . One person said, 'I keep thinking they're really going to get going and then they slow down again,' and one man felt the 'culture' was too much and didn't return after intermission."[45]

The most egregious example of incomprehension was provided by Albert Goldberg, a *Los Angeles Times* critic who reviewed Angel's West Coast premiere of the *Concierto de Aranjuez* at the Hollywood Bowl in July 1964, with Eleazar de Carvalho conducting a Spanish-themed program of Albéniz, Falla, Ravel, and Rodrigo. I note here that Celedonio was to have played this premiere, but Mamá did not want him to appear as a concerto soloist because she feared that he might succumb to the temptation of an encore with one of the attractive young female musicians. Angel stepped forward to take his place.

Now, Goldberg was a knowledgeable and astute critic, as well as a very good writer—which makes it all the more incomprehensible that he could get something so utterly wrong, at least about the music, if not the musician.

> One difficulty is the inherent nature of Spanish music; like Spanish dancing, it consists mainly of variations on a single theme, and these are not the best possible variations. It was like a meal in which every course from soup to dessert is spiced with the same sauce; the seasoning may be interesting, but a little goes a long way. The hit of the evening was Angel Romero's guitar playing in Joaquin Rodrigo's Concerto [sic] de Aranjuez. According to the composer, the piece is "meant to sound like the hidden breeze that stirs the tree-tops in the parks, and it should be only as strong as a butterfly, and as dainty as a veronica." This is a flossy description of music of such triviality that its appearance on a symphony concert could only be justified by the kind of playing young Mr. Romero brought to it. He could not make it sound better than it is, but he did excite unreserved admiration for his disciplined, incisive rhythm, his authority, surety and taste, and the manner in which he projected the tinkling, fragile tones of one of the most delicate of instruments in one of the world's largest amphitheaters.[46]

ROYAL FAMILY OF THE GUITAR

Despite such an errant critique, the American public tended to associate the Romeros' homeland with tradition and nobility, of either the comical Don Quixote variety or something out of a Velázquez painting of the royal family.[47] This association may have derived precisely from the way they handled the adversities elaborated upon above, with a commendable blend of humor and grace. Thus the *New York Times* noted of their 1967 Carnegie Hall appearance that "since their artistry is rooted in dignity, they are a deeply satisfying group of instrumentalists."[48] Again, the Cal Tech review cited earlier praised Celedonio as "distinguished and aristocratic in bearing and appearance." In fact, words such as *dignity*, *aristocratic*, and *nobility* flowed from the critics' pens, and already in the early 1960s, the Romeros were dubbed the Royal Family of the Guitar (and later, in German, Die

PART 2. SOUTHERN CALIFORNIA

königliche Familie der Gitarre), which in a purely artistic sense was true but in another quite ironic, given their actual origins among the Andalusian peasantry and their proletarian political sensibilities.[49] The Kennedys were the closest thing to royalty the United States had to offer, and thus the assassination of first JFK (1963) and then RFK (1968) came as a rude shock to the Romeros. This sort of thing wasn't supposed to happen here! Pepe wrote a letter to his parents on June 11, 1968, commenting on the assassination of Robert Kennedy, for whom both he and Celin had already voted in the primaries.

However, what mattered most to them, then as now, was music. The *Victoria (BC) Daily Times* declared that their recital at the appropriately named Royal Theatre "sent a large audience to its feet in one of the most spontaneous demonstrations of enthusiasm [the reviewer had] ever seen in a local concert hall."[50] This had nothing to do with royalty, though all four members of the quartet would eventually be knighted by King Juan Carlos of Spain.

* * *

In the 1960s, during the Romeros' meteoric rise to celebrity, some observers thought that theirs was simply a novelty act that would soon lose its luster, that the quartet's fifteen minutes of fame were nearly over. But the Romeros were just warming up. From a permanent base in Del Mar, near San Diego, they would expand their activities in teaching, recording, and international touring, achieving a degree of professional renown even Celedonio and Angelita had scarcely dreamed possible, much less probable.

CHAPTER 7

DEL MAR

The Romeros have resided in Del Mar for almost fifty years, making it the place the family has lived longer than any other, including Málaga. But their move there was not deliberate but rather the result of coincidence and quick thinking on the part of Celin, who has a nose for real estate and the sense to take advantage of a good deal when he sees one. An avid chess player, he has a knack for checkmate.

In 1986, the *San Diego Tribune* featured an article on the Romeros from which we learn that in July 1969, the quartet gave the premiere of a new concerto written for them by Morton Gould. The Romeros appeared with the San Diego Symphony, and the concert was part of a celebration of the city's two hundredth anniversary. Celin was driving back to Hollywood and pulled off the road to buy a cup of coffee at a 7-Eleven store in the suburban beach community of Del Mar. "It was about the only thing there at the time," he recalls. He was enchanted with the surrounding town, and by the time he left, a few hours later, he had purchased a house. The next day, his brothers and father bought lots and built their own houses. "It's a wonderful place," enthused Celin. Celedonio was especially smitten with this locale and supervised construction of a three-story Spanish-style white-stucco house, with outdoor walkways featuring patterns of inlaid stonework reminiscent

PART 2. SOUTHERN CALIFORNIA

of the Alhambra. But the *pièce de résistance* was indoors: "Look—look around you at that view. From the third floor, I can see from La Jolla to San Clemente. Where else can anyone see something like this? I bought this lot and designed this house myself, all of it. This is where we have remained and will remain. It is our *home*." As far as he was concerned, "This is paradise. . . . I love every hour that I am here."[1]

Four years earlier, Pepe had explained in an interview with the *Los Angeles Times* the family's enduring attraction to Del Mar: "It is very similar to Spain, to the city in which we lived, Málaga, a coastal city. We live in different places in Del Mar but we get together constantly to keep the feeling of the family very much alive."[2] The house is now occupied by Celin, Claudia, Pepe, and Carissa, and for years it accommodated the workshop where Little Pepe and Bernardo build guitars. (They now have a large studio in Oceanside, north of Del Mar.)

Of course, there were downsides. As Pepe once complained to Akron's *Beacon Journal* about the Romero children: "The problem is they don't practice as much as they should. When you live in Del Mar and you have an easy life and a life full of whatever you want, you get lazy and you don't need music as much. Music is to me a very spiritual thing, and some people only turn to it in times of problems."[3] In the end, the kids nonetheless turned out just fine.

One of the notable effects of this move to Del Mar was an increasingly close association with San Diego, which was much smaller than Los Angeles and far less saturated with celebrities. As a result, when the *San Diego Union-Tribune* wanted a piece on Spanish cuisine for its Food section, it needed to look no further than the Romeros in Del Mar. In one issue, for instance, Pepe offered this sage counsel: "The most important ingredient in the paella is love. That's my specialty. I stand here showering the ingredients with love and the cooks with love. I think, when food is prepared to the sound of beautiful music, it always tastes better."[4]

Mamá was a virtuosa in the *cocina*, but on the road it wasn't always possible to get the sort of meals the family preferred. Ever resourceful, Mamá began bringing along a hot plate in her suitcase so that she could prepare paella and other Spanish dishes in hotel rooms. These feasts often led to rather spirited gatherings, but hotel managers were generally understanding. However, in Germany, where the family often toured, management was a little stricter. When telltale scents prompted a confrontation, the Romeros would deny cooking in the room, insisting that the odor was nothing more than "garlic perfume"!

Departing from the topic of food preparation, in this same *Union-Tribune* article Celin expatiated on his feelings about the United States, a country he had come to know very well in his travels: "The beauty of this country is incredible. I love autumn in Connecticut, the South, the flat plains of the Midwest and the place where the Rockies start." All the touring that had provided Celin an intimate familiarity with his adoptive country's natural splendor had also generated something at least as attractive: income.

"PROSPEROUS, EH?"

The move to Del Mar was made possible not only by Celin's quick thinking but also by the Romeros' increasing affluence. They had managed their money well, made some good investments in real estate, and were busy giving concerts on average once every two days, appearances that paid increasingly well. Three concerts at the Ambassador Auditorium in the early 1980s netted the quartet the then-handsome sum of $30,000. Thanks to such performance earnings, royalties from recordings, and fees from teaching, they were living the American dream and then some. They enjoyed fine homes in an upscale community and had enough money to indulge their passion for collecting guitars and driving Mercedes-Benz automobiles. They weren't in 1940s Málaga anymore. True, they still felt a profound attachment to their native country, but now they could and did visit there whenever they wanted. As Celin said in 1970, "Spain has changed. Things are milder now politically, and we have returned there to play. But to live we like America. We married American girls and have five children among us who are Americans."[5]

This new reality surfaced in an interview with the *Herald* in Everett, Washington, when Pepe asked the journalist, "'How do you like my cigar? Prosperous, eh?'"[6] *Próspero, sí, señor*. The Romeros had entered a socioeconomic stratum only their very distant, landowning ancestors had occupied, but now with a degree of celebrity no one in their clan had ever achieved.

PART 2. SOUTHERN CALIFORNIA

Smoking a Cuban *puro* was one way to revel in this new status, and it continues to bring the Romero boys considerable satisfaction on a daily basis.

However, prosperity also entailed a certain noblesse oblige. First Celedonio and later the quartet had always been available for benefit concerts, even during those difficult decades in Málaga. That generosity has continued unabated throughout all their years in America. Celedonio was particularly supportive of the Catholic charity Fundación Esperanza (Hope Foundation), and the Mexican newspaper *El Mexicano* reported on his third benefit concert for this charity, which was building a medical clinic in Tijuana.[7] Celedonio eventually became a member of the board of trustees of this organization. Always quick to remember Spain, the quartet also gave a concert to benefit the Asociación Española Contra el Cancer (Spanish Association against Cancer), on this occasion accompanied by the Murcia Symphony Orchestra. On August 21, 2004, their concert proceeds were used to promote research at the Salk Institute in nearby La Jolla (Jonas Salk is famous for developing a polio vaccine). Various museums and children's hospitals were also the grateful recipients of their assistance.

Other benefit appearances were for fellow performing artists and organizations, such as the Santa Barbara Symphony. As noted above, the *San Diego Union-Tribune* published a favorable review of their appearance at the Old Globe Theater in Balboa Park to raise money for the School of Music and Dance at San Diego State University.[8] Ever an avid sports fan, Angel Romero was only too happy to perform a benefit for the San Dieguito Surf Soccer Club on May 22, 1982, at the Performing Arts Center in El Cajon. His performance received a very favorable and appreciative review in the local newspaper.[9]

The Romeros may not have been model Catholics, but the religion was a central part of their culture, and they occasionally attended and gave a number of benefit concerts at Saint James Catholic Church in nearby Solana Beach, for which it was understandably grateful. One appearance, in July 1981, merited an especially appreciative letter from the church's pastor. In fact, during their early years in the U.S. they were already active assisting the Catholic Church in its charitable activities. Cardinal Spellman sent them a letter dated April 12, 1965, expressing "gratitude for giving [their] time and talent to the special television program on behalf of the New York Catholic

7. DEL MAR

Charities Fund Appeal." He added, "We appreciate your generosity and the difficult trip you made to reach the studio."[10]

Generosity took different forms. Sometimes the Romeros were called upon to serve as diplomats, not only for Spain but also for their new *patria*. Presidents of the United States would serve up the Romero Quartet at diplomatic functions to showcase the best that this country had to offer. For instance, they were the musical centerpiece of a program honoring the president of the Republic of Korea and Mrs. Park on August 21, 1969, at the Saint Francis Hotel in San Francisco. They played their usual and successful assortment of works by Telemann, Vivaldi, Sor, Tomás Bretón, and, of course, flamenco. President Richard Nixon sent them a letter of thanks dated August 23, 1969, enthusing that they had "provided a superb musical experience for all . . . who were privileged to hear [them]. Nixon stated, "I am grateful to you for the generous gift of your time and your talent."[11] They later appeared in a program honoring His Royal Highness the Prince of Wales on February 20, 1986, in Austin, Texas, performing Rodrigo's *Concierto andaluz* with the Austin Symphony.

Perhaps their most notable presidential appearance, however, took place at the White House itself. President Jimmy Carter was a fan of the classical guitar, and he had already seen the Romeros perform in Atlanta. So when he held a state dinner for Premier Tito of Yugoslavia on March 7, 1978, he invited the Romeros to provide the entertainment. They were only too happy to oblige. Making a mistake one comes to expect after reading a few hundred of such reviews, the *Washington Post* noted that Carter especially liked *Recuerdos de la Alhambra* by Albéniz (the reader knows by now that it is by Tárrega). Carter joked that his main instrument was the ukulele, on which he "did about the same thing as they."[12] He went on to explain that while he was in Hawaii, he studied ukulele and his wife, Rosalynn, learned the hula. Pepe recalls that, years later, he met President Carter on a flight out of Atlanta, and Carter embraced him. He genuinely admired the Romeros and loved their music.

Appearances like this one help explain why they were on the mailing lists not only of Presidents Nixon and Carter but also Bill Clinton, all of whom routinely sent them Christmas cards. Clinton sent Celedonio greetings for his eightieth birthday, dated March 26, 1993. Celedonio responded on June

PART 2. SOUTHERN CALIFORNIA

7 with thanks, accompanied by some recordings. "My family and I and our guitars are at your complete disposal," he graciously declared. (On this occasion, Celedonio also received felicitations from the Spanish secretary of state.)

In 1987, the Romeros played for the king and queen of Spain at a reception held in their honor at the Los Angeles County Museum of Art. A letter from the Los Angeles County Office of Protocol dated September 29, 1987, advised them that the Royal Family of the Guitar should address the Royal Family of Spain initially as "Your Majesty" and subsequently as "Sir" or "Madame."[13] On another occasion, the Spanish consul in Los Angeles asked the Romeros to attend a reception for a descendant of Columbus, which would be held at the Cabrillo National Monument on Point Loma in San Diego. The Romeros truly were the cultural ambassadors of Spain in Southern California.

In recognition of his signal accomplishments as a cultural ambassador sui generis, in 1981 King Juan Carlos bestowed on Celedonio the Cruz del Caballero de la Orden de Isabel la Católica, a Spanish knighthood, later upgraded to Knight Commander (Comendador de Número) in 1988.[14] An earlier Spanish musician by the name of Isaac Albéniz had been similarly honored. The *Los Angeles Times* reported on the presentation of the knighthood, which took place at Cal Tech's Beckman Auditorium. This occasion included music provided by the Romeros, though Celedonio himself could not play because of the excitement and pressure of the day. Reviewer John Henken's tongue-in-cheek commentary noted that the brothers delivered their "standard Iberiana with personable zest and varying degrees of accuracy, happily churning through Telemann and Bach with out-of-tune vigor."[15]

Celedonio proudly explained this honor to the *San Diego Tribune* in the January 13, 1986, interview cited at the outset of this chapter: "I am in Spain like someone who has been decreed a Lord in England. The king, he implores me to come back, to come back to Spain, my homeland. Franco is gone now, of course, and I would be welcome. But I don't go. *This* is home." As indeed it now was.

* * *

The Romeros had performed a remarkable balancing act: retaining a strong sense of their cultural identity as Spaniards, while feeling completely at home in and committed to the United States. This dual identity provided a sturdy foundation for taking their music to a global audience.

CHAPTER 8

THE WORLD

Del Mar is the branch on which our Romero nightingales finally came to rest and where they have remained over the subsequent decades. But it was also the place from which their international careers took flight, taking their road show through the air to all the places where Celedonio might have dreamed of performing but would never have had the chance had he not flown the Spanish coop.

Indeed, during the 1960s, their concertizing had been confined largely to North America. The quartet did not make its London debut until 1971, at Queen Elizabeth Hall. During that same 1970–71 season, concert destinations also included Holland, Belgium, and Germany. Pepe made his first European tour as a soloist in January 1982, giving thirty concerts in seven countries; the following year, he played in Spain. He was quoted at the time as saying, "This is great and that's what I live for."[1] During this period, they also began making numerous recordings for Philips, a prestigious European label. Angel would eventually cut a separate recording deal with, appropriately enough, Angel/EMI.

In 1979, they toured Australia for the first time. The local newspaper in Sydney eagerly conveyed their opinions on Australia, its concert public, and indigenous music: "The brothers' first encounter with an Australian was in California, where they heard an Australian musician play the didgeridoo.

Their verdict: 'Tremendous.' They also approve of Australian audiences. Pepe commented: 'They're very easy to play for. They get involved with you very quickly.'"[2] Sincere, no doubt, but also very diplomatic.

DEUTSCHLAND ÜBER ALLES

Over the years, the Romeros have proved especially popular in Germany, to a large extent because they had a very enthusiastic and effective manager in nearby Salzburg, Joachim Schlote. As a result, they have performed more in that country than perhaps anywhere else outside the United States, including Spain. The *Berliner Morgenpost* called them the "Paganinis of the guitar," though German journalists more often referred to them as "die Könige der klassischen Gitarre," or the Kings of the Classical Guitar.[3]

Celedonio in particular returned the compliment, as he had a special love of German music, especially Beethoven, whose Seventh Symphony and Violin Concerto were among his favorite works. He firmly believed that Germany was the "divine fatherland of music."[4] In the family archive is a photo of him in Vienna, standing proudly in front of Beethoven's tomb in the Zentralfriedhof, the city's main cemetery.

A sampling of a concert itinerary from 1975 gives some idea of the rigors of this sort of touring and also the kind of saturation the Romeros achieved, performing in major cities and *Kuhdörfer* (cow towns) alike, just as they did in the United States, from Wuppertal to Düsseldorf, from Linz to Tübingen, along with Berlin, Ulm, Munich, Hamburg, and many others.

Pepe's itinerary from 1994 is typical of the killing schedule all the Romeros maintained during the 1970s and beyond. During one five-month period, from March 1 to July 19 of that year, he gave fifty-one solo recitals, and a little arithmetic soon reveals that he was thus giving a concert in a different venue nearly every night—in different cities, states, and countries. Considerable travel time was required, leaving relatively little time for practice, rest, and relaxation.

Starting in California on March 1, he performed on consecutive nights in San Luis Obispo, Pasadena, San Diego, Santa Barbara, Los Angeles, and Irvine, moving on to Tempe and Tucson, Arizona, then San Antonio and Dallas, Texas, followed by a whole assortment of U.S. cities: Saint Paul, Des Moines, Green Bay, Madison, Rock Island, Milwaukee, Kalamazoo,

8. THE WORLD

Ann Arbor, New York City, Morristown, and Denville. After a two-week break, he was entertaining audiences overseas in Singapore, Taipei, Gifhorn, Hamburg, Zürich, Veldhoven, Rotterdam, Berlin, Bottrop, Mülheim, Ahlen, Hamelin, Graz, Germering, Regensburg, Munich, Schweinfurt, Kempen, Neuenhagen, Bad Lauchstadt, Langenhagen, Hildesheim, Murrhardt, once again Pasadena, and finally Victoria, on May 26. Then, on to Echternacht, Germany; Córdoba, Spain; Colmar, France; and Arcata, California.

Reviews in German newspapers were nearly always encomiastic, as was the German public. Celedonio once remarked, "Munich audiences react like Spanish ones. They let us know right away if they don't like something, but they are inspired to stay with us. That to me is the ideal public."[5] They liked him well enough to give him the keys to the city in 1970. A critic in another city marveled that "each member of the quartet listens not only to his own instrument but also to what the others are playing. One breath moves the river of music making, a single heartbeat the dynamic interplay of voices."[6]

Not all the critics were won over, of course. One groused that the Telemann D-major concerto "sounded like finger exercises."[7] Another reviewer, in Kassel, compared the Romeros unfavorably to Segovia, finding the former less intellectual and more prone to playing music that was idiomatic to the guitar and full of feeling but without the spiritual profundity and technical brilliance of Segovia.[8]

What I distinctly remember is a 1985 Romero performance in the smallish city of Sindelfingen, near Stuttgart in southwestern Germany. Germans love to vacation on the Costa del Sol in order to escape the cold and clouds that characterize the climate in their country throughout the winter months. On this occasion, though, the Costa del Sol came to them, in the form of four Andalusian guitarists. The German language has a word for listening intently to something, *lauschen*, a verb for which there is no one-word equivalent in English or Spanish. I witnessed a demonstration of *lauschen* on this evening, when Pepe played *Recuerdos de la Alhambra*. Complete silence reigned in the hall, and one could have heard the proverbial pin drop. But what really brought the house down was Mamá's appearance in a black dress and lace mantilla playing her equally black castanets. Here was the real Spanish deal, and the audience ate it up. Such appearances prompted a newspaper in Münster to explain that "this [was] the kind of bubbling, unrestrained joy in making music one associates with Spain."[9]

PART 2. SOUTHERN CALIFORNIA

Los Romeros: The Royal Family of the Guitar was the subject of a PBS documentary that aired in September 2001 and was later issued on DVD (see appendix 4). The only country outside the United States to do them a similar honor was Germany, whose Norddeutscher Rundfunk broadcast *Los Romeros: Die Gitarren-Dynastie* in October 2004. (The DVD itself was made in 2003. See appendix 4 for more information.)

There is some irony in the fact that though the Romeros were cultural emissaries par excellence of their native land, they were by this time quite at home in Southern California. Pepe once admitted, "Though I love Spain and would not think twice about going there, I love this country too. I consider myself very much at home in America. People are just people everywhere."[10]

Fortunately, no Romero has to choose between America and Spain, and the Romeros would never abandon their Spanish roots and identity, especially not when they were concertizing in Spain. A Spanish newspaper once admiringly interviewed the expatriate musicians, carefully noting that Celedonio and his sons still spoke an Andalusian dialect, whose accents were detectable even when speaking English. Celedonio knew just the right notes to sound when he assured his interviewer, "I believe that when we Spanish musicians play abroad, we conquer new hearts for Spain everyday." In fact, he went on to disclose, 70 percent of their repertoire was Spanish.[11]

It's interesting to note how these new-and-improved Romeros were received in the town that knew them way back when. A Málaga newspaper featured an extensive interview with the now-famous foursome that sheds interesting light on their touring in Spain. As the reporter noticed, "Though *malagueño* by birth, [Celedonio] makes grammatical errors as a result of his familiarity with the language of Lincoln. 'After we left for America, it would be twelve years before we returned to Málaga, though we performed in Madrid before then. From 1966 onward, we have returned to Spain several times. Of course we feel ourselves to be Spanish, and *malagueños* 100 percent.'" And here is where the interview gets interesting, because for the first time, Celedonio became a cultural ambassador for the United States, vociferously defending its musical life against the uninformed insinuations of his interlocutor:

> **INTERVIEWER:** You were telling me about the Yankee's love of art. Does the American really love music?

8. THE WORLD

CELEDONIO: That's a barbarity! There is a wonderful selection of orchestras, marvelous orchestras in all the states. And the concert public is exquisite. The musical education and love of the American are due to two things: there is a large number of musical societies in American cities, and schools train musical tastes. Every day all students are required to listen to an hour of classical music.[12]

He then went on to declare that many universities have orchestras that are just as good as the official orchestras of the respective cities.

I have noted on a few occasions that Celedonio was not averse to stretching the truth a little bit in order to make a point. That tendency is on display here, especially in his claim that students were required to listen to sixty minutes of classical music every day. What matters in this case, however, is the intent of his remarks, not their content. He now strongly identified himself as a citizen of the United States and was prepared to defend its reputation, regardless of how worthy of defense it might actually have been in specific instances.

Still, Málaga's *Sur* reported that at many of their Spanish concerts with Spanish orchestras the Romeros requested that the orchestra play the Spanish national anthem, "revealing the love they [bore] the land of their birth."[13]

A PROPHET WITH HONOR, IN HIS OWN COUNTRY AND EVERYWHERE ELSE

As a result of his accomplishments in Spain, the United States, and now the world at large, Celedonio (and his sons) received many honors. A sampling of these here will provide some visual illustration of the high regard in which the five-feet-six-inch guitarist who once introduced his diminutive self to the skeptical Gallego sisters on Carretería Street was now held, namely, he was a musical colossus standing astride oceans and continents.

1. Celedonio awarded Cruz del Caballero de la Orden de Isabel la Católica by King Juan Carlos of Spain, January 5, 1981. Later upgraded to Comendador de Número (Knight Commander of Number) in 1988.
2. Museo Celedonio Romero opens in Málaga, 1988.
3. Celedonio's Curso Superior de Guitarra begins in the Teatro Cervantes, June 26, 1989.
4. Celedonio receives the Diocesan Medal "in recognition of the many musical gifts he has shared with the Catholics of San Diego," January 14, 1990.

PART 2. SOUTHERN CALIFORNIA

5. Proclamation of Celedonio Romero Day on January 14, 1990, by San Diego mayor Maureen O'Connor.
6. Celedonio receives the Beethoven Award from the San Diego Catholic radio station KFSD-FM, January 14, 1990.
7. Celedonio named Hijo Predilecto con la Medalla de Oro, Málaga, August 7, 1990.
8. Celedonio and Angelita appointed Caballero y Dama del Santo Sepulcro Internacional de Roma y Jerusalén, by the Vatican on May 22, 1992.
9. Proclamation of Celedonio Romero Day on March 27, 1993, by San Diego mayor Susan Golding.
10. Pepe receives an honorary doctorate from the University of Victoria, June 1994.
11. Celedonio receives an honorary doctorate from the University of Victoria, November 25, 1995.
12. Pepe receives the Premio Andalucía de la Música in June 1996, in recognition of his contribution to the arts.
13. Plaza in the barrio de Capuchinos in Málaga named after Celedonio, November 24, 1999.
14. Celin, Pepe, and Angel awarded Cruz de la Caballero de la Orden de Isabel la Católica by King Juan Carlos of Spain, in a ceremony at the University of Southern California on February 11, 2000.
15. Grammy President's Merit Award to the Romeros on February 7, 2007, at the Biltmore Hotel, Los Angeles.
16. Pepe receives an honorary doctorate from the San Francisco Conservatory of Music, May 20, 2011.
17. La Guitarra Lifetime Achievement Award to Celedonio Romero, February 25, 2015, at California Polytechnic University, San Luis Obispo.
18. Pepe receives Premio Huella Cultural 2017 from Club Rotario de Málaga, May 25, 2017.
19. Celin receives honorary doctorate from the University of Oklahoma City, May 13, 2017.
20. Pepe is awarded a gold medal and the title of Académico Honorario by the Real Academia de Bellas Artes de Granada, 2018.

Other awards given to Celedonio include

1. Medalla del 200 Aniversario de los Conquistadores Españoles, San Diego.
2. Placa de Artista de Honor de la Fundación Méjico-Americana.
3. La Orden del Colmillo de Alaska.

4. Medalla del President de Méjico José López Portillo y Placa, awarded to him by the Red Cross of Mexico.
5. Gold Medal of the Japan Festivals.
6. Insignia de Santiago el Mayor.
7. Artista de Honor y Amigo de San Diego, given by the Mexican and American Foundation.

* * *

The year 1990 represented the high-water mark of the original quartet. In over three decades of residing in the United States, the Romeros had taken their music to all venues great and small. And much of their success could be explained not just by the fact that they were a family but that they were a family of four distinctive and unique individuals, with just enough in common to make them an ensemble and enough setting them apart to keep them interesting.

1. Ruins of a church in the now-deserted village of Jotrón, in the mountains north of Málaga. Celedonio's maternal grandparents and mother were from Jotrón. It was also the first place he lived in Spain after arriving from Cuba in 1919. (Unless otherwise noted, all photos are from the Romero family archive or by the author.)

2. Situated between mountains and the Mediterranean, Málaga occupies a commercially and militarily advantageous position. Viewed from the Moorish Alcazaba above the city, the bullring is visible at the base of the hill on which the medieval fortress stands.

4. Josefa Pinazo Gutiérrez (1871–1942), mother of Celedonio. Her facial features bear a marked resemblance to those of Celedonio and Angel.

3. José Romero López (1866–1932), father of Celedonio and a renowned architect and builder active in both Málaga and Cuba.

5. House where Celedonio was born, in Cienfuegos, Cuba. He spent the first six years of his life (1913–19) in Cuba.

6. Salvador Gallego Rivera (1884–1964), a carpenter, and his wife, Encarnación, enjoy their baby daughter, Inez de los Ángeles Gallego Molina ("Angelita"), born in 1910.

7. Around the time of her marriage to Celedonio, in 1934, young Angelita looked radiant in traditional Spanish attire.

8. The aspiring virtuoso was passionately devoted to Angelita. He holds a guitar by Antonio de Lorca Ramírez.

9. A city of tree-lined boulevards and bustling commercial districts, Málaga also has a thriving cultural life, one in which Celedonio's early career flourished.

10. Celedonio (right) in an army uniform. During the Spanish Civil War, Celedonio's brothers fought for the Republic, while he was conscripted first into the Loyalist and then the Nationalist forces. Health problems kept him safely out of combat.

11. Little Celin (b. 1936) gets acquainted with the instrument that would be the focal point of his life.

12. Young Pepe (b. 1944) familiarizes himself with *Don Quijote*, a work much loved by the family.

14. Celedonio practices on the patio of his house on Málaga's Calle Rafaela, where Pepe was born.

13. Angel's (b. 1946) zest for life is apparent in this early dance move.

15. Angelita and her three sons, in 1955 in Seville. Pepe's baggy woolen pants were very uncomfortable.

16. Young Angel serenades his adoring mother in a park near their new home in Santa Barbara, California.

17. Not to be outdone, Celedonio serenades Mamá in front of the Santa Barbara Mission.

18. The historic Lobero Theatre in Santa Barbara, where Celedonio gave his U.S. debut concert on June 13, 1958.

19. The successful immigrants enjoy a picnic in their newly adopted country.

20. Celin cut a handsome figure in his army uniform in 1960. Fortunately, the closest he came to combat was on a firing range.

21. The Romeros proudly display their first-ever albums (1960), featuring Celedonio and Celin playing Spanish classics (left) and Pepe's flamenco interpretations (right).

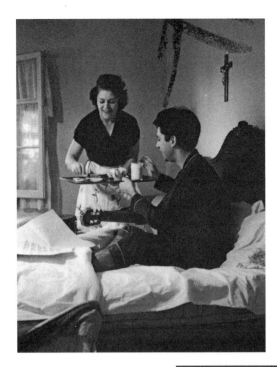

22. Mamá serves her Pepe breakfast in bed, while he practices. She provided the necessary support for four blossoming careers.

23. During their concert tour of the United States in 1961, they were justly hailed as "second to none." In fact, as a guitar quartet, they were unique.

24. An early performance on television, one of many such appearances they made, especially on *The Ed Sullivan Show* in 1967. They brought the music of Spain into living rooms across the U.S.

25. The Romeros drove the length and breadth of the United States, giving concerts in cities both large and small. The Holiday Inn was more than happy to welcome them wherever they went.

26. Disagreements about interpreting music got intense during rehearsals, but on stage, harmony reigned supreme.

27. The Romero sons all married American women (from left to right in back row, Angel and Wendy, Celin and Laurie, Mamá and Papá, and Pepe and Kristine). "Be fruitful and multiply" (Genesis 1:28) was one biblical injunction with which they were only too happy to comply.

28. The Romeros entertain President Jimmy Carter, Yugoslavia's Premier Tito, and guests at the White House in 1979.

29. From the 1970s onward, the Romeros were international celebrities. In 1986 they performed for Pope John Paul II at the Vatican.

30. The Romeros have collaborated with some of Spain's leading composers and are seen here with Joaquín Rodrigo after performing the *Concierto andaluz* in 1992 at the World Expo in Seville.

31. As Pepe's and Angel's solo careers blossomed, so did tension between them, egged on by managers and audiences who wanted to see concerts become contests.

32. Angelita was a virtuosa on the castanets and often appeared with the quartet in concert. Here she refines her interpretation of some music by Federico Moreno Torroba, with the composer at the piano.

33. Celedonio's technique remained limber right up to the end of his life.

34. With the departure of Angel from the quartet in 1990, Celin's son Celino (second from left) took his place. Angel's son Lito (second from right) took Celedonio's place shortly before his passing in 1996. Photo courtesy of Mark Johnson.

35. The Romeros receive a Grammy President's Merit Award in 2007.

36. Pepe (left) and Celin (center) have devoted a significant part of their careers to teaching, both privately and, as shown here, in master classes. Photo courtesy of Laurel Ornish.

37. Pepe's son, Pepe Jr. (center), builds fine instruments that are in demand around the world, and especially at the Romero home in Del Mar, where father Pepe (left) and uncle Celin (right) show their appreciation.

38. Pepe's grandson Bernardo is now also building beautiful guitars and shares a workshop in Oceanside with his cousin Pepe Jr.

39. Three generations of Romeros show their pluck: Celin (left), son Celino (center), and grandson Nino (right).

40. The saga of the Romeros is essentially the story of one man, Celedonio, a truly inspired and inspiring poet of the guitar. Photo courtesy of David Gersten.

PART 3

PROFILES

And with their spurs to the wind
There are four troubadours
Guided by fortune
To sing their loves
With magical instruments.

[Y con espuelas al viento,
cuatro son los trovadores
regidos por la fortuna,
para cantar sus amores
con mágicos instrumentos.]

—Celedonio Romero, from "Caballos de Media Luna (Fantasía)"

CHAPTER 9

CELEDONIO AND ANGELITA, THE POET AND HIS MUSE

Though one often thinks of the Romeros in a collective sense, by this point it should be obvious that each of the original members of the quartet was/is also a unique individual. As *Music of the West Magazine* observed in a review of the Romeros' first Los Angeles concert, "Each possesses a different technique and a highly individual approach to the guitar."[1] The same is true of them as people, and in the next four chapters, we will explore their personalities in some detail.

I have chosen to focus in each case on a characteristic that stands out as definitive of the person: Celedonio approached life and music with the soul of a poet, and his muse was Angelita, the mother of his talented progeny: Celin, who remains a committed romantic; Pepe, an inveterate philosopher by nature; and Angel, whose protean energies suggest his appellation. But it is important to understand that each of these individuals exhibits all these characteristics to one degree or another, even if a single trait emerges as dominant in every case. In particular, each son accentuated or amplified elements of Celedonio's character that were already evident in his youth; Angelita also exerted a powerful formative influence on them. In this way the Romeros remain a readily collective entity without losing their individuality.

PART 3. PROFILES

* * *

We recall that during his early concert years, Celedonio often appeared on stage with poets, who would read from their own or others' works, and whose readings he would occasionally embellish with musical accompaniment. It says something significant about Spanish culture that ordinary people would seek out this sort of entertainment, that their idea of pleasant recreation would include an evening of classical music on the guitar interlaced with readings of poems by authors past and present. Indeed, in the period in which Celedonio was active, literature was the queen of the arts in Spain. And poetry was the king of literature.

Not only did Spain possess a rich heritage of novels, drama, and poetry from the golden age of the seventeenth century, including the works of Miguel de Cervantes, Lope de Vega, Tirso de Molina, and Luis de Góngora, but its authors, novelists, poets, and dramatists—and especially its philosophers—were among the leading lights of European literature in the early twentieth century. A simple exercise in name-dropping will establish this point: Vicente Blasco Ibáñez, Federico García Lorca, Miguel de Unamuno, and José Ortega y Gasset, for starters. Celedonio exhibited a passionate love for his Castilian language, especially its Andalusian dialect. Though this was a defining trait of his character, it was far from unusual among his compatriots. Thus it comes as no surprise that he would never be content merely to read and listen to the poetic outpourings of others; instead, when he wasn't creating music, he was expressing himself through the distinctive rhythms and melodic intonations of his native tongue.

In my Granados biography, I had occasion to note that the composer of *Goyescas* was frequently referred to in the Barcelona press as the "Poet of the Piano."[2] Several decades later, Celedonio made a CD on the Delos label titled *The Poet of the Guitar*. The attractiveness of this synaesthetic metaphor is easy to understand: during Granados's lifetime, poetry occupied an exalted place among the arts in Spain, and that moniker was the highest accolade he could have received. A reverence for poetry persisted well into the twentieth century and permeated the Spanish-speaking culture in which Celedonio came of age.

Yet a poetic temperament doesn't necessarily equate with dreamy otherworldliness. In fact, Celedonio had an enormous capacity for hard work

9. CELEDONIO AND ANGELITA, THE POET AND HIS MUSE

and for "delivering the goods" under pressure. He was an intense man with piercing dark eyes and a sinewy build, like a coiled spring under tension. His tremendous reserves of energy and will prompted Sabine Max at Phonogram to marvel at "that typical Romero energy. The amount of work—and work of what quality!—[he has] done during the past two months can inspire any normal human being with wonder and admiration."[3]

Although Celedonio never lacked for musical occupations to fill his time, writing served a therapeutic purpose, for as I have occasionally noted in this narrative, Papá could be moody and prone to angry outbursts. In short, he could be feisty. On one occasion, a young lady wanted a refund on lessons for which she had paid in advance but didn't take. Her feckless boyfriend confronted Celedonio to demand the money back and soon discovered what Papá was made of, as the older man chased the younger down the block, brandishing as a weapon a cast on his arm resulting from a recent auto accident. On an earlier occasion, while still in Spain, he was engaged in a dinner conversation with a flamenco guitarist who made the mistake of dismissing "classical music [as] flamenco badly played"! The man was perhaps referring to classical works inspired by flamenco but constituting, for his taste, feeble imitations of the real thing. Celedonio nonetheless took umbrage at this slight on the honor of Albéniz, Falla, Turina, and Torroba, among others, and promptly removed himself from the table, hissing, "I will not eat with a pig!" Celedonio had a genteel, even aristocratic air about him, but the "poet of the guitar" also had his limits, and woe to that person who crossed them.

Celedonio found that writing poetry in particular had a restorative effect on his psyche. And he was nothing if not prolific in this regard, eventually releasing a book of his poems and other writings titled *Poemas, Prosas, Pensamientos y Cantares* (1995).[4] This effort made it possible to preserve and make more widely available his writings. He was also an avid gardener, and puttering around the yard helped equilibrate his mood; of course, a glass of his favorite Marqués de Riscal wine could work wonders as well.

Whether motivated by anger or pure inspiration, Celedonio produced a steady profusion of poetry and prose, which he hastily jotted down on the nearest available writing surface, usually Holiday Inn napkins or stationery in such far-flung and exotic locales as Albuquerque, New Mexico; Twin Falls, Idaho; Rolla, Missouri; Manchester, New Hampshire; and Westbury-Stowe,

Vermont. One effusion, committed to a piece of stationery provided courtesy of the Ponderosa Best Western Motel in Billings, Montana, laid bare some rather bleak ruminations at that moment: "I have seen a tower of passed centuries converted into nothing. I know of mountains that were very tall and are now nothing, as well as great cities and lovely beaches. But the passage of time respects nothing."[5] Perhaps there was something about Billings that put him in a nihilistic mood, but it is more likely that this was an instance when, despite his outward sanguinity, he was wrestling with various inner demons.

Of course, there are demons, and there are demons. The original word in Greek, *daemon*, does not necessarily have a pejorative connotation, referring simply to a spirit being that is superior to humans but not quite a god. In Spanish, the word *duende* refers to a spirit that descends on an artist in the heat of creative inspiration. As Celedonio himself explained, "The *duendes* are little people, who are invisible, but they stand, conduct, and direct the performance of the music in your mind."[6] Celedonio's music and poetry exude *duende*, and he composed or wrote when a *duende* moved him, especially in the quiet of the night or early morning. But it could strike anywhere, anytime, provoked by a concert with his sons, a sunset or a sunrise, our ineluctable mortality, the Divine, or endearing reflections on his life companion, Angelita.

The depth of his *duende* is in evidence on the Mercury two-LP set *World of Flamenco* from 1967. On this remarkable recording, the family plays a wide variety of traditional genres of music and dance, called *palos*, accompanied by singers and dancers. An added attraction is the inclusion of a couple of numbers featuring Celedonio's recitation of poetry by Federico García Lorca, accompanied by Pepe. This is exactly the sort of thing Celedonio had done during the 1930s in Málaga, except that now he was reading rather than playing. As one hears him solemnly intone "La guitarra" from *Poema del cante jondo*, to the sounds of Pepe's intricately crafted *soleares*, it is hard to suppress a chill running up one's spine:

> Empieza el llanto
> de la guitarra.
> Es inútil callarla.
> Es imposible
> callarla.

9. CELEDONIO AND ANGELITA, THE POET AND HIS MUSE

[The weeping of the guitar begins.
It is useless to silence it.
It is impossible
to silence it.]

Though his own poetry was in most respects a private affair, he was not averse to sharing it with a receptive public. On some occasions, only poetry will do! For instance, at a ceremony on November 25, 1995, when he received an honorary doctorate from the University of Victoria, he recited a poem he had written for the occasion, titled "La guitarra es mi vida." The guitar was indeed his life and his soul. In his acceptance remarks, he felt compelled to offer these observations: "Music is, as we all know, the spiritual bridge that brings us to the Divine and transports us by mysterious and beautiful paths of spiritual feeling . . . ever closer to that which is good. There is a marvelous triptych to which I am completely devoted: Music, Bach, and above all, God!"

Such convictions led him to reflect ruefully on the consequences of art's absence, or worse, its decadence: "The lack of culture in all respects is one of the worst enemies of man, and in the majority of cases, it is what leads people down the error-strewn path of brutal violence. [Our goal must be] to create great cultural centers where concerts of beautiful music are given and conferences are held dealing with every aspect of art."

Celedonio's poetic nobility and electric personality often suggested to critics and interviewers characters from Spanish literature and history. For instance, an article in Spanish by Eduardo Garrigues, director of the Casa de América, compares Celedonio to Francisco de Ulloa, Hernando de Alarcón, Francisco Vázquez de Coronado, and Juan Rodríguez Cabrillo, "who took great risks in crossing seas and mountains with very scarce resources. Celedonio Romero sailed in his fragile little boat of a guitar to achieve international recognition." Indeed, the author continues, Celedonio was like Don Quijote himself, accompanied by his ever-faithful and admiring Dulcinea, Angelita. "Celedonio had the bearing and profile of those knights errant: the lean and sinewy body, not very tall, loose-limbed and agile, with regular, dignified features, a broad forehead, and an aquiline nose."[7]

Another example of this sort of rhapsodizing is at hand in an interview that appeared in the *Monitor*, in McAllen, Texas. Though it is replete with essentializing stereotypes, it nonetheless gives us a window on the way people perceived Celedonio and his family. And the interviewer was not necessarily far off the mark when he observed,

> A last-minute interview with four fiery Spaniards who also happen to be very famous is intimidating. . . . Though obviously of retirement age, [Celedonio] bristles with energy and life force. There is the dignified face of a Don Quixote, but he is short like Sancho Panza. Unlike the mule-mounted sidekick, Papá Romero is slim and graceful as a dancer and speaks with his entire body. Eloquently. The black eyes sparkle and change color. All prepared questions are jettisoned and a delicious visit ensues. He has made you his intimate friend. Finishing our visit was difficult: Romero's love of life and state of happiness are genuine and contagious.[8]

This state of happiness was not something he cultivated so much as it was simply his *manera de ser*, or way of being. And it emanated from his love of the musical art. As Celin would recall years later,

> He had a special personality, a presence, an aura about himself that was very contagious. He was one of the most natural musicians I ever knew, and his lyric sense was very beautiful. It was the way he approached the instrument, his elegance. To me, he had a touch that was unequalled. I think that all this did cultivate something in us. Very important, too, was his love for all music, how he exposed us to other kinds of music, not only guitar but also opera and symphonies. After dinner, we would listen to an opera with him. He made us listen to Schubert *Lieder*, for instance, because he approached the guitar as a singing, sustaining instrument, not just plucking. That was a great atmosphere in which to learn to play the guitar.[9]

Celedonio himself explained to the Mexican newspaper *El Mexicano* that "music is a thing of emotion, and it affects a gardener or a duke the same way. . . . Art is an anarchy where there are no borders, a giant world ocean in which Africa, China, Argentina, Spain and England are all the same."[10] Multiculturalists will take umbrage at such a homogenization of disparate cultures, but to Celedonio, the unity of the arts equated with the unity of humanity.

In addition to unity, however, the poet and composer required solitude, and he further informed *El Mexicano* that he preferred writing music "when [he was] completely alone and usually in the late hours of the night, in the early morning, at one or two when there is no noise and the night has

9. CELEDONIO AND ANGELITA, THE POET AND HIS MUSE

magical sounds." He explained, "Where I live, I hear the sound of the ocean waves, and I like to look at the stars, the universe."[11] Of course, the Pole Star in his private universe was Angelita.

ANGELITA

I have made much of Celedonio's imperishable passion for the guitar, but his real muse was his wife, lover, friend, advisor, and traveling companion of sixty-five years, Angelita, the mother and mentor of his exceptional offspring. A press release (quoted below) from Lucas Management during the early years speaks volumes about the somewhat ambivalent social status of a woman like Angelita, who was a person of artistic and intellectual substance but whose talents had to be constrained within a sturdy frame of female domesticity. This was especially true of Spanish society under Franco, in which the ideal of womanhood was the wife playing a supporting role at home and never competing with her husband in any professional way. In fact, one of the main reasons Angelita wanted to abandon Spain for the United States was the subordinate status and treatment of women in her homeland. She wanted a better life not only for her husband and sons but also for herself. The United States was undeniably superior to Franco's Spain in this regard, but it was far from ideal.

Any cultural historian surveying the television programs of the 1950s and 1960s, for instance, *I Love Lucy*, *The Donna Reed Show*, *Leave It to Beaver*, or *Father Knows Best*—not to mention *The Flintstones* and *The Jetsons*—is struck by the fact that the ideal woman, no matter how smart or capable, contented herself with tending to housewifely duties. Shows featuring liberated, independent females didn't establish a secure beachhead in American popular culture until the 1970s, with *The Mary Tyler Moore Show* and its spinoff *Rhoda*.

In 1961, manager Jim Lucas understood these gender realities as well as anyone, so in his press release of that year he wrote, "Señora Romero is a former film star and leading zarzuela singer in Spain." This was a slight but permissible exaggeration of her actual accomplishments, though not her talent. Still, it couldn't be allowed to put the menfolk into anything like the shade, so Lucas added: "She cheerfully picks up after them when they are untidy, and singlehandedly looks after details of the household. 'In

America, I hear men help with the housework,' she says, 'but I don't seem to be able to impress mine with this fact. And, after all, the younger boys have their school studies, and all of them have hours of daily practice as well as teaching at our guitar school, so since servants are so expensive in this country, I do the rest.'"[12]

This was absolutely true, and in the photo gallery of this book one will find a picture of her bringing Pepe breakfast in bed, while he practices his guitar before school. The Romero Quartet needed a support system, and its name was Angelita. Taking another stab at her artistic worth, the press release revealed that "Angelita misse[d] the way the Spanish gypsies [sic] gathered at the Romero home in Málaga to play, sing and dance. She often join[ed] Pepe in informal occasions, singing flamenco songs, etc."[13] True, but it would still be a few years before she actually joined her men onstage, playing the castanets.

Fortunately, her hearth-and-home responsibilities also provided ample scope for deflected professional creativity. The press release further described her as "a superb cook [who] regularly serves traditional Andalusian dishes to her family and friends." As it turned out, this close proximity to food had some unfortunate side effects. "Señora Romero regrets that she is not as slender as the men in her family. 'We all eat about the same amount,' she sighs, 'but they stay thin and I do not. In Spain this never bothered me, but now that I am here I would like to have a more American look.'"[14] Angelita may have lost her "starlet" good looks after giving birth to three boys, but Celedonio seems never to have been much bothered by that. In his mind's eye, she was still the fetching young *chiquitita* who had enchanted him in old Málaga. And she always found him handsome.

One hastens to add that the Romero men in general are far too complex and demanding to remain fascinated for very long by a woman whose only virtues are physical. They prefer strong, capable, independent mates, as we shall also see further on. According to Pepe's wife, Carissa, "Mamá was very intelligent, she read a lot, and she had a large conception of God. Papá deeply loved her and always preferred to have her company," especially when he attended *tertulias* and other cultural gatherings.

For instance, Mamá loved literature and would read to the family in the car on their trips. She would also read Papá to sleep, since he was a light sleeper and often required help to sleep soundly. If she stopped, he would

9. CELEDONIO AND ANGELITA, THE POET AND HIS MUSE

wake up and tell her to keep reading. However, she got very tired of this routine, so she started to make tape recordings that could be played for him. Since he also liked Gregorian chant, she would sometimes have records of chant playing in the background while she read. This lent the house an eerie atmosphere during the wee hours of the morning, which could and did prove unsettling to anyone who got up in the middle of the night to go to the bathroom. Mostly she preferred to read the Spanish classics, and he shared her tastes. She thus helped not only Celedonio but also her children, who credit her with giving them a solid grounding in the Spanish language and its literature. Pepe later recalled, "My father and my mother loved [*Don Quijote*] so much, especially my mother. When she was teaching me how to write in Spanish, she dictated the whole book to me as I wrote it in long hand. It took us five years."[15]

In fact, the Romero boys were all homeschooled, by Mamá. As she herself reported many years later: "My children never went to elementary school [*colegio*]. . . . I taught them. I was the tutor. But they took all the same subjects as the children in the official schools to be prepared for high school. During the day, they would study continuously in the house, and then they would go to the concert [in the evening]." Her interviewer on this occasion was Laurel Ornish, who offered this helpful explanation: "In those days in Spain, it was not obligatory for 6–10 year olds to attend school. But each year, they had to take a test at an official school and pass it, in order to advance to the next grade."[16]

In addition to all this, Mamá's castanet playing was a powerful inspiration. After one of her many appearances with the quartet, Celedonio perfunctorily jotted down on a Crest Hotels envelope that "Mother Romero played the castanets with expert rhythm, precise delicacy, and a grand tone." After another concert, he enthused: "Angelita's castanets are sent by heaven and therefore blessed."[17] This spontaneous observation was prompted by her participation in the quartet's arrangement of numbers from *Carmen*. As Celedonio himself wrote: "It is a very *young* older woman who plays the castanets. Castanets that come flying over the Atlantic, crossing oceans of dreams to play again."[18]

To be sure, Celedonio was not the only one to esteem her virtuosity. One of Angelita's most rewarding moments was performing at the Vatican for Pope John Paul II in 1986, where he gave a special blessing to her castanets.

Even into her seventies, she was capable of eliciting the following encomium from critics: "Sultry beyond her years, in a black-and-red gown, Angelita sat motionless through the first two sections of the work while most of the audience wondered what she was doing there. Then suddenly her hands flew out of her lap and she began a breath-taking accompaniment with castanets, with a machine-gun precision and fire that would have put the hot-blooded Carmen to shame."[19]

A review of a concert at the Ambassador Auditorium in Pasadena exclaimed that she was a delight as she "clickety-clacked in dead earnest through minimal chores in Celedonio's two-guitar [arrangement] of Rodrigo's *Aranjuez* and Moreno Torroba's Sonatina."[20] A German review summed up her participation in a single word: *ruhrselig* (soul stirring).[21]

As good as Angelita was with the castanets, her greatest musical achievement was of another order of magnitude altogether. As the boys themselves disclosed to another critic, "We always tell her that the instrument she plays is the quartet. The four of us are her instrument."[22]

Thus, on her eightieth birthday, the Vatican awarded her the title "Lady of the Equestrian Order of the Holy Sepulchre of Jerusalem," in recognition of her extraordinary accomplishments.[23] Perhaps the greatest of these was that in choosing a mate, she had gambled on an impecunious guitarist who had little more than poems and tangos to offer her. But she resolutely placed all her chips on his number, and her bet paid off far beyond their wildest dreams. A lady, yes; one smart cookie, too.

CHAPTER 10

CELIN, THE ROMANTIC

In 1978, *Fono Forum* noted that Celin was like his father in at least one important respect: he had a contemplative streak and was a romantic.[1] However, though Romero friends and family enjoyed Celedonio's poetic effusions, on one occasion he showed Celin a poem, which failed to impress his eldest son. Celedonio bitterly complained to Pepe that Celin possessed no appreciation of culture! This was far from true, but Celin's romanticism follows a slightly different course.

My first impulse was to label Celin as "the Leader." Celin was an accomplished guitarist and potentially as good as the others. Anyone who listens to some of his earliest solo recordings will be left with no doubts about the Romeroness of the technical execution. The *Los Angeles Examiner* wrote of his playing in the early years that "Celin wove another intoxicating spell with dazzling technical figurations . . . wide leaps accomplished with consummate control."[2] However, he early on understood perfectly well that in a guitar quartet, someone must be willing to play a supporting role, to provide the bass notes while the others glitter in the upper register. In the early years especially, when his maturity and fluency in English made him the natural choice to manage the quartet's complex business, Celin had to accept a musically subordinate position, one that would not entail a thriving solo career that would compete with the quartet, especially as Pepe's and Angel's solo careers began to assume a life all their own.

PART 3. PROFILES

As his companion Claudia has noted of him: "Celin always looks for a solution that is best for all. He carries the group on his extensive wings without putting himself to the fore. His concern is for the happiness of all, because that affects his happiness." Still, one must never underestimate the crucial role he has played in the quartet. Pepe explained it to me by using an apt metaphor: "He has done so much in the background and in the foreground. He has been the catcher in a trapeze act. Angel and I were the fliers. Without a great catcher, the fliers would not last very long!"

In fact, complex situational dynamics require a complex mind to handle them, and despite his jovial and easygoing manner, on the inside, where it counts most, Celin is a very complex person and functions comfortably within various shades of gray. He is a natural-born diplomat and mediator. Moreover, he always had a good head for business, finance, and real estate. Thus much of the family's material prosperity was the result of his wise management of their resources.

I finally settled on "Romantic" to describe Celin, however, after ruminating at length on a conversation I had had with him many years ago, during which he referred to the *tradition* of the guitar. The way he intoned the word *tradition* made a deep impression on me, as if he had been pronouncing the name of some sacred thing, not at all in vain but rather with the deepest reverence and respect. Only in more recent times have I come to understand the reason for this attitude. Next to his parents, Celin is the Romero most connected to and rooted in the land and culture of his upbringing. José Manuel Gil y Gálvez, whose family has lived in Málaga for centuries, believes that Celin is the most *malagueño* of all the Romero boys. He speaks using local words and expressions common in the 1950s, and in fact he sounds just like José Manuel's grandfather.

Even when he was almost sixty years old, Celin would recall with intense longing the simple pleasures of his early life, when "the baker would come with his donkey" every day delivering bread. "The nights were so hot and so fragrant," he enthused. The interviewer who elicited this response concluded: "Evincing a sense of nostalgia for an era that is disappearing into the homogenized sameness of Western civilization, he considers himself a curator for the richness of what once was."[3] Similar sentiments were expressed by Torroba, which may help to explain Celin's deep rapport with that composer's music.

10. CELIN, THE ROMANTIC

His nostalgia for the irretrievable past gives rise to intense romanticism in his personality. In a sense, there is no contradiction between Celin as leader and Celin as romantic, because his job as leader was to convey the family tradition to his younger brothers and to all those students and audiences who would come after. And that family tradition was grounded in romanticism, in the heritage of the period in which Tárrega had brought the guitar to new prominence. It was this romantic tradition that imbued the life and work of Celedonio, and which he transmitted to Celin and expected him to carry on.

Yet we must add another ingredient to the recipe for Celin's personality, and that is humility. Romantic affectations, pretense, and self-mythologizing are definitely not his style. Thus he demurs when asked about his instruction of Pepe and Angel: "The guitar was always at the center of our lives, but I can't say for certain how much I actually taught them. Because I am six and a half years older than Pepe, and nine older than Ángel, I became my father's lieutenant, so to speak. My father gave me some responsibility for taking care of my younger brothers. Yet, over time, we developed a very hierarchical system, in which I was responsible for Pepe, and Pepe was responsible for Ángel."[4]

Beyond giving them guitar instruction, Celin had to assume actual parenting responsibilities when his parents frequently availed themselves of Málaga's many cultural attractions, such as the *tertulias* mentioned earlier.

Possessed of a keen memory, Celin has very distinct recollections of those early years in Málaga and Seville, and a wistful sense for a world and way of life that have passed away but which live on in the music he prefers to play. Not for him the avant-garde, atonality, and musical modernity. As he once commented to me, "The so-called new music I don't enjoy so much. Some of it is good, and some is not; that has been true in every generation. But some of this very dissonant music has never moved me very much." Rather, he is

> very committed to the music of the great Spanish masters such as Tárrega, Albéniz, Granados, Torroba, and Rodrigo. For example, in the case of Torroba, he was one of the last Romantics, and I feel that the world is losing a lot of that Romanticism, which people of my generation experienced. I have lived in the places in Andalusia so often depicted in the music of these

composers, and I have seen it in a more pristine condition, many decades ago. Andalusia is now quite different; the essence is still there, but it's more difficult to perceive. In Sevilla, for instance, you see electric buses; it's not the old Sevilla anymore, with horses, the scent of fresh-baked bread, and streets without cars. The music of Albéniz and others evokes that old Andalusia, and that is the music in which I am now most interested. I want to convey my thoughts and impressions of that earlier time to a new generation.[5]

Thus Celin's musical tastes reflect his passion for the traditions that informed the culture in which he came to maturity. He recalls with fondness his early years in Málaga:

When I was still only two or three, I remember noticing the devastation caused by the bombing and ambulances coming from the front filled with soldiers going to the hospital. I remember seeing all that. But my father kept on playing, no matter what. He had great devotion to the guitar, always making transcriptions and learning new repertoire. By a very early age, I knew a lot of music by Tárrega and Sor. I always saw my father practicing in the kitchen, and I even remember him making a transcription of Albéniz's "Cádiz" there. For years we were hungry because the only thing we had to eat was bread. All we had was a daily bread ration, a little piece of roll for each of us, and my mother had to go buy food from the soldiers. At the same time, though, I was very close to my father and his music. He would take me outside the city to the fields and generally devoted a lot of time to me. My childhood was nice. It was poor, but there was a lot of love. I felt good about it.[6]

Amid all this privation, with so much time and energy devoted to a struggle for sheer survival, the guitar might not have been the first thing on a boy's mind. But Celin's early and total immersion in the guitar shaped his personality in ways that set him apart from his friends. He once told a Seville newspaper that the guitar was "probably in the genes," and he would go to watch guitars being built the way other kids went to the park to play.[7]

As we have noted, the Romero home was a popular meeting place for singers and dancers, so much so that it was like a daily fiesta. Here again, though, the flamenco to which he was exposed in the 1940s and 1950s was of a kind that had emerged only a few decades earlier but was already considered traditional. The flamenco fusion of today, with its extroverted admixture of elements from pop and jazz, holds no fascination for him

10. CELIN, THE ROMANTIC

at all. One might wonder why he doesn't just move back to Spain, but the truth is that his life is in the United States. This is where his children and grandchildren are, and he wants to be with them. But he also wants to be sure they know Spain, his Spain, the Spain of his memories. This Spain may gradually be disappearing, but it will never vanish.

And the United States has treated the Romeros well. Why change horses in the middle of a stream?

> We have been lucky. Audiences have been very nice to us, largely because we have been able to transmit to them the fun that we are having. That's what it is. Music is a serious thing, and we have to take the process of study and preparation seriously. But at the same time, it's great fun. It's serious business practicing scales, repeating exercises, playing passages hundreds of times to get them right. But once you have finished that, you want to share this with others. The joy that the music is giving us is something we then convey to other people.[8]

When asked what he considers the single most important quality that a guitarist must possess to succeed today, his response displays his romantic inclinations:

> You have to be able to transmit your feelings to the audience. You have to move them. You have to love what you're doing, to be passionate about it, and for the right reasons—not fame or money but rather a love of the instrument and its music. You are there to share that love with the audience. As I said earlier, I always feel that the guitar is a *romantic* instrument, and as such, I don't think we should be nasty to it. We have to be gentle, we have to bring out the most volume from it, and to enjoy the special beauty that the guitar has, that wonderful range of sounds it can produce. That is what I truly feel. Just learn to enjoy one note. That is the main thing: just give me a beautiful note![9]

A Zen-like principal is at work here, one that informs Celin's approach not only to the guitar but to life itself, which can and should be a chain of beautiful notes encircling all the good, bad, and neutral experiences of our time on earth. If we focus on creating beauty in this instant, the future will in large measure take care of itself. In any case, that philosophy has worked very well for the Romeros.

CHAPTER 11

PEPE, THE PHILOSOPHER

Celin isn't the only romantic in the family. As this chapter will make obvious, Pepe also has a powerfully romantic streak in his musical personality. But it is not so much connected with a nostalgic yearning for an irretrievable past as it is with a philosophical outlook that views the guitar as a passion inseparable from life itself. Learning the guitar is simply part of learning how to live a human life. Of course, it is a very large part of Pepe's life, especially considering the breadth of his musical tastes, embracing five centuries of classical music as well as the folklore of his native Andalusia.

Pepe's interpretations of the Spanish classics are informed in no small measure by his profound knowledge of flamenco. And yet, as he insisted to *The Ledger*, flamenco is not the main emphasis of his work: "Classical music is what I am devoted to, and what I perform and practice. . . . I don't consider myself a gifted composer, but I am a gifted interpreter." At the heart of gifted interpretation is absolute focus on and commitment to the music at hand: "Whichever piece I'm playing at the time, that is the main piece. And whether it is in Carnegie Hall, or whether it is in my own living room, it's the same."[1] At the heart of great music making, of course, is red-blooded human emotion, the principal reason the music came into existence in the first place.

11. PEPE, THE PHILOSOPHER

One of the most notable and insightful things anyone ever said of Pepe's playing was uttered by Habichuela el Viejo, the grand patriarch of the Habichuela clan, one of Spain's leading flamenco dynasties. Pepe told the following story: "About 2:00 a.m., after everyone had played and sang and read poetry, a man dressed in black came forward—he'd been sitting there the whole evening smoking—and he said to me, 'When you play classical music, it becomes flamenco.'"[2] Pepe considers that to be one of the highest compliments he has ever received.

It bears noting at the outset, though, that Pepe is, like his father, a poet, except that he uses brushes instead of words to express his feelings. We said previously that his artistic talent manifested itself early on, and that he was even being groomed for art school and a possible career in that area. In fact, one of his impressionistic landscapes is in the Lehman Collection of the Metropolitan Museum of Art. Several of his paintings of flamenco dancers adorn the walls of his Del Mar home, and he has a tendency to think of music in visual terms, once observing that "art is everything: hearing with the eyes and seeing with the ears."[3] He might well have had a career as an artist, but that is inconceivable in light of his illimitable passion for musical sound.

Of Pepe, a reviewer said, "He is a born communicator, a man who seems thoroughly to enjoy the act of performance and who exudes enormous confidence and polish in the most uncomplicated, laid-back manner. Beyond this, he has a quality that is often missing in artists on this series, and that is charm. There is charm in his presence and in the curve of a phrase. He puts not only a face on the music he performs, but frequently a smile as well. And he does this with crystalline clarity and an unforced expressiveness."[4]

The *Tucson Citizen* noted of a Pepe concert that "the music seemed to come as naturally and easily to [him] as water to a spring, flowing in a braided stream of color, mood and historic nuance. Romero's tone maintained its unsullied luster, warmth, evenness, balance and appropriate character."[5] Needless to say, he also played fast, but that wasn't uppermost in the reviewer's recollections. And neither should it have been, for truly consummate technique is invisible. As the great guitarist and composer Fernando Sor once noted: "I have always preferred hearing it said of a performance, 'He appears to be doing nothing, that appears so easy'; than to hear it said, 'Oh! How difficult that must be! for he appears to have given proofs of it.'"[6]

How does one achieve this state, aside from relentless practice? When Pepe isn't playing the guitar, he is thinking about it. And at the same time he is thinking about the guitar, he is pondering life and considering how the vectors of the guitar and a human life intersect. This reflection leads him to many philosophical insights. For instance, he once told a reviewer, "Life is a constant evolution; life never stands still. It's not a change that I am aware of as it happens. . . . As you grow, as you experience life, as your reservoir of emotions is enriched by the years that one lives, the music that one plays, changes."[7]

His own life and career provide the answers he seeks, which he passes on to his students. Again, this impulse was characteristic of his father as well, but Pepe's facility with English enables us to understand this Romero trait in some depth. As Pepe told the *Shanghai Daily*, "My father taught me the power of music as a fountain of love and wisdom guiding us towards enlightenment. As far as I remember, I thought of myself as a guitarist. It was something I was, not something I was to become. My family encouraged and nurtured every aspect of my artistic life. I experienced an incredible bonding with my father that grew into a feeling of being like one guitarist with two bodies."[8]

Just how interconnected life and the guitar become in Pepe's thinking is evident from another quote: "Everything that has happened to me has had a significant effect on my music . . . whether it is falling in love, falling out of love, falling in love again, having a child, having an accident, being happy, being sad. When I walk onto the stage, it's a complete sharing of my feelings, and I feel very much united to the audience when I'm playing."[9] He relayed similar sentiments on another occasion: "To me, the guitar is more than any one thing. It can be a woman or a small child or a wise old friend that at the time of need you can go to it and it gives you just the right advice. The guitar is my closest friend."[10]

This sort of intimacy with an inanimate object may strike the uninitiated as somewhat strange, but it is ultimately not the physical object of the guitar itself that Pepe considers to be his confidante, any more than he would consider a piece of furniture to be a "wise old friend." No, the guitar is simply the medium for the music that arouses these feelings of intimacy

11. PEPE, THE PHILOSOPHER

and bonding. It is not the guitar itself with which he is in communion but rather five hundred years of musical genius. When he plays a *fantasía* by Alonso de Mudarra, a *canarios* by Gaspar Sanz, a sonata by Fernando Sor, a prelude by Francisco Tárrega, or a *bulerías* by Sabicas, he is in essence having a séance with a mind, a heart, a soul that live on inside him. As he explained at length on another occasion:

> I will always continue to perform and record the music of Giuliani, and Sor, too. I love those two composers very deeply. . . . I think that for a performer to give the best possible interpretation of a work, he must look as deeply as possible into the details of the composer's life and try to see life as the composer must have seen it. You have to get as close as you can to the feelings they had. . . .
>
> These were men with a great capacity to love. I think that anyone in our business must start out with a tremendous love inside, and a need to express it—the need to embrace more people that you can embrace with your arms. . . . In a sense, a musician is no different than an actor. If an actor is playing Macbeth, he must become Macbeth. At first, the music is in the cosmos. The composer receives it, and passes it on to the performer, whose job it is to take the audience back to that place where the composer gets his inspiration. That's why when you hear a beautiful performance, you feel that you are in some sort of timeless, spaceless place. It's a release of one's soul. . . . To me it's one of the clearest manifestations of God.[11]

Music is an inexhaustible font of beauty and inspiration that continues to drive him forward, in performing and teaching. And it doesn't matter how many times he has played a particular piece. Every time he finds some new inspiration in it. He once remarked to an interviewer with the Madrid newspaper *El Mundo* that though he has performed Rodrigo's celebrated *Concierto de Aranjuez* thousands of times, every time he plays it, "it captivates [him] completely."[12] In fact, he was eight or nine years old when he first played through the *Aranjuez*'s guitar part. He listened to the earliest recording of the piece, by virtuoso Regino Sáinz de la Maza, who premiered it in 1940. He also heard it played by his father.

> Every time I play it, or I think of it, it's new, it's different. It brings new feelings, new ideas. It does exactly what music should do: make people feel good. Music has a purpose in Creation. Sound is a very important part, and music plays a very important role, far more important than most people realize. For that reason, it's very important to use it always with respect,

with compassion, and—above all—with love. The *Concierto de Aranjuez* is actually a key to a door that opens up into a different state of being, a beautiful state. It's the kind of music that is like a key to a state of grace.[13]

Despite the quasi-mystical overtones of these revelations, this work has more-earthly associations for Pepe as well. In a *Gramophone* interview from 1981, John Duarte noted, "In [Pepe's] earlier recordings, I had heard technical perfection but little love of the music, but this seemed to have changed during the last two years." To this observation, Pepe responded:

Perhaps, as one gets older, one becomes more in tune with one's own love, felt inside oneself, and is able to put it more into music. I do feel that musicians have different periods and get fascinated with different aspects of making music, and I feel I have come into a different phase in my career. Something did happen to trigger it off and it was about two years ago. I feel the composer who writes the music and the artist who plays it are like a man and woman. There are better and worse looking women, but there is something you see in her that releases the fragrance of your love for her.[14]

This observation by the very perceptive Duarte was no coincidence. Pepe had indeed found a new source of romantic inspiration in his life, namely, his current wife, Carissa, and more will be said of her in part 4.

Part of his enduring attraction to the music of Torroba and Rodrigo involves his personal relationship with the composers themselves. Pepe was chosen by Rodrigo and the government of Spain to be one of the major participants in the worldwide celebration of that composer's ninetieth birthday year, in 1991. Among other appearances in connection with this occasion, he performed tributes with the Orpheus Chamber Orchestra at Carnegie Hall, at the Berliner Philharmonie, in the Musikverein in Vienna, and at Moscow's Great Hall of the Pillars. Not surprisingly, his close relationship with musical giants like Torroba and Rodrigo provoked a philosophical response from Pepe:

To me, it has been a wonderful experience to see how they can transform everyday emotions that we all feel; we all love our children, but very few people can touch the face of the grandchild and have that feeling become the second movement of the four-guitar concerto. That has been the most valuable lesson to me—the realization that music is love, music is those feelings. Then, as a performer, I have to take that piece of music and transform

11. PEPE, THE PHILOSOPHER

it back into those feelings, so that the public receives the love that inspired the music, in that way finishing the magic circle that music is. Music is, to me, the voice of God. It is a means we are given to break barriers, to communicate with people who speak other languages and become one heart. It is what we can use to find a spiritual being inside of ourselves. These men were living examples of that inspiration.[15]

As with any complex and difficult task, there is an element of Zen centeredness and conscious awareness one has to attain before achieving mastery. As the guru explains:

You almost have to forget any preconceived idea [and] come with an empty mind so the piece can speak to you each time for the first time. The more you can experience that passion and that love for the country, its history and people, the more you can have a real affinity, and it cannot help but come out in the playing. If you're not from Spain, it doesn't mean you cannot play Spanish music. It just means perhaps you'll have to eat extra Spanish food, drink extra Spanish wine, watch more flamenco, and read more Lorca and Cervantes! If your heart is touched by music, that's what counts.[16]

Now that's the kind of spiritual discipline most of us can readily embrace. The guitar requires many things, but abstention from sensual pleasures is not one of them. Still, it does entail a certain level of idealism, unsullied by quotidian concerns. "Being a guitarist does not mean having a career. It's having a relationship with music. Music is a companion to take with you. It comforts you when you're sad, and when you're happy, you share it. It's a wonderful friend. And like a friend, it'll never betray you."[17] And this idealism extends to the whole notion of competition: "I feel music, not competition. It is the expression of human emotions and, particularly, music is love. Many musicians take music in a competitive way. I feel very sad about that. Competition is a thing of the ego. Musicians should be servants of the music and give their all and not worry about being better than someone else."[18]

Can someone be born a guitarist? I claim no expertise in genetics, but I suspect that one can be born with the ingredients that, under the right circumstances, will produce a great guitarist. Had Pepe been forced to work in a coal mine at age ten, no amount of natural talent would probably have saved him. But without an innate gift, no environment would produce a

Pepe Romero. Thus he has no conscious memory of learning to walk, speak, or play a guitar. As he once observed, "I always knew when I was very young I'd be a guitarist. I felt meant to do it. I remember as a little boy, listening to my father play. Those were the best memories. . . . But it doesn't matter what you play, classical, flamenco or whatever, just as long as the music touches your heart."[19]

But our philosopher was not content with such a forensic analysis. All of this has to mean something; it has to serve some higher purpose. He has stated this firm belief: "When things are tough, the arts come to the rescue of the people. That's what I would like to see now. Unfortunately, we need a little more awareness that the arts are a necessary part of feeling, of energizing the soul, energizing the spirit. Without the spirit and the soul taking a strong part of our conscious awareness, we really are not that ready to meet the challenge of our times. We need the music. It's a very important part of the energy we need."[20]

Pepe's entire philosophy of music could be summed up in a single word: love. Now academics and intellectuals will find that a disturbingly simplistic formulation, but it is a driving force that does not conduce to simplistic results, musically or otherwise. Without that insatiable passion *for* what he does, Pepe (and the other Romeros) could simply not *do* what he does. In 1982, he reported to the German press that he was giving 250 concerts a year, half solo, half quartet.[21] That's a concert once every 1.46 days. The sheer number of notes he has to keep in mind is difficult to comprehend, but added to the normal pressures of performance are the logistical complications of getting from one place to the next, by car, trains, and planes, checking into and out of hotels, keeping social engagements, practicing, and rehearsing—not to mention family obligations and teaching. That he kept up such a schedule when he was forty years old was remarkable if not extraordinary, but that he does it still in his seventies is a testament to something other than a need to make money. Only a person consumed by a passion for what he does would subject himself to this sort of life. It's clearly something he and his brothers relish, though with an element of stoicism. As he once noted, "This is a busy life, but when you become a musician this is what you do."[22]

But stoicism combines in Pepe with a penchant for mysticism, outside the boundaries of any definable set of religious beliefs but very concrete

11. PEPE, THE PHILOSOPHER

nonetheless. "When Pepe Romero plays the guitar, he believes he is at the center of the universe. He feels playing the guitar before an audience is almost a mystical experience. 'The music is like a circle. A divine inspiration comes to the composer, who puts it down on the paper. The player receives it from there, but must go back to the original inspiration to carry it to the audience. Then the audience and musician can be inspired to a divine feeling of joy and of peace. It is a beautiful feeling.'"[23]

Statements such as these (and he repeated these same basic ideas in many interviews) reveal an inexhaustible love of music, one that is the central organizing reality of his existence. And in that same year of 1983 he declared in another interview that

> I think the main ingredient for a successful performance is a lot of love for the music. The music must become an expression of your own inner self. You must combine that with a lack of fear of the public and a lack of fear of the platform. The concert must be a friendly occasion, a gathering of people in a common cause: to share in the love and beauty of music. You can say that the artist and the audience have to become as one in the friendly embrace of music. Too often musicians set themselves apart from their audience, which immediately opens up the way for nerves.[24]

Perhaps Pepe himself provided the best summary of his philosophy of performance: "I don't like comparisons: when a man falls in love with a woman the worst thing he can do is to make love to her and think of someone else. When you walk on stage to play a work you are in love with it. When you walk with the woman you love it doesn't matter what someone else thinks. I feel the same way about music. At the end, on the day when I play my last note, I want to go with the thought that I have played what I liked, when I liked it."[25]

No, comparisons and value judgments are not his style, but they are inevitable in a family of four guitarists, each with a distinctive musical personality. That can become a source of great inspiration and a source of conflicts that even a philosopher cannot ultimately forfend. For as Pepe has said, "God put me in a family where I learned I can never be the greatest. And, so long as I'm alive and in this family, I know that none of them can be the greatest, either!"[26]

CHAPTER 12

ANGEL, THE PROTEUS

By nearly any standard, whether in terms of technical virtuosity, musical versatility, number and quality of recordings, concert appearances, or contributions to the repertoire, Pepe and Angel have made an indelible mark on the guitar's history and development. In recognition of this fact, along with Celin and Pepe, in February 2000 Angel was honored by the Spanish king with the Cruz del Caballero de la Orden de Isabel la Católica, a knighthood.

Again, though, these sons are quite different people and personalities. To be sure, their sense of humor (often very earthy) and outlook on life are thoroughly "Romero," but in sketching profiles, we focus on what sets them apart from one another. The labels for Celedonio/Angelita, Celin, and Pepe sprang readily to my mind; however, I struggled to find a one-word description for Angel. I had known Pepe and Celin for many years, and from all I had read about and by him, I felt that I knew Celedonio reasonably well, though I had only met him a couple of times, and then just briefly. But I only made Angel's acquaintance in the course of researching this book, and I found him to be harder to essentialize. He was, I had always known, a phenomenal guitarist and a very refined musician. He epitomized the term *child prodigy*. And unlike many prodigies, he didn't fizzle out after adolescence but just kept getting better.

12. ANGEL, THE PROTEUS

Still, how does one characterize a person who has done so many different things, whose energies seem to spread out in time and space like a burst of gamma rays from a supernova explosion? That was my quandary. Not content simply to play the guitar at the highest level of virtuosity, Angel has built guitars, flown airplanes, earned a brown belt in karate, demonstrated genuine artistic talent in numerous drawings and paintings, sung on stage with Plácido Domingo, collected Arabian horses, won an award for a film score he composed, tried his hand at writing a script, studied acting and appeared in a Hollywood film, and most notably, taken up the baton in a second career as a conductor.[1] He may not have succeeded in any of his avocational endeavors to an extent that comes even close to rivaling his accomplishments as a guitarist, but what is intriguing is not how well he has done all these things but rather that he has done them at all.

So I eventually settled on the name of Proteus, an ancient Greek god of rivers and seas, known for his ability to change shape. Not surprisingly, our aqueous shape-shifter relishes very close proximity to the ocean, as a place not only for meditation but also for work. He once remarked to a German journalist that he often goes to the beach and watches the waves of the Pacific, to contemplate the grandeur and power of the ocean, which puts things in perspective for him.[2] As he explained to the local newspaper in Escondido, California, "You look at the ocean, so vast and powerful, and you know how small we really are. Any human assumption of how big or famous you are has to go when you look at the ocean. Here man is only one little element of God's creation."[3]

Angel's impulse to excel in a variety of undertakings is a defining characteristic, but there is a countervailing impulse in his temperament, and that is a commitment to absolute excellence as a guitarist. He may spread himself thin at times but not at the expense of his first passion: the guitar.

GUITARIST

Angel characteristically establishes both his kinship with as well as his unique position in the Romero family: "I was inspired by my father, but I created my technique on my own when I was 14 or 15 years old—or even possibly 12 or 13 years old. I made my first solo recording at 14 on The Royal Family of the Guitar."[4]

PART 3. PROFILES

A particular trademark of Angel's is the *Concierto de Aranjuez* by Joaquín Rodrigo, of which he gave the West Coast premiere in 1964, at age eighteen, and which he has made his own in innumerable performances, several recordings, and a published edition.[5] He has also arranged themes by Rodrigo into a new concerto, *Rincones de España* (Corners of Spain), which he has premiered (more will be said of this in the chapter on the Romero repertoire). He recalls the first recording of the *Aranjuez*, in 1967 with the San Antonio Symphony: "Even today, the guitar world still considers it to be a very explosive interpretation, which is totally uninhibited, both emotionally and technically, by a very young man.... It was recorded in one take. I did a second recording in 1976 with the London [Symphony Orchestra] and Previn. The *Aranjuez* is one piece that I never forget; I never have to practise it."[6]

One isn't quite sure how to understand these assertions, but it might be what provoked *Los Angeles Times* reviewer John Henken to remark, in a 1984 review, that when Angel played it with the Los Angeles Philharmonic, "there was more than a hint of automatic pilot about the performance. But his technical control never wavered."[7] Then again, Henken might have mistaken insouciance for indifference. The *Central Florida News-Journal* reported on his performance of the *Aranjuez* with the late Rafael Frühbeck de Burgos and the London Symphony Orchestra: "It was his relaxed and seemingly carefree demeanor that endeared him to the audience. In only a moment he had broken down the barrier that often rises up between musician and audience."[8] Having recently attended a performance by him of this work, with the same Los Angeles Philharmonic that accompanied him over fifty years ago, I can testify that his execution has lost none of its verve.

Yet despite this apparent nonchalance, Angel has admitted to me that he gets nervous a week or two before a concert, especially recitals, which feel to him like a "circus-clown stand-up bit." In fact, he does not consider the stage "a normal place to be. Making money is superficial. Playing your best for a review. Everything about a stage sucks." This aversion is reminiscent of Glenn Gould's expressed distaste for live performance, though Angel much prefers performing in public to playing in a recording studio, because people provide warmth and feedback.

Angel's preconcert jitters, driven in large measure by a perfectionist streak in his personality, occasionally wake him up in the middle of the night, as he counts the days before the performance. He still has vivid memories of his Town Hall debut when, at age fifteen, he was so nervous he paced around the block three times before his curtain call. But once the fateful moment itself has finally arrived, he says that he's "cool as a cucumber and can't wait to go on stage." He "feels hands on him that this is where he is supposed to be." By 7:00 p.m., he can't wait to play. The sweetest words he knows are "maestro, five more minutes." He feels like "a hungry man hearing 'dinner in 5 minutes,' and it's gonna be his favorite meal."[9] Nonetheless, "when you start wondering what the audience will think of you, what the press will say, worrying about the mistakes you may make, you are lost."[10]

Despite his apparent ambivalence about solo performance in particular, Angel claims never to have had a technical problem, something reviewers have never had any trouble believing. The *Austin American-Statesman* exclaimed that "guitarist Romero plays with genetic insight," and Angel himself feels that he was drawn to the guitar almost as if it had been "genetically programmed."[11] As he claimed in the interview for the *Times-Advocate* cited earlier, "Even now I pick up a new piece, and it feels like I've already played it. My hands go to where they should and I feel the comfort that it's not a new piece in my subconscious because I've heard my father play it. And it's freaky how it seems to be in my genes."[12]

In short, Angel is doing what he was cut out to do, and he knows that perfectly well. As he states in the *Escondido (CA) Times-Advocate* article, "To do something else [other than play the guitar as a profession] would be like stopping breathing. I have thought about it, and if I came back 1,000 times to earth, I would choose to be exactly the same—a musician."[13] Maybe so, but he has spent decades trying to serve two or more masters simultaneously. And to a remarkable degree, he has succeeded.

ARTIST

We will now examine in greater depth some of his protean activities, focusing on his art, his Hollywood connections and projects, and especially his conducting. Aside from flying planes, surfing, practicing karate, and a brief stint collecting horses, Angel's most serious avocations have not strayed outside the realm of the arts: painting, writing, acting, building guitars, composing/arranging, and especially conducting.[14]

PART 3. PROFILES

Pepe has built a house on the Sacromonte in Granada, with a breathtaking view of the nearby Alhambra. Celin relishes the time he spends in Málaga and fantasizes about living there. Angel, more Americanized than his brothers, feels far less nostalgia for the Old World and instead bought a vacation home on some beachfront property in Hawaii, on the north shore of Oahu, where he could surf. He and his family enjoy the seclusion of that locale. But for many years now, Angel has maintained homes that have taken him out of the immediate residential orbit of his family in Del Mar, for a time inland to Ramona during the late 1990s, and then in San Marcos, just north of Del Mar. In 2016, he and his family relocated to Hollywood.

Angel's hilltop home in San Marcos, in northern San Diego County, offered a breathtakingly panoramic view of the Pacific. The ocean is a sort of talisman for this family of *malagueños*, and they seem to draw strength from it. But what most fascinated me was the interior of his house. One work in particular attracted my attention, and that was a large abstract oil painting that he calls the *Concierto de Aranjuez*. The vibrant colors and dynamic brushstrokes coalesce into abstract patterns and suggest nothing of the actual palace and gardens there, though there is a guitar in the middle of the composition. This expressionistic work conveys his inner response to Rodrigo's music. He painted it around the time that he was first performing and recording this piece in the United States, during the late 1960s, and his "brushes" included the feet of his baby boy, Lito. Other remarkable works include pencil drawings of famous musicians, including Paganini. These he did from memory during flights or other times when he was not otherwise occupied.

Angel feels a special affinity for Mexican art (and music), and he also likes to display several of Pepe's paintings. Overall, though, his tastes diverge from those of his brothers in that he is much more attracted to modern art than they are. Just as Celedonio wrote poetry as a necessary diversion from the stresses and strains of life, so Angel has made it clear that he paints for relaxation—and that when he is painting, music takes a back seat. He has to "switch off completely" and doesn't even play music in the background, focusing exclusively on the task at hand. His preferred subjects are landscapes and seascapes, locales far removed from Hollywood Boulevard.[15]

12. ANGEL, THE PROTEUS

HOLLYWOOD STAR

I noted in part 2 that the Romeros quickly established relationships with Hollywood celebrities and even provided music for some films. But Angel is the only Romero who continued to cultivate these relationships beyond the 1960s and to enlarge his career in the direction of Hollywood. Angel recounts with considerable relish his many associations with legendary Hollywood celebrities. In fact, when he played the *Aranjuez* at the Hollywood Bowl as a lad of eighteen, he himself achieved instant notoriety in La La Land, and this exotic wunderkind with movie-star good looks turned many a celebrity head. One reviewer even compared him to Rudolf Valentino.[16] The *Ridgecrest (CA) Valley Independent* thought Angel "so handsome that he might be called a Rudolph Valentino of the concert stage. Many of the women in the audience wound not have cared if he only played the scales."[17] The *Pasadena Star-News* perceived a resemblance to "a young Omar Sharif," declaring, "[He] has the charisma of a star."[18]

Angel later asserted that his fan base included such glitterati as Woody Allen, Whoopi Goldberg, and Patrick Stewart, as well as fellow Spaniards Pedro Almodóvar and Carlos Saura.[19] He also says that he was a close friend of Frank Sinatra, liked to hang out with Desi Arnaz (who was "like his uncle"), and would visit Jimmy Durante. He counted Jack Benny, Lucille Ball, Ginger Rogers, and Bob and Dolores Hope among his friends; in addition, he used to play chamber music with Isaac Stern and Dudley Moore. Angel's guitar artistry gained a truly mass audience in 1977 when he played an arrangement of the middle movement of the *Aranjuez* to accompany a television commercial for the Cordoba automobile, a spot famously narrated by Ricardo Montalban. Angel and Ricardo traveled together to La Mancha, Spain, where the commercial was filmed, and became fast friends in the process.

Thus his later activities in acting, film scoring, and even writing screenplays flowed naturally from such associations. In an extensive interview with the local *North County Times*, he revealed that "what excites him more than his recent recordings of some Bach and a new Rodrigo concerto is his budding career as an actor. 'I've been taking acting lessons with Jeff Corey in Los Angeles, the man who taught James Dean and Jack Nicholson.'"[20] In fact, he had already landed a cameo part as an American senator in the 1993 film *Bound by Honor (Blood in, Blood Out)*, directed by Taylor Hackford. But in this same article, Angel expressed reservations about the acting profession: "He believes an actor's career is more difficult than a musician's because once you peak, mere artistry won't keep you aloft. 'Musicians either lose their passion or they lose the physical side.' He remembers seeing 89-year-old Segovia in New York. He fell asleep on the stage. But when it was time to play a Bach fugue, something triggered in his brain. He was marvelous, says Romero. 'The public is kinder to musicians. They allow you to grow old. I hope when I reach that point, the audience will remember me in my prime.'"[21]

Composing and performing music for films posed no such risks, and he wrote the score for the 1994 Gabriele Retes film *Bienvenido-Welcome*, which opened the Muestra del Cine Film Festival in Guadalajara. For that composition he won the 1995 Ariel (the Mexican equivalent of an Academy Award) in the category of music written originally for film. He contributed to the score for *Young Guns II*, with music by Alan Silvestri. The filmmaker played the film for him, and he improvised some music for the opening shot of the desert. In addition, he performed and recorded the Bill Conti score for the 1991 movie *By the Sword*, and he also supplied memorable guitar stylings for Robert Redford's 1988 film, *The Milagro Beanfield War*. Thanks in part to Angel's playing, Dave Grusin's score for this film won the Oscar in 1989.

An extension of Hollywood-related musical activities is apparent in his various guitar arrangements of pop songs and melodies, some of them from famous movie scores. One particularly moving such transcription is the theme song from *Somewhere in Time*, on his album *Bella* (named after his daughter). He also effectively arranged the theme song from *The Deer Hunter*. Another album features a remarkable collaboration with jazz artist Claude Bolling, about which I will say more in chapter 14. Angel is not the first Romero to plug his guitar into American popular culture in this way; recall that shortly after their arrival in 1957, Celin arranged "Stormy Weather" for guitar. But Angel is the only one of the brothers who has continued down this path. Still, his flirtation with American popular culture has its limits. When asked by the *New York Times Magazine* if he would get into rock, as Anglo-Australian guitarist John Williams was doing, he resolutely replied, "Never!"[22] Still, he came close on November 7, 2015, when he played "Sloop John B" with the Beach Boys and John Stamos at the Goodwill Gala in Orange County.

12. ANGEL, THE PROTEUS

CONDUCTOR

It is Proteus on the podium that most intrigues me. As Angel told the *North County Times*,

> I think I've wanted to conduct since I first fell in love with the symphony orchestra when I was a kid. I realized the power of music, and I wanted to be a part of that power. I try to recreate parts of the orchestra on the guitar. I imitate the sound of the strings, the harp. I also love opera. The human voice is the greatest instrument, and I try to reproduce that sound when I play. My guitar becomes a small orchestra, and it depends on how I feel as to what instrument I imitate.[23]

Though most conductors play either the piano or an orchestral instrument, usually violin, it's not unheard of for a guitarist to lead an orchestra. For instance, Hector Berlioz played the guitar and was also one of the greatest conductors of the nineteenth century. And there isn't as much disconnect between the guitar and the orchestra as one might suspect. Angel has revealed that "for [him] the guitar has always been like a small orchestra and the orchestra has always been like a big guitar."[24] As he said on another occasion, "When I conduct, I have all the instruments at the same time. I can decide the coloration of the sound, of the music. It is not a feeling of power but of responsibility."[25] As a guitarist, he has told me that he prefers playing concertos to giving solo recitals because in collaborating with an orchestra, there's "more variety of sound and human interaction."

Although Angel never had any formal education in conducting, he studied privately and associated himself with several noted figures in the profession. When performing with the Knoxville Symphony, he was delighted to play under the baton of former music director Zoltán Rozsnyai (1926–90), who returned as a guest conductor on this occasion. Angel told the *Knoxville News-Sentinel*, "Zoltán is an old friend of mine. He was my teacher in conducting [when Rozsnyai was conductor of the San Diego Symphony]. I moonlight as a conductor sometimes and Zoltán gave me private lessons."[26] Angel was also proud of his association with other conductors, telling another newspaper that like his "adopted grandfather," Arthur Fiedler, he loves travel and meeting people.[27] Morton Gould was also a good friend. Most of all, Angel is proud of the guidance he received from Eugene Ormandy, who gave him an autographed eight-by-ten photo as his "diploma," on which he wrote, "To Angel Romero, with the greatest respect from one conductor to another." Angel thus considers his conducting technique Hungarian. He is also a close friend of Gustavo Dudamel, conductor of the Los Angeles Philharmonic, and he has conducted the Simón Bolívar Youth Orchestra in Caracas, at Dudamel's invitation.

As a conductor, Angel feels a special affinity for Beethoven, who was also his father's preferred composer. The Fourth Symphony is a particular favorite, and so great is his rapport with this work that he needs to kiss the score and ask Beethoven to come out with him before conducting the symphony. Once, having neglected this little ritual just before going on stage, he raced back to the dressing room to deliver the indispensable *beso*. He is perhaps most fond of the Seventh Symphony, however, and particularly the allegretto movement, though he brings a whirlwind of passion to the fourth movement. (Angel's *Bella* album features his surprisingly convincing transcriptions for solo guitar of the slow movements from both the "Pathétique" and the "Moonlight" Sonatas.)

Angel has conducted a number of other ensembles on a guest basis, including the Pittsburgh Symphony, the Academy of St. Martin-in-the-Fields, the Royal Philharmonic Orchestra, Germany's NDR Symphony Orchestra, the Berliner Symphoniker, the Beijing Philharmonic, the USC Thornton Chamber Orchestra, the Singapore Symphony Orchestra, the Euro-Asia Philharmonic Orchestra, the Shanghai Symphony, the Bogotá Philharmonic, the Chicago Sinfonietta, the Orquesta de Baja California, the Santa Barbara Symphony, the San Diego Symphony, and the San Diego Chamber Orchestra, among others. Many times he appears in a dual role as both guitar soloist and conductor. Following a 2002 performance, a critic in Flagstaff noted approvingly that "when performers also conduct, most construct a program which allows them to safely play on the first half and then switch their attention to the baton for the second half; not Romero, who moved back and forth with ease in a remarkable feat of concentration and musicianship."[28]

His first major gig as the conductor of a large symphony orchestra took place in the summer of 1981. The *Los Angeles Times* published an article announcing his debut as conductor, at the Open Air Theatre of the San Diego Symphony, in a program of Spanish music, noting, "These concerts will mark the first time in his professional career that Romero has conducted purely

12. ANGEL, THE PROTEUS

orchestral music and not just a guitar concerto while he was playing."[29] He also conducted the Louisville Symphony Orchestra that year.

Many seasons later, in 1996, when Angel was fifty, he auditioned for the San Diego Symphony, against nine other candidates. He conducted the *Nutcracker* Suite, Beethoven's Seventh Symphony, and the Vivaldi D-major Concerto for Lute (arranged for guitar), in which he also soloed. The reviewer for the *San Diego Union-Tribune* noted a number of things about his appearance:

> Nothing seemed difficult for him. As conductor, Romero proved charismatic, despite his interpretive quirks. . . . Equipped with a fluid baton technique and an expressive left hand, he coaxed and cajoled the musicians into giving him what he wanted. At times, as in the Beethoven, he leaned forward as if to pull the sound from the players and their instruments. Romero was also something of a speed demon, and he encouraged uncommonly fast tempos in portions of both Beethoven and Tchaikovsky. The Nutcracker's March was unabashedly brisk, and the Sugar Plum Fairy seemed quick enough to spin sugar into cotton candy. It's just as well there weren't any dancers on stage. Given the pace, they might have toppled over.[30]

As encouraging as that review was in many respects, it suggests why Angel never got the job. Orchestral musicians rebel against tempos they find inappropriate or uncomfortable.

In 2002 he again auditioned for the job of conductor of the San Diego Symphony and announced to the local press, "I have a dream of people in Berlin going to see the San Diego Symphony. I would love for them to play in the great music halls of Vienna. With the benefit of my international fame, we would be welcomed all over the world."[31] However, that particular dream was never realized.

Another big potential break came in the 2005–6 season, during which the San Diego Chamber Orchestra auditioned six guest conductors for the post of artistic director. As Angel told the *San Diego Union-Tribune* at the time, "I am interested" and "I like the orchestra." He had already made a favorable impression on the critic, who shared that "there was much to like about Monday's program, titled 'Ode to Joy!,' which was presented at Sherwood Auditorium. Romero . . . displayed the suave dynamism that distinguishes his musicianship. The man has charisma to burn. . . . But [he] also savored subtlety. He emphasized the alluring rhythms and tone colors of Turina's 'La Oración del Torero.'"[32] However, for whatever reason, he did not land the SDCO job.

Angel's first steady conducting gig was as music director of the Orquesta de Baja California (established in 1990), beginning in 2005. He took it to Lincoln Center that same year to perform an all-Revueltas program, and he continues to direct that ensemble on occasion as a guest conductor. He has also served as conductor and musical director of the West Los Angeles Symphony Orchestra, at Royce Hall on the UCLA campus.

Having witnessed Angel conduct, on DVD and in person, I can attest to his excellent baton technique, the clarity and reliability of his cues, and his charismatic aura. He is a leader and commands respect. He also gets very good results from the "troops," in large measure due to his meticulous score preparation. In short, he's an exciting presence on the podium. This makes it all the more difficult to explain why he does not now have a regular position with a major orchestra, though he remains convinced that he will land one.

THE DAREDEVIL

One of more notable aspects of Angel's personality is a striking juxtaposition of almost diffident humility, on the one hand, and exuberant self-esteem, on the other. As his own mother pointed out, when he was young, "If he did something great, he would say, 'This is great!' But the [other boys], if you say, 'That's great,' they say, 'No, no importa. It's all right. It's normal, no big deal.' But to Angel nothing was ever normal."[33] This trait can prove bewildering to those who don't know him personally or well. For instance, a quote like the following is uncontroversial: "I am a musician first and a guitarist second." But then informing the newspaper's readers that "others are guitarists first" no doubt raised some eyebrows.[34]

The following is typical of the sort of press statements Angel has sometimes made, statements that may strike the reader as unnecessarily dismissive and perhaps a bit unfair: "There's a lot of hype surrounding guitarists. And it's destructive. Audiences come to the concerts, frequently because of the hype. They don't like what they hear and then don't come to the *good* concerts. It puts people like me in a position of having to defend myself...."

12. ANGEL, THE PROTEUS

And, to add insult to injury, it's not uncommon for performers who don't have good technique to do away with it altogether and focus on interpretation. . . . Slow down here, pick up there."[35]

Not one to hide his candle under a bushel, Angel knows his own worth, and he's not reluctant to let people in on something that is far from a secret.[36] However, a certain insecurity lurks just behind the self-promotion. So though this tendency may seem to border on egotism at times, it actually poses a deeper question: why?

Angel himself has nicely encapsulated the origin of his overarching ambition and uninhibited self-regard, which he disclosed years ago in an interview with the *Mercury News*: "'I had to prove myself, as the youngest must. It makes you excel more. I started out in the shadow of my older brothers, and I had to work that much harder. . . . I wanted to show everyone what I could do,' [Angel] says, brimming with self-confidence."[37]

Carissa once confided to me that she would not have wanted to grow up with Celin and Pepe as her older brothers. These brilliant and powerful males would make it difficult to establish one's own identity, to get parental attention in the face of such competition. And even if one could escape their shadow, he would still be in his father's. Angel recalls that when he was about three years old, far too young to defend himself, his brothers hoisted him on a table and began to dig their fists into his flesh, not to massage but to torment. Early conflicts like these have remained etched in Angel's memory.[38]

Thus it seems that Angel is driven to do what he does because his status as an autonomous and unique individual depends on it. It would never be enough simply to fit in, to fulfill the role cut out for "the baby" of the family, Mamá's *Benjamín*. It would never be enough simply to be as good as his brothers. He would have to find ways to set himself apart, and this necessity resulted in a notably competitive streak in his personality.

Still, though he may insist that, as a result of his diverse activities, he is more multifaceted and interesting than his brothers, he is still proudly Romero and will assert the following, without being at all inconsistent:

> Pepe and I are great competitors, which keeps both of us on our toes, but let me tell you that there's nobody on this planet that Pepe loves more than me; and there's nobody on this planet that I love more than Pepe. We are

like one person; we love each other, we respect each other, we smoke cigars together; since I was a baby we slept in the same room until I was almost 18 years old. And we're both very close to Celin. He is my most valuable and annoying critic; he freely gives me his criticism.[39]

I wrote the preceding observations before discovering a book about this very subject, one recommended to me by a colleague in the University of California, Riverside psychology department as serious and credible research and not merely pseudoscientific psychobabble. The book in question, *Born to Rebel: Birth Order, Family Dynamics, and Creative Lives* by MIT research scholar Frank J. Sulloway, sheds considerable light on the issue of siblings and personalities, especially among males. As it turns out, the Romero family makes for a case study supporting the findings of this remarkable book, confirming the conclusions I had reached through a far less systematic approach involving observation and intuition. As the youngest of five boys, I have some understanding of the complex dynamics of sibling rivalry, but scientific affirmation of my educated guesses is reassuring.

As Sulloway makes clear:

> Birth order merits our special attention because it encapsulates disparities in age, size, power, and privilege. The typical firstborn strategy is to align his or her interests with those of the parents, adopting the parents' perspective on family life. The family status of firstborns is primary, and they seek to maintain this primacy by defending their niche against encroachments by younger brothers and sisters. Laterborn offspring face a different developmental challenge. Their most pressing problem is to find a valued family niche that avoids duplicating the one already staked out by the parent-identified firstborn. Instead, they seek to excel in those domains where older siblings have not already established superiority. Laterborns typically cultivate openness to experience—a useful strategy for anyone who wishes to find a novel and successful niche in life. Consistent with these exploratory tendencies, laterborns take greater risks, endeavoring to achieve through openness and diversity what firstborns gain through territoriality and conformity to parental expectations. For each family niche, there are different rules of the sibling road.[40]

Here is a vital key to the brothers' personalities, especially Angel's protean proclivities. Celin adhered most closely to the cultural patterns established

12. ANGEL, THE PROTEUS

by his parents, and he played the role of surrogate father, as needed. Seeking to establish a separate identity, one consistent with his preternatural inclinations, Pepe delved more deeply into flamenco than any other Romero. He also cultivated a talent for art not exhibited by his father or older brother. Angel, facing an almost insurmountable barrier of classical and flamenco expertise on the part of his father and brothers (recall the final quote in the previous chapter), not to mention Pepe's artwork, would seek to establish *his* identity by taking even greater risks (such as playing the Bach Chaconne in New York at fifteen or the *Aranjuez* in Los Angeles at eighteen) and by diversifying his activities to include not only a wider range of musical endeavors, for example, jazz, conducting, and film scoring, but also nonmusical pursuits, for instance, karate, flying, and acting.

Not without reason has he identified himself to the *Cleveland Plain Dealer* as the "daredevil" in the family, though from my point of view, the gutsiest thing any Romero ever did was to uproot his family in middle age and relocate to a part of the world where he knew almost no one and could not speak the local language.[41] Celedonio defined the word *daredevil*, but Angel is the proverbial acorn that did not fall very far from the paternal oak tree. In fact, we have already observed that a willingness to take big risks is a trait common to all the Romeros, a trait largely responsible for their success.

* * *

In any case, a healthy competition spawned by sibling rivalry would provide the impetus for some truly great music making after the family settled in the United States. Sadly, it would also contribute to a widening rift in the ensemble that would ultimately tear it apart, as we shall see. Nonetheless, the family had by then established a formidable legacy that would outlive the dynasty's founder and that will endure for the foreseeable future. In addition to their numerous recordings, teaching and new repertoire constitute the foundation on which this legacy securely rests. But the quartet is not finished yet, and despite dramatic changes in personnel, new generations of Romeros have stepped forward to continue the dynasty. Proteus continues to flourish as well.

PART 4

LEGACY

With my three sons, I have played where no one had played before, and together we have crossed prairies, rivers, and mountains.

[Con mis tres hijos toqué, donde nadie antes tocara, todos unidos cruzamos praderos, ríos, montañas.]

—Celedonio Romero, written on stationery from the Golden Eagle Inn, Niles, Michigan

CHAPTER 13

THE ROMERO TECHNIQUE

Among the Romeros' most significant accomplishments of lasting importance is the development and promulgation of a highly systematic, clearly defined, and consistently successful technique of playing the classical guitar. Though this was the creation of Celedonio, his sons, principally Celin and Pepe, have elaborated on the "Romero method" over several decades of influential teaching, not only privately but also in leading university music programs. Celin taught at San Diego State University from 1979 to 2013, and at the University of California, San Diego (UCSD) from 1980 to 2009. Most recently, he has been on the faculty of California State University, Los Angeles. Pepe taught at UCSD from 1982 to 1991 and at the University of Southern California (USC) from 1975 to 1982. He resumed teaching at USC in 2004 and remains there today, as a Distinguished Artist-in-Residence at the Thornton School of Music. Pepe has been among some esteemed company at this institution and fondly recalls being welcomed to USC in 1975 by the likes of Gregor Piatigorsky, Jascha Heifetz, and Gabor Rejto.

Celin and Pepe were hired at SDSU and USC, respectively, because students were going to them for private lessons in order to prepare for recitals. The schools found this situation more than a little embarrassing and made the wise decision to hire them. In the process of teaching at these institutions and in giving master classes around the world, Pepe and Celin have directly conveyed the Romero technique to thousands of aspiring guitarists. Now, with the assistance of Celino and Lito, their method spreads ever outward in expanding ripples through succeeding "generations" of students and those students' students. Of course, the potential for the Romero method to be diluted and misrepresented over time would be very great if it were not for the fact that they have codified their approach, over three generations, in method books and instructional DVDs by Celedonio, Pepe, Angel, and Celino (see appendix 4 for a list of these). It will thus always be possible for someone to access their teachings from the source, not just through a long succession of followers.

For precisely this reason I will not dwell at great length here on the fine points of guitar technique, since that information is readily available in the aforementioned sources, as well as from the Romeros themselves and their leading disciples, about whom I will have something to say at the conclusion of this chapter. It would also be of minimal interest to the general reader. Thus I have chosen to focus for the most part on those aspects of the Romero method that seem to me to be applicable to other varieties of musical or creative performance, and even to life itself. These have come largely from periodicals not readily available or even known to most readers.

For no other reason than a love of novelty and sheer caprice, I have elected to freely adapt the Noble Eightfold Path of traditional Buddhism to suit the exigencies of the moment here (with apologies in advance to the Buddha and his many followers). This "path" consists of a progressive series of exhortations toward right understanding, thought, speech, action, livelihood, effort, mindfulness, and concentration. I am not an adherent of Buddhism (or any other religion), but there is a persistent strain of spiritual/mystical thinking in the Romero approach to the guitar, and this quality lends itself to a quasi-Buddhist explication of their technique. I hereby make no attempt to contribute anything meaningful to the already-vast body of exegetical literature concerning Buddhist doctrines, of which there is a bewildering multiplicity of schools and styles.

Wherever possible below, as I have done before in this book, I use the exact words of the person being quoted rather than paraphrasing what he or she has said, in order to avoid any miscommunication. The Romeros choose their words carefully, and these require no distillation by me. Because Pepe

13. THE ROMERO TECHNIQUE

and Celin have invested a great deal of time and energy in teaching and have been consistently active in this arena for many decades, dedicatedly carrying on the pedagogical tradition of their father, the majority of the following insights originate with them. But when Angel has something to say about playing the guitar, it's worth paying close attention to. The same is true of Celino.

However, I begin with a quotation from the writings of the Dalai Celedonio himself. This seems to say everything, though it will hardly prevent us from attempting to gild the lily thereafter.

> Dear Guitarists, this is how it is:
> If, with great devotion, you dedicate many hours of your life to the guitar,
> She, in turn, will take you to the very heights
> With her six divine princesses.[1]

RIGHT UNDERSTANDING

"With all thy getting," urges Proverbs 4:7, "get understanding." This is easier said than done, but it is where we must begin. By right understanding, I mean here a working comprehension of how to learn and play the instrument. A debate has raged for eons among performers about the role that actual repertoire plays in developing technique. Should one use concert literature to develop one's technique or stick to exercises and etudes for cultivating dexterity? This is an artificial dichotomy. Any concert work will pose distinctive technical challenges, and in the process of overcoming these, a performer will improve her or his technique. And some etudes are intended to serve two masters simultaneously, that is, develop technique and fill out a concert program. Where Pepe draws the line is in matters of interpretation: "Technique should never dictate interpretation. Technique is governed by the subconscious in response to interpretative dictates of the conscious mind."[2] In short, if one's interpretation of a work is to some extent the result of technical limitations, then that work is not ready for public performance.

Celedonio was very strict about not playing a piece before one was ready. For instance, young Pepe was dying to play *Recuerdos de la Alhambra* and *Capricho árabe*, two warhorses by Tárrega, but Papá would not permit it until he was really ready. As it turned out, he was finally allowed to learn *Capricho árabe* about the same time he got his first watercolor set.³ It thus comes as no surprise that Pepe often expatiates on this subject, as he once did in a master class:

> You should not develop your technique through repertoire, but rather use repertoire as "treats" after you accomplish a certain part of your technique. . . . Everybody should eat and drink and dream and live for a good two or three years with Carcassi and Sor studies until you have Carcassi and Sor coming out of every pore of you.⁴ Carcassi, Sor, and Giuliani are magic names. . . . Never play pieces that you cannot do well, because you get used to compromising, to doing things against your own musical instincts just because you cannot do them any better.⁵

Of course, all of this poses another immemorial question: what is technique? In a *TV Shopper* cover story, Angel pithily defined it as the ability "to play many notes accurately in a short amount of time."⁶ And how does one develop such velocity? Angel explains a crucial principle in cultivating celerity, and that is maintaining a minimum of distance between finger and string. His maxim, "the shorter the distance, the faster the speed," is basic physics.

Angel revealed a key ingredient in the development of this ability, telling Henry Adams that "any classical guitarist from southern Spain has a flamenco background to one degree or another, which, in part, means fast scales. This is a must in good flamenco playing, but for many classical guitarists, this is their greatest weakness."⁷ The connection with velocity has to do with the flamenco guitar's emphasis on strumming as well as plucking. *Rasgueo* (strumming) exercises the extensor muscles in the right arm, which in turn enable a player's fingers to return faster to the point where they are ready to pluck anew. It also helps to develop independence of the fingers. In fact, flamenco has played a decisive role in the evolution of the Romero technique, and a critic for the *St. Louis Post-Dispatch* rightly observed that, in contrast to "the tighter, less-mobile hand position championed by Segovia, [the Romeros employ] a righthand technique that, in plucking as much as in strumming, owes a great deal to the flamenco style."⁸ One hastens to add here, however, that some legendary flamenco guitarists did not have remarkable *picados*. One such was maestro Diego del Gastor (1908–73). Knowledge

13. THE ROMERO TECHNIQUE

of *compás* and effective *rasgueo* are the two indispensable ingredients in accompanying flamenco *cante* and *baile*.

However, if we identify technique with velocity, then Angel's technique is by any definition superlative. But that is not how Angel actually plays. Listen closely to any performance by Angel Romero, and you will perceive, in addition to lightning speed, a kaleidoscope of tone colors and nuances in phrasing, articulation, and dynamics. This does not derive from flamenco playing or proximity to Andalusia. Clearly, technique is the mechanism by which a performer conveys to others the full range of musical thoughts and feelings within himself or herself. Velocity may be a part of that aesthetic equation, but it is not the only element. In a very real sense, technique is inseparable from musicality, as they form an unbroken continuum from means to end. And for a discerning audience, blinding speed served up without genuine feeling is a form of musical necrophilia. What makes the Romeros' renditions of the Spanish classics so memorable is not just their technical legerdemain but also their absolute commitment to and belief in the music itself, emotionally and intellectually.

Preoccupation with technique is a major contributor to nervousness in performance. Even the technically perfect Pepe has mentioned to me that "every artist experiences some trepidation, some apprehension before going on stage." Enrique Granados, one of the leading pianists of his epoch, used to become so discomposed before going on stage that his friends literally had to shove him in the direction of the piano. Then, after playing a few bars, he would recover.[9] Pepe experiences the same sensation of recovery, partly because he has come to learn that even if he doesn't play as well as he would like, he does no one any harm. Nothing bad will happen! After all, it's not as if he were operating on someone's heart or brain or flying a jet fighter in combat.

I clearly recall a lesson during which Pepe applied the following corrective to my outlook on performance: "You think of mistakes as bad guys, but the audience loves it when you make a mistake, because it reminds them that you're human." Funny, I never had any difficulty reminding audiences that I was human. I always thought that was blindingly obvious!

In fact, Pepe's seeming nonchalance requires some qualification. If he misses a note or has a brief memory lapse, everyone will see it as an exception to the rule of excellence he has established over decades, in thousands of concerts and numerous recordings. He practices a lot to ensure that mistakes are rare, but the occasional faux pas doesn't trip up the rest of his performance or disturb his sleep. Hey, the audience loved it! However, an up-and-coming artist can afford far fewer such butt flops because professional competition is fierce, and she or he does not have a large cushion of reputation to absorb the fall.

Of course, there are two different types of performances, live and recorded. If one fudges a passage while making a CD, the miracle of modern recording technology can readily fix the problem. Nonetheless, Angel points out that there is another difference between recordings and performances because recordings pick up every little sound, including ambient sound, things that no one would notice in a concert, which can lead to a certain self-consciousness and consequent anxiety. As noted earlier, he prefers the human connection that only live performance provides.

In the end, all of one's technical and psychological preparations arise from and rest on a foundation of love, love of the instrument, the music, and the fellow human beings one seeks to entertain and inspire. This is the operative principle in achieving right understanding of the guitar and the Romeros themselves. As John Harris noted concerning the PBS documentary he made about the family: "The program shows how the young Romeros are taught music through *love*. The children are placed on the knees of an elder and shown how to strum the guitar. This allows kids to see the love and warmth the instrument can bring."[10] Such a formation leads to the right way to think about what one is doing.

RIGHT THOUGHT

The Noble Eightfold Path in Buddhism encourages the aspirant to maintain a correct mental posture in relation to life and life's experiences. Of course, exactly what "right thought" might mean in the esoteric realms of Buddhist practice is beyond our purview here, but the Romeros are in no doubt as to what this constitutes in making music, and one suspects that the Buddha would agree.

Right thinking basically boils down to maintaining a positive outlook concerning your own playing and that of others. In fact, the two are inseparable. People with a healthy self-concept are more likely to be affirmative in their

13. THE ROMERO TECHNIQUE

dealings with others. Cultivating a positive attitude toward others can also reinforce beneficial feelings about one's own worth. This is basic psychology but far from insignificant because a positive self-image is a vital component of self-confidence, a necessary ingredient in any recipe for successful performance. The Romeros believe that this sort of right thinking is something that can and must be cultivated. In the eulogy he delivered at his father's funeral in May 1996, Pepe recalled the following illustrative incident:

> One of the first lessons that he taught me, I remember, was he used to talk very well about a guitarist from Granada. And finally, this guitarist from Granada came over to the house. And my father had said many, many nice things about him. And this gentleman played. And I told my father—when I was a very little boy—I said, "Papá, he is the worst guitarist I have ever heard!" And he said to me, "You didn't look, you didn't listen to the gentleness of his thumb." To me that was a great lesson.[11]

Even a little meditation on this anecdote will make plain the reason for Papá's perspective. At every juncture in life, we have a choice, to dwell either on the negative or on the positive. Focusing on the good in others will help us do the same for ourselves. I remember going to a Segovia concert in Chicago in the mid-1970s, when the legendary maestro was, by almost any measure, well past his prime. I much later mentioned to Pepe that Segovia had seemed to be practicing on stage, that he would forget passages and have to stop and start over, and that it was a little embarrassing. Far from chiming in with my critique, Pepe immediately averred that he saw Segovia perform around that same time and marveled at his "very fluid left hand." Obi-Wan had taught Pepe well.

Of course, this attitude isn't the same as being a Pollyanna. It may well be necessary, even inevitable, to form a negative opinion about what someone is doing. We have no choice but to judge, and we will also be judged, regardless of what we think and do. The psychology of critical assessment is indeed tricky, because we clearly learn by negative as well as positive example. The late violist Paul Doktor once told me of an instance where he took his students to see someone perform, and the performance was, as he had anticipated, not very good. When the students asked why he had taken them to such an unsatisfactory concert, Doktor told them it was so they could learn what *not* to do.

PART 4. LEGACY

All of this relates to our evolutionary penchant for competition, the process by which we establish our place in the pecking order. There's no getting around the fact that festering just beneath every limpid pool of Buddhistic idealism in our cerebral cortex is a fetid swamp of jungle logic in the more primitive regions of the brain. This area is where the mammalian propensity for butting heads and establishing dominance hierarchies is lodged. A guitar teacher in Germany once complained to me that he no longer attended guitar conventions and their attendant competitions because every player seemed intent on demonstrating *"ich* bin der schnellste" (*I'm* the fastest!). A fixation on sheer athleticism at such events can seem to some the very antithesis of high art.

The late flamencologist Donn E. Pohren humorously, though ruefully, summed up this attitude in a way that has always made me laugh uproariously, except when it makes me sob inconsolably. Referring to the modern school of flamenco-guitar super-virtuosity promulgated by Sabicas and others, he pitied the poor up-and-coming guitarist facing such daunting competition: "His guitar, constantly nagging, seems to say 'practice me, you bastard, practice me, four, six, eight hours a day, or you'll never catch up with Sabicas or Escudero or Vélez or Serrano. You'll be second rate, a failure, your children won't eat. Practice, *venga*, get flashier, faster, screw the emotion, that doesn't sell, add some more notes to that *falseta*. . . . Put on that Sabicas record Jesus Christ how does he do it, he must never let up practice practice PRACTICE.'"[12]

Obviously, this is a somewhat extreme example of not-right thought. Fortunately, such impulses can be transcended. As Pepe said in the *Akron Beacon Journal* piece cited earlier, "I've never felt competitive toward anyone else but myself. I go as far as not liking guitar competitions. I've only judged one, just to make sure I really felt how I felt. Music is not a competitive thing. It's self-expression and a means of reaching your own soul."[13] Of course, music consists of sound, and only the right sound will reach our souls.

RIGHT SOUND

I have replaced the word *speech* with *sound* for the simple reason that the sound of the guitar is tantamount to the speech of an actor or the brush-

13. THE ROMERO TECHNIQUE

strokes of a painter. The sounds produced by the play of the fingers on the strings, directed by the mind, are the principal means of expression at a guitarist's disposal. But not just any sounds will do, and separating sheep sounds from goat sounds is what we are concerned with here. The kinds of sounds a musician elicits from the instrument say something about his or her state of being, and in turn they affect the performer's consciousness and that of others. In Indian classical music, the melodic element is called *raga*, a word that literally means "that which colors the mind." And so it does.

While still living in Hollywood, Angel used to go to the old DeKeyser music store to purchase Segovia's recordings because he admired his tone production and was influenced by it. Angel says that his father did not approve of this, but recall that Celedonio himself had spent hours listening to Segovia recordings when he was a young guitarist in Málaga. In truth, many guitarists have found Segovia's distinctive colorations very seductive.

Much of this effect involves the way one places the fingers on the strings, at the precise point where flesh and nail meet. This observation about fingers and strings has a lot to offer our conception of right sound. As Pepe reported in *Guitar Player*, Celedonio

> began his studies without nails and began teaching his sons the no-nail style "so that we would develop a good fingertip position and learn to color the sound using only the flesh. It's a lot harder to color with flesh, but once you've mastered it and you add just enough nail to make it possible to color with both flesh and nail, you find that you have a tremendous variety of color with the minimum change of hand position. I don't think I had nails until I was nine years old—and I was already playing concerts by then. When I play Renaissance music, I tend to use much more flesh than I use in later music. Here's where the ability to control the right hand is very important, because while Renaissance playing calls for this weak/strong alternation, the ideal of modern guitar playing is to be able to go from finger to finger with no audible difference—to carry a beautiful, legato line."[14]

It merits mentioning here that this statement reveals a subtle difference between Pepe's playing and Angel's. As he explains here, Pepe tends to keep his right hand in one place relative to the sound hole and achieve coloration through his fingertips. Angel prefers more dramatic contrasts in tone color and moves his right hand farther toward or away from the sound hole in order to achieve this effect (toward the sound hole, mellower; toward the bridge, more strident). In fact, he compares his coloration to Pepe's by contrasting Van Gogh's use of color to that of Monet. (For his part, Pepe is only too happy to be compared to Monet.)

Regardless of one's approach to tone color, one of the biggest sonic challenges the guitar has faced in the modern era is that of filling large concert halls. Here is where right sound has a crucial role to play, as Pepe explains: "If you have good projection and quality of tone, you can be heard in the biggest hall; you can make it feel like a living room. I strive to play in the same manner as when I'm alone."[15]

The heart of the matter is that whether one is playing in Carnegie Hall or the hallway of one's apartment, the sound should be the same. Achieving that consistency, Pepe contends, is possible only through the act of listening: "The silence upon which the work is preconceived in the performer's mind is like a painter's canvas. . . . The main thing I'm trying to do is awaken your sense of hearing. Really listen to yourselves when you play, the same way you hear other people play. . . . Desire for the sound triggers the movement, not vice versa."[16]

As the Romeros adjure their students, if your sound changes as you go faster, you are going too fast. The quality of the sound should remain the same, regardless of tempo. I recall once talking with a street musician in Munich years ago. He played classical guitar very well, and after giving him some money, I complimented him on his playing. I then told him that I had studied with Pepe Romero. His eyes lit up, and I fully expected that the next words out of his mouth would be about how fast Pepe could play. He surprised me by admiring instead the consistency of Pepe's tone production, that no matter how fast he played, each note had the same golden luster.[17] As Celin said, "Just give me a beautiful note!" Right sound is a beautiful sound, one whose fullness expresses a broad spectrum of overtones, from low to high, as a result of the proper placement of both flesh and nail on the string at the point of attack and a rapid follow-through. Ultimately, however, all the sounds one makes spring from the womb of inner silence, by means of right action.

13. THE ROMERO TECHNIQUE

RIGHT ACTION

Pepe has said that there are two ways to go out on stage: "One is believing you're the greatest guitarist in the world, and the other is simply to love the music and want to share that love with the audience. The first way is valid but will eventually fail you. Only the second way endures."[18]

Many players want to impress more than to move their listeners, and this preference can lead them to try to play faster than they are actually able to do. Pepe warns against this sort of forced effort because it will produce tension and strain that will wear out the mechanism. In a sense, it's like getting a loan you can't afford or maxing out your credit card, he says. Also one must maintain the proper hand position to avoid developing tension. As he once told me, cultivating a tense hand position is "like trying to walk in a very unnatural way."

Consequently, the Romeros promote a hand position that they view as distinct from that of Segovia, which, in Angel's opinion, can produce "a quite high-wristed, twisted kind of a hand."[19] Celin explained his father's approach to this crucial aspect of technique: "[Celedonio] always talked about the proper alignment of the right hand, not to do anything that was awkward or to make abrupt movements with the wrist. Rather, he emphasized holding the hand in the same way playing the guitar that one does for daily movements. It is very important never to hit the string with the fingers of the right hand when plucking them but rather to be firm but gentle. Projection is also important, to be able to project without forcing."[20]

Celino offers a valuable elaboration on this approach in his method book, *The Art of the Spanish Guitar*, in which he advises that "all our movements on the guitar have to feel like everyday movements, and most problems start when we think we have to do something 'fancy' or out of the ordinary.... Anyone can find a comfortable guitar position for their body type, as long as they do not disturb the natural movements of the arms, forearms, wrists, or hands."[21]

Augmenting one's sense of urgency about developing fleet fingers is a preoccupation with having a career. Here is where the Taoist method of "doing by not doing" is central to the Romero technique. This axiom, articulated by Lao-tzu in his *Tao Te Ching*, bears a strong resemblance to passages in chapter 2 of the *Bhagavad-Gita*, in which Krishna enjoins his disciple Arjuna to act without desire for the "fruits of action." This neatly defines right livelihood.

RIGHT LIVELIHOOD

Marsha Sinetar has written a self-help book titled *Do What You Love, the Money Will Follow*. To which my response is, maybe. History is replete with examples of people who were forced into occupations they didn't necessarily love but at which they became successful, and of ardent idealists who wound up starving in an unheated garret. Nonetheless, that title basically sums up this step on the Romero path. In *Vista Magazine*, Pepe explained,

> In order to study with me, a student must understand that he may never make a penny out of it, that he may never play a solo concert, and feel that that is not a problem for him . . . for the purpose of having a career that puts music in a place where it really is unnatural. You have to play for the moment and for the beauty exclusively, for the feeling it brings you. And then, if other people enjoy listening to what you have, you become a concert player. That's the way it was for us.[22]

Celin made this abundantly clear in a 1993 interview:

> To me, a good student is a person who really loves playing music, instead of talking about careers. If you love it, and you're good, your chances are pretty good for success. I like to record. I like to perform. I like to teach. At the same time, I'm not crazy about any of those things, either. I do it because I love it, but I'm not a fanatic about it. I play concerts for the fun of it, I teach for the fun of it. I like to record when it's fun. The moment those things are not fun, I don't like to do them.[23]

After all, the Romeros succeeded by putting first things first. As Pepe remarked about their ascent to fame, "We didn't really leave Spain to launch an international career. We left in search of freedom. An international career came after that."[24] But they never actually sought an international career; it sought them. Pepe expatiated on this principle thus: "I don't think any arts should be looked into as a business. If it happens, fine, but you have to go into it for what it does for you—like a religion or a marriage."[25]

13. THE ROMERO TECHNIQUE

An almost mystical principle is at work here, and most religions provide some scriptural reference to it. The basic idea of being "in the moment" is central to many spiritual traditions, especially Zen Buddhism, and has filtered into popular culture via such books as Alan Watts's 1971 classic, *Be Here Now*, and the late Robert Pirsig's equally renowned *Zen and the Art of Motorcycle Maintenance* (1974). Phil Jackson, the former head coach of the Los Angeles Lakers, cultivated such practices and encouraged his championship teams to embrace them, leading some to refer to him as the "Zen master."

Regardless of our relationship to Tao, Zen, and yoga (or the Lakers), the Romeros also emphasize a guitarist's need to remain focused on what really matters in the present. Zen masters, yogis, and the Romeros are not the only ones who have taught this truth. The sayings of Jesus include similar injunctions, for example, "Sufficient unto the day is the evil thereof" (Matt. 6:34). As with evil, so with psychophysiological tension, which grows more intense with our fixation on the future. "Tak[ing] therefore no thought for the morrow" (Matt. 6:34) may ultimately not seem like an entirely practical way to live, but as with most metaphysical maxims, there is a deeper kernel of meaning here that one has to extract from the coarse husk of literalism. Many people are not prepared to take this crucial step, however, a fact that led the gentle Galilean master to lament, "They seeing see not; and hearing they hear not, neither do they understand" (Matt. 13:13). No doubt the Romeros have harbored similar feelings after more than a few of the lessons and master classes they have given over the years!

In any case, that such admonitions can be found in very different religious and philosophical traditions, across large spans of time and space, suggests something derived from and universally applicable to human experience, not as a rigid dogma or revealed truth but in a spirit of thoughtful awareness.

At this point, some readers will protest that it is easy for someone to be this high-minded when he basically had a career before he knew there was such a thing as a guitar career. Celin once related to me that, in those early years in the United States, the Romeros were incredulous that anyone would actually pay them to do something they would gladly do for free. It was like being paid to smoke a cigar! In the end, careers are what happen when, like Celin, you're so absorbed in the creative act of music that others are drawn into your orbit by the gravitational pull of the effort you're making, assuming it's the right kind of effort.

RIGHT EFFORT

As the old saying goes, the only way to get to Carnegie Hall is practice, practice, practice. But practice does not make perfect. Only perfect practice makes perfect enough to get one to Carnegie Hall. Practice is not an absolute good, as poor practice can actually reinforce bad habits and retard progress. Toward the end of his life, Enrique Granados gave up practice altogether, not because he was in the habit of practicing poorly but because it forced him to think too much about what he was doing: "The more I practice, the worse I play," he said, with a mixture of exasperation and self-deprecating irony.[26] This is, in some respects, an enviable problem to have.

In any case, having achieved some measure of perfection, a performer need not try to overawe the audience with a demonstrative stage presence. As the *Omaha World-Herald* noted: "That [Pepe] Romero greatly admires pianist Arthur Rubinstein is not difficult to understand. Neither artist impresses with showy, virtuosic flourishes. His easy demeanor masks his considerable technique."[27] This is true of all the Romeros.

Above and beyond all other things, Pepe insists that "when you play [music], there's a feeling of joy." The master class in which he made this remark was covered by a Hartford, Connecticut, newspaper, which went on to report,

> Romero alternated between sitting in the front row and before the performing student to sitting alongside the student on stage. At times he snapped his fingers or slapped a chair back to capture the beat for the student, saying, "every note has a purpose—it comes to you and it comes from you." "Trust your instinct, really trust your feeling." "You have to give up the fear of making a mistake." "Now do it again and this time let it play you. You know what is missing? Magic! Let it happen to you." One student observed that "When he plays in concert, he opens the music *to* us. When he teaches us, he opens the music *in* us."[28]

There is something very Socratic about this process, but the only way the "inner" guitarist can emerge is through disciplined self-effort. Granados once warned his students to "continue working methodically, or you will get absolutely nowhere."[29] Angel has several times averred that though he is "a very emotional and sensitive person . . . at the same time in [his] guitar practice [he is] like Pythagoras, extremely mathematical."[30] He clearly acquired this penchant from Celedonio, who said that "studying the instrument is a step-by-step process which requires dedicated, systematic work with studies before [one] can approach the more demanding works."[31] However, he also advised those studying his method book "not to study too much, because the brain tires, and the body's strength does not have a chance to recover. A short, thorough period of study gives better results than a longer study of less depth. Use exactly the correct amount of strength, so as not to create tension and tiredness."[32] Pepe maintains that the "most important point is to be patient."[33]

Pepe further believes that one learns twice, as he remarked to me, "once when you're young, and again when you're old. There is inevitable wear and tear on the joints, and you have to adjust." He still practices several hours a day, not just repertoire but also technique, in order to stay in fighting trim. He believes his own fingers are as nimble as they ever were, but he is aware that they work differently than they did when he was young. Thus he is very devoted to the assiduous practice of scales, arpeggios, and etudes, especially those by Mauro Giuliani, Fernando Sor, and Matteo Carcassi.

Perhaps Angel, in an interview with Cindy Shubin, summed up right effort best: "There are a great deal of mathematics in the techniques that have to be solved so that you have to put your complete concentration and use your utmost common sense."[34] Concentration and common sense go hand in hand and are approached by becoming very conscious, very mindful of what one is doing.

RIGHT MINDFULNESS

Pepe says that he was born knowing how to play the guitar, which is quite an assertion. One doubts that knowledge of guitar playing per se can be genetically transmitted, as this would be consistent with the now-discredited theories of Jean-Baptiste Lamarck (1744–1829), who claimed that acquired traits could be passed from one generation to the next (in this case, from Celedonio to Pepe). Darwin later demonstrated, however, that what *can* be transmitted are genetic predispositions to pitch discrimination and memory, digital dexterity and coordination, and general intelligence. Possessing these traits in abundant measure and nurturing them in an environment conducive to their development will probably leave one feeling that she or he was born knowing how to play the instrument. It would induce Pepe to declare that he could play the guitar "almost as soon as [he] could pick it up," asserting, "It was actually my first language. It has been such a part of me from such an early age, that although I have fooled around with it, trying to learn another instrument, like a cello or piano, was an impossible struggle."[35]

Nonetheless, these advantages will count for little without right mindfulness, without careful attention to and conscious awareness of one's actions. Thus Pepe further reports that he would simply visualize what his father was doing and imitate it; he didn't have to be told, even if he was at times given specific instructions by his father and older brother. An adept learner, he early on became an equally adept instructor. Celedonio started giving Pepe students when he was only about nine years old. The way he taught his students then is the way he teaches them now: he observes, or is mindful of, what they are doing that differs from his own technique and then helps them to do it his way. This doesn't mean that he is forcing hands and fingers to look and function exactly like his own. Rather, he studies what does not seem to be working as effectively as it could and then derives from his own technique how this aspect of the student's playing could function most efficiently. There is an element of mechanical reasoning here, of understanding how things work, that we have observed in earlier generations of Romeros, even if it was applied to construction projects and not music.

Mindfulness is not restricted, however, to technique. One has to be similarly conscious of the realities that each piece of music presents. In an interview with *Guitar Player*, Pepe crystallized this aspect of right mindfulness: "I think that for a performer to give the best possible interpretation of a work, he must look as deeply as possible into the details of the composer's life and try to see life as the composer must have seen it. You have to get as close as you can to the feelings they had. In a sense, a musician is no different than an actor. If an actor is playing Macbeth, he must become

13. THE ROMERO TECHNIQUE

Macbeth—not himself, and not Shakespeare, but Macbeth. Therefore, . . . I must become the Gran Sonata."[36]

This process of being aware of the composer's intentions is much easier if the composer is still alive! Pepe goes on to note, "With Medina, Torroba, and Rodrigo, I studied specific musical problems and worked on things like counterpoint, harmony, and instrumentation. . . . We would talk about the kind of emotion each work triggers, and he would recollect how he felt when he was composing." And right mindfulness extends to playing music in a group. In this same article, Pepe discusses actual techniques for developing ensemble togetherness. The net effect of such awareness is that "when [the Romeros] work together, [they] know each other so well that a fifth personality emerges."[37]

It becomes clear that mindfulness involves an ability to project one's own consciousness into another person's body and mind, even his or her world, whether the person is living nearby or flourished hundreds of years ago. This requires what one might call "informed intuition." However, there is an even subtler aspect to this, and that is mindfulness of the phenomenon of the music itself, as something that seems to happen almost independently of human agency. Pepe expatiated on this facet as follows: "The sound of the guitar is like a very minute raindrop coming down from an absolutely clear sky—not out of the clouds, but out of nowhere. And when it hits the sea, it creates a tremendous explosion that envelops all of you, and that sound can have all the colors, all the emotions, everything in it. It is a magical, a wondrous sound."[38] What one takes away from such remarks is that there is an almost disembodied dimension to our experience of music, that it has an existence independent of our will or representation. Our job, ultimately, is to become mindful of the music that is *already there*, with or without us, and to become a sort of channel for it.

I clearly remember one lesson with Pepe where I was about to play a piece by Bach on which I had recently been working very hard. Just as my fingers approached the strings, Pepe abruptly stopped me, protesting that I was "thinking too much." I was somewhat nonplussed to discover that he could actually read my thoughts, though perhaps it wasn't too difficult a feat at that particular moment. Anyway, he then asked me to visualize the plane of the strings forming a window and to imagine that my fingers were raindrops striking that pane of glass. Where the music became more intense, the drops would strike the window more rapidly, and vice versa for less-intense passages. Of course, there were no markings in the score to guide such a visualization, so I would have to resort to spontaneous intuition, a modus operandi that was not customary for me.

Much to my surprise, I got through the piece with a good deal less effort and anxious suspense than usual. The music almost seemed to play itself—almost. Clearly, my careful preparation of the notes had made possible such spontaneity, but without the visualization, my rendition would have remained studied and somewhat labored. Only much later did I learn that this was also the way Granados taught, by giving his students visualizations as a guide, even (especially) if they had nothing to do with the music per se.[39] All of this can be summed up in a time-honored maxim: learn everything you can about a piece of music, and then be spontaneous.

Intellectual study and intuitive spontaneity thus constitute two sides of the mindfulness coin. Properly directing one's attention, that is, remaining mindful of what is truly important in both technique and repertoire, results from and contributes to the most important ingredient in the recipe for success: right concentration.

RIGHT CONCENTRATION

I distinctly remember a conversation with Celedonio many years ago in which he averred, in his calmly intense way, that the best antidote for nervousness was concentration. Angel said as much in an interview around that time: "Everything depends on concentration. Every piece of music is like an animal that can sense if a guitarist is afraid, like a dog that perceives a person's fear and bites him."[40]

But right concentration will prove elusive if one is not sure exactly what to concentrate on. Pepe explains this in a way that resembles *pranayama*, a means of yoga meditation involving control of the breath and "life force" (*prana*): "Concentrate not really on the playing, but on getting a smooth, even breath. As you play one string take the complete time to inhale, and on the next string take the full time to exhale. As you play, imagine your breath going into your forearms, making them warm."[41]

13. THE ROMERO TECHNIQUE

The meditative aspect of this teaching is abundantly clear in what he next counsels his students to do, namely,

> to visualize the notes written on a large staff, as if it were flowing above their heads. They are playing now with the eyes closed. He instructs them to keep their eyes shut and look about them, then to "read" the music from the visualized score. "Concentrate on feeling the string with your finger, its thickness and tension against the finger. Then push it. Memorize what it takes to move the string. Direct the energy from your mind into your fingers and not too much goes into your body—then you become tense. It is very, very important that the abdomen is relaxed at all times. Where the fingers are when they are inactive is very important. Tactual memory can really carry you through the performance. It leaves your mind free to be just a conductor, to be completely detached from your hands."[42]

Indeed, visualization is the key to right concentration, and Pepe makes this point over and over again. About forty years ago, his instructions to students were reported in the *La Jolla Light*: "Visualize perfection and develop the ultimate in concentration. Your fingers are ballet dancers. You make a mental movie of where they are to go and run this as you play. Visualize someone playing beautifully, imitate the facility with which s/he plays, and that person will become you."[43]

This undertaking may sound simple enough, but simplicity is not synonymous with ease. It requires concentration sired of repeated practice. Still, the method has worked innumerable times, and there are many Romero students today whose performing and teaching constitute an enduring testament to the efficacy of the Romero technique.

FOLLOWING IN THEIR FOOTSTEPS

As long ago as 1971, Celedonio remarked to the *Odessa American*, "We have past pupils in many leading universities throughout the country, Tokyo and Hong Kong, who are now leading professors of guitar."[44] The intervening forty-five years have witnessed a steady increase in the number of such successful "past pupils." Notable among these from the early years in Hollywood is Christopher Parkening (1947–). He started studying with Celedonio in 1958, at age eleven, and was soon taking lessons with Pepe as well. Although many commentators have made much of his later association with Andrés Segovia, by Parkening's own admission, the Romeros "were wonderful teachers who helped [him] lay a strong technical foundation."[45] Thus equipped, at age fourteen he was the first guitarist to win the Young Musicians Federation competition in Los Angeles, and the following year he performed the Concerto in D Major by Mario Castelnuovo-Tedesco, all before participating in a Segovia master class at Berkeley in 1964. His discography is long and distinguished, and he has also published a popular method book, as well as several volumes of music he has edited and arranged. He taught for several years at USC and Montana State University, Bozeman, and he now heads up a very successful guitar program as Distinguished Professor of Music at Pepperdine University in Malibu.

The highly influential guitar pedagogue Frederick Noad also studied with the Romeros during their early years in the United States. He went on to publish very popular guitar methods as well as several volumes of music from the Renaissance, Baroque, classical, and romantic periods, which he edited. Other successful concert artists indebted to formative Romero guidance include Vincenzo Macaluso, recording artist and master of the ten-string guitar, and Robert Guthrie, a renowned recitalist who has also performed on National Public Radio and was the subject of a PBS documentary. He has taught at Yale University, the Boston Conservatory, and the Aspen Music Festival. He is now head of the guitar program at Southern Methodist University in Dallas, Texas. I studied briefly with him in 1978 and can attest to his excellence as a teacher and performer.

Given Pepe's long association with USC, it comes as no surprise that the guitar program there has produced a bumper crop of leading guitarists, most notably William Kanengiser and Scott Tennant, the founding members of the celebrated Los Angeles Guitar Quartet (LAGQ). This ensemble was formed in 1980 and has charted its own course, emphasizing crossover arrangements and original transcriptions rather than simply becoming clones of the Romeros. Among the LAGQ's many successful recordings, the 2004 CD *Guitar Heroes* won a Grammy for Best Classical Crossover Album. John Dearman, who plays the seven-string guitar, is also a Romero disciple and longtime member of the group. He is on the guitar faculty at California State University, Northridge, as well as at El Camino College in Torrance. Rounding out the quartet is Matthew Greif, who studied in Spain with Cel-

13. THE ROMERO TECHNIQUE

edonio and Pepe and is on the guitar faculty at California State University, Dominguez Hills. He also teaches guitar at El Camino College. Greif joined the LAGQ in 2006, taking the chair previously occupied by Romero protégée Anisa Angarola (1980–90) and then Andrew York (1990–2006).

The Romeros never require conformity, instead seeking to bring out each person's own musical personality. At the same time, they also recognize that imperfect technique will impede rather than facilitate one's development. Thus despite Pepe's indifference to such events, both Kanengiser and Tennant have won prestigious international competitions, in Toronto and Tokyo, respectively, and they maintain thriving solo careers alongside their activities with the LAGQ. In addition to their solo albums, both have made signal contributions to guitar pedagogy, Tennant with his multivolume method *Pumping Nylon: The Classical Guitarist's Technique Handbook* (Book/DVD/CD, Alfred Music, 1995–) and Kanengiser with his educational videos *Classical Guitar Mastery* (DVD, Hot Licks, 2005), *Effortless Classical Guitar* (DVD, Hot Licks, 2006), and *Classical Guitar and Beyond* (DVD, Mel Bay, 2007). They are both professors of guitar at the USC Thornton School of Music and give master classes nationally and internationally. (I studied privately with Kanengiser in the early 1980s, in preparation for entering the master's program at UCSD to work with Pepe and Celin. He is a superb teacher.)

Other Romero students who head guitar programs in Southern California include Martha Masters, at California State University, Fullerton (she has also served as president of the Guitar Foundation of America); Randy Pile at Saddleback College; Scott Morris at California State University, Dominguez Hills; and Eric Foster at the University of San Diego. Pepe's son-in-law Greg Shirer is an associate professor in the San Diego Community College District and has a large online presence teaching Pepe's method. And the Romero-family tradition of influential teaching has not ended with Celedonio's sons and their students. Celino Romero has emerged as a sought-after teacher in his own right, and he teaches master classes across the United States and abroad, often with his cousin Lito.

It's safe to say that, sixty years after their arrival here, the Romeros have basically colonized Southern California, but their domain extends throughout the United States and to Europe and Asia. Alex Dunn, who studied with Pepe and Celin at UCSD, has taught guitar for many years at the University of Victoria in British Columbia, Canada, and he played a crucial role in arranging for the honorary doctorates awarded Celedonio and Pepe by that school. Robert Ward teaches at Northeastern University in Boston, while Hadley Heavin is a guitar instructor at the University of Nebraska, Omaha. William Krause, a former Romero student at USC, is an outstanding performer and teacher at Hollins University in Virginia, and he is also the leading musicological authority on Torroba, having coauthored (with me) an Oxford biography on that topic; he is also conducting extensive research on Turina, in preparation for a book on that composer.

Pepe has taught at the Salzburg Summer Academy, the Schleswig-Holstein Festival, and the Córdoba Guitar Festival; along with the quartet, he has given master classes elsewhere throughout Europe and in China, Korea, and Japan. Every summer the quartet conducts a weeklong master class, named after Celedonio, at Oklahoma City University's Wanda L. Bass School of Music, which awarded Celin an honorary doctorate in 2017. They also teach similar classes in Málaga. Among Pepe's most notable disciples in Spain is Vicente Coves, who collaborated with his guru on groundbreaking recordings for the Naxos label of guitar works by Torroba, whose concertos are conducted by Vicente's gifted brother, Manuel Coves, a great champion and interpreter of Spanish opera and zarzuela. Vicente's accomplishments have won recognition from Moscow's Tchaikovsky Conservatory, which conferred on him the Rubinstein Medal, one of the most prestigious awards in the world of classical music. Alexander Sergei Ramírez studied in master classes with Pepe first in Düsseldorf and then at the Mozarteum. He is now professor of guitar at the Robert Schumann Hochschule in Düsseldorf and has made numerous recordings.

* * *

Of course, having elegant technique is pointless without having an equally elegant—and original—repertoire to play. The Romeros have enriched the guitar's literature with numerous works for solo guitar, guitar quartet, and concertos. It is this enduring aspect of their legacy to which we now shift our mindful awareness.

CHAPTER 14

THE ROMERO REPERTOIRE

Despite the guitar's five-hundred-year pedigree, the instrument's repertoire has pursued a course rather consistently on the margins of mainstream classical music, largely because the only people who composed for it were themselves guitarists. Every major guitarist of the twentieth century has had to confront and address this condition if she or he wanted spend time "downtown" rather than remain in the musical "suburbs." And this meant persuading nonguitarist composers to write for an instrument with which they were not familiar: because it is not an orchestral instrument, writing for it was not taught in traditional classes on instrumentation. Thus any guitarist who wanted to commission works from mainstream composers would also have to provide some guidance along the way. And many leading guitarists have been willing to do so. Of course, as they have done throughout history, guitarists continue to compose music for their chosen instrument, and the Romeros are no exception.

In addition to the composition of new works, transcribing and arranging opened up vast tracts of virgin territory for guitarists to cultivate; moreover, there were neglected byways and roads less traveled in the guitar repertoire itself that guitarists could explore, discovering noncanonic works of interest to revive and make their own. Finally, though improvisation increasingly became a lost art among classical performers in the twentieth century, any guitarist with a deep understanding of folk and popular musical traditions might well be able to spice up her or his program with a perfunctory rendition of something almost certain to please an audience. For guitarists, flamenco was an obvious, if not easy or common, choice. In the era of recording, improvisations and unnotated music could also take on a permanence they never had previously.

In short, the five principal ways of expanding the repertoire during the last century have been commissioning, composing, arranging, reviving, or improvising it. The Romero repertoire embraces all these approaches, and I survey them below. Their repertoire is at once deeply connected to traditional guitar music and yet departs from it in distinctive, even innovative, ways.

As soloists, the Romeros have tended to emphasize the music they love most, and that is the core Spanish repertoire from the sixteenth to twentieth centuries. This music is their meat and potatoes. They are great interpreters of the works of Milán, Sanz, Sor, Tárrega, Rodrigo, Turina, and Torroba, as well as Albéniz and Granados, not to mention flamenco. Celedonio has written several very effective solo pieces and concertos as well. In addition, they display a remarkable affinity for the music of Bach, as well as the Italian Mauro Giuliani. Pepe goes so far as to assert that "Giuliani is the strongest pillar in the guitar world, in his use of technique, blending of the guitar with other instruments, and his flair for composition."[1]

By contrast, rigorously atonal, serial, or aleatoric music is simply not to the Romeros' liking, and they would bring no conviction, much less love, to it if they programmed it, which they do not. In this sense, their solo programming strongly resembles Segovia's. Speaking of his years teaching at the University of California, San Diego, which has a large reputation for avant-garde music, Pepe explained, "Contemporary music per se is neither more nor less difficult than other music. As in any period, we have to be selective, to find music with which we identify, music we can make our own."[2]

This was a politic and somewhat circumlocutive way of saying that they do not identify with contemporary music à la UCSD, and it is not their own. Rodrigo more directly summed up their feelings, as well as his own, when he referred to contemporary music as "excessively cerebral" and called for a music that was more "humane, more attentive to natural sensibilities,

14. THE ROMERO REPERTOIRE

more expressive and less driven by a desire for novelty, and above all more independent of what many have called the 'tyranny of modern art.'"[3]

Seneca the Younger famously remarked that "he who is everywhere is nowhere."[4] This axiom can be adapted to many purposes. "He who loves everything loves nothing" might well apply to the Romeros. They have succeeded in large measure because they don't pretend to love all kinds of music or attempt to play it simply to satisfy the preferences of some people in the audience. As Pepe once adjured me, "Play the music you love the way you love to hear it played." This is a variation on the Golden Rule, and audiences respond favorably to such genuineness.

Not everyone approves of these rather conservative inclinations. In fact, guitarists already steeped in the canon are often on the lookout for new repertoire, for music they can play that will separate them from the herd. As a consequence, they may gravitate toward more experimental programming. Thus the *Arizona Daily Star* reported the following concerning a solo recital by Pepe: "One of Tucson's leading guitar mavens tried to stifle his disappointment when he saw the program—an almost all-Spanish and Latin American affair typical of Segovia and the first generation of his followers. No, Romero did not play Britten or Walton or Henze," unlike Julian Bream, for instance. However, the reviewer went on to note that "in his chosen repertory, he was masterful."[5]

It is no wonder that, concerning a Pepe recital at a Guitar Foundation of America convention, one reporter noted, "The audience Friday night contained a larger proportion of non-guitarists than did [Michael] Lorimer's. Accordingly, Romero chose music that could be readily understood and appreciated by such an audience."[6] In a review of Pepe's album *La Paloma*, a recording of Spanish and Latin American favorites, critic John Duarte identified one persistent reason for this approach: "Efforts to persuade guitar-lovers to embrace the unfamiliar are all too often box office failures or produce, at best, minimal profit."[7]

None of this was lost on the *New York Times*, which remarked in 1976 that "since their debut [in 1961, they have been] offering shrewdly devised programs that do not change essentially in content. In this they are undoubtedly wise, for their latest concert here, in Alice Tully Hall on Thursday night, was enjoyable. . . . Together they created a wonderful racket." However, "if there was any dissatisfaction with the evening, it was in the conventionality of the program. In the last few seasons, the Omega and Zarate Guitar Quartets have made their debuts here, bringing a more sophisticated and contemporary repertory and playing it with a chamber-music delicacy. It has made the Romero kind of concert a bit old-fashioned."[8] And that was over forty years ago!

Indeed, going through Romero programs from the 1960s to the present day reveals a striking consistency in this regard. The quartet programs remain a bit like a vaudeville show in that they consist of a variety of musicals "acts." A Romero Quartet concert features a cornucopia of pieces for one, two, or four guitarists. There was even a time when they played trios, if one member of the group was unavailable. But although the solos may have conformed more or less to the Segovia repertoire, there was an obvious difference here, and that was the idea of a quartet. As Pepe explained to one reviewer, this sort of ensemble "did not exist before. Composers wrote for one or two guitars, not four." The only real precedent for a guitar quartet per se was in flamenco performances where, in earlier times, the absence of amplifiers might well necessitate four guitarists to prevail over the clamor of voices, hands, castanets, and feet. As Pepe himself clarified in this same interview: "Only when flamenco was taken to the concert stage did the dancers, who wanted more sound, use more than one guitarist. But the guitarists played almost the same thing in unison. In the 19th century there were almost always two guitars, sometimes three guitars, but almost always two."[9]

Imitation is the sincerest form of flattery, and in the past three decades there has been a proliferation of guitar quartets, not only in Los Angeles but also in San Francisco, Minneapolis, Stockholm, and many other locales. The Romeros created not only a new kind of ensemble but also an entirely new repertoire. Yet, though there are now many guitar quartets in the world (and, yes, the Zarate and the Omega Quartets are still around), the Romero Quartet remains unique.

Nonetheless, some may have felt in the beginning that the Romero "show" was a flash-in-the-pan phenomenon that would not last, that once the newness of it wore off, audiences would lose interest. Instead, the Romeros are still going strong because there is an enduring, transgenerational appeal to the music they play and the way they play it. If there is a notable persistence of a core repertoire in their programs over the decades, it results from practical necessity. First, the guitar repertoire is finite and includes certain standards guitarists love to play and audiences want to hear. Second, when a performer is giving 150–200 concerts a year, half of them solo appearances, she or he simply doesn't have time to prepare completely different programs each season. Keeping in mind these two facts will make all the more remarkable the sheer quantity of new or obscure music the Romeros have actually premiered and recorded over the years.

In truth, the Romeros *have* been a driving force in the creation of serious new repertoire and are not simply purveyors of guitar classics. But they have chosen to do this mostly in the sphere of collaborative music, as a quartet and particularly with orchestra.

COMMISSIONS

Our focus in this section will be on several of the enduring works the Romeros have commissioned for their quartet or for one or more guitars and orchestra. The survey will embrace not only works that they themselves requested but also those that may have been commissioned by others but were written for them. In a couple of instances, the works were actually written for other artists to premiere, but the Romeros have made what I consider to be definitive recordings of them.

The Romeros long had a close and productive relationship with Rodrigo, one of Spain's leading composers in the twentieth century. Blind from age three, Rodrigo nonetheless forged ahead to compose numerous works for piano (which he played very well), orchestra, guitar, and especially guitar and orchestra. Rodrigo's most celebrated work is undoubtedly his *Concierto de Aranjuez*, inspired by the famous palace and gardens south of Madrid, where the composer and his wife spent many pleasant hours.

Though the work was premiered in Barcelona by Regino Sáinz de la Maza in 1940, we have seen that first Angel and then Pepe championed it in several classic recordings and in innumerable performances (Celino now performs it regularly). This fact, in tandem with the sheer novelty of a guitar quartet and a growing friendship with the Romeros, persuaded Rodrigo to compose works for them.

In the mid-1960s, Celedonio wrote to Rodrigo asking him to compose music for the quartet, an invitation Rodrigo fortunately accepted. Celedonio introduced himself by reminding the composer that they had met many years earlier, at an event sponsored by the Ateneo de Sevilla in which Rodrigo spoke and Celedonio played. Rodrigo immediately saw the potential of a collaboration with the Romeros and set about writing music for them. He wrote the following to the Romeros' Columbia Artists manager, Herb Fox, on October 29, 1966: "As I said in my former letters, I have decided to start immediately with the composition of the four guitar Concerto for the Romeros, postponing the composition of all the other works I was commissioned with."[10]

This work was the *Concierto andaluz*, for four guitars and orchestra, which they premiered on November 18, 1967, with the San Antonio Symphony, under the baton of family friend Victor Alessandro (Angel played the *Aranjuez* on this same program). The title of this major work was actually Celedonio's idea, as he wanted a musical homage to his native Andalusia that would include characteristic songs and dances, as a sort of musical portrait of the region. The Romeros soon went on to record the *Andaluz* and *Aranjuez* on the Mercury label, and this album remains one of their best and most iconic recordings.[11]

The concerto sounds very Spanish from the first note to the last, but it is not based on preexisting melodies; rather, Rodrigo has freely composed themes that nonetheless evoke the bolero, *sevillanas*, *zapateado*, and fandango. As was the case with the *Aranjuez*, Rodrigo adheres to the traditional concerto structure of three movements, fast, slow, fast. Those familiar with the *Aranjuez* immediately note, however, that this middle movement is not nearly as dramatic, as it does not climax in a sort of cri de coeur laden with tragic desperation followed by muted resignation. Nonetheless, it produces a lyrically tranquil mood that contrasts effectively with the very dancelike outer movements, brimming as they are with the sort of flamenco effects one anticipates in an "Andalusian concerto."

It is more than a little ironic that a fan of the *Andaluz* was none other than Generalísimo Francisco Franco. Rodrigo's wife, Vicky, wrote to the Romeros on August 4, 1972, concerning a ballet choreography of the *Andaluz* for a performance at the Palacio de La Granja. The occasion was an annual reception that Franco held there for members of the government and diplomatic corps. The production, using recorded music, proved to be a hit, which was really saying something in the case of the Franco, who took little interest in music. Vicky notes that the dictator, who almost never attended concerts, actually congratulated the dancers and said he would like to see it again sometime. Rodrigo was very pleased with the results of their collaboration, and Vicky reported on his plans to write another concerto

14. THE ROMERO REPERTOIRE

for the Romeros, whom he "love[d] and admire[d] so much." As it turned out, he composed a solo concerto for Pepe and then provided thematic raw material for another, fleshed out and premiered by Angel.

One might well wonder how Rodrigo, a blind nonguitarist, was able to compose so effectively for the guitar. Having worked closely with him, Pepe states that he had a special Braille machine for sketching out his ideas. As he explained to the Ambassador Auditorium's newsletter, "Then he dictates the whole thing, without the Braille reminders, to a copyist. He dictates the piccolo, first flute, second flute, etc., right down the score. Everything is in his mind. I take the music he sends me and I play it for him. In some places, I come up with alternate ways to play certain passages, closer to what I think he wants to say—maybe some re-voicing of chords or perhaps a little different technique to use on the guitar."[12]

The *Concierto para una fiesta* was composed for Pepe but commissioned by William and Carol McKay of Fort Worth on the occasion of their two daughters' debutante ball, in 1983 (the "fiesta" to which the title refers). The McKays were a prosperous ranching family who clearly thought this would be a very distinctive and classy way to introduce their daughters to polite society. Pepe gave the premiere on March 5, 1983, with the Fort Worth Chamber Orchestra at the McKays' debut party in the ballroom of Redglea County Club.

During this period, there was a very popular prime-time television soap opera called *Dallas*, starring Larry Hagman. It presented viewers with a weekly glimpse into the supposedly sordid and selfish world of well-to-do Texans. The genesis of this concerto provides a refreshing rebuttal to that tawdry narrative. In fact, one journalistic commentator at the time remarked, "The composition already is going a long way toward changing the image of Texas."[13] The *Dallas* TV series was a huge hit in Germany, so not surprisingly an article in *Stern* magazine commented that

> *Dallas* fans have to change their views. Those who were pretty sure all the time that Texas' high society is satisfying its cultural needs only with cocktails, intrigues, and country music are set right by a colleague from the same branch as J.R. The reason is: oil millionaire William McKay has two charming daughters, Alden Elizabeth and Lauri Ann, who were allowed a small wish from Papá on the occasion of their debutante ball. They had no Porsche, no diamonds from Tiffany on their wish list, but a guitar concerto for them by Joaquín Rodrigo.[14]

PART 4. LEGACY

To be sure, Rodrigo received $20,000 for his composition, and the entire event cost the McKays upward of five times that much—more than either a Porsche or Tiffany jewelry would have cost at that time. Concerning the music itself, Pepe declared that the Rodrigo *Fiesta* is "by far the most difficult piece ever written for the guitar."[15] Pepe once confided to John Duarte something of the work's genesis,

> [Rodrigo and I] always had a ritual of smoking cigars together. [The composer said,] "You know I am going to die soon, but, you will die soon too because everyone dies. And then think how much fun we are going to have smoking our cigars and saying—'Look at those poor bastards down there trying to play our piece.'" . . . Though standards rise from year to year, it may be near the truth for some time. After some 35 years of reviewing I am left without an adequate superlative to describe Pepe Romero's performance.[16]

The first movement features themes from Valencia, which is logical insofar as Rodrigo himself was also Valencian. The restlessly introspective second movement provides more rhythmic than lyric interest and is animated by the alternation of 6/8 and 5/8 and complex groupings of beats within each measure. The final movement bursts forth with *sevillanas*-inspired rhythms and tunes, which provide the musical "fiesta" we have awaited.

Another Rodrigo concerto merits our brief attention here, and that is the *Concierto madrigal* for two guitars and orchestra. This was originally composed for the duo of Ida Presti and Alexandre Lagoya, but it was the duo of Pepe and Angel that finally premiered and recorded it (Pepe and Celino have now performed it several times). This piece celebrates the Spanish musical heritage by using historical melodies and rhythms in the context of a neoclassical language that is distinctively Rodrigo's. It also features some of the most breathtakingly difficult guitar music written up to that time. John Duarte was moved to say of this recording that "as a display of guitar playing it is staggering."[17]

During the 1983–84 season, the Ambassador Foundation in Pasadena presented a program of works in honor of "the two great romantic Spanish composers of our time, Rodrigo and Moreno Torroba." Though Rodrigo was still alive and composing, Torroba had passed away in November 1982. The program would feature the *Concierto andaluz* and Torroba's *Tonada concertante*, with Angel as soloist. Pepe also invited soprano Elly Ameling to sing songs by

14. THE ROMERO REPERTOIRE

Rodrigo; in addition, Pepe and that composer's son-in-law, violinist Agustín Leon Ara, gave the world premiere of Rodrigo's *Serenata al alba del día*.

In the Ambassador publicity materials cited earlier, Pepe observed, "Torroba was a little more placid, with a somewhat nostalgic quality to his music, while Rodrigo has a certain feeling of unrest. I believe Torroba composed thinking of the past, and Rodrigo was always searching for the future."[18] On another occasion, Pepe remarked, "If we think of the guitar as a temple, I would say two of the strongest pillars are Rodrigo and Torroba."[19]

Indeed, Federico Moreno Torroba was another towering figure in twentieth-century Spanish music, and Rodrigo held him in affectionately high regard.[20] Pepe reports that when Torroba died in 1982, Rodrigo called him with the news, crying as he announced, "A giant has died." Pepe said that it was "amazing to see the warmth between these two great men, how they spoke and felt about each other."[21] Although I digress a bit in doing so, it merits pointing out that composers like Torroba and Rodrigo had been on the other side of the political divide from the Romero family during the civil war. I once inquired of Celin if the subject of political allegiances ever come up, or did it just not matter? He responded, "I don't recall hearing any political discussion, any talk about the Franco regime, between those composers and us. Torroba talked a lot about music as well as the difficult situation musicians in Spain faced, how hard it was to survive. But there was no discussion of politics per se." As mentioned in an earlier chapter, this silence was part of a larger trend in postwar Spain called the Gran Olvido, or "great forgetting," by which these contentious subjects were simply not brought up for fear of resurrecting ghosts of the past. The Romeros' collaboration with Rodrigo and Torroba remained untainted, or at least unstrained, by politics. It was focused on music and friendship.

Torroba composed about one hundred works for the guitar or guitars, but his musical legacy rests very securely on the nearly seventy works he composed for the stage, mostly a type of Spanish operetta called zarzuela. The period 1850–1950 was the golden age of the zarzuela, and Torroba was one of the most prolific and successful of zarzuela composers, known for such masterworks in the genre as *Luisa Fernanda* (1932) and *La chulapona* (1934). Segovia approached him as early as 1920 to compose for the guitar, and Torroba complied with a collection of pieces that are now standard repertoire. However, unlike Rodrigo, he was slow to write for guitar and orchestra, not meeting this challenge until the 1960s. He composed the brilliantly virtuosic and evocative *Diálogos para guitarra y orquesta* for Segovia, who never performed it. Though Michael Lorimer premiered it in 1977, Pepe made the first recording in 1980, on the Philips label, one that Segovia apparently found not only impressive but also deeply moving.[22]

Constructing a concerto as a series of "dialogues" between the guitar and the orchestra is not only an appealing idea but also the best way to allow the guitar to be heard. Regardless of this work's rather abstract title, however, its Spanish character is unmistakable. Torroba's orchestra includes the usual complement of strings and woodwinds, in addition to trumpet, percussion, celesta, and harp. This distinctive ensemble provides plenty of tone color but is not so large as to overwhelm the soloist.

The first movement is marked "Allegretto, comodo" and commences with a lighthearted melody in the winds and celesta, which prepares the way for the solo guitar's presentation of yet another component of the opening theme group. Its symmetrical phrasing and modality suggest Spanish folklore. The guitarist also introduces a contrasting secondary theme, in triple meter and more reflective in nature. Throughout Torroba skillfully develops his themes in both the guitar and the orchestra. The second movement is marked Andantino mosso and exhibits the triple meter typical of Spanish folk music. Again Torroba makes colorful use of woodwinds and percussion in laying out Spanish rhythms reminiscent of the *seguidillas*, though his harmonic idiom is very modern. The guitar soon answers with its distinctively folkloric theme; in fact, solo-guitar passages dominate this movement, though occasional interjections from the orchestra continue the impression of a dialogue.

An atmospheric Andante precedes the finale. This captivating essay is an arrangement of *Romance de los pinos*, a solo composed for Segovia in the 1950s. A dreamy, meditative mood prevails, and everything about the writing suggests a true romance of the pines. The movement is basically a series of variations on this number.

The lighthearted Allegro wastes no time shifting into high gear, with its rocketing scales in the winds and syncopated punctuations in the strings. The music has a strongly flamenco character, and the digital pyrotechnics this movement demands of the soloist constitute the supreme test of a guitarist's agility.

John Duarte was a critic not always easy to please, and one certainly unafraid to provide an unvarnished critique of anything that did not pass

14. THE ROMERO REPERTOIRE

muster with him, especially in regard to repertoire he considered too conventional, as well as to tempos he deemed inappropriate. Thus it really meant something when he wrote of the *Diálogos* recording,

> Pepe Romero plays with stunning skill and, this being very much his home ground, considerable sensitivity and elegance; his rapid passagework has the cleanness of a surgeon's scalpel—I'm sure Segovia would have taken it with the cursor higher up the metronome [i.e., slower]—and his tone is of unexceptionable purity. I number this among the finest guitar-concerto recordings I have ever heard—no profound message but warmly attractive music, marvelously played by all concerned and incredibly well balanced and recorded.[23]

Torroba wrote two guitar concertos for notable flamenco guitarists. One was the *Fantasía flamenca*, which premiered in 1976 at Carnegie Hall, with Mario Escudero as soloist. But the first such work he composed emerged perhaps two decades earlier and was dedicated to the great virtuoso Sabicas: the *Concierto en flamenco*. Writing a "flamenco concerto" is difficult because it requires a soloist of exceptional abilities. Most flamenco guitarists are not accustomed to operating in the classical milieu of the symphony orchestra, and classical guitarists generally do not play flamenco. This sort of music making is as alien to the classical guitarist as a symphony orchestra is to the flamenco guitarist. Pepe is justly famous for his masterful interpretations of both classical and flamenco repertoires; thus his rendering of Sabicas's inspirations conveys not only the precision of his technique but also the emotional directness and sincerity of Sabicas's music.[24] There are hazards inherent in this repertoire for a person of Pepe's talents, however; as he has confessed, he does not play any flamenco concerto from memory but rather uses the music so that his natural tendency to improvise does not lead him astray!

The first movement begins with an orchestral introduction that is both reflective and emotionally charged. The guitarist and orchestra then elaborate on themes from the *fandango de Huelva*. The second movement presents a stirring rhapsody on the *farruca*, a *palo* in duple meter that is only danced, not sung. The third movement is a beautiful *alegrías*, whose very name suggests the mood of gaiety and high spirits that prevails here. The *bulerías* is the most animated of *palos* and dominates the final movement, bringing this flamenco concerto to a thrilling conclusion.

In fact, by the 1970s, the Romeros had taken Segovia's place as the go-to guitarists for Torroba's musical inspirations, and in a letter of January 5, 1977, Torroba wrote to Celedonio explaining that though Segovia had previously provided the impetus for his guitar compositions, now "[the Romeros were] all of extraordinary value to [him], not only as artists but also as promoters of a modern repertoire" that he had have written for them "with the greatest devotion."[25]

During the period 1975–80, Torroba composed a concerto titled *Tonada concertante*, a *tonada* being a type of theatrical song of the eighteenth century. In 1982, Angel premiered the *Tonada concertante*, dedicated to Celedonio, and made the first recording of the *Homenaje a la seguidilla* (premiered by Irma Constanzo in 1975 but later dedicated to Angel). Torroba had every reason to be completely satisfied with these renditions, and the Romeros thus developed a very close and warm friendship with him. (Pepe has recorded these concertos on the Naxos label. See appendix 3 for information on all these recordings.) This resulted in, among other collaborations, a concerto composed specifically for them, the *Concierto ibérico* for four guitars and orchestra. The Romeros actually requested the work from him in a letter dated May 10, 1973, and in a response of January 3, 1974, he said he had completed the work.

The *Ibérico* was clearly inspired by Rodrigo's *Andaluz*, and Torroba found writing for this combination rewarding because four guitars can hold their own against an orchestra more effectively than one. His "Iberian Concerto" contains evocations of flamenco but also of Castile and even the Basque country, thus embracing his peninsular subject.

The Romeros premiered the piece in Vancouver on November 19, 1975, and it went on to several subsequent performances in North America. Its Spanish premiere took place on November 17, 1979, at the Teatro Real, where it again received critical acclaim. One critic commented that the concerto's "structure is well defined and the work is very accessible, as the public demonstrated with repeated manifestations of its enthusiasm."[26]

I note that this preference for formal clarity was a trait of musical aesthetics during the Franco era and the neoclassicism embraced by many of the composers of that epoch in Spain, all of whom were influenced to some extent by Falla's example. Torroba himself shed valuable light on the *Concierto ibérico* in a 1980 interview, just after the works were recorded by the

Romeros on the Philips label, with Neville Marriner leading the Academy of St. Martin-in-the-Fields: "I particularly like to compose for orchestra and guitar, but even more so for four guitars. . . . So many Spanish composers like myself have written concertos for guitar and orchestra because the music embodies the characteristics of the traditional Spanish sound. It is full of life, both gay and happy. It represents Spain."[27] The composer went on to assert that this rendition of the *Concierto ibérico* was the best that he had heard and that he was "tremendously satisfied" with it.[28]

The Romeros themselves were deeply convinced of the merit of Torroba's concerto. "'People were very enthusiastic when they heard it,' said Celedonio Romero. 'Ibérico' is a jewel of a piece for the soloists. It represents different parts of Spain, Castile and the Basque country, and for example in the last movement some of the rhythms come from Andalusia. This concerto delves deep into the 'feeling' of Spain.'"[29]

Pepe, the soloist for this recording, explained: "Torroba is a very nationalistic composer. He is a man who has never left the roots of traditional Spanish music. Because he has written so much music for the voice, he writes for the guitar in a way that makes use of actually the most difficult thing to do with it—the legato—to make the guitar sing."[30]

Torroba chimed in: "'Ibérico' is traditional Spanish music. Listen to its modulations, cadenzas, cadences, rhythms, and neo-classical harmonies. I have illustrated the harmonic evolution which has taken place in Spanish music during my own lifetime."[31]

Ever an astute observer of contemporary Spanish music, musicologist and composer Enrique Franco offered this praise: "Those staves, intended for those who play them today, the Romeros, obey the premises of simplicity, *españolismo*, popular traits, and suitable instrumentation typical of Moreno Torroba, spontaneous composer, of a fluid vein."[32] Unlike Rodrigo, however, Torroba wrote music for the quartet by itself, especially the suites *Ráfagas* (1976) and *Estampas* (1979). A *ráfaga* is a sudden, strong wind, and these pieces present gusts of lyric inspiration based, as always in Torroba, on Spanish folklore, though its four movements bear rather generic labels: Adagio, Allegretto calmo, Allegertto mosso-Allegro, Vivace. On the other hand, *Estampas*, or "prints," are brief vignettes of daily life and feature very evocative titles: "Bailando un Fandango charro" (Dancing a cowboy fandango); "Remanso" (Quiet place); "La ciega" (The blind woman); "Fiesta en el pueblo" (Village festival); "Amanecer" (Dawn); "La boda" (The wedding); "Camino del Molino" (Mill Road); and "Juegos infantiles" (Children's games). Another quartet work, *Sonatina trianera* (1980), was inspired by the Triana district of Seville, a cradle of flamenco and also an area in which the Romeros lived for a time. The *sevillanas* and *bulerías* provide musical inspiration here. The work is dedicated to Celin, who plays the bass part, and also features castanets, to be played by the one and only Angelita, of course. Yet another quartet composed by Torroba for the Romeros was *Sonata-Fantasía II* (1976), a sequel to his first *Sonata-Fantasía* (1953), for guitar solo, which had provided much of the thematic material for the *Diálogos* concerto. One other Torroba orchestral work closely associated with the Romeros is the composer's arrangement of his evergreen favorite *Sonatina* as a sort of concerto. This is one of Celin's specialties, and having seen him perform the work in Pasadena, I can see why Torroba was pleased with the effect it produced.

Though Rodrigo and Torroba are undoubtedly the two most famous Spanish composers with whom they have collaborated, the Romeros have also commissioned and/or premiered original works by other distinguished compatriots, including Francisco de Madina, José Muñoz Molleda, Xavier Montsalvatge, and especially Lorenzo Palomo.

Francisco de Madina (1907–72) was actually a priest and hailed from the Basque region (his Basque name was Aita Madina). The Romeros met him quite by chance in New York in 1967, where he was the father superior of a Residence House in the Bronx. They soon developed a fast friendship, and he was inspired by the Romeros to dedicate himself to guitar composition, his first work being a solo suite (*Bucolic Suite*) for Celedonio. This piece was followed by the *Danza rapsódica* for four guitars, which the Romeros took on their first European tour, in 1970–71.

Madina's musical style is conservative and draws inspiration from the folklore of his country, particularly the Basque region. Thus it comes as no surprise that his first concerto for them was the *Concierto vasco* (Basque concerto), whose four movements are named after songs and dances popular in the Basque country: "Arin," "Zortziko," "Eresia," and "Fandango." They debuted this concerto in 1970 with the San Francisco Symphony Orchestra under the baton of Arthur Fiedler (Pepe and Angel debuted Rodrigo's *Madrigal* at this same time). Of this work, the *Newark*

14. THE ROMERO REPERTOIRE

Star-Ledger said, "It is a 'hot' piece of music, full of an Iberian feeling of temperature and warmth, and it certainly warmed up the . . . audience, [which] was moved to applaud heartily after two of the work's internal movements."[33] Madina did not restrict himself to penning evocations of his ancestral ground, however. Pepe performed his *Concierto flamenco* at the Santa Barbara County Bowl on August 9, 1973, and its three movements, "Seguidillas," "Sentimiento," and "Anda jaleo," proved a hit with the audience (however, Pepe had already given the work its world premiere with the Honolulu Symphony, conducted by Pascual Marquina, in 1972). Madina has also composed for the quartet by itself, especially the Quartet no. 1, subtitled *Angelita*, after the Romero matriarch. The quartet interpreted its four movements, Allegro, Gavota, Nocturno, Final, for the Kansas City Guitar Society on September 23, 1988.

Another Spanish composer and Romero collaborator was José Muñoz Molleda (1905–88), whose colorful *Tríptico* for guitar quartet consists of "Elegia 'Seguiriya'"; "Tientos," and "Baile." The Romeros gave a very successful rendition of this piece on December 31, 2009, at the Ninety-Second Street Y in New York City, a leading venue at which they have frequently performed as soloists as well as as a quartet.

Although Narciso Yepes gave the 1981 premiere of *Metamorfosi de concert* by Catalan composer Xavier Montsalvatge (1912–2002), Pepe revived it for the composer's ninetieth birthday and subsequently made the only available recording, with the Orquestra de Cadaqués conducted by Gianandrea Noseda (Trító, 2003). This intriguing work combines inspirations from Caribbean music with Montsalvatge's own modernistic style to create music that is both abstract and compelling. This piece is not typical of those in which the Romeros have specialized, but it is yet another indication of their flexibility and willingness to cross aesthetic boundaries.

Of special importance has been the Romeros' relationship with Spanish composer and conductor Lorenzo Palomo (1938–). Their first collaboration was *Nocturnos de Andalucía* for guitar and orchestra, which premiered in Berlin on January 27, 1996, with Rafael Frühbeck de Burgos conducting the Rundfunk-Sinfonieorchester Berlin. Pepe solicited this "suite concertante" from his friend Lorenzo, who lived in San Diego from 1976 to 1981. Like Pepe, Palomo spent his childhood in Andalusia, specifically Córdoba, and he feels a profound attachment to this part of Spain. That sentiment is on display in each of the work's six evocative movements: "Brindis a la noche" (A toast to the night); "Sonrisa truncada de una estrella" (Shattered smile of a star); "Danza de Marialuna" (Dance of Marialuna); "Ráfaga" (Gust of wind); "Nocturno de Córdoba" (Nocturne of Córdoba); "El tablao" (The flamenco stage). The score is replete with echoes of Andalusian folklore, especially flamenco; moreover, the "Danza de Marialuna" was inspired by Juan Ramón Jiménez's poem *La niña de blanco*. The *Nocturnos* are scored for a large orchestra, including low brass and a large battery of percussion instruments, and normally this would not bode well for the soft-spoken guitar. But Palomo skillfully reduces the orchestral forces when the guitar is front and center, saving *tutti* passages for effective contrast.

Palomo's *Concierto de Cienfuegos* for guitar quartet and orchestra follows in the footsteps of the *Conciertos andaluz* and *Ibérico*, by Rodrigo and Torroba, respectively. It premiered at the Teatro de la Maestranza de Sevilla on June 14, 2001, with Rafael Frühbeck de Burgos conducting the Real Orquesta Sinfónica de Sevilla. Of course, Celedonio was born in Cienfuegos, and this work is an homage to him; thus it embraces traditional musics of both Spain and Cuba. The colorfully inventive allegretto opening movement, "Noche, lago de mil fantasías" (Night, lake of a thousand fantasies), explores the rhythms and modalities of the *bulerías*, as a tribute to the Romeros' native Andalusia and also to Palomo's hometown, Córdoba. In this nocturnal reverie, the dancers on this musical occasion are fairies! The following movement, "Canto a la noche—arrullos" (Song to the night—lullaby), is marked *calmo* and evokes the habanera, a classic example of the phenomenon that Spaniards refer to as *ida y vuelta* (round-trip), whereby Spanish songs and dances made their way to Cuba, blended with African rhythms, and then returned to Spain as something quite distinctive and new. This lyrical interlude exudes an intoxicating tropical languor and nostalgia. The closing Allegretto con anima, "Las dos orillas" (The two shores), is a riotous celebration of Afro-Cuban rhythm and percussion, evoking the sycopations and instruments (conga, bongo, claves) characteristic of a musical heritage with which Celedonio proudly identified.

However, the Romeros' promotion of new music for guitar and orchestra has by no means been confined to fellow Spaniards, and in fact this aspect of their repertoire reflects their dual identity as U.S. citizens, too. Thus it comes as no surprise that they have been very involved with composers

14. THE ROMERO REPERTOIRE

on this side of the Atlantic. And as one might well expect, these works do not celebrate or evoke Spain. They reflect a wide variety of other musical inspirations, especially but not exclusively from the United States.

One of their most important American (meaning U.S.) collaborations was with Morton Gould (1913–96), a prominent composer, conductor, arranger, and pianist. Gould composed a concerto for the quartet that lies well beyond the Spanish pale and provides further indication of the Romeros' willingness to step outside their comfort zone and try something completely different. *Troubadour Music* is inspired by the traditional role of the guitar in accompanying song, and one of the innovative aspects of the work is that it calls for the quartet to start playing offstage and then to casually come on stage two by two, still playing their guitars, in the manner of wandering minstrels. They leave the stage the same way, providing a distinctly spatial element to the performance. The music itself often has a jazzlike flavor combined with some very modernistic touches in the harmony and rhythm.

In the Romero archive is a letter from Gould in New York, dated September 21, 1968, in which he provides some insights into the music. He says that he had "attempted a formal work with popular vernacular—an old combination of [his]." As for the music itself, he states, "Altho [sic] there are many rhythmic changes I think familiarity will bring comfort and a natural ease and feeling to the varied pulses I have employed. I have used the four guitars about equally. There there is a lot of interchange and passing of one leading line to another."

The Romeros found Gould's work thought provoking, to say the least. Pepe said that it was "descriptive of our times," while Celedonio described as "original" and Celin, as "impressionistic." Pepe declared, "Gould's piece is revolutionary for the guitar. He has included completely new techniques in fingering, arpeggios, things like that." So much so that Celedonio averred that the Romeros "invented new techniques to play this."[34]

The Romeros premiered the work with the San Diego Symphony in July 1969 at a concert celebrating the city's two hundredth anniversary. A *Los Angeles Times* review of the new piece as performed at the Hollywood Bowl shortly thereafter perceived that "the competitive element, which might have created excitement by pitting the players against each other, was lost in utilizing the guitarists most of the time as an ensemble unit rather than as four soloists." (Angel played the *Aranjuez* on this occasion, and this same review praised his "deft virtuosity and a sensitivity that stamped him as a true musician.")[35]

A number of other works merit a brief overview here. Though they have not found a permanent place in the repertoire, they are remarkable for their musical diversity and provide further evidence of the Romeros' stylistic range. Pepe premiered a concerto by Loris Tjeknavorian at the Kimball Recital Hall on the campus of the University of Nebraska, Lincoln, in November 22, 1988. Titled *Zareh*, the melodies are based on ancient Armenian religious chants. The *Lincoln Journal-Star* reported that Pepe was a friend of Tjeknavorian's, liked the concerto, and agreed to perform it at the premiere. He further revealed it was a very difficult piece and has required a lot of practice. "Although it's very modern, it's very melodic," said the composer to the newspaper.[36]

Angel premiered Christopher Fazzi's *Guitar Concert, Western Suite*, with the Phoenix Symphony. He also premiered and recorded a concerto by Lalo Schifrin (b. 1932), the renowned Argentine pianist, arranger, conductor, and composer. Although John Henken, music critic for the *Los Angeles Times*, found it "overtly popular in style, and unduly reminiscent of both Rodrigo and Mancini at many points," it was also, in his opinion, "tuneful and intelligently wrought."[37] Schifrin recently completed a second guitar concerto for Angel, *Concierto de la amistad*, premiered by the dedicatee with the Los Angeles Philharmonic at the Hollywood Bowl on August 2, 2016. This work, inspired by the composer's long friendship with Angel, is Schifrin's survey of guitar music through the ages. Though eclectic in approach, it bears the stamp of the composer's distinctive musical personality. *Los Angeles Times* critic Mark Swed praised the concerto's "lyrical solos for Romero, allowing his beautiful tone to peal across the acres, very much larger than life over the loudspeakers."[38]

Two Latin-themed efforts merit mention here. Ernesto Cordero (b. 1946) is a Puerto Rican composer whose delightfully Caribbean-flavored *Concierto Festivo* (2003) was commissioned by the University of Puerto Rico. Dedicated to, premiered, and recorded by Pepe, it was nominated for a Latin Grammy in 2012.[39] The *New Haven Register* reported on the premiere of Michael Zearott's *Concierto Mariachi*, with Pepe in the demanding solo role accompanied by the New Haven Symphony Orchestra conducted by Michael Palmer. The composer said of this piece, "One day I mentioned to [Pepe] that for a long time I had wanted to write a piece using mariachi themes and rhythms. That brought an instant gleam to his eye and he said, 'Then why don't you write a mariachi concerto for me?'"[40] Another work for guitar and orchestra to receive the Pepe treatment was Paul Chihara's 1975 *Guitar Concerto*, which he premiered with Neville Marinner conducting the Los Angeles Chamber Orchestra and later recorded under that conductor's baton with the London Symphony Orchestra.

One final and very notable work is Claude Bolling's *Concerto for Classic Guitar and Jazz Piano*. Angel played this work at the Hollywood Bowl in the summer of 1979 and became fast friends with Bolling as a result of that collaboration. In fact, Bolling later wrote an additional movement for the concerto, the "Finale," which he dedicated to Angel. Appropriately enough, Angel recorded this work on the Angel label in 1980, with pianist George Shearing, percussionist Shelly Manne, and bassist Ray Brown. This is the most conspicuous and noteworthy foray into the realm of American popular music, specifically jazz, that any Romero has ever made. The *Contra Costa Times* interviewed Angel on this very topic: "Angel calls jazz 'a sensuous, melodious medium, very similar to the Folklorico of Spain. He [Bolling] is very much in the tradition of dixieland, and I'm a lover of that music. Jazz is an improvisational medium—that's my attraction to it.'"[41]

Of course, the very idea that jazz is "popular" music is debatable, and one could argue that, at least since the advent of bop and cool jazz in the 1940s and 1950s, it has become a sort of classical music in its limited appeal. It is for this reason that jazz and classical styles have become increasingly compatible, resulting in a hybrid known as "Third Stream" jazz. Among the chief exponents of this style were Dave Brubeck and Claude Bolling. His concerto starts out with a "Hispanic Dance" featuring a South American idea in 5/4 meter interlaced with a bluesy theme. The second movement, "Mexicaine," has an introspectively Mexican flavor, with a light jazz salsa. As one might expect from the title, "Invention" mimics the imitative counterpoint of a Bach invention, with some jazz-style improvs between the piano and bass. The "Serenade" has a bossa nova swing to it, while the ensuing "Rhapsodic" foregrounds the guitar in music of a Spanish flavor. "Africaine" highlights the guitar and piano, while the "Finale" composed for Angel presents variations on the previous six movements, in a virtuosic recapitulation.

PART 4. LEGACY

COMPOSITIONS

The principal composer in the Romero family was Celedonio, though Pepe and Angel have also been active in this arena. Certainly Celedonio's works deserve a separate and serious analysis, but that is beyond the scope of the present volume. Celedonio composed numerous solo pieces for the guitar in addition to several works for guitar and orchestra. Among these are Andalusian confections such as the *Concierto de Málaga* (1978). This work is inspired by and based on flamenco themes, and because the first movement is actually a *soleares*, he preferred the title *Concierto por soleares*. However, in deference to his hometown, he eventually settled on *Concierto de Málaga*. Celedonio declared that the *soleares* "is the mother of the cante jondo. It represents the melancholic and profound sentiments of [the] ancient Andalusian race. It has been, is, and will continue to be one of the richest fountains of inspiration of our country." He added, "As an Andalusian who loves his country . . . I wanted to start my concerto with a soleares."[42] In fact, it was Torroba who suggested to Celedonio that he transform elements of his *Suite andaluza* into this concerto and offered to help with the orchestration.

The second movement is an arrangement of his ever-popular *guajira*-inspired *Fantasía*. Concerning this movement, the composer recalled his childhood in Cienfuegos:

> In the afternoons my father used to take me for walks in the beautiful Cuban countryside with its great fields of corn and sugar cane. There the peasants sang of love at the end of their daily chores. . . . The tropical nights were unforgettable, filled with very brilliant stars and the great moon that shines as much as the sun. All this became embedded in my heart when I was a boy and the remembrance, together with great nostalgia and love for this beautiful island, have stayed with me throughout my life.[43]

The third movement is titled "Tangos y tientos," with a *bulerías* cadenza at the end. Celedonio realized that this work would be the perfect vehicle for displaying Pepe's talents, so he dedicated it to him, "with all my love and admiration." Indeed, this is a work that requires someone who is equally adept at classical and flamenco styles, and since such guitarists are few in number, that may explain why this captivating work does not enjoy wider circulation.

14. THE ROMERO REPERTOIRE

Another of Celedonio's concertos that Pepe has promoted is *El Cortijo de Don Sancho*, which he premiered with the American Sinfonietta on August 16, 1996, at the Mount Baker Theatre during the Bellingham Festival of Music in Washington, shortly after Celedonio's death. The inspiration for this colorful work is Don Quixote's reliable sidekick Sancho Panza and his *cortijo*, or farmhouse (*cortijo* is a word common to Andalusia and Extremadura and means the same thing as *finca* in Castilian). Celedonio felt a certain sympathy for the humble Sancho, since so much attention had been paid to Don Quijote over the centuries at the expense of his loyal companion. Celedonio would rectify this situation by focusing on Sancho.[44]

In addition to concertos, Celedonio composed a plethora of pieces for solo guitar, which his sons have programmed and recorded. Prominent among these is the *Suite andaluza*, mentioned above, which was inspired by assorted flamenco dances: "Soleares," "Alegrías," "Tango," and "Zapateado." It concludes with his "Fantasía." In addition to flamenco, Bach's music was a major passion of Celedonio's (as it is with all the Romeros), and this inspired him to compose a Baroque-style suite named after the famous Gothic cathedral in Cologne, Germany. Angel recorded it on an album devoted exclusively to his father's music (see appendix 3), and the liner notes of this disc inform us that *The Cathedral of Cologne* "was inspired by an early-morning visit to that remarkable edifice in 1980, when he fell under the sway of the organ of the cathedral and wrote this long (25:43) work as a homage to Bach."

La Catedral de Colonia is laid out like a dance suite by Bach and consists of a Preludio, Sarabande, Bourrées I and II, Minuettos I and II, and Giga. One conspicuous anomaly here is the insertion of an "Oración (Adagio procesional)" in between the Bourrées and the Minuettos. This may have been inconsistent with the dance suites of Bach but not with Celedonio's penchant for creative whimsy and devotional sentiment. This disc also includes two waltzes. As Angel reported, "I said to him, there in the Capitol Studios, 'Papá, we're a little short of music for this record,' and straight away, he found some sheets of stationery and wrote these two charming waltzes for me," *Angel Vals nos. 1 and 2*.[45]

In the manner of Tárrega, Celedonio was drawn not only to the waltz but also to the mazurka, and he composed two of them dedicated to the great Spanish pianist and Hollywood film star José Iturbi, a close friend of the Romeros. These are now a staple in Celino's repertoire as well.

PART 4. LEGACY

Celedonio also composed a work dedicated to Celin, the *Suite madrileña no. 1*, whose five movements evoke the Spanish capital: "Entrada" (Introduction); "En el Retiro (Añoranza)" (In the Retiro Park, nostalgia); "El chótis de la bombilla" (The schottish of the light bulb); "En las Cibeles (Nocturno)" (In the Plaza of Ceres, nocturne); and "En el Prado (Cantando la rueda)" (In the Prado, the singing wheel). This work is a musical recollection of his visit to Madrid in the wake of the civil war (and after recovering from a severe case of typhus), where he had gone to pick up a new guitar made especially for him by Santos Hernández and paid for by admirers in Seville. On this trip he took his young son, Celin. As Pepe has said of this work (in the liner notes of his DGG recording from 2010), "'El chótis de la bombilla' represents Celin as a handsome, seductive, debonair young man. In this suite we can also hear the love and passion my father felt for the Romantic piano composers Schumann and Brahms."

Pepe has specialized more in arranging rather than composing, but following in his father's footsteps, he composed *De Cádiz a la Habana* for guitar quartet, inspired by his admiration for Sabicas and Carmen Amaya. Based on the *colombianas*, it suggests cultural exchange between Spain and the New World, something his own family knows very well. Angel has also been active as an arranger and composer. In 1991, he premiered the concerto *Rincones de España* (Corners of Spain), based on themes by Rodrigo. About five years before Rodrigo died, Angel asked him to write a concerto, but the venerable composer demurred, citing his advanced age. However, not wanting his beloved guitarist to go away empty-handed, Rodrigo sent him some harmonized themes, including a *jota* and other Spanish-style melodies.

As is his wont, Angel has occasionally broken the mold with creations attuned to contemporary popular culture. Especially effective in this regard is the title cut from his 1995 CD *Remembering the Future*. This hauntingly beautiful piece features tablas, vocals, and electric guitar.

ARRANGEMENTS/TRANSCRIPTIONS

The Romeros didn't create a guitar quartet so that they could play the existing literature; they created the existing literature so that their quartet would have something to play. We have already seen that they have made a singular contribution to the repertoire for guitar and orchestra, integrating the guitar into the mainstream symphonic tradition. What

14. THE ROMERO REPERTOIRE

may be less obvious, however, is the extent to which they have integrated that mainstream symphonic tradition into the guitar repertoire. And by symphonic tradition, I mean any sort of symphonic works, whether standalone pieces from the concert literature or orchestral numbers from operas and zarzuelas. It is their arrangement of all this symphonic music that I focus on here.

In the beginning, there was Bach, though the guitar repertoire extends back to the early 1500s, about two centuries before Bach was in his prime. But the canonic orchestral repertoire one hears at symphony concerts begins with the late Baroque, with Bach and Vivaldi, especially. Guitarists had been transcribing Bach's lute, violin, and cello music for solo guitar since the 1800s, and Vivaldi's concertos for lute and mandolin were fair game. But the quartet made it possible to play late-Baroque orchestral music independently of an orchestra. Celedonio was always a great lover of this music, and among his earliest arrangements were works by Telemann, Vivaldi, and Bach.

A specialty was Bach's Brandenburg Concerto no. 3. This was a logical choice because it is for strings only and readily lends itself to a guitar-quartet arrangement in a way that the concerto grosso–style no. 5 would not. A Vivaldi lute concerto could now be rendered for guitar solo and three-guitar "orchestra." As Celin told the *Wichita Eagle* in regard to the Romeros' Vivaldi transcriptions: "We were inspired by Bach's version transcribed for the harpsichord." Celedonio chimed in, noting that "The sounds of harpsichords and guitars are similar, and [the D-major lute concerto] is one of Vivaldi's most beautiful concertos."[46] In contrast to Vivaldi, Telemann was a somewhat controversial choice in the 1960s because his reputation was only slowly emerging from Bach's shadow. But Celedonio saw attractive qualities in this music as well and transcribed for quartet the D-major concerto for four violins and orchestra. This certainly provided a model and much of the inspiration for the four-guitar concertos that were soon to flow from various composers' pens. In 1960, Angel also arranged a soprano aria from Bach's Cantata no. 68 for the quartet.

A remarkable piece arranged by Pepe for guitar and orchestra is Rodrigo's evocatively programmatic *Sones en la Giralda* (Sounds in the Giralda), a work descriptive of the imagined spirits residing in the landmark Moorish minaret, preserved as a campanile and incorporated into Seville's magnificent cathedral. Rodrigo suggested this arrangement to Pepe as a case of "turnabout is fair play." Spanish harpist Nicanor Zabaleta had secured Rodrigo's permission to transcribe the *Aranjuez* for harp, so Rodrigo thought it only fair that his *Sones en la Giralda* for harp and orchestra be similarly arranged for guitar, courtesy of Pepe. It remains one of the most unusual and extraordinary works in the guitar repertoire.

Three generations of Romeros have been great lovers of opera and zarzuela, largely because they have always been great lovers of the human voice, of a gorgeous melody sung by a gorgeous voice. They grew up listening to both kinds of musical theater, so it was only logical that early on in the quartet's career they would choose some of their favorite instrumental numbers to arrange. Among their favorite zarzuela composers are Tomás Bretón (1850–1923), Ruperto Chapí (1851–1909), Amadeo Vives (1871–1932), and Gerónimo Giménez (1852–1923). They have memorably interpreted Lorenzo Palomo's arrangements of selections from Bretón's *La verbena de la paloma*, Chapí's *La revoltosa*, and Vives's *Bohemios*. Pepe has effectively arranged numbers from Giménez's *El baile de Luis Alonso*. Manuel de Falla is naturally a favorite, and they bring new life to Spanish dances from his opera *La vida breve* and ballet *El sombrero de tres picos*, as well as Pepe's arrangements of the "Jota," "Nana," and "Polo" from the *Siete canciones populares españolas*. They also feel a real affinity for the music of Turina, and Pepe has transcribed his orchestral work *La oración del torero* (The toreador's prayer) for quartet.

Some American musicals—the rough equivalent of zarzuelas—are suitable for transcription because of their Latin flavor. Conspicuous in this regard is *West Side Story*, a medley of numbers from which Angel arranged for guitar and violin in the 1960s and which, according to the *Seattle Times*, he performed very effectively there.[47] (The film was released in 1961.)

However, perhaps the most ambitious and triumphant arrangement they made—and one of the most logical and predictable—was of selections from Bizet's *Carmen*. In performances of this work, Angelita often appeared, playing castanets. The arrangement was a group effort, in which Torroba's son, Fede, made the first arrangement, after which Angel and Pepe embellished it; Romero student Robert Wetzel transcribed the Interlude. Pepe emphasized, "With *Carmen*, we tried to present it as it would have been improvised by flamenco players."[48] The Romeros feel a special rapport with this work because of their long connection with Seville, where the opera's

14. THE ROMERO REPERTOIRE

action is set. As mentioned earlier, they lived not far from the cigarette factory associated with the notorious femme fatale of the 1845 novel by Prosper Mérimée, on which Bizet based his 1875 *opéra-comique*.

As Pepe told interviewer Wilhelm Hellweg for a press release regarding the 1984 Philips recording, "In order to really understand *Carmen*, you have to go back to Seville. . . . Carmen is very Spanish, a very free woman, who really uses jealousy, creates jealousy, in order to experience love. It is a very typical trait of the Andalusian woman; the ultimate proof of love is when her lover loses his mind through love of her." Celedonio concurred, adding, "It comes so naturally to the Spanish temperament that, for years, a crime of passion was not really punishable by the law. It was almost forgiven."[49]

In this same press release, Angel asserted that "in a way, Carmen was one of the first feminists." Growing up in their Spanish milieu gave them a special rapport with this opera. As he went on to recall, "I remember as a child my parents and my brothers listening to great singers singing habaneras, seguidillas, and boleros. I remember the bands playing pasodobles, seeing the people dancing to the pasodobles, going to a bullfight and hearing the orchestra playing pasodobles. So, when you play the Toreador song, it is instinctive." This arrangement is one of the Romeros' most effective and delectable confections in the realm of arranging and transcribing. But there was also plenty of music written for the guitar that had been overlooked and which they brought to light.

REVIVALS

I have noted previously that the Romeros are not attracted to avant-garde music, for example, atonal or electroacoustic works. Angel made this very clear in an interview with Henry Adams: "We feel that there is so much good music of the past that hasn't received enough attention by performers."[50] He goes on to credit the duo of Presti and Lagoya with reviving interest in music for two or more guitars, of which much was written in the nineteenth century. So if a performer is less than enthusiastic about "experimental" music, then in addition to transcribing and arranging works of a more traditional type, seeking out lesser-known, or unknown, works from earlier periods is a good way to enrich the repertoire. This is also a type of "new music," and the public is generally very supportive of this approach.

PART 4. LEGACY

This is where musicologists have an important role to play. They may have little expertise in composing or arranging music, but they are (or should be) good at identifying, locating, and editing neglected works by established composers like Sor or Giuliani or pieces by unjustly neglected contemporaries who simply lack name recognition. The past few decades have witnessed very fruitful collaboration between music scholars and performers in this regard. For instance, Richard Stover almost singlehandedly rescued the Paraguayan Agustín Barrios (1885–1944) from obscurity, and guitarist John Williams was quick to exploit Stover's discoveries by recording his editions. The Romeros have also shown an interest in Barrios. Thomas Heck made the first serious modern editions of Mauro Giuliani's large corpus of solos, while Brian Jeffery has performed yeoman service for the works of Fernando Sor in his critical editions of this music. Frederick Noad also made available to guitarists modern editions of historical music.

In an insightful article, journalist Allan Kozinn grappled with "what conservatory catalogues call 'the Segovia repertory' which has tied that majority of guitarists who conform to it to the concert literature of the 1940s—Turina, Torroba, the Villa-Lobos Preludes." Kozinn was critical of Segovia's practice of programming movements and short pieces rather than longer works and whole suites. But he happily noted that many guitarists were now leaving the "grab bag" approach behind, thanks to an enlarged repertoire made available by Heck, Jeffery, and Noad. "It is a revolution in performance standards, programming philosophies, contemporary repertory expansion and, most significantly, it is the start of a kind of musicological exploration the likes of which the instrument has not seen since the early 1920s when Segovia and Pujol began searching Europe's libraries for the lost music of the lute and vihuela composers."[51]

Though the Romeros were certainly capable of grab-bag programming, they have also stayed abreast of all these developments and have played a leading role in resurrecting uncelebrated masterpieces from the past. And they have made a point of programming substantial multimovement works, especially chamber and orchestral works. Their discography reveals many first recordings of works by Francesco Molino, Mauro Giuliani, Luigi Boccherini, and Ferdinando Carulli, as well as by contemporary masters such as Rodrigo and Torroba.

14. THE ROMERO REPERTOIRE

A *Los Angeles Times* critic noticed in Pepe's performances a very marked element of "intellectual introspectiveness mixed with concern for musicology and accuracy." As Pepe explained to him, "I have been very much involved in bringing a lot of forgotten music back into the concert hall—especially music from the 19th Century."[52] Among this "forgotten music" are three guitar concertos of Mauro Giuliani. Both Pepe and Angel have made landmark recordings of these works, which had received scant attention from earlier generations of guitarists. Giuliani was a contemporary of Rossini and wrote in a style very reminiscent of what one hears in *La cenerentola* and *Il barbiere di Siviglia*. Inveterate opera buffs, Pepe and Angel's attraction to Giuliani's music is thus readily understandable. Other guitar concertos were even more obscure before Pepe brought them to light. They included works by Giuliani's contemporaries Ferdinando Carulli (1770–1841) and Francesco Molino (1768–1847). Pepe recorded two substantial and delightfully lyrical Carulli concertos, in E minor, op. 140, and A major, op. 8a, as well as Molino's E-minor concerto, op. 56. All exude the sprezzatura and bravado of opera buffa.

Pepe was also responsible for resurrecting the previously unknown Fantasia in D Minor for guitar solo by Fernando Sor. The manuscript made its way from Sotheby's in London to J. & J. Lubrano in the United States and thence to Pepe via John King. Pepe edited the work and made the premiere recording of it on his 1994 Philips CD *Noches de España: Romantic Guitar Classics* (Philips 1994). He had premiered it in concert in 1992, in Atlanta. As he relayed to the *Atlanta Journal-Constitution*: "When I was in Atlanta last year, I fell in love with Spivey Hall. I thought: This is where the premiere has to be. Acoustically, visually, spiritually, the ambience of Spivey Hall provides the right setting for this piece. I hope the muses that inspired Sor to write such a beautiful work will inspire me to do it justice."[53]

Although not the only guitarist to revive them, Pepe has made a specialty of the guitar quintets by Luigi Boccherini. There are eight extant Boccherini quintets for guitar and string quartet from the late 1700s, and they are colorful evocations of the Madrid soundscape, which he knew from living and working in the Spanish capital for many years. Pepe recorded all the quintets with a chamber ensemble from the Academy of St. Martin-in-the-Fields on the Philips label. A German review of these historic recordings gave them "straight 10s for interpretation, value of repertoire, recording quality, and design."[54] Especially effective is "La Ritrata di Madrid" (The night-watch of Madrid) from no. 9 in C, which depicts the military unit on nighttime parade. The twelve variations in this number gradually increase in intensity as the soldiers approach, then fade away as the marchers disappear into the night. This is a delightfully suggestive bit of program music. The Fandango from no. 4 in D is also very popular, so much so that the Romeros arranged it for guitar quartet, with Angelita crafting a castanet part for an additional splash of local color.

We noted earlier that Pepe has an enduring love of the human voice and, by extension, of opera. As he explains in the liner notes of his 2009 Philips recording *Opera Fantasy for Guitar: Pepe Romero*, this "great passion" was first aroused at age thirteen when Celin bought him a recording of *La bohème* with Renata Tebaldi and Carlo Bergonzi. "I was immediately in love with opera, a love which I feel to this day and cultivate at every opportunity," he declared. This passion inspired him to record some guitar "fantasies" on operatic themes that had fallen by the programming wayside. In the nineteenth century, it was common for instrumentalists to arrange or write sets of variations on popular operatic airs. Liszt's "concert paraphrase" on *Rigoletto* comes to mind as a conspicuous example. Although this might seem a feat much harder to accomplish on the guitar, that didn't deter Johann Kaspar Mertz (1806–56) from composing virtuosic *Fantasies* on themes from Verdi's *Rigoletto* (op. 63) and *Il trovatore* (op. 8, no. 27), as well as Mozart's *Don Giovanni* (op. 28). Tárrega composed a *Fantasy on Themes from [Emilio] Arrieta's "Marina,"* while Arcas wrote a similar work on themes from Verdi's *La traviata*. Manuel Ferrer (1828–1904) was a very accomplished Mexican guitarist, composer, and pedagogue active in the Los Angeles area, and he composed the *Fantasy on the Quartet of Verdi's "Rigoletto."*

As we know, Giuliani was deeply influenced by his compatriot Rossini and wrote several guitar works based on themes from his operas. Each of these "fantasies" bears the title *La Rossiniana*, and Pepe plays the first of these (op. 119) on this CD, which also features pianist Wilhelm Hellweg's arrangement of waltzes from Gounod's *Faust* for guitar and piano. It goes without saying that these showpieces require consummate skill and were intended, then as now, to impress the public with a performer's technique. But they are also affectionate evocations of a repertoire that was once a sort

14. THE ROMERO REPERTOIRE

of popular music known to the butcher, baker, and candlestick maker as well as the upper crust. One last revival by Pepe that merits our attention here was the *Introduction to the Chôros* for guitar and symphony orchestra by Heitor Villa-Lobos, which had apparently languished in obscurity for decades before being discovered in the possession of the Parisian publisher Max Eschig.

IMPROVISATIONS AND UNNOTATED MUSIC

Improvisation does not consist simply in making stuff up out of nothing. It always takes place within some system or structure in which there are "rules of the road." This is as true of a Baroque trio sonata by Corelli as it is of *Take the A Train* by Strayhorn—or a *bulerías*. There are preexisting melodies, embellishments, chord progressions, rhythms, and meter(s) that define any particular genre and on which the performer then elaborates. An audience assesses a performer's improvisatory skill within the boundaries imposed by any particular style or form. It is this dynamic tension between constraint and invention that makes such a performance a sort of tightrope act.

Someone improvising on a *bulerías*, for example, must first and foremost respect its *compás*, or metric structure, which consists of twelve beats with accents on 12, 3, 6, 8, and 10. In Western notation, this would equal 6/8 alternating with 3/4. The tempo of the *bulerías* is lively, and certain rhythms and melodic embellishments are associated with it as well. It can be played in almost any key, though it is often played in an "Andalusian mode" starting on A and going upward through B-flat, C-sharp, D, E, F, G, A, and then downward the same way except with C-natural rather than sharp. The underlying harmonic progression in this modality is something called a descending minor tetrachord, proceeding from A major to D minor to C major to B-flat major, and back to A. Got that? Now, improvise!

This is where many classical guitarists freeze up like a deer caught in the headlights of an oncoming semitrailer. They have had it drilled into them that they must respect the notes on the page and do what the music tells them to do. As Celin has observed, "In the classical form, you have to stick to the printed music, and whether you feel that specific spark at that moment or not, you have to play that phrase."[55] But sticking to the printed music creates a dependency on notation that can be hard to overcome. It certainly won't help with a *bulerías*. And that's just one *palo*. There are numerous others, each with its own distinctive characteristics in rhythm, melody, and harmony. If that still isn't challenging enough for you, try negotiating a *palo* along with a singer and/or dancer(s), who will also be expected to improvise.

Thus playing flamenco guitar involves far more than dishing out a few spirited bars of Ernesto Lecuona's *Malagueña*, as much as I love that piece and despite the fact that its vivacious measures started me on my lifelong path, at age fourteen. Improvising flamenco requires a deep knowledge of the entire art form, not just serving the audience fast-fingered ear candy. As Pepe has explained it: "Flamenco, in fact, portrays the Spanish mentality, especially the southern one, their way of loving, the way men feel about women, women about men . . . to the southern Spaniards, there is no happiness without tragedy, no love without the loss of sanity, no truth without lies."[56]

To be sure, a guitarist's *falsetas* (solo passages) very often are worked out in advance because in the rapidly changing environment of a performance, it's best not to leave everything to chance. Some ideas require development and refinement beforehand. But this type of "composition" not only allows for extemporaneous revisions and additions on stage; it also benefits from them. As the *Arizona Daily Star* noted of a Romero concert, "The fancy stuff was what people wanted to hear, and the Romeros' lightning-fast flamenco improvisations drew the most applause."[57]

All the Romeros are comfortable with improvisation, and the classic example of this would be the quartet's two-LP Mercury recording from 1967, *World of Flamenco*. Notable here are three things: (1) the wide variety of *palos*, including standards (*sevillanas*, *malagueñas*, *bulerías*) along with some less frequently heard numbers, for example, *caracoles* and *milonga*; (2) the participation of singers, dancers; and (3) readings by Celedonio of poetry by Federico García Lorca, who was from Granada and deeply influenced by the flamenco culture that surrounded him there. The recording was made in Los Angeles using local singers and dancers, who were nonetheless handpicked by the Romeros themselves and of very high caliber.

To give some idea of how American audiences responded to this facet of the Romeros' "act," the *Dallas Morning News* reported the following: "Dallasite Betty Jo Hay wouldn't think of missing the Galaxy Ball Saturday in

14. THE ROMERO REPERTOIRE

Forth Worth. The ball is an annual fundraiser for the Texas Mental Health Association, for which Betty Jo has served as president."[58] Another Dallas daily announced at this same time, "The highlights will be many. Principal performers will be the classical guitarist Pepe Romero and an ensemble of his family members, accompanied by a troupe of flamenco dancers and singers. The Romeros will set the scene for re-creating the atmosphere of a Spanish *bodega* (wine cellar) where entertainment is presented."[59] Though this may seem kitschy, the Romeros were happy to play along, especially if it would benefit a worthy cause.

As I have already established, Pepe is the only Romero who performs flamenco regularly, not only alone but also with groups called *cuadros flamencos*. His first recording, ¡*Flamenco fenómeno!* (for Contemporary Records), is remarkable enough for a fifteen-year-old, given not only the impressive technical display but also the knowledgeable and maturely sensitive renditions of traditional *palos* such as the *seguiriyas*, *soleares*, and *bulerías*. This recording was followed in 1962 by *Pepe Romero Plays Flamenco* on the Mercury label. But his classic recording may well be the one he made with the legendary singer Chano Lobato and dancers Paco Romero (no relation) and María Magdalena in 1991 on the Philips label. In addition to *alegrías*, *farrucas*, *bulerías*, *soleares*, and *zapateado*, this disc offers moving interpretations of *granadinas*, *tanguillos*, and even *cantinas*. His creative ease in blending with singers and dancers in the performance of a wide variety of standard flamenco *palos* is really quite remarkable. Pepe explained his stylistic approach on this CD as follows: "There are two types of flamenco: traditional flamenco and a new wave of flamenco music, which is inspired by music of the popular and rock fields. My record is of the traditional flamenco music from Andalusia by the old masters."[60]

Years ago I had the privilege of performing with the very accomplished *cantaora* La Cordobesa. After one rehearsal I told her that I had studied with Pepe Romero. She immediately shot back that of all the guitarists she had worked with, he was her favorite. This was high praise. From a singer's or dancer's point of view, the guitarist's job is to accompany and support them, not so much to play flashy solos. An accompanist ideally carries the others along with the force, confidence, and solidity of his or her playing. A good accompanist knows and anticipates the vocal inflections and complex footwork and heelwork (*zapateo* and *taconeo*) of those he or she is accompanying and can provide a rhythmically intricate counterpoint to them without ever disrupting the *compás*. The accompanist must also have a good ear for the subtle tonal shifts in the singer's florid runs, to stay on top of the harmonic changes. All this work requires a keen rhythmic sense, a good ear, and most of all experience.

When such a person can also play a *malagueña* by Albéniz, he or she will bring a special savoir faire to it that someone beyond the flamenco realm will not be able to duplicate. As Pepe himself opined, "All the best Spanish guitar music is based on flamenco in its purest form, so you must understand flamenco to play it well. Who would understand better how to sing 'Porgy and Bess'—someone who has never heard American music, who doesn't know the spirituals, or someone who loves it and has experienced it?"[61]

Although Angel has not specialized in flamenco, he is more attuned to current fashions than his brothers, and thus he finds *nuevo flamenco* more attractive than Pepe does. An example is his recording of a *rumba gitana* (Gypsy rumba) titled "Rhumba" on his album *Remembering the Future: Angel Romero* mentioned above. Clearly indebted to Paco de Lucia's new-style rumbas and accompanied by rhythm guitar, vocals, and *cajón* (an Afro-Peruvian box drum), Angel's rendition is notable for its musical inventiveness and stupefying virtuosity. Of course, one might well wonder just how much of this is improvised and how much has been composed in advance. We may never know, and that's exactly the way it should sound.

There is one other type of improvisation in which the Romeros indulge from time to time, and that is adding embellishments and flourishes not indicated in the score. Sometimes this addition is perfectly consistent with commonly accepted performance practice, especially in early music (i.e., composed before 1750). Angel's beautiful interpretation of the slow movement of the Concerto in A Minor from Vivaldi's *L'estro harmonico*, op. 3, is made all the more expressive, and at the same time probably more authentic, by his addition of ornamentation, something typically done during the Baroque era. He recorded this with the Academy of St. Martin-in-the-Fields (conducted by Iona Brown) and revealed to me that the embellishments were not merely a matter of musicological calculation but rather spontaneous outpourings of emotion.

Adding a fast run at the end of a piece by Sor and Giuliani may seem to some a controversial practice, but Pepe disagrees. For instance, he adds a

14. THE ROMERO REPERTOIRE

blistering scalar flourish to the end of Giuliani's *Handel Variations*, a flourish not specified in the score. When an interviewer asked him about this, he replied, "Yes, that was my own addition. I feel that it does not change the character of the piece. And in that period it was customary; you could add this or that. Even the composers themselves often did so."[62]

COLLABORATIONS

The essence of the Romero legacy is collaboration, with one another and with other musicians, including not only composers but also conductors, singers, and other instrumentalists. In addition to all those mentioned above, their collaborators include vocalists Victoria de los Ángeles, Phyllis Curtain, Jessye Norman, Elly Ameling, and Plácido Domingo, as well as cellist Gabor Rejto and numerous orchestras and chamber ensembles, even the Canadian Brass. Pepe participated in a "Guitar Summit" in 1994 that featured Leo Kotke and Joe Pass, as well as fellow flamenco guitarist Paco Peña. In characteristic fashion, Pepe said of this encounter, "It doesn't matter what you play, classical, flamenco or whatever, just as long as the music touches your heart."[63]

* * *

If I have demonstrated nothing else in telling this story, it is that the Romeros have touched innumerable hearts with the many kinds of music they play. And they have done this despite adversities and setbacks that would have ended most collaborations.

CHAPTER 15

BREAKIN' UP IS HARD TO DO

Yes, breakin' up is hard to do, but sometimes it is easier than the alternative, which is to stay together under increasingly conflictive circumstances. It is a well-known fact that in 1990, after a remarkable thirty-year run, the Romero Quartet underwent a wrenching change in personnel, one that threatened the very existence of the group. For a variety of reasons that we will explore here, it was no longer possible or even desirable for Angel to continue with the quartet. To deny that sibling rivalry played a role in the breakup would be naive, but to claim that this was the sole cause of it would be absurd. We need to adopt a somewhat postmodern view that looks at the event from multiple perspectives, without privileging any particular narrative.

It is good to recall that for years the Romeros had managed to control the tensions inherent in their professional life on the road. Pepe was being completely sincere when he denied feeling competitive with anyone, insisting instead to the *Akron Beacon Journal*, "We all are very dear friends. We do share the love for the instrument. As players, we are quite different. As people, we are quite different, too. I have always enjoyed listening to . . . my brothers and father."[1]

Perhaps there was something slightly tongue-in-cheek about the following assertions, made by and to Canberra's *Sun*, but they were probably not too far off the mark: "Emotionally . . . the Romeros brothers are ex-

15. BREAKIN' UP IS HARD TO DO

traordinary—they hardly ever argue and never, never fight. 'If we have an argument it is a very superficial one,' Pepe . . . said at the Windsor Hotel yesterday. 'It's unthinkable to us that we could ever become involved in a serious disagreement, we enjoy being together.'"[2]

In 1989, Celin let the *San Antonio Light* in on the following family secret, a throwaway bit of PR that humanized their otherwise superhuman feats on stage: "We tease each other so much (I love to make Angel mad) that our father is always saying, 'Why don't you grow up!' We do have fun, and it extends especially to the stage. Even when we get mad over some little thing backstage, when we go out there, one of us breaks a little smile and the whole thing is over. We look at each other, and an amazing thing happens because of the music. Music has been very good for us."[3] Truly, the family that plays together stays together. Pepe once admitted, "We argue a lot. About everything. We argue over which restaurant to go to, how we are going to perform, which tempo, what piece of music we should use, who is going to play which part . . . but it is always in a healthy manner."[4]

Federico Moreno-Torroba Larregla witnessed firsthand such arguments, even under circumstances that warranted one-pointed attention rather than disputation:

> Once, my father and I were assisting the quartet at Celedonio's home in Del Mar as it rehearsed my father's *Ráfagas* for a concert in Pasadena that very evening. Angelita was preparing a meal for us and at one point interrupted the rehearsal to ask whether we wanted mayonnaise on our fish. This provoked an intense debate: Celedonio did not want any, Pepe did, Celin wanted only a little, and Angel wanted a spicy sauce. As the controversy continued, my father grew concerned because valuable practice time was being lost in the process. Pepe reassured him, saying, "Patience, maestro, everything will turn out fine." After several minutes elapsed, it was decided that each could have his fish according to his own taste. The rehearsal resumed, but not for long. The unforgettable Angelita soon reappeared to inquire of my father how he wanted his fish, because he had not registered an opinion. This initiated a new round of discussion, as the Romeros counseled him one way or the other. He didn't care about the sauce, because all he wanted was to rehearse! Pepe decided the issue for him, telling Angelita that the maestro would take his fish with mayonnaise. Music making got underway yet again, but after a short time, one of Pepe's daughters rushed in to inform us that Angel's car was blocking a neighbor's driveway and that it would have to

be moved. My father was once more feeling distress, and he now resigned himself to a performance that would be adequate but nonetheless reveal a lack of preparation. When concert time arrived, however, the Romeros executed *Ráfagas* as if they had practiced it all day long, without any distractions concerning mayonnaise. Frankly, my father and I were dumbfounded, because we had never witnessed such a prodigious rendition without the benefit of sufficient rehearsal.[5]

It was one thing for intimate friends of the family to undergo such a trial, but for a total stranger, it could be positively unnerving. Illinois journalist G. B. Appleson once went to interview the family at the East Peoria Holiday Inn, where they were staying. As the intrepid reporter gingerly approached room 204, the presence of the Romeros became clearly audible:

> No sooner did the harmonies lure you forward than a burst of shouting made you wonder if you were about to walk in on a violent family squabble. That's the Romeros . . . four very talented, very romantic and very hotheaded men. "There are four generals and no soldiers," says Angelita. She sat patiently in the cluttered room reading a book, while her husband and sons screamed at each other in Spanish about how a composition should be played. "It is like this all the time," said Mrs. Romero. "There is never a dull moment." It was amazing the four ever finished anything. It is amazing they have any hearing left. But when they play, there is nothing else in the room. For you or for them. It is their blood and their heritage speaking. "We all feel in love with the guitar," said Pepe. "It is an instrument in which the sound becomes an extension of your body." At one extreme, the four seem so intent, so diligent, so self-disciplined, practicing whenever there is a spare moment. But then again, they are so uninhibited, so fun-loving, so very natural, it is hard to believe they are such a renowned group of musicians. "Fame is something other people feel more than the ones who are famous. You never even think about it," said Pepe, joining in an argument with his brothers over whether a bedspread should be replaced over a sheet-music-covered bed while a photographer shot pictures. Like anxious schoolboys, they eagerly made up tales about each other. Most of the jabs were directed towards the youngest, Angel, who is notably handsome and apparently knows it.[6]

On smirking display here is the then-prevailing stereotype of Latin men as instinctive rather than intellectual, hot-blooded and temperamental in the mold of Ricky Ricardo ("Luuuucy, you got some 'splainin' to do!" "Noooow, Ricky," etc.). As well-intentioned as all the above observations were, they barely concealed the potential for serious divisions in the quartet once Pepe and Angel became stars not only of the ensemble but also, and each in his own right, of the music world.

AMOK TIME

In one of the best-known and most popular episodes in the original *Star Trek* television series, Captain James T. Kirk and his first officer, Mister Spock, engage in mortal combat on the planet Vulcan. The reason for the conflict is Spock's highly illogical mating frenzy, which compels him to return to Vulcan in order to duel with a rival Vulcan for the hand of a young woman. Captain Kirk offers to substitute for the rival, thinking that he can somehow throw the match and thereby ensure Spock's survival. Only too late does he learn that, according to Vulcan custom, this is a fight to the death. Although in the end Spock appears to have killed his commanding officer and friend, Dr. McCoy has cleverly given Kirk a drug that only simulates death. Ultimately, all three are joyously reunited on the starship *Enterprise*.

The scenario of two brothers, friends, or colleagues of roughly equal abilities fighting each other has an inherently dramatic appeal, one going all the way back to Cain and Abel. It certainly made Roman gladiatorial contests more interesting, not to mention the movies *Ben Hur* and *Spartacus*. By the second and third years of the original *Star Trek* series, the characters of Kirk and (especially) Spock had become so popular with viewers that nearly every episode dealt with *them*, putting them into and getting them out of some dangerous situation. In similar fashion, by the 1980s, Pepe and Angel were clearly the dominant members of the quartet, each with his own thriving solo career. And whether or not a rivalry really existed between them, that was what audiences increasingly wanted to see. They wanted to see which one was best. They wanted some "amok time." The quartet's managers were not slow to recognize the commercial advantages of subtly highlighting a competition between them, to see who could perform the more spectacular feats of technical derring-do. As Carissa Romero summarized it to me, "Audiences more and more wanted to see competition between Angel and Pepe. Managers fuel this sort of thing because it brings in audiences."

Understandably, Pepe tried to tamp down any public perception that there was rivalry, though some journalists would remain unconvinced:

Is there any kind of rivalry?

"No. This is something felt by others—by managements and music critics. We've grown up doing the same thing, you know, as children who loved music and loved doing the same thing. I never saw Angel as a rival, but as a partner and as a brother."

It was just a thought.

"It's a thought in many people's minds!"

When your first Giuliani record was issued I said to my wife, 'Wait a bit and Angel will follow'. Quite soon he followed with 'The Divine Giuliani'. Then you recorded a Rodrigo concerto, and Angel followed. It seems that Angel is always one step behind you.

"Yes, that's funny, somehow. You're right."[7]

Managers had other ways of sowing discord in the group. They would sing the siren song of a solo career to the Romero sons, with the prospect of greater fame and fortune than could be had as a member of the quartet. Pepe's perspective is that managers believe they will make more money from a soloist's career, so all the Romero sons have felt pressure to do this, starting with the oldest, Celin. For a variety of reasons, Angel finally decided to strike out on his own. As he himself later explained, "When you are a part of a team—like the quartet—if you fall it affects everyone. As a soloist that pressure is not there. I can experiment all I want, which is much more fitting for my personality. I am independent, the daredevil of the family."[8]

One notes an almost eerie prescience in a review from the *Chicago Daily News* in 1966 that observed, "The most interesting musician (as distinct from guitarist) to hear at the moment proved to be young Angel. Angel will be doing other, *lonelier* things in the recital world."[9]

The conflict finally reached a critical mass in the late 1980s with vehement disagreements between Pepe and Angel and Celedonio and Angel. In particular, Angel did things that antagonized Celedonio, who expected people to fulfill their commitments. Instead, Angel's scheduling conflicts caused him to become increasingly unreliable, and he would sometimes not show up for concerts or would send students to substitute for him at the last minute. These were often serious contractual violations, which were noticed by the press. Germans generally place a high premium on punctuality, so one critic disapprovingly noted Angel's tardy arrival at a concert in Gevelsberg. "It adversely affected the whole evening," she scolded.[10]

15. BREAKIN' UP IS HARD TO DO

Celedonio was fond of an old Spanish saying: "A los tuyos con razón o sin ella" (Stand by your own, whether they are right or wrong). Family loyalty was the most important thing, and from his point of view, the increasing conflict within the quartet bordered on disloyalty, not to mention the threat it posed to the family business.

Angel had and still has his own point of view on the split. In the fall of 1992, John Henken reported in the *Los Angeles Times* on a talk he had with Angelita's "Benjamín":

> Angel Romero sees it more as a matter of his own growth. In addition to his solo career and duo performances with his son, he is composing, conducting and even acting—purely for recreational release, he said. "The main issue is that I have so many things going," he said by phone. "I'm very diversified, and it was just time to break loose. My solo schedule has become so hectic that I was having to come back all the way from Europe or the Orient to play just one performance with the quartet. My management is different from that of the quartet, and it became very difficult to schedule." Angel lays much of the blame for the frequently rumored family feuds with the competing managements and record companies. "Managers and record companies started all this screwed-up competition between me and Pepe. Since I've been away from the quartet, I'm enjoying my relationship with my brothers better. I love everybody in the family, and I respect them all, but music to me is not a democracy, it is a dictatorship within yourself. I feel like a racehorse that wants to run in the Kentucky Derby, but is also pulling a wagon. I think teamwork is wonderful. It gives much strength, but it also restricts creativity. It's nothing to do with ego," said the most volatile of the famously emotional clan. "It has to do with contentment."[11]

Of course, Clydesdale Pepe also had a Secretariat solo career, but the quartet remained a priority, and he found a way to interlace the two commitments. However, this interview makes it clear that Angel accused the Romeros' management agency of essentially playing favorites, accommodating Pepe's solo-concert dates to the quartet's touring schedule while doing little to avoid conflicts in his own itineraries. He preferred his own manager.

From Angel's perspective, he was pushed out of the quartet, and there seems to be some truth to this, though it only occurred after a certain limit had been reached and breached. In the family archive is a letter from Columbia Artists Management, Inc. (CAMI) threatening Angel that if he did not cooperate fully, he would be replaced by Celin's son, Celino. (As we will see in the next chapter, this is what eventually happened, and one can safely say that Celino thereby saved the Romero Quartet.) The conflicts resulted from the fact that Angel had signed with a rival agency, International Creative Management (ICM). Thus, a letter to Celin from Herbert O. Fox at CAMI of January 4, 1990, complains, "Several things have happened recently regarding the Quartet that result in our need to know, once and for all, who the members of The Romeros Quartet are and what is its availability. At this moment, 'confusion reigns supreme' and we must get this settled." But though Celin was the quartet's leader, he could no longer predict—much less control—what Angel would do.

Managerial blood boiled as rival agencies fought over Angel. For instance, CAMI had booked the quartet for a date at the Ambassador Auditorium in February 1991, but Angel's new solo manager, ICM, went ahead and told the Ambassador that that date was no good because Angel had a solo date in Flint, Michigan, at the same time. According to Fox's letter, CAMI found this "very disturbing, as the Ambassador date was the first one [CAMI] booked this year, and [the agency] had told [ICM] about it quite a while ago." Fox further asserted, "[ICM] did not tell us at that time that Angel was not available."

Matters had gone from bad to worse when CAMI discovered that ICM had called the Ambassador to inform it that "Angel would not play the date with the Quartet next season unless he was booked for a solo date the following season." Fox lividly declared, "This is absolutely reprehensible. We cannot afford to have a competitor calling clients negotiating side deals that affect Quartet dates, particularly when such side deals might effectively eliminate bookings for other members of the Romero family. And we certainly cannot have a competitor calling a client to inform them whether or not Angel will perform a date with the Quartet. That is our job."

A subsequent fax from ICM to CAMI, dated January 12, 1990, effectively severed Angel's lifeline to CAMI and the quartet: "Aside from the aforementioned dates, please understand that Angel Romero will no longer be a part of the Romero's quartet engagements. This decision was not reached easily and many serious conversations took place before this decision was jointly made between Angel and [us]." This was fine by CAMI, as Fox had already concluded the following: "After having been informed that, for

15. BREAKIN' UP IS HARD TO DO

next season, Angel wants to make the decision city by city as to which Quartet dates he will graciously consent to play, other members of the Quartet and Columbia have agreed that no member of the Quartet can pick and choose dates in this manner. The Quartet either exists as a unit or it does not exist at all. We have all also agreed that if Angel will not do every date, we have to find someone who will. The family has suggested Celino."[12]

Given all these professional and psychological crosscurrents, the question is no longer why the original quartet broke up but rather how it stayed together for so long. Part of the answer is that Celin was an effective diplomat and held everything together; however, he could not do this indefinitely. It comes as no surprise that Papá and Mamá took the breakup very hard, and much of their disappointment was simply concern for Angel's welfare. The general feeling in the family was that, despite his several public pronouncements to the contrary, Angel was better off with the quartet. As Pepe once remarked to me, "I believe completely that the power we each have as solo performers comes in a big way from each other."

Now as before, there is a deep and abiding love between the Romero brothers that no outsider can fully comprehend. But though fraternal waters run deep, on the surface, where people are paying the most attention, things can seem to get choppy at times. Angel in particular often feels estranged from his brothers, who, he complains, do not maintain a degree of contact with him that he would like. Pepe is constantly engaged with his family and students, and he performs and travels too much, in Angel's opinion. For their part, Angel's brothers believe that he made a serious mistake in leaving the quartet, and that reality may continue to cast a shadow over their relationship.

* * *

Angel understandably feels that "the family as it was has pretty much ended." Perhaps the family as it *was* is no more, but the Romeros have been nothing if not fruitful, and they have multiplied. Thus, they and the quartet are very much alive.

CHAPTER 16

THE NEXT GENERATIONS

With the departure of Angel and the passing of Celedonio six years later, major gaps in the quartet were filled by two very gifted Romeros: Celin's son Celino and Angel's son Lito. Rather than parachute them into the narrative at this point, I will first relate the passing of the patriarch and the matriarch of the Romeros, then backtrack a bit to survey the major relationships in the lives of Celin, Pepe, and Angel, some unions of which produced a new and thoroughly American generation of Romero music makers. I conclude with some observations about the family today.

EXIT, STAGE LEFT

Celedonio Romero y Pinazo closed his eyes to the changing scenes of this world on May 8, 1996, at the age of eighty-three. This was not his first serious brush with death, only his last. Recall that he had had heart problems going back to his army days in the 1930s. In 1978, he suffered an attack of pitting edema of the ankles and bilateral basal pulmonary rales. His final illness was a protracted and painful one, as he had contracted lung cancer in early 1995. He was never a regular smoker, and this cancer was a rare type that had a genetic origin unconnected with his environment. Celedonio was a fighter to the end, and it took more than cancer to dampen his love of music. He gave his last formal concert on May 12, 1995, playing Rodrigo's

16. THE NEXT GENERATIONS

Concierto andaluz with the quartet. He performed an encore with the quartet in nearby Oceanside only two months before his passing, just after his eighty-third birthday. (He had given his final concert in Málaga in 1991.)

During the waning months of his life, and especially on his deathbed, when he could no longer play, he wanted particular pieces played for him as he faded away, including his beloved *Fantasía XVI* by Luis de Milán, the Bach Chaconne, and the *Fantasía* by Sor that Pepe had resurrected. Pepe performed these and other works in bedside concerts shortly before Celedonio's death, but he wasn't alone in keeping Papá company. As their father lay dying, Celin entertained him with Torroba's *Sonatina*, though he maintained such a determined vigil that he fainted from exhaustion. Angel was touring in Europe when he got word of Papá's precipitous decline, and he immediately canceled his appearances to return to California. He arrived just before his father died.

Celedonio's funeral service was held at 10:00 a.m. on Monday, May 13, at Saint James Catholic Church, in Solana Beach, near Del Mar. It featured a reading of his poetry and concluded with Beethoven's "Ode to Joy." The two hundred people in attendance, including numerous family members and friends, represented a cross section of the vast number of lives he had touched during his forty years in Southern California. This was the church with which Celedonio had been associated for many years, for which he had given benefit concerts, and where he had many friends and admirers. That Saint James (Santiago) is the patron saint of Spain was a happy coincidence. True, the family did not attend Mass on a regular basis, as the experience of life in Spain, especially during the civil war, had left them with deeply ambivalent feelings about the faith. Like many Catholics, participation arose more out of a desire to maintain appearances than out of any metaphysical convictions. Nonetheless, he clearly believed in, or at least fervently hoped for, an afterlife, and before he died, he told his sons that he would meet them in another place. Until then, he wanted peace and love to reign supreme in the family. As Pepe explained in his eulogy: "And at the very end, he could not breathe at all, there, he could not produce a sound, so he just moved his lips to tell what he wanted. And what he wanted was peace between my brothers and me forever, and he wanted that we should protect each other and we should protect our mother, that we should protect our children and love them."[1]

In the family archive are many cards and telegrams offering condolences on the death of a towering figure in the twin worlds of music and the guitar.

PART 4. LEGACY

Among these are missives from Michael Lorimer, Manolo Sanlúcar, the Los Angeles Guitar Quartet, and guitar societies in Saint Louis, Florida, and Dallas, as well as the Seville Royal Symphony Orchestra, city government of Málaga, and Palau de la Música Catalana. A year later, President Bill Clinton would add his eloquent voice to the chorus in praise of our fallen nightingale: "Throughout our history, our nation has been blessed with great musicians like Maestro Romero, visionaries who have told us not only who we are, but also who we can become. They have distilled our emotions, clarified our thoughts, and renewed our spirits with the vigor of their music and the freshness of their perspective."[2] *Muy bien dicho* (very well said), but Celedonio himself gets the last word here:

> When I die, the stars will shine more brightly upon you,
> Because all my love will be in them.[3]

The stars indeed shone more brightly on Mamá, to light the difficult path ahead of her now. She struggled valiantly to persist in the face of this great loss, and with the support of her family, she was able to soldier on for another three years before succumbing to heart disease on March 10, 1999, in San Diego. As was the case with Celedonio, however, it was not her first encounter with mortality. She had suffered a serious stroke in 1988, while accompanying the quartet during a tour that took them to Bob Jones University in Greenville, South Carolina, where she fell ill. Though she spent some time recovering in a wheelchair, she eventually was back to her old self and playing the castanets with renewed vigor, especially in the guitar-quartet arrangement of the famous "Fandango" from Boccherini's Guitar Quintet no. 4 in D. Her funeral service took place at Saint James in Solana Beach on March 15, 1999, and her devoted sons serenaded her one last time as she lay in her casket.

No one could possibly take the place of these two larger-than-life figures, but the sound of guitars and castanets would not cease with their passing, thanks to a new generation of Romeros who rode to the rescue.[4]

GENERATIONS TO THE RESCUE

Leo Tolstoy quotably begins his novel *Anna Karenina* with the observation that "all happy families resemble one another; each unhappy family is un-

16. THE NEXT GENERATIONS

happy in its own way." Literary critics may deem that a suitable opening in the context of the story, but as much as I love the rest of the book, that particular maxim has never rung true with me. Most families are a blend of happy and unhappy, and each one is unique. This understanding will inform our exploration of the many Romero *families*.

One indelicate reality any chronicler of the Romeros must eventually confront is that none of the first marriages of the Romero sons survived the stresses and strains that constant touring places on a family. All the "boys" married in their twenties, and these youthful unions proved especially vulnerable to long absences, inevitable changes in outlook and direction, and infidelity. Whatever incompatibilities may have lain dormant beneath the joyful surface of matrimonial celebration eventually reared their heads with a vengeance as the reality of this situation asserted itself.

The Romeros, as an ensemble and as soloists, were giving at least two hundred concerts a year, usually more. Sometimes spouses could go along, and Mamá nearly always did. But the sons' young wives usually had pressing responsibilities on the home front, especially with the arrival of children. Frequent and sometimes lengthy separations were as painful as they were unavoidable. And it is not hard to imagine the temptations that the Romero sons encountered in their travels. Handsome, charming, young, and famous, they were essentially rock stars and effortlessly attracted the kind of companionship they were disinclined to go without for very long.

The very real toll these innumerable, if fleeting, liaisons took on their marriages is undeniable. And it was only a matter of time before some liaisons would prove less fleeting than the others. Only with advancing age, more maturity in mate selection, relative freedom from child rearing, and the consequent ability of spouses to go on tour would the hanky-panky subside and allow for stable, supportive, and satisfying relationships. However, those initial marriages produced numerous offspring, among them several who would play a decisive role in advancing the family legacy.

CELIN, LAURIE, CELINO, AND CLAUDIA

On May 7, 1966, Celin married Laurie Wanda Barc. Barc is a Polish name, and her grandparents were from Poland. A gifted soprano from Phoenix, Arizona, she had a music degree from the University of Arizona and had performed some major roles on the West Coast. She was six years younger than Celin and caught his roving eye in 1963 while enrolled at the Academy of the West, as a result of winning the regional Metropolitan Opera auditions.

He spied her on the beach one day and made his move. She was reclining in the sand while studying an opera score when he delivered his thickly accented pickup line, "You look like a girl who plays tennis!" This may not have been the most original introduction in the history of dating, but he was darkly handsome, and it worked. He soon invited her over to a barbeque at a house that the three sons had bought in Montecito. Laurie actually found Celin a little, well, strange, but her girlfriends were all highly impressed, as the Romero boys were considered very eligible bachelors. Although Laurie wasn't much of a tennis player after all, she did sing opera, and that was even more attractive to the opera buff Celin. As it turned out, she wound up sacrificing her opera career to marry him and bear their two children: Angela (b. 1966) and Celedonio ("Celino") (b. 1969).

However, this situation didn't mean the end of Laurie's musical career. She could still teach and give recitals, which she did (Columbia Artists was also her agent). In particular, she and Celin performed arrangements for guitar and voice. For instance, a program in the archive from the 1981–82 concert season features them both. Laurie was also an accomplished keyboardist, and she played harpsichord while accompanying Celin in the Vivaldi D-major lute concerto, arranged for guitar. Celin then played a solo set, and the recital concluded with several songs featuring Laurie singing to Celin's accompaniment, including works by Giuliani, Villa-Lobos, and Rodrigo.

Angela inherited her father's passion for history and politics and went on to study political science at Columbia and then MIT, where she received her doctorate. She is a professor of sociology at San Diego Mesa College and is married to Carl Robert Sanchez. Together than have three children, Carlos Emilio (b. 1994), Emilio Celin (b. 1996), and Marina Isabella (b. 1998).

Celino (yet another nickname for Celedonio) took over for Angel in 1990 and has since become a regular and reliable member of the quartet, one with a thriving career as a recitalist as well as a soloist with major orchestras in Houston, San Francisco, Munich, and elsewhere. Indeed, as we saw in the previous chapter, he had big shoes to fill and did so under extreme pressure. There was not much time to learn difficult music and execute it with typical

16. THE NEXT GENERATIONS

Romero élan and panache. Twenty-five years later, he has proven himself more than equal to this task, the result of native talent and persistent hard work.

Yet Celino resembles his father in that he is more a man of action than one of words. He is not prone to self-aggrandizement and will not crow about his achievements unless pressed to do so. For example, he once described his early years with characteristic modesty: "When I was young, I thought about being a pilot. And I was really into soccer and baseball. But when I started going to junior college at Palomar, I began listening to a lot more music. And when Angel left the quartet, I went over to his place, got all his music and just fell in love with it."[5] This autobiographical dispensation gives the somewhat misleading impression that he came late to the guitar, which was not true. The year before he had told *On the Air Magazine*,

> When I was a little baby, I had the ear already, just from listening to it. When I was around four years old, I got my first little miniature guitar, and I started playing a little flamenco. I would be on the road all the time with them and I was getting lessons from all of them. My first concert was when I was six at a church Christmas festival. I played the Little Drummer boy. As I was growing up, I started playing a lot of sports and didn't play the guitar as much. . . . I was a little shy, and I always felt, "There's no way I'm ever going to be as good." Pepe would always say to me, "Don't blow such a great talent."[6]

Celino did not "blow" a great talent. In the beginning of his quartet career, he was understandably diffident and even reluctant to go onstage, but that was a quarter of a century ago. He now matches his uncle Pepe stride for stride in the most difficult works, including Rodrigo's *Concierto madrigal*. A review of a recent performance in San Francisco confirms his arrival as a seasoned and secure professional: "Pepe was joined by Celino on his slightly smaller instrument for Rodrigo's 'Tonadilla,' originally written for the mid century guitar duo of Ida Presti and Alexandre Lagoya. Uncle and nephew shared the fascinating close intervals that begin the piece, flowing into impressionistic takes on a variety of Iberian modes. In the chamber-music like exchanges, the pair's synchronization was impressive, and their pleasure in the process was apparent on their faces."[7]

In any case, having him in the quartet in the early 1990s intrigued audiences with the spectacle of three generations of Romeros; understandably, it was an emotional experience for Pepe to have his father on one side and his nephew on the other. Papá himself was sometimes reduced to tears at the sight. Celin took understandable pride in his son's talent and courage, remarking in 1993, "He's really maturing very, very fast. He has a complete and natural instinct. He's a very good musician. He's a hard worker. He's unbelievable. He surprises all of us, all the time."[8]

In addition to playing with the quartet, performing concertos, and giving solo recitals, Celino likes to . . . fish. He has a Boston whaler and enjoys catching yellowfin and bluefin. Being thirty miles or more out on the Pacific puts things in perspective for him, as it has done for generations of sea-loving Romeros. Like his grandmother, he also enjoys cooking and has a number of fish recipes that have proven popular with his family.

His most notable catch, however, was not a fish but rather his wife, Michelle. Her maiden name is Zubia, a Basque surname, though her recent ancestry is a mixture of Mexican, Irish, and Austrian. He met her in 1996 at Chico State University in Northern California, where he was performing at the time. They were married two years later. She is an accomplished jewelry designer but has devoted herself to raising their children. Celedonio (so named in honor of Papá) was born in 1998. His nickname is Nino, to avoid confusion with three earlier generations of Celedonios. Maximino ("Maxi"), named after Papá's brother, was born in 2001; Raquelle Angela arrived in 2006. Nino plays ukulele and various styles of guitar, while Maxi plays classical guitar. Raquelle Angela is an award-winning dancer.

Maxi has had the benefit of excellent instruction. His father displays a real love of pedagogy, explaining the attraction this way: "The guitar can be a nightmare!" To help himself and fellow aspirants wake up from this bad dream, he has carefully analyzed the Romero technique, which fascinates him. He also just likes helping people and hopes to publish a second edition of his 2006 *The Art of the Spanish Guitar*. True to Romero form, Celino has rather traditional tastes in repertoire, and his favorite composers include Sor, Tárrega, and Torroba.

Celin's marriage to Laurie ended in a permanent separation, though Laurie reports that they are much better friends now than when they were together. Both have very independent temperaments and "fought all the time." Laurie lives quite happily in Santa Fe but still occasionally visits Celin and their children and grandchildren in Del Mar. For the past twenty-three

16. THE NEXT GENERATIONS

years, Celin has enjoyed the companionship and love of Claudia Tornsäufer, originally from the Düsseldorf area in northern Germany. An accomplished guitarist, she graduated from the Robert Schumann Hochschule in Düsseldorf and once performed for German president Dr. Richard von Weizäcker. She was then inspired to move to San Diego in order to study with the Romeros.

Claudia had attended a summer academy at Salzburg's Mozarteum in 1989 and again in 1990, where she studied with Pepe. The following year she visited San Diego during Christmas vacation. In 1990, she met Celin at a New Year's party, and they felt an immediate rapport. A hallmark of true love is that their friendship and attraction deepened over time. In the summer of 1991, she returned to San Diego to study with Pepe and then continued her lessons with Celin starting in the fall of 1992, at San Diego State University, where she received a scholarship and became a teaching assistant. In due course, she and Celin fell in love.

Claudia is now a professor for the San Diego Community College District, where she teaches courses on opera and music appreciation. In addition, she has completed a doctorate in educational leadership at SDSU. Disciplined and sedulous, she also manages the quartet's schedule, along with Celino's solo engagements, and balances her many responsibilities with graceful aplomb. Among her other qualifications is a knack for being able to calm Celin and comfort him, which he appreciates very much. For her part, she loves the "depth of his soul, his philosophical nature, his noble, generous heart, as well as his romantic and passionate side." And he has the all-important ability to make her laugh.

PEPE, KRISTINE, PEPE JR., AND CARISSA

Pepe's first marriage was to Kristine Meigs Eddy, a talented musician who started out on violin and piano but eventually switched to guitar. She came from a very musical family: her father was a professional opera singer, while her mother conducted a choir at Santa Barbara City College. Celin joined this choir to establish contacts with local musicians, and though Kristine's mother actually took some lessons with him, she soon concluded that the guitar was too difficult and gave it up. Kristine attended Celedonio's 1958 debut recital and fell in love with the guitar. She also developed a major crush on Celin, but he soon entered the army, and since Celedonio did not speak English, she wound up taking lessons with Pepe, who was her age (though she was seven months younger).

Pepe and Kristine were married at All-Saints-by-the-Sea in Santa Barbara on December 18, 1965, when they were both twenty-one years old. They eventually had four children: Cristina (Tina) (b. 1967); Maria Angelina (b. 1969); Susanna (b. 1972); and Pepe Jr. (b. 1978). Tina has a son, Bernardo (b. 1994), by an earlier marriage. She is now happily married to Greg Shirer, a Pepe student and music professor in the San Diego Community College District. Angelina is an accomplished pianist and a charming dancer who is now married to Joseph Kressin and has two children: Jacob (b. 1995), who has studied voice and Spanish in Granada, aspires to sing opera, and has appeared in concert at the Performing Arts Center in nearby Escondido; and Leah (b. 1998), who is a talented ballerina. Susanna is a schoolteacher and counselor for underprivileged children and is married to Lane Reiss; they have a daughter named Kristina (b. 2006).

Pepe Jr. is married to Kimberly Joolingen, an avid practitioner of yoga and former schoolteacher who now homeschools their two children: daughter Sophia (b. 2007) and son, Owen (b. 2013). Pepe Jr. recalls, "If I didn't hear the guitar when I got home from school, something was wrong."[9] Not surprisingly, he took an early interest in playing the guitar, but over time, it became clear that his real talent was for making rather than playing the instrument. In junior high, he won an award for a cabinet he made in wood shop. Papá looked into his crystal ball and saw a future of Romero guitars, so he decided to establish a shop in his home where Little Pepe could build them.

Little Pepe got his initial training with Dake Traphagen in the state of Washington. He then apprenticed with some of the best builders in Europe, one of whom was Edmund Blöchinger in Germany, near Munich. He then learned from master builders in Spain, including Miguel Rodríguez and José Luis Romanillos. On June 12, 1997, at the tender age of nineteen, he sent a postcard to his grandma telling her that he was in Madrid studying guitar building with Pablo Contreras, a very famous *guitarrero*. Not surprisingly, given this background, Pepe Jr. builds his instruments in a traditional Spanish manner, though he is not afraid to experiment.

16. THE NEXT GENERATIONS

His finely crafted and beautiful-sounding instruments have thus achieved international celebrity, and he has about three years' worth of backorders. Unwilling to compromise on quality, he makes only eight to ten guitars a year, each currently costing about $12,000. Inspired during a visit to Hawaii in 2011, he has also gone into building ukuleles and has even started a ukulele business in Vietnam. Pepe Jr. clearly inherited the Romero knack not only for construction but also for business. But he's not alone in this regard.

According to Little Pepe, Tina's son Bernardo is a natural at building guitars. Having played one of his first creations, I can attest to the truth of that observation. He shares Pepe Jr.'s studio, which for many years was located in the house that Papá built and that is still occupied by Pepe and Celin; however, they have moved to a new studio in Oceanside. As Little Pepe puts it, his father taught him out of love, and that's how Pepe Jr. is bringing along his nephew Bernardo, who studied Spanish and guitar building in Granada, at the University of Granada and with luthier Juan Miguel Carmona, respectively.

Pepe Sr. and Celin both play Little Pepe's instruments, but not solely out of family loyalty. They have too much at stake to appear on stage with an inferior instrument. No, as Pepe told the *Ann Arbor News*, "The guitar of my son will have to stand up to the greatest instruments ever built. Even with my son, I would not play it unless I loved the instrument itself. It is not enough to love the maker."[10] I have also played a few of Little Pepe's instruments, and I can certify that it is very easy to love them.

Pepe and Kristine married very young, so it is not surprising that they gradually grew apart. She would have preferred that he spend more time at home, but his career would not permit it. The divide between them became irreparable as Pepe found new companionship, though this attachment would develop gradually over several years. In the early 1980s, Pepe cultivated a relationship with a student he met in Houston, Carissa Sugg, and this union grew into a thirty-years-and-counting love affair. Carissa is twelve years younger than Pepe, and they married on May 16, 1987. They remain a very happily married couple.

Ironically, it all started with a smashed dream: by the time she was sixteen, Carissa Sugg knew she wanted to be a dancer; however, her religiously orthodox father forbade her to be a dancer on stage, despite a family history that included professional dancers, among them her mother and grandmother. Fortunately, Carissa had a plan B, as she also loved classical and flamenco guitar and had a sizable collection of LPs. She started taking lessons in 1973 at the Guitar Gallery in Houston, run by Romero disciple Terry Gashen. He and his wife (Susan Lamborghini, by now their manager) opened her world, as they were very liberal and open-minded. Of course, she heard all about the Romeros and became such a fan that she had a big poster of Angel in her bedroom (though her father made her take it down). She was planning to attend an Angel concert, but he canceled the tour due to illness. Pepe substituted for him at Jones Hall, a prestigious venue in Houston. She recalls laughing from pure joy throughout the program. The following summer Pepe gave a weeklong master class at Rice University, under the auspices of the Guitar Gallery. Although she was not enrolled in the class, she learned a lot from observing him teach. One thing she noticed was that students really improved as a result of his guidance.

Pepe and Carissa began to socialize and felt a mutual attraction, not just physical but in every way. Fortunately, Pepe's travels required him to go through Houston a lot, so he had many opportunities to spend time with Carissa. Still, he was married with children, and there seemed to be no real way forward for them, so Carissa studied premed at the University of Texas Health Sciences Center, where she earned a bachelor's degree in nutrition and then a certificate in dietetics. But by 1980, things had gotten very serious with Pepe, and he was now separated from Kristine. The following year Carissa moved to California to be with him, and that is where she has remained. Pepe eventually divorced Kristine, and though she says that it was "amicable," it was also "horrendous," especially since neither party wanted to hurt the children.

Carissa and Claudia hold the Romero "act" together and collaborate closely in managing the quartet. Pepe readily admits, for example, that he doesn't remember words nearly as well as he remembers musical notes. That's the way his brain is wired. But it means that without an amanuensis, he's in serious trouble. Correspondence, for example, is the lifeblood of a career such as his: emails and letters constantly pass between him and his various managers and collaborators. A series of perfectly remembered musical notes will simply not suffice as a response.

16. THE NEXT GENERATIONS

Fortunately, Pepe has a wife who is an exceptionally capable manager of his career. As Pepe himself has said, her chief motivation is to be of service. I have already alluded to the famous picture of Mamá bringing Pepe breakfast in bed so that he could keep practicing through the meal. Carissa keeps this picture by her bed for inspiration. As Pepe noted, Mamá "protected the time and the space" in which the Romeros could do what they have done. Carissa and Claudia both lovingly carry on in that role for their mates and the family at large.

ANGEL, WENDY, LITO, AND NEFRETIRI

Angel married Wendy Winkelman in Las Vegas, on November 14, 1966. Two years younger than Angel, she was an aspiring actress in Los Angeles, and they first met while attending Hollywood Professional School. Together they had three children: Angelito, known as Lito (b. 1967), and twins named Celina and Josefa (b. 1971).

Both Lito and Celino were good at soccer and thought that they wanted to play professionally. They had early exposure to another way of life, however, and would be excused from grade school to go on tour with the quartet, giving them the opportunity to watch the goings-on backstage. During those formative years, Lito began to imagine himself performing with his dad, uncles, and grandpa. He started playing the guitar at the tender age of four and received instruction from his father, grandfather, and uncles. His technique, however, most closely resembles that of his father, though he has always had a great love of flamenco and worked with Pepe on that technique. In fact, he absorbed the Romero method and style by ear, since he was taught by rote and did not learn to read music until much later.

After high school, he attended Mira Costa College and SDSU for a while, but an academic career was clearly not in the cards. A major turning point was making the Telarc recording *A Touch of Class* with his father in 1991. He also performed many duo concerts with him about that time and still feels very close to Angel, who was a great teacher and role model. They have continued to perform and record together, including the Vivaldi Concerto in G Major for two mandolins and orchestra, with the Academy of St. Martin-in-the-Fields. Thus, unlike his younger nephew Celino, Lito actually had a concert career before he joined the quartet, to take the place of Papá, in 1995. He fondly recalls going on a European tour with them that year and then returning to the United States to entertain at the 1996 Olympics in Atlanta.

Lito continues to be attracted to flamenco and flamenco-inspired classical music, including works by Falla, Turina, Rodrigo, and Torroba. He especially enjoys interpreting Papá's music, as well as Pepe's arrangements of Sabicas's flamenco creations.

Lito is happily married to Ruth María Fernández, who is of 100 percent Puerto Rican ancestry.[11] They met in 2002 in rural Ramona, where Angel had bought a house. She was a barista in the only espresso place in Ramona, and loving espresso as much as Lito does, it would only be a matter of time before he loved his server, too. Although not a musician, she is a very good salsa dancer and has tried to teach him some moves, with varying degrees of success. She is now an esthetician and owns her own business, the very suitably named Andalucia Beauty Lounge. They have a son named Joaquín (b. 2004) and a daughter, Valentina Lucia Romero (b. 2012). They now live in Escondido, where her business is located, about twenty miles inland from the coast.

Possessing an unusual degree of physical and personal charm, Angel found the constraints of matrimony a bit too confining. He and Wendy eventually parted ways, though they remain good friends. After many other liaisons, some more enduring than others, true love and even fatherhood entered his life story again.[12] This time the attraction was to a woman much younger than he was, though a person of more than enough strength and self-confidence to hold her own.

The *Modesto Bee* offered Angel's description of their meeting: "[Angel] found a love [in Modesto] a decade ago. After finishing his solo, he went outside for a smoke and saw some attractive ushers. "Being the person I am, I said, 'Ooh, what cute young girls,'" So I said, 'Good evening, good evening.' The most serious in the group was 1995 Downey High School graduate and music student Nefretiri Morte. . . . Nefretiri's parents [are] Barry and Gloria Morte, who still live in Modesto."[13]

Nefy sang Rapunzel in the Downey High production of *Into the Woods* and studied music briefly at Modesto Junior College. She went on to perform in Falla's *El amor brujo* with the Norddeutscher Rundfunk and the Chicago

16. THE NEXT GENERATIONS

Sinfonietta, with Angel conducting on both occasions. She also performed García Lorca's *Canciones españolas antiguas* at the Koblenz Festival, again with Angel, in his arrangement for voice and guitar. They have a daughter named Bella (b. 2001), who has inherited her parents' musical talent and plays piano as well as guitar. She exhibits a preference for classic pop, especially Aretha Franklin, Tony Bennett, and Elvis Presley. Having heard her sing, I can testify to the attractiveness of her voice. Angel recently moved his family to Hollywood in order to facilitate her career.

THE QUARTET TODAY

As the *St. Louis Post-Dispatch* noted, "It used to be that Pepe and Angel Romero laid equal claim to being the group's flashiest member. Now unchallenged by his brother, Pepe tends to be the center of attention whenever the music gets wildly virtuosic."[14] Some things have not changed over the decades, regardless of changes in personnel, and the *Toronto Star* got it exactly right when it observed,

> What makes a Romeros concert memorable . . . is the interplay between the foursome and how democratically it operates. Pepe may be the leader, but he is not the star. The spotlight moves from the quartet to the individual then to a duo. Each gets his turn to play the solo and to accompany. But without the right stuff, it will remain a bit of a novelty act, almost as much fun to watch as to hear. But too often, we find ourselves responding to the virtuosity rather than the music. Oh, and to the person whose phone went off during Lito's solo, hang up![15]

Among the Romero guitarists today, Celedonio lives on in collective memory. As Pepe has noted, "We continue to study with [him] because anytime there is a problem we encounter in learning new music, we still always think, 'How would you have done it?'"[16] Such enduring counsel has helped the quartet stay together and prosper. Another vital ingredient in its continuing success is the uniformity of musical approach among its members, one handed down across generations. In a real sense, it is a family business, and it has endured and prospered far beyond what even the most optimistic observers might have predicted back in 1960, not to mention 1940.

PART 4. LEGACY

* * *

In 2013, I was witness to a Romero Quartet concert at the Lobero Theatre in Santa Barbara, where it had all begun fifty-five years earlier, in 1958. It was given in honor of Celedonio, who would have been one hundred years old. On this evening, Celin, Pepe, Celino, and Lito were joined in an encore by several younger Romero guitarists. It was a rare sight and brought to my mind words from the Catholic Mass: "As it was in the beginning, is now, and ever shall be: [Romeros] without end."[17] Amen to all that.

ENCORE

> I desire that, by night,
> [My guitar] will sound out very long notes
> And that they will fly through the heavens.
> [Yo quiero que por las noches,
> Sueñe con notas muy largas
> Y que vuelen por el Cielo.]
> —Celedonio Romero, from "Yo quiero"

In a letter of August 21, 1990, the Romeros' European manager, Joachim Schlote, wrote the following to Celedonio from Salzburg: "Your activities with concerts . . . all over the world, your compositions, your interpretations of great Spanish music and your educational merits simply make you one of the outstanding personalities in the world of guitar music. To reach the hearts of thousands of people and to make their lives happier by music can be considered a great present to everybody."[1] Multiply that assessment several times over, and you have a tidy summary of what the Romero family has accomplished. John Paul II anticipated this sentiment in fewer words when, after the Romeros played for him at the Vatican in 1986, he declared: "How much goodness you give to humanity with your music!"[2]

This concert was among the most meaningful events of their careers, one they fondly and proudly recall. Photographs of it grace the walls of their homes, as it seemed somehow a fulfillment of what they had been taught to expect. Indeed, the Catholic theology on which generations of Romeros were nurtured posits the existence of an omniscient Creator who presides over the destinies of all things, right down to two sparrows being sold for a farthing (Matt. 10:29). Celedonio often felt that the course of his life was guided by this almighty hand of Providence, and he was understandably thankful for it. In fact, on one occasion he wrote that "the universe . . . is marvelously ordered by the sublime Creator."[3] This ordering included his family, as on another occasion, he confidently asserted that "my sons are a gift of God. They are a miracle. We are all very close, very loving. They were born with the ear."[4]

Of course, all the good things that happen to us are fully compatible with belief in a benevolent deity. Less comprehensible is all the nastiness that life dishes out, in the form of death, disease, natural disasters, and the tremendous capacity of human beings for wanton cruelty and destruction. Celedonio had certainly witnessed all this darkness firsthand, but it never disrupted his fundamentally grateful and optimistic outlook on life. As he wrote in one of his poems, "I have known great wars, immense cataclysms, devastating earthquakes, and many assaults on humanity, but I carry on just the same, unalterable."[5] If we have learned nothing else from this story, by now we must surely know that the nightingale looks only skyward as it sings its songs.

But there are other ways to view the history presented in the preceding pages. From a Buddhist perspective, transience is the one unalterable characteristic of life, and far from being part of a divine scheme, mutability ensues from the interaction of preexisting conditions without any preordained or even necessarily predictable outcome. Buddhism obviously thereby makes no provision for the sort of god that Saint Thomas Aquinas envisioned, namely, an uncreated creator, an uncaused cause, a supreme being who perpetually presides over and guides its creation. All life may be sorrowful, as the First Noble Truth declares, but that suffering does not result from a supernaturally originated design. Karma is simply because it is, as a condition and consequence of human consciousness and action, not because any sentient entity willed it to be so. All we can do is learn to modulate our response to the ineluctable realities of this world, in a gradual—or sudden!—process of transcendence.

I do not presume to see deeply enough into the fabric of reality to know if either of these two views, Catholic or Buddhist, is correct. The Cistercian monk Thomas Merton built a sturdy philosophical bridge from Catholicism to Buddhism, while Zen Buddhist monk Thich Nhat Hanh has done the same from the other side of the chasm separating these two ancient traditions.[6] To be sure, there are many other paths to deconstructing the "nature of things," as Lucretius put it. For their part, the Romeros have always tended toward heterodoxy in religious matters, and as the sons get older, their spiritual attitudes become less and less distinct. Angel has described himself as someone who, if he were religious in any conventional sense, would "probably be a Buddhist with a tinge of Catholic surrounding it," an observation that inspired the preceding paragraphs. Though Pepe and Celin believe there "must be something," they aren't sure how to articulate it. In sum, the Romeros' spirituality is now more a feeling than a thought, an experience rather than an idea. It is a "something" they perceive most intensely while making music, and it defies description.

However, one would not have to be a Buddhist to conclude that contingency plays a central role in our earthly existence, that all history, human and natural, is but a lengthy concatenation of such contingencies. Even the author of Ecclesiastes 9:11 was apparently persuaded of this idea when he wrote that "the race is not to the swift, nor the battle to the strong, neither yet bread to the wise, nor yet riches to men of understanding, nor yet favour to men of skill; but *time and chance* happeneth to them all" (emphasis added).

History may not reveal its alternatives, but it is safe to say that had one José Romero López *not* decided in 1880, at age fourteen, to leave rural day labor behind and seek a better life for himself in the city of Málaga, the Romeros as we know them would never have existed. As a result, the ensuing evolution of the classical guitar's pedagogy, repertoire, and discography would have been impoverished to a conspicuous degree. I would certainly not be writing this book; indeed, though I grew up in Minneapolis, Minnesota, far from the mountains of Málaga, the entire trajectory of my life and career would have been radically different—and as a direct result of the neural synapses, a century earlier, in the prefrontal cortex of an illiterate teenage Spanish peasant of whose ignominious existence I would never have known and whose life choices would have seemed to be of no consequence whatsoever to (an equally ignominious) me.

In reality, an uninterrupted skein of causality connects the first step that José took on the path to Málaga one fateful day and my typing of the period at the end of this sentence. Here is a classic example of the sort of "cosmic irony" one often perceives in the novels and poems of Thomas Hardy. In fact, had our young José the Obscure decided to remain a farmhand, not only my own life but also the lives of thousands of other people would be very different today.

> Alien they seemed to be:
> No mortal eye could see
> The intimate welding of their later history,
> Or sign that they were bent
> By paths coincident
> On being anon twin halves of one august event.[7]

Such are the vagaries and vicissitudes of our contingent life on earth.

And so our saga ends where it began, in the sylvan solitude of a mountainside north of Málaga. Night is coming on, and the air grows cooler now as slanting rays of a setting sun bathe my surroundings in an almost ethereal radiance. Celedonio always maintained that each note one plays lives in eternity, traveling ever outward into the cosmos.[8] The laws of physics stipulate a different outcome: sound waves cannot move through a vacuum, and they dissipate over time and space. Alas, nothing endures forever. But Celedonio was a poet, not a scientist. Long may his cosmic notes live!

Taking some poetic license of my own, I now imagine that, in the secret stillness of the night, these delicate *romero* plants that encircle me here exude not only fragrance but also a sort of music that soars into the heavens, where iridescent tones scintillate in the firmament like mystic stars, suffusing the frigid blackness of outer space with Andalusian warmth and color. Our belovèd poet Antonio Machado heard this celestial music long ago: "Today the stars sing / And nothing else."[9]

* * *

Be that as it may, here below, in all times and places, the love of music has remained a defining characteristic of our species. This immemorial passion for musical warmth and color found and still finds one of its most beautiful expressions in the twenty-four-string guitar known as Los Romeros.

APPENDIX 1

CHRONOLOGY

Year	Event
1913	Celedonio Romero Pinazo born in Cienfuegos, Cuba, to José Romero and Josefa Pinazo, March 2.
1919	Except for the father, the entire Romero family returns to Málaga. Settles for a time in rural Jotrón, in the mountains north of the city, then returns to the city of Málaga.
1924	Papá Romero returns from Cuba and is reunited with the family in Málaga.
1928	Celedonio gives his first public concert, at age fifteen, in Málaga.
1932–35	Celedonio studies *solfège* and harmony at the Málaga Conservatory.
1934	Celedonio marries Angelita, November 29. Drafted into the Spanish army but discharged due to heart ailment.
1936	Outbreak of Spanish Civil War in July. Nationalist bombing of Málaga begins in August and continues until the city capitulates six months later. Celin Romero is born November 23, during a bombardment of the city by Franco's air force.
1937	Málaga falls to Franco's forces in February. Celedonio is drafted into the Nationalist army but manages to escape frontline duty through the intervention of friends in Franco's medical corps. Spends rest of the war in Málaga, out of harm's way, though his three brothers continue to fight on the Republican side.
1939	End of Spanish Civil War; Celedonio resumes his concert career, touring throughout Spain.
1944	José Luis (Pepe) Romero born March 8.
1946	Angel Romero born August 19.

APPENDIX 1

1951	Celin performs on Radio Málaga.
1954	Romeros meet Evelyn and Farrington Stoddard, who will assist them in moving to the United States. First, the family moves to Seville.
1957	Romeros finally succeed in arranging their escape from Spain, with help of the Stoddards and highly placed officials in the Spanish government. Leave from Lisbon for the United States on a TWA flight to New York and then Los Angeles. Settle in Santa Barbara, California, with the Stoddards.
1958	Celedonio gives his debut recital in the United States, at Santa Barbara's Lobero Theatre on June 13. Family moves to Hollywood and establishes guitar school there.
1959	Celin is drafted into U.S. Army and sent to Fort Ord in Monterey, California, for basic training.
1960	Quartet makes first appearance, Lobero Theatre in Santa Barbara. Earliest recordings made with Contemporary Records. Celin completes active duty and enters U.S. Army reserve.
1961	Now managed by James Lucas, Romeros perform at Wilshire Ebell Theater in Los Angeles, January 21. Go on to perform in San Francisco, Chicago, Boston, and New York. Appear on *Jack Paar* television show.
1962	Quartet appears again at Town Hall in New York.
1964	Angel, age eighteen, gives West Coast premiere of Rodrigo's *Concierto de Aranjuez* with Los Angeles Philharmonic at Hollywood Bowl. The quartet appears on the *Hootenanny* television show.
1965	Quartet appears on *The Tonight Show*.
1967	Quartet appears on *The Ed Sullivan Show*. Death of Farrington Stoddard. Premieres Rodrigo's *Concierto andaluz* with San Antonio Symphony. Lito Romero born August 15. First recordings with Mercury Records. Romeros are now managed by Columbia Artists.
1969	Celino Romero born May 21.
1969–70	Celedonio builds home in Del Mar, California, and his sons find houses there as well.
1975	Angel premieres Torroba's *Tonada concertante*, dedicated to Celedonio.
1979	Quartet performs at the Carter White House at a state dinner for Premier Tito of Yugoslavia. Premieres Torroba's *Concierto ibérico* in Vancouver.
1970s–present	Pepe and Celin hold a variety of teaching positions, at University of Southern California; San Diego State University; University of California, San Diego; California State University, Los Angeles.
1981	Celedonio is knighted by King Juan Carlos of Spain, January 5.
1982	Death of Federico Moreno Torroba, September 12.
1983	Pepe premieres Rodrigo's *Concierto para una fiesta*.
1984	Celedonio receives Orden de Alfonso X el Sabio.
1986	Quartet plays for Pope John Paul II at Vatican.
1988	Celedonio's knighthood is upgraded to Comendador de Número.
1990	Angel leaves quartet; Celino takes his place; San Diego declares January 14 Celedonio Romero Day.

CHRONOLOGY

1991	Angel premieres his *Rincones de España*, a concerto on themes by Rodrigo.
1993	San Diego declares March 27 Celedonio Romero Day.
1994	University of Victoria confers honorary doctorate on Pepe in June.
1995	Lito takes Celedonio's place in quartet; University of Victoria confers honorary doctorate on Celedonio in November.
1996	Celedonio dies on May 8.
1999	Angelita dies on March 10. Death of Joaquín Rodrigo, July 6.
2000	Celin, Pepe, and Angel knighted by King Juan Carlos of Spain, February 11.
2001	PBS airs documentary on Romeros on September 14.
2004	German Norddeutscher Rundfunk airs documentary about Romeros on October 30.
2005	Angel becomes conductor of Baja Symphony Orchestra.
2007	Romeros receive President's Merit Award from Grammys on February 8.
2011	San Francisco Conservatory of Music confers honorary doctorate on Pepe in May.
2012	Pepe's recording of Ernesto Cordero's *Concierto Festivo*, with I Solisti di Zagreb, is nominated for Latin Grammy.
2015	Celedonio is posthumously awarded La Guitarra Lifetime Achievement Award in February.
2016	Angel premieres *Concierto de la amistad* by Lalo Schifrin, August 2, at Hollywood Bowl.
2017	In May, the University of Oklahoma City confers honorary doctorate on Celin, and Pepe receives Premio Huella Cultural from Club Rotario de Málaga.
2018	Pepe is awarded a gold medal and the title of Académico Honorario by the Real Academia de Bellas Artes de Granada.

APPENDIX 2

ROMERO GENEALOGY

23andMe DNA testing has revealed that the Romeros' ancestry is largely European, including a trace of Ashkenazi Jew. Rather surprisingly, the family is distantly related to country singer/songwriter Jimmy Buffett on the maternal side.

CELEDONIO'S ANCESTORS

(all locations in the province of Málaga)

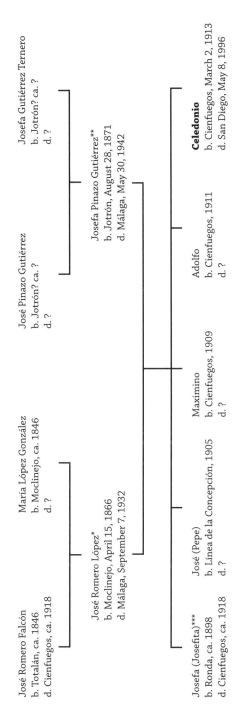

* José had three siblings, named María, Enriqueta, and Antonio, but we know nothing more about them.
** Josefa had three siblings, named Dolores, Rafael, and Isabel, but we know nothing more about them.
*** There were three children before Josefa and three right afterward, but they all died in infancy. One was to have been named José, but the others' names are unknown.

CELEDONIO'S DESCENDANTS

(grandchildren and great-grandchildren were all born in Southern California, unless otherwise indicated)

Salvador Gallego Rivera
b. Málaga, 1884
d. Málaga, 1964

Encarnación Molina Cuevas
b. Jaén, ?
d. Madrid, ?

Inez de los Ángeles Gallego Molina (Angelita)*
b. Málaga, January 4, 1910
d. San Diego, March 10, 1999

Celedonio Romero Pinazo (cont.)

Celedonio Gustavo Adolfo (**Celín**)
b. Málaga, November 23, 1936

José Luis (**Pepe**)
b. Málaga, March 8, 1944

Miguel Ángel Leonardo (**Ángel**)
b. Málaga, August 17, 1946

* Angelita had a biological sister named Dolores (Loli) and an adopted sister named Rosario (Rosa).

Celin Romero Gallego (cont.)
    ⎡ Laurie Wanda Barc
    ⎣ b. Phoenix, 1942

- Carl Robert Sanchez
  b. Canal Zone, Panama, 1962
- Angela
  b. 1966
  - Emilio Celin
    b. 1996
  - Marina Isabella
    b. 1998
  - Carlos Emilio
    b. Arlington, Virginia, 1994

- Michelle Zubia
  b. Newport Beach, 1970
- Celedonio (Celino)
  b. 1969
  - Celedonio (Nino)
    b. 1998
  - Maximino (Maxi)
    b. 2001
  - Raquelle Angela
    b. 2006

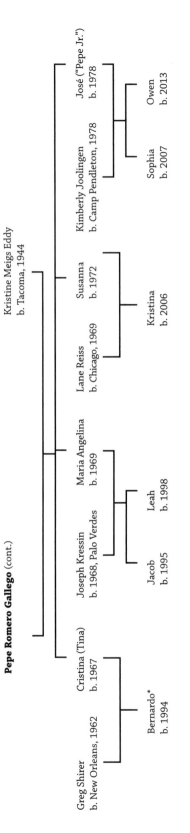

* Bernardo is Tina's son by a previous marriage.

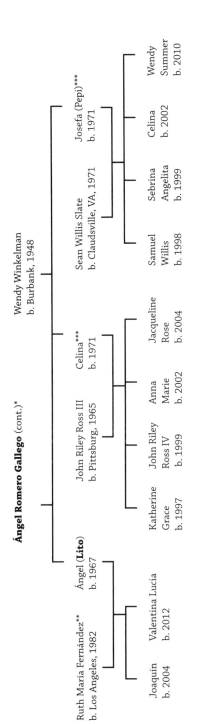

Ángel Romero Gallego (cont.)*

Ruth María Fernández** b. Los Angeles, 1982 — Ángel (**Lito**) b. 1967

John Riley Ross III b. Pittsburg, 1965 — Celina*** b. 1971 — Sean Willis Slate b. Claudsville, VA, 1971 — Josefa (Pepi)*** b. 1971

Wendy Winkelman b. Burbank, 1948

Joaquín b. 2004   Valentina Lucia b. 2012

Katherine Grace b. 1997   John Riley Ross IV b. 1999   Anna Marie b. 2002   Jacqueline Rose b. 2004

Samuel Willis b. 1998   Sebrina Angelita b. 1999   Celina b. 2002   Wendy Summer b. 2010

* Angel and Wendy are divorced; a subsequent marriage to Susan Parker ended in annulment, without children.
** Lito and Virginia dissolved their relationship before Lito married Ruth María (this is out of chronological sequence in the chart, per Lito's request).
*** Celina and Josefa are twins.

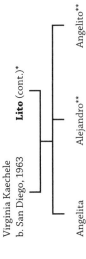

Virginia Kaechele b. San Diego, 1963   **Lito** (cont.)*

Angelita Natalia b. 1992   Alejandro** b. 2000   Angelito** b. 2000

* See note ** in preceding chart.
** Alejandro and Angelito are Lito's twin sons by a previous relationship.

THE THREE BROTHERS TODAY

Celin (cont.) ——————————— Claudia Tornsäufer
b. Essen, Germany, 1966

Pepe (cont.) ——————————— Carissa Romero (née Sugg)
b. Dallas, Texas, 1956

Angel (cont.) ——————————— Nefretiri Romero (née Morte)
b. Hayward, California, 1977

Isabella Susanna
b. 2001

APPENDIX 3
LIST OF ALBUMS

This list does not include every recording on which a Romero is featured, as the number of rereleases and compilations is very large. Presented below are original recordings and reissues of entire albums, especially those in other formats (e.g., LP to CD). The list begins with the quartet, then various Romero duets, and finally solo recordings. Duo and solo recordings are further subdivided by performers. Entries within each category proceed in roughly chronological order, from earliest to most recent, and each entry includes the album title, label name, serial number and year of first release, followed by notes about the recording, especially pertaining to collaborating musicians. The list does not include every individual number on every album, as doing so would overwhelm the necessary limits of this appendix and even the book itself.

QUARTET

Title	Label	Serial no. / Release	Notes
The Royal Family of the Spanish Guitar	Mercury	MG-50295/1963	
The Royal Family of the Spanish Guitar	Mercury Golden Imports	SRI-75027	Rerelease of above
The Romeros, Spain's Royal Family of the Guitar: Baroque Concertos and Solo Works	Mercury	SR-90417/1965	

APPENDIX 3

Title	Label	Serial no. / Release	Notes
An Evening with the Romeros	Mercury Golden Imports	SRI-75022	Rerelease of above
An Evening of Flamenco Music: The Romeros, the Royal Family of the Spanish Guitar	Mercury	SR-90434/1965	
The Romeros Play an Evening of Flamenco	Mercury Golden Imports	SRI2- SRI-75073	Rerelease of above
The Romeros: The World of Flamenco	Mercury	SR2-9120/1967	
The World of Flamenco	Mercury Golden Imports	SRI2-77007	Rerelease of above
Die Könige der spanischen Gitarre	Philips	CD 422 164-2	German rerelease of above
The Romeros, Spain's Royal Family of the Guitar: Vivaldi Guitar Concertos	Mercury	SR-90487/1968	With V. Alessandro, conductor, San Antonio Symphony
The Romeros Play Vivaldi	Mercury Golden Imports	SRI-75054	Rerelease of above
The Romeros Play Baroque Guitar	Philips	LP 6572.012/ 1963, 1965, 1968	Rerelease of solos and concertos, with V. Alessandro, conductor, San Antonio Symphony
Vivaldi Guitar Concertos, Los Romeros	Philips	CD 426 076-2	Rerelease of above on Concert Classics label
Vivaldi Konzerte für 1, 2 und 4 Gitarren	Philips (Germany)	CD 434 545-2	German rerelease of above
Rodrigo: Concierto Andaluz *for Four Guitars and Orchestra*	Mercury	SR-90488/1968	Premiere recording, with V. Alessandro, conductor, San Antonio Symphony
Rodrigo: Concierto Andaluz *for Four Guitars and Orchestra*	Mercury Golden Imports	SRI-75021	Rerelease of above
Rodrigo: Concierto Andaluz *for Four Guitars and Orchestra*	Philips	CD 434 369-2	Rerelease of above
The Romeros Play Classical Music for Four Guitars	Philips	LP 9500 296/1977	
Los Romeros-Telemann/ Bach/D. Scarlatti/ Loeillet/Dowland	Philips	LP 9500 536/1978	
"Concierto Andaluz," Los Romeros	Philips	Cassette 7300 705/1979	With Neville Marriner, conductor, Academy of St. Martin-in-the-Fields
Francisco de Madina: Concierto vasco para cuatro guitarras y orquesta	Polygram Ibérica	LP FM-68743/1986 Cassette FM-68750/1987	Pepe, Celin Romero with students Randy Pile and Lisa Smith, with Lorenzo Palomo, conductor, Orquesta Sinfónica de Bilbao
"Concierto Andaluz," Los Romeros	Philips	UPC 028940002427/ 1983	Rerelease of above

LIST OF ALBUMS

Title	Label	Serial no. / Release	Notes
"Concierto Andaluz," Los Romeros	Philips 446 804-2	PHCP-20364/1999	Japanese release of above
Joaquín Rodrigo: Conciertos "Aranjuez," "Madrigal," "Andaluz," "Para una fiesta"	Philips	LP (set of 3) 412 170-1 Cassette (set of 3) 412 170-4	Rerelease with Neville Marriner, conductor, Academy of St. Martin-in-the-Fields
Rodrigo: "Concierto de Aranjuez"; "Fantasía para un gentilhombre"; "Concierto Madrigal"	Philips	CD 432-828-2 CD (Spain) 434 208-2	Rerelease of above on Splendour of Spain label
Joaquín Rodrigo Conciertos: "Aranjuez," "Madrigal," "Andaluz," "Para una fiesta," "Fantasía para un gentilhombre," and works for guitar solo	Philips	CD (set of 3) 432 581-2	Rerelease with Neville Marriner, conductor, Academy of St. Martin-in-the-Fields
Torroba: "Concierto Ibérico"- Los Romeros	Philips	LP 9500 749/1980 Cassette 7300 834	With Neville Marriner, conductor, Academy of St. Martin-in-the-Fields
Vivaldi Guitar Concertos, Los Romeros	Philips	LP 412 624-1/1985 CD 412 624-2 Cassette 412 624-4	With Iona Brown, conductor, Academy of St. Martin-in-the-Fields
Mad about Vivaldi	Deutsche Grammophon	CD 439 516-2/1993	Rerelease of Vivaldi collection, including Pepe Romero performing Guitar Concerto in C, RV 425
Bizet Carmen Suite–Falla Dances	Philips	LP 412 609-1/1985 CD 412 609-2 Cassette 412-609-4	
The Royal Family of the Spanish Guitar	Mercury Living Presence	CD 434 385-2/1997	Rerelease
Guitar Festival: Vivaldi/Telemann/Bach/Flamenco, Los Romeros	Philips	CD 422 275-2 Cassette 422 275-4	Rerelease on Touch of Classics label with V. Alessandro, conductor, San Antonio Symphony, including Pepe flamenco solos from Mercury SI-75092
Guitar Festival: Vivaldi/Telemann/Bach/Flamenco, Los Romeros	Philips	Cassette 416 232-4	Rerelease of above on Classics on Tour label
Festival der klassischen Gitarren Los Romeros	Philips	CD (set of 3) 432 371-2, 432 372-2, 432 373-2	Rerelease in Germany; contains Aranjuez, Fantasía, Madrigal, Andaluz, and Pepe solos
High Tech Gitarre	Philips	CD 422 914-2/1983	Rerelease in Germany; contains "Carmen Suite"; duos with Celin/Pepe; flamenco and so on

APPENDIX 3

Title	Label	Serial no. / Release	Notes
The Storm at Sea (Vivaldi Concertos-Golden Baroque label no.13)	Philips	CD 454 415-2/1996	Rerelease compilation; contains Pepe and I Musici, Angel and St. Martin-in-the-Fields
The Romeros: Generations	CPA Hollywood Records	CD 2003	First recording with Lito Romero in quartet
Homenaje a Joaquín Rodrigo: Los Romero con Orquesta Sinfónica de RTVE (Spanish Radio and Television Symphony Orchestra)	RTVE	65136 OSyC-022/2001	Live performance at the Alhambra in Granada Festival 1997; with Edmon Colomer, conductor
Joaquín Rodrigo Homenaje	Deutsche Grammophon	0028946564523-AX/2000	Rerelease compilation of *Concierto para una fiesta*, *Andaluz*
Essential Guitar: 33 Guitar Masterpieces	Decca	289 470 477-2/2002	Rerelease compilation; 2 CD set, including Pepe and Quartet
Aita Madina: Concierto vasco para 4 guitarras y orquesta. *Euskadiko Orkestra Sinfonikoa/Los Romero/Mandeal*	Claves	CD 50-2517/18/2005	
Los Romeros: Golden Jubilee Celebration	Decca	478 0192/2008	Rerelease; fiftieth-anniversary recompilation
The Romeros: Celebration	Sony RCA Red Seal/NDR Kultur	88697458272/2009	
Palomo: "My Secluded Garden," "Madrigal and Five Sephardic Songs," Concierto de Cienfuegos	Naxos	8.572139/2009	Los Romeros, Pepe Romero, María Bayo, Rafael Frühbeck de Burgos, conductor, Seville Royal Symphony Orchestra
Christmas with Los Romeros	Deutsche Grammophon	477 9365/2011-12	Pepe, Celin, Lito, Celino and Angel Romero, with Massimo Paris, conductor, Concerto Málaga. Recorded at Santa María Cristina, Málaga

DUET

ANGEL AND CELEDONIO

Title	Label	Serial no./Year	Notes
Granados: "12 Danzas Españolas"	Telarc	CD-80216/1991	

LIST OF ALBUMS

ANGEL AND PEPE

Title	Label	Serial no./Year	Notes
Rodrigo: "Concierto Madrigal" for Two Guitars	Philips	LP 6500.918/1975 Re-release CD 400 024-2/1983	With Neville Marriner, conductor, Academy of St. Martin-in-the-Fields
Rodrigo: "Concierto Madrigal" for Two Guitars	PentaTone	PTC 5186141/2004	Rerelease on super-audio CD

CELEDONIO AND PEPE

Title	Label	Serial no./Year	Notes
Works for Two Guitars: Diabelli, Giuliani, Carulli	Philips	LP 9500 352/1977	

CELIN AND CELEDONIO

Title	Label	Serial no./Year	Notes
Celedonio Romero and Celin Romero: Spanish Guitar Music	Contemporary	LP M-6502/1960 Re-release CCD 14069-2/2004	

CELIN AND PEPE

Title	Label	Serial no./Year	Notes
Famous Spanish Dances: Albéniz, Falla, Granados	Philips	LP 6514.182/1981 Re-released CD 411 432-2/1982	
Famous Spanish Dances: Albéniz, Falla, Granados	Splendour of Spain	CD 432 827-2/1991 (Spain: 434 207-2)	Rerelease of above
Pepe Romero: Guitar Solos	Philips	CD 434 727-2/1992	Rerelease on Insignia label. Contains solos and duos w/Celin
Flamenco	Ethnic Folkways Library	LP FE-4437/1956	Release of live performances on Málaga radio. Celin (14 years old) plays *Rumores de la caleta*; Pepe (10 years old) plays *Recuerdos de la Alhambra* and *Alegrías*

SOLO

CELEDONIO

Title	Label	Serial no./Year	Notes
Guitar Music from the Courts of Spain	Mercury	LP SR-90296/1963 (MG 50296)	
Guitar Music from the Courts of Europe	Mercury Golden Imports	LP SRI-75126/n.d.	Rerelease of above
Celedonio Romero, "Poet of the Guitar"	Delos International	LP DEL-25441/1981	
Celedonio Romero: An Evening of Guitar Music	Delos International	D/CD 1004/1986	

APPENDIX 3

Title	Label	Serial no./Year	Notes
Celedonio Romero Plays J. S. Bach, Gaspar Sanz	Delos International	D/CD 1005/1986	
Celedonio Romero: Poet of the Guitar	CPA Hollywood Records, Inc.	1996	Produced by James Hunley, Alta Nova Productions

PEPE

Title	Label	Serial no./Year	Notes
¡Flamenco fenómeno!	Contemporary	LP S-9004/1960; also available on CCD 14070-2/2004	
Flamenco!	Mercury Living Presence and Golden Imports	LP MG-50297/1962; SR-90297; SRI-75092; 434 361-2; also available on CD 434 361-2/1995	
Giuliani Guitar Concerto, op. 30; Rodrigo: "Concierto Madrigal" for Two Guitars	Philips	LP 6500.918/1975	Angel and Pepe Romero in first Philips recording of the *Madrigal*, with Neville Marriner, conductor, Academy of St. Martin-in-the-Fields
Rodrigo: "Fantasía para un gentilhombre" Giuliani: "Introduction, Theme with Variations and Polonaise," op. 65	Philips	LP 9500042/1976	With Neville Marriner, conductor, Academy of St. Martin-in-the-Fields
Famous Guitar Music, including Tárrega: "Recuerdos de la Alhambra"/Albéniz: "Asturias"/Villa Lobos/Lauro/Sagreras/Sor	Philips	LP 9500 295/1977	
Giuliani Guitar Concertos op. 30 and op. 70	Philips	LP 9500 320/1977 Re-release CD 420 780-2	With Neville Marriner, conductor, Academy of St. Martin-in-the-Fields
Giuliani: Concerto for Guitar in A, op. 30; Rodrigo: "Fantasía para un gentilhombre"	Philips	LP 6514.296	Rerelease
Giuliani: Concerto for Guitar (op.30), Introduction, Theme and Variations and Polonaise (op.65)	Philips	LP 9500 046	Rerelease in France on Tresors Classiques label
Mauro Giuliani: Guitar Concertos (op. 30, op. 36, op. 70, op. 65)	Philips	LP (set of 2) 6770 012 Cassette (set of 2) 7650 011 Re-release compilation, 1996	With Neville Marriner, conductor, Academy of St. Martin-in-the-Fields

LIST OF ALBUMS

Title	Label	Serial no./Year	Notes
Works for Guitar from Renaissance to Baroque: Sanz, Milán, Mudarra, Narváez, Pisador, Valderrábano	Philips	LP 9500 351/1977	
Guilani: Handel Variations, op.107; Gran Sonata Eroica in A; Variations on "I bin a Kohlbauern Bub," op. 49; La melanconia; Grande ouverture, op. 61	Philips	LP 9500 513/1978	
Flamenco–Pepe Romero, Guitar (includes "Suite Andaluza")	Philips	LP 9500 512/1978 Cassette 7300 672	
Rodrigo: "Concierto de Aranjuez"	Philips	LP 9500563	With Neville Marriner, conductor, Academy of St. Martin-in-the-Fields
Rodrigo: "Fantasía para un gentilhombre," "Concierto Madrigal"	Philips	LP 6514295	Rerelease, with Neville Marriner, conductor, Academy of St. Martin-in-the-Fields
Rodrigo: Complete Concertos for Guitar and Harp, includes "Aranjuez," "Madrigal," "Andaluz," "Para una fiesta," "Fantasía para un gentilhombre"	Philips	CD (set of 2) 462 296-2/1998	
Rodrigo: "Fantasía para un gentilhombre," "Concierto de Aranjuez"	Philips	CD 4114402	Rerelease, with Neville Marriner, conductor, Academy of St. Martin-in-the-Fields
Rodrigo: "Concierto de Aranjuez," "Fantasía para un gentilhombre"	Philips	CD 426 008-2	Rerelease on Academy Jubilee label, with Neville Marriner, conductor, Academy of St. Martin-in-the-Fields
Sor Guitar Sonatas op. 22 and 25	Philips	LP 9500586/1979	
Torroba: "Diálogos"–Pepe Romero	Philips	LP 9500749/1980 Cassette 7300834	On same LP as *"Concierto Ibérico" for Four Guitars and Orchestra*, with Neville Marriner, conductor, Academy of St. Martin-in-the-Fields
Boccherini Guitar Quintets nos. 4, 5 and 6	Philips	LP 9500789/1980 CD 4203852/1980	With Academy of St. Martin-in-the-Fields' Chamber Ensemble
Boccherini Guitar Quintets nos. 3 and 9	Philips	LP 9500789/1980 CD 4260922/1980	With Academy of St. Martin-in-the-Fields' Chamber Ensemble

APPENDIX 3

Title	Label	Serial no./Year	Notes
Boccherini Guitar Quintets nos. 1, 2 and 7	Philips	LP 9500985/1981	With Academy of St. Martin-in-the-Fields' Chamber Ensemble
Boccherini: The Guitar Quintets	Philips	LP (set of 3) 6768268	Rerelease of previous three
Boccherini: The Guitar Quintets including "La ritirata di Madrid" and "Fandango"	Philips	CD (set of 2) 438 7692	Rerelease in 1993 of Quintets 1, 2, 3, 4, 5, 6, 7, 9
Boccherini Quintets nos. 1, 2, 5, 6	Philips	CD 4566372	Rerelease in Italy on Amadeus label
Boccherini: The Famous Fandango. Guitar Quintets nos. 4 and 5 and "La ritirata di Madrid"	Philips	LP (Netherlands) 6833267	Rerelease in Netherlands in 1980
Best of Boccherini (includes guitar quintets nos. 4, 9)	Philips	CD (set of 2) 438 3772	Rerelease 1993
Joaquín Rodrigo/Pepe Romero (solos)	Philips	LP 9500915/1981 Cassette 7300915/1981	
Pepe Romero: Bach Partita BWV 1004 and Suite BWV 1009	Philips	LP 6514183/1982 CD 4114512/1982	
Carulli 2 Sonatas Diabelli Sonata op. 68, Grande Sonate brilliante op. 102	Philips	LP 410 396-1/1983 Cassette 4103964/1983	With Wilhelm Hellweg, forte piano
Jeux Interdits, Recuerdos de la Alhambra, Asturias	Philips	LP 6514381/1983 CD 4110332/1983 Cassette 4110334	
Jeux Interdits and Other Guitar Favorites	Philips	CD 4565522	Rerelease of above on Eloquence label
Rodrigo: "Concierto para una fiesta," Romero/Torroba: "Concierto de Málaga"	Philips	LP 4111331/1984 CD 4111332/1984 Cassette 4111334/1984	With Neville Marriner, conductor, Academy of St. Martin-in-the-Fields
Villa-Lobos, Castelnuovo-Tedesco Guitar Concertos Rodrigo: "Sones en la Giralda"	Philips	LP 4163571/1986 CD 4163572/1986 Cassette 4163574/1986	With Neville Marriner, conductor, Academy of St. Martin-in-the-Fields
"Aranjuez," "Sones en la Giralda," Villa-Lobos and Castelnuovo-Tedesco Concertos"	Philips Japan	PHCP 10538	Japanese rerelease
Pepe Romero Guitar: Albéniz/Tárrega/Moreno Torroba/Romero	Philips	LP 4163841/1986 CD 4163842/1986 Cassette 4163844/1986	
Villa-Lobos: Five Preludes, Etude no. 1, "Suite Populaire brésilienne"	Philips	LP 4202451/1987 CD 4202452/1987	

LIST OF ALBUMS

Title	Label	Serial no./Year	Notes
Pepe Romero: Flamenco Chano Lobato, Maria Magdalena, Paco Romero	Philips	CD 4220692/1988 Cassette 4220694/1988	
Baroque in Our Time (includes Ciaconna from Violin Partita in D Minor)	Philips	CD 4544272/1996	
Carulli, Molino: Guitar Concertos; Mozart: Adagio KV 261, Rondo KV373	Philips	CD 4262632/1990	With Neville Marriner, conductor, Academy of St. Martin-in-the-Fields
La Paloma: Spanish and Latin American Favorites	Philips	CD 4321022/1991	
Vivaldi Guitar Concertos: I Musici, Pepe Romero, Massimo Paris	Philips	CD 4340822/1992	
Rodrigo: "Concierto de Aranjuez," "Fantasía para un gentilhombre," "Cançoneta," "Invocación y danza," "Trois petites pièces"	Philips	CD 4380162/1994 Cassette 4380164/1994 Laser CD 0702631/1994	With Agustín León Ara, violin, and Neville Marriner, conductor, Academy of St. Martin-in-the-Fields
La Guitarra de Aranjuez	Philips	CD 4380162/1994	German release of above
Noches de España: Romantic Guitar Classics	Philips	CD 4421502/1994	World-premiere recording of Sor Fantasie in D Minor
Opera Fantasy for Guitar: Pepe Romero	Philips	CD 4460902/2009	
Songs My Father Taught Me	Philips	CD 4565852/1998	Last Philips production
Boccherini: Quintetti con chitarra n. 2, 6, 7, 4	UNICEF	DC-U31/2000 by Il Canale	Pepe Romero with Quartetto Stadivari
Pepe Romero Spanish Nights	Philips	CD 4467592/ recordings from 1976-1994	Rerelease compilation on Harmony label
Pepe Romero: Guitar Solos	Philips	CD 434 72722/1992	Rerelease on Insignia label; contains solos and duos with Celin
Homenatge a Montsalvatge Metamorfosi de concert	Tritó	TD 0010/2003	With Gianandrea Noseda, conductor, Orquesta de Cadaqués
Chihara: Guitar Concerto	Albany Records	TROY724/2005	With Neville Marriner, conductor, London Symphony
Giuliani Guitar Concerto no. 1	PentaTone	PTC 5186141/2004	Rerelease on super audio CD
The Art of Pepe Romero	Philips	CD (set of 2) 475 6360/2005	Compilation of earlier recordings
Corazón Español	CPA Hollywood Records	CD 2005	
Classic Romero	CPA Hollywood Records	CD 2007	

APPENDIX 3

Title	Label	Serial no./Year	Notes
Palomo: Andalusian Nocturnes; Spanish Songs	Naxos	CD 8.557135/2006	With María Bayo, soprano; Rafael Frühbeck de Burgos, conductor, Seville Royal Symphony Orchestra
Palomo: "My Secluded Garden," "Madrigal and Five Sephardic Songs," "Concierto de Cienfuegos"	Naxos	CD 8.572139/2009	With María Bayo, soprano; Rafael Frühbeck de Burgos, conductor, Seville Royal Symphony Orchestra
Cordero: Caribbean Concertos for Guitar and Violin	Naxos	CD 8.572707/2011	With Guillermo Figueroa, I Solisti di Zagreb. Nominated for 2012 Latin Grammy "Best Classical Album"
Pepe Romero: Spanish Nights	Deutsche Grammophon	CD 4790073/2012	All Spanish repertoire, not previously recorded. World premiere recording of *Suite madrileña, no.1* by Celedonio Romero
Pepe Romero: Master of the Guitar	Decca	CD 4785669/2013	Rerelease compilation. 11- CD set celebrating Pepe Romero's seventieth birthday
Guitar Works by Federico Moreno Torroba: Diálogos, Aires de la Mancha, Suite castellana, Concerto flamenco	Naxos	8.573255/2014	Pepe Romero, Vicente Coves, guitars; with Manuel Coves, conductor, Orquesta Sinfónica de Granada
Guitar Works by Federico Moreno Torroba: Homenaje a la seguidilla, Tonada concertante, Concierto de Castilla	Naxos	8.573503/2017	Pepe Romero, Vicente Coves, guitars; with Manuel Coves, conductor, Extremadura Symphony Orchestra

ANGEL

Title	Label	Serial no./Year	Notes
Concierto de Aranjuez	Mercury Golden Imports	LP SRI-75021/1968	With V. Alessandro, conductor, San Antonio Symphony Orchestra
Angel Romero: Spanish Guitar Virtuoso	EMI Seraphim Classics	CD 54505/2001	Originally released 1976 and 1978 LP, Angel: S-36094
Angel Romero: Spanish Guitar Virtuoso, vol. 2	EMI Seraphim Classics	CD 74505/2001	Originally released 1976 and 1978 LP, Angel: S-36094
Angel Romero: Classical Virtuoso	Angel Classics	LP S-36093/1976	

LIST OF ALBUMS

Title	Label	Serial no./Year	Notes
Rodrigo: Elogio de la Guitarra *and Moreno Torroba:* Piezas Características	Angel Classics	LP S-37132/1978	
The Divine Giuliani	Angel	LP SZ-37326/1979	
Moreno Torroba and Castelnuovo-Tedesco: Guitar Concertos	Angel	LP DS-37880/1982	With Federico Moreno Torroba, conductor, English Chamber Orchestra
Music of Celedonio Romero	Angel	LP DS-37311/1983	
Guiliani: Guitar Concertos 1 & 3	His Master's Voice	LP ASD-1435581/1983	With Raymond Leppard, conductor, English Chamber Orchestra
Guiliani: Guitar Concertos 1 and 3 Grande Ouverture	EMI	CD 7479862/1987	Rerelease of above
Schifrin and Villa Lobos: Guitar Concertos	Angel Classics	CD 4DS-38126/1985	Jesús López-Cobos, conductor, London Philharmonic Orchestra; George Shearing, piano; Shelly Manne, drums; Ray Brown, bass
Rodrigo: Concierto de Aranjuez, Fantasía para un Gentilhombre, Elogio de la guitarra	Angel/EMI	CD 724358506327/2004 CD 47693/1986 CD S-37440/1985	With André Previn, conductor, London Symphony Orchestra
A Touch of Class: Popular Classics Transcribed for Guitar	Telarc	CD 80134/1988	Lito Romero, second guitar
A Touch of Romance: Spanish and Latin Favorites Transcribed for Guitar	Telarc	CD 80213/1990	
"Cavatina" from *The Deer Hunter*, on the album *Movie Love Themes*	Telarc	CD 80243/1991	Guest artist with Erich Kunzel, conductor, Cincinnati Pops Orchestra
Angel Romero Plays Bach: The Music of Bach Transcribed for Guitar	Telarc	CD 80288/1993	
Noël	RCA Victor Red Seal	CD 09026-62683-2/1994	Guest artist with Canadian Brass
Vivaldi Concertos	RCA Victor Red Seal	CD 09026-68291-2/1995	With the Academy of St Martin-in-the-Fields, Angel Romero, guitar and conductor
Remembering the Future	RCA Victor Red Seal	CD 09026-68268-2/1995	Academy of St. Martin-in-the-Fields; Lito Romero, guitar; Norbert Blume, viola d'amore; Kenneth Sillito, violin; John Constable, harpsichord; Graham Sheen, bassoon

APPENDIX 3

Title	Label	Serial no./Year	Notes
Concierto de Aranjuez	Polygram	CD 434369/1996	
Concierto de Aranjuez	Mercury Living Presence	CD 4756184/2004	Rerelease of above
Romero & Rodrigo: Solo Works for Guitar	BMG Music	CD 09026-68767-2/1997	
Claude Bolling: Concerto for Classic Guitar and Jazz Piano	Angel	CD 72435/1998	With George Shearing, Shelly Manne, Ray Brown
Bella: The Incomparable Artistry of Angel Romero	Delos	CD DE-3294/2001	
Villa Lobos: Concerto for Guitar and Small Orchestra	EMI Classics	CD 5008432/2007 CD 0947032/2011	With Jesús López-Cobos, conductor, London Philharmonic Orchestra
Concierto de Aranjuez	Helicon Records	CD 02-9662/2013	With Ryan McAdams, conductor, Israel Philharmonic Orchestra

APPENDIX 4

SOURCES AND PUBLICATIONS

PRIMARY SOURCES

The principal location of primary sources pertaining to the Romero family is Special Collections of the Libraries at the University of California, Riverside. This collection was donated in 2013 by the family to UCR and consists of an abundance of relevant materials. A more detailed listing of contents is available at the Special Collections website for the Romero archive, http://www.oac.cdlib.org/findaid/ark:/13030/c8057mh2/. The archive includes

1. Correspondence: letters, telegrams, postcards, greeting cards. Many of these are from famous individuals, including Spanish composers Joaquín Rodrigo and Federico Moreno Torroba, as well as from U.S. presidents Nixon, Carter, and Clinton.
2. Periodicals and newspaper clippings: actual periodicals as well as numerous clippings from magazines and newspapers going back to the 1920s.
3. Programs: hundreds of programs from solo and ensemble appearances from 1958 to 2012.
4. *Memorias de un septuagenario por José Romero Pinazo* (photocopy). Málaga, September 7, 1983. Memoirs of Celedonio's oldest brother.
5. Poems, diary entries, personal and official documents, assorted memorabilia.

APPENDIX 4

DVDs

Angel Romero: The Art of Classical Guitar. Ninety-minute instructional video from Hal Leonard, 2011.

Los Romeros: Die Gitarren-Dynastie. A film by Michael Valentin and Martin Feil. NDR (North German Radio), 2003.

Los Romeros: The Royal Family of the Guitar. Directed and produced by Bill Chayes and John Harris. Written by John Harris. Public Broadcasting System, 2008.

Pepe Romero Live in Granada, May 21, 2010. "Celebration of Romantic Spain." A Tribute to Albéniz and Tárrega on the 100th Anniversary of Their Deaths. CPA Hollywood Records-Caja Granada, 2012.

Pepe Romero Plays Cordero's Concierto Festivo *with I Solisti di Zagreb*. Mel Bay, MB22202, 2011.

Rodrigo: Concierto de Aranjuez *and Shadows and Light*. A film tribute to Rodrigo by Larry Weinstein and Rhombus Media, 1992/94.

Torroba's Guitar. Halpern Productions, 2012. Features Pepe Romero playing Torroba's music.

Lalo Schifrin's *Concierto de la Amistad for Guitar and Orchestra*, with Angel Romero, soloist. Featured on *Tango under the Stars: Gustavo Dudamel, Los Angeles Philharmonic, Live at the Hollywood Bowl*. Bernard Fleischer Moving Images, 2017.

PRINT PUBLICATIONS

(Method books, editions of music, and original compositions)

ANGEL ROMERO

Angel Romero—Bella: The Incomparable Artistry of Angel Romero. Hal Leonard Publications, 2011. Arrangements from his recording *Bella*.

Angel Romero: In Concert. Mel Bay Publications, 2013. Arrangements of his concert favorites.

Concierto de Aranjuez by Joaquín Rodrigo. Piano reduction published Mainz: Schott, 1984. Includes Angel's fingerings.

CELEDONIO ROMERO

Angel Vals no. 1. Unión Musical Española, 1986.
Angel Vals no. 2. Unión Musical Española, 1986.
Sonata Scarlatta no. 1. Unión Musical Española, 1986.
Sonata Scarlatta no. 2. Unión Musical Española, 1986.
The Celedonio Romero Method for the Classical Guitar. Tuscany Publications, 2012. Revised version of earlier edition, published by Juan Orozco, 1980.

CELINO ROMERO

The Art of Spanish Guitar: A Method by Celino Romero. With accompanying CD of the author performing selections from the method. Music Sales America, 2006.

SOURCES AND PUBLICATIONS

PEPE ROMERO

Danzas españolas by Gaspar Sanz. Tuscany Publications, 2000.
Guitar Solos and Duets: Works by Albéniz and Sanz. Bradley Publications, 1982.
Isaac Albéniz. Favorite Spanish Pieces (Asturias, Cádiz, Córdoba, Rumores de la caleta, Sevilla). Tuscany Publications, 2005.
La Guitarra: A Comprehensive Study of Classical Guitar Technique and Guide to Performing. Tuscany Publications, 2012. Revised and expanded version of *Pepe Romero's Guitar Style and Technique*, 1982.
Partita no. 2 by Johann Sebastian Bach. Tuscany Publications, 2000.
Tango Angelita. Tuscany Publications, 2000.

ROMERO WEBSITES

http://www.romeroguitarquartet.com
http://www.peperomero.com
https://www.facebook.com/peperomeroguitar
http://www.peperomero.com/luthier/
http://www.angelromero.com
https://www.facebook.com/Bernardo-Romero-Guitars-1866407130312549/

NOTES

The epigraph was written by Celedonio Romero, apparently from memory and without attribution, on an undated piece of stationery from the Holiday Inn in Dayton, Ohio. Document in the family archive.

FOREWORD

1. "Grandes orquestas internacionales nos piden que toquemos un concierto español para cuatro guitarras y orquesta y nadie mejor que Vd., Sr. Rodrigo, para escribir este concierto, pues Vd. es la cumbre y gloria del mundo."

2. "¡Bravo, Pepe sale muy bien!"

INTRODUCTION

1. As Pepe noted in an interview with Wayne Harada (*Honolulu Advertiser*, October 25, 1972), "It's 'easy to play, hard to know how.' Once you find out how to relax and manipulate the guitar, you learn how to understand the message in your mind, and transfer this feeling down to your fingers. Playing the guitar is easy. Very easy. But knowing how to play it is very hard."

2. According to Celin, as Celedonio lay dying, he requested that Celin play the *Sonatina* for him. He adjured his son to play it every day after he was gone, and it thus retains much sentimental significance for Celin.

3. For a classic study of this phenomenon, see John Storm Roberts, *The Latin Tinge: The Impact of Latin American Music on the United States*, 2nd ed. (New York: Oxford University Press, 1998).

NOTES TO CHAPTERS 1 AND 3

CHAPTER 1. FROM MÁLAGA'S MOUNTAINS

1. "Stille, stille, laß uns lauschen," from *Abendständchen* (Evening serenade). Brentano (1778–1842) was a leading German Romantic poet.

2. From the first of a series of poems titled *Del Camino* (1902). For a deeply insightful biography of this fascinating figure in Spanish literature (b. 1875; d. 1939), see Ian Gibson, *Ligero de equipaje: La vida de Antonio Machado*, 4th ed. (Madrid: Prisa Ediciones, 2014). His citation and discussion of these poems appear on pp. 147–53.

3. I was privileged to be present at the public presentation of his volume of poems titled *Sueños de luna* (Málaga: Ediciones del Genal, 2014), at which Pepe played the guitar to accompany José's reading of his own poems. This delightful fusion of poetry and guitar music is a Romero-family tradition, as we shall later see.

4. The historical discussion of Málaga here is greatly indebted to Andrés Sarriá Muñoz, *Breve historia de Málaga* (Málaga: Editorial Sarría, 2004).

5. Ibid., 114.

6. According to the Central Intelligence Agency's *World Factbook*, https://www.cia.gov/library/publications/the-world-factbook/fields/2103.html, accessed December 6, 2017, literacy is "the ability to read and write at a specified age." The current literacy rate of 98.1 percent is for those fifteen years and older.

7. Uncle Pepe cites this letter, without date, in his Memoirs.

8. For a comprehensive study of this tragic phenomenon, see Henry Kamen, *The Disinherited: Exile and the Making of Spanish Culture, 1492–1975* (New York: Harper, 2007).

9. Sarriá Muñoz, *Breve historia de Málaga*, 83.

CHAPTER 3. THE CITY OF PARADISE, REGAINED

1. Excerpted from "He andado muchos caminos," in *Soledades, gallerías y otras poemas* (1899–1907). See Antonio Machado, *Border of a Dream: Selected Poems*, trans. Willis Barnstone (Port Townsend, Wash.: Copper Canyon Press, 2004), 9.

2. See Sarriá Muñoz, *Breve historia de Málaga*, 111.

3. In the Romero archive (hereafter RA) is a business card from Niña de los Peines (Pastora Pavón Cruz) and José Torres Garzón (Pepe Pinto) expressing their affection. The Romero family was very well connected to leading *flamenquistas* in Málaga, Seville, and elsewhere in Andalusia.

4. In an interview with M.C., "Romero: 'Para tocar bien a Bach a la guitarra hay que saber bulerías,'" *Sur* (Málaga), September 22, 1990.

5. Disclosed in an interview with Robert Finn, "Guitar Virtuoso Shows Precision in Technique," *Cleveland Plain Dealer*, October 23, 1988.

6. Interview by Barbara Zuck, "Papa's Passion: Family Quartet Carries on Legacy of Love for Guitar," *Columbus (Ohio) Dispatch*, November 14, 1996.

7. Interview with Paul Bernstein, "The Royal Family of the Guitar," *New York Times Magazine*, November 29, 1981, 106.

8. Ibid.

9. Exam results from 1933–34 course in *solfeo* ("segundo and tercero de solfeo, primero de armonía") from Málaga Conservatory, dated September 8, 1934.

10. The clipping in the RA, titled "Velada en la Sociedad 'Anhelos,'" gives no specific date other than the year.

11. L.J.P., "Concierto del guitarrista Celedonio Romero en el Centro Artístico," *Ideal de Granada*, May 15, 1929.

12. "Notas Teatrales," *ABC*, August 4, 1934.

13. Fortea stated this in a letter to Celedonio dated "Madrid May 1936." Letter in the RA.

14. In a small booklet of encomiastic statements from critics and musicians assembled and published by Celedonio during these early years, for the sake of publicity. Copies of this document are in the RA.

15. From the transcript of an interview on National Public Radio's *All Things Considered*, Sunday, September 9, 2001, in connection with the Romero documentary that aired the following Friday, September 14, on the Public Broadcasting System. The pupil in question was Brojelle Molina.

16. Alfonso XIII visited Málaga from April 28 to May 1, 1904.

17. Reported to Marcia Fulmer, "Guitar Quartet a Celebration of Artistry," *Elkhart (IN) Truth*, March 6, 1997, D5. Malats's *Serenata* "was the first piece my father played for my mother."

18. Nevada Smith, "All in the Family," KPBS's *On Air Magazine*, June 2001, 13.

19. Angel recalls that during Encarnación's final years in Madrid, she lived in a penthouse, six stories up, and she never used the elevator, preferring instead to walk. She died after being run over by a car on her way back from the supermarket. She was eighty-three years old and in perfect health.

20. Agrupación Profesional de Periodistas of the Federación Gráfica Española. Earlier such events had taken place on August 2, 26, and 27, 1936.

21. According to family lore, Celin was nursed for over three years, Pepe for two and a half, and Angel for a little over one. By that point, Angelita was too tired to continue.

22. These records are located in the Archivo Militar in Guadalajara, along with those of Celedonio's three brothers.

23. Years later, the Falangist newspaper *Patria: Diario de Falange Española Tradicionalista y de las J.O.N.S.* would publish an interview with Celedonio titled "Celedonio Romero aprendió solo a tocar la guitarra" (Celedonio Romero learned alone how to play the guitar), in which he reminisced about an unforgettable meeting with Segovia, who embraced him affectionately and told him that he was his equal. Whether or not this anecdote is reliable, it nonetheless shows the high esteem in which Celedonio held Segovia. Undated clipping in the RA.

24. I am deeply indebted to Álvarez's septuagenarian daughter, Rosa María Álvarez Campos, and her grandson, Pedro Ángel González Mazone Álvarez, for hosting me and the Romeros one unforgettable afternoon at her home in Seville and the nearby Real Venta Pilín restaurant. She provided many fascinating recollections and insights into her father's career and relationship with Celedonio.

25. Pepe still has the music that Álvarez kept in his guitar case, including transcriptions by Fortea and Segovia of pieces by Beethoven, Chopin, and other Romantics.

26. Walter Aaron Clark, "The Romeros: Living Legacy of the Spanish Guitar; An Interview with Celín Romero," *Soundboard Magazine: The Journal of the Guitar Foundation of America* 36, no. 2 (2010): 60–61.

27. The critic was "Manolo," who titled his review "Celedonio Romero, guitarrista genial."

28. Felipe Corradi, "Algunas notas sobre el concierto de Celedonio Romero," unidentified newspaper clipping in the RA.

29. E.M., "El guitarrista Celedonio Romero en la Peña Trianera," unidentified and undated clipping in the RA.

30. *Patria, Diario de Falange Espanola Tradicionalista y de las J.O.N.S.* Undated clipping in the RA. When asked for an anecdote, he recounted that at a recent concert, after playing some Bach, a petulant man in the audience asked him to please play "some little piece. He apparently thought very little of Bach's music."

31. The clipping is an announcement of his forthcoming appearance at the Teatro Coliseum in Salamanca, on the twenty-seventh. This concert was yet another benefit to combat infant mortality.

32. Ration cards from that time for Angel and Pepe confirm their birth dates and addresses: for Miguel Ángel Romero Gallego, born August 19, 1946, living at Diego de Vergara 41. Pepe's is dated somewhat earlier and gives Rafaela 38 as the address. However, Angel's birthday is actually the seventeenth and is celebrated as such by the family. This is another instance in Romero annals where registration of a birth was postponed to make sure the infant would survive.

33. Clark, "Romeros," 61.

34. Jeff Walker, "All-in-the-Family: The Romero Guitar Quintet," *San Marcos (TX) Daily Record*, March 20, 2011.

35. Interview with Pepe by Pedro González Mira, "O el amor por la guitarra," *Ritmo*, no. 640 (February 1993): 8.

36. Channing Gray, "Romeros: A Classic Happy Family," *Providence (RI) Journal-Bulletin*, 1988. Clipping with incomplete date in the RA.

37. Lydia Martin, "What It Means to Be a Romero: You Play Guitars; If Not, You Make Them," *Miami Herald*, September 12, 2001, 1E.

38. Interview by Alison Bert, "Guitarist Offers a Taste of Classical Romance," *Tallahassee Flambeau*, 11. Undated clipping in the RA.

39. Letter dated March 16, 1999, in the RA. Carissa had translated this story from Mamá for Robin.

40. Interview with Joan Mooney, "Brothers Have Been in Tune since Childhood," *Sunday Telegraph* (Sydney), July 1, 1979, 49.

41. Excerpted from comments submitted to me by Torroba's son.

42. One of his performances, along with one by Pepe, has been preserved on the Ethnic Folkways Library *Flamenco* LP (FE-4437) of 1956. Celin plays Albéniz's *Rumores de La Caleta* and Pepe plays *Recuerdos de la Alhambra*.

43. He was no stranger to this venue, however, and had already played there in August 1940, in a program organized by the Delegación Provincial del Frente de Juventudes. In truth, movie theaters hosted a variety of cultural attractions besides films.

44. As they reported to Gerald Brennan, "The Classical Guitar Quartet: Romero Clan's Unique Legacy," *Ann Arbor (MI) News*, January 25, 1995.

45. Letter in the RA, dated January 28, 1953.

CHAPTER 4. SEVILLE AND ADIÓS

1. "Hoy, Celedonio Romero, en el Centro Artístico," *Ideal de Granada*. Undated clipping in the RA.

2. We learn from the substantial documentation in the RA of the Stoddards' assistance with the Romeros' emigration, in particular a letter from Evelyn of July 15, 1957, that she was born Evelyn Merritt Hardiman, December 5, 1907, in Merritt, British Columbia, Canada, and naturalized a U.S. citizen on September 12, 1941, in Los Angeles; that Farrington F. Stoddard is American by birth in the United States; and they live at 1315 De La Vina Street. The State Department document approves the affidavit of support for the parents and children only if they are admitted as immigrants from Spain.

3. Farrington was very well connected with people in the U.S. government and its diplomatic and military personnel overseas, which led the family to suspect that his job as radio operator might have been a cover for being an intelligence officer of some kind.

4. In 1984, the Romeros gave a benefit concert for the Santa Barbara Symphony. An article titled "Local Residents Helped Orchestrate Romeros' Escape from Spain in '50s," *Santa Barbara News-Press*, May 2, 1984, B-4, told the story of the Stoddards' role in bringing the family to the U.S. Evelyn was by then a widow and living in nearby Carpinteria. She joined the Romeros backstage after the concert.

5. When in Granada, the family would stay at the Hotel Washington Irving, conveniently located right next to the Alhambra. It was also owned by a guitarist, Antonio Velásquez.

6. Letter from Lecea dated November 27, 1953, in the RA.

7. By an interesting coincidence, Claudio Boutelou (1774–1842) was a botanist from a family of gardeners who had worked on the Aranjuez estate, later the inspiration for Rodrigo's celebrated *Concierto de Aranjuez* for guitar and orchestra, a Romero-family specialty.

8. Kenneth LaFave, "Spanish Guitar Is 'Los Romeros' Family Dynasty," *Arizona Republic*, September 23, 2001.

9. Interview by Derrick Henry, "Quartet Celebrates Joy of Guitar," *Atlanta Journal*, December 29, 1995, P7.

CHAPTER 5. SANTA BARBARA

1. Interview by Holly Johnson, "The Guitar Master: The Classical Sound of Pepe Romero Reveals a Genius at Work," *Sacramento Bee*, January 1995. Clipping without precise date in the RA.

2. Undated letter to her sister-in-law Lola, shortly after her arrival in the United States. Subsequent quotes are from this letter.

3. One of the Romeros' neighbors in Del Mar is a former airline pilot, with an obvious proclivity for poetic metaphors. I am grateful to him for this description.

4. "Local Residents Helped Orchestrate Romeros' Escape from Spain in '50s," *Santa Barbara News-Press*, May 2, 1984, B-4.

5. This correspondence can be consulted in Alcalá de Henares at the Archivo General de la Administración, in files (10)26 54/08730, (10)26 54/08642, and (10)26 54/08646.

6. The story is set in Spain during the Napoleonic invasion of Iberia in 1808–14 and involves a love triangle between a British officer (Cary Grant), a Spanish guerilla (Frank Sinatra), and his mistress (Sophia Loren), who falls for the Englishman.

7. The series was based on the popular Zorro stories by Johnston McCulley (1883–1958).

8. L. Caballero, "Celedonio Romero prometió triunfar en America y lo ha complido," *Sur* (Málaga), April 24, 1960.

9. The manuscript in which this observation appears is now in the RA.

10. Mamá kept a notebook with Spanish words and their English equivalents, dated "27 de julio 1958." Her attempts to acquire English were not altogether successful, and she would always speak in broken English, though she preferred communicating in Spanish. Papá's English was better, but neither became as fluent as the sons.

11. Celin elaborated on his early experiences behind the wheel in an interview with Linda Williams, "The Guitar As an Art," *You: People, Places, Things*, October 16–22, 1976.

12. Eusebio Rioja Vázquez, "Celedonio Romero, el mago gigante de la guitarra," *Sur* (Málaga), June 25, 1989, 6.

13. Ronald D. Scofield, "Celedonio Romero Recital Hailed," *Santa Barbara News-Press*, June 14, 1958, A-2.

14. Press release in the RA.

15. L. C., "Celedonio Romero, Triunfador en América." *Sur* (Málaga), October 31, 1958.

16. Announcement in the RA.

17. An audio recording of Pepe's performance on the steps of the mission that day is available on YouTube, "Pepe Romero's Opening Perfomance, in the 1950s," www.youtube.com/watch?v=JjzDhX8K9Yg, accessed December 6, 2017.

18. Announcement in the RA.

19. Purchased from Reliable Auto Sales on Vermont Avenue in Los Angeles. It cost $530.80, with $300 down, including $100 for the used car.

20. Letter in the RA.

21. Walker, "All-in-the-Family."

22. Both of these undated letters are in the RA.

23. Letter in the RA.

24. Letter in the RA.

25. "Spanish Concert Classical Guitarist Takes Basic Tng [Training] with 3d Bde Unit," *Fort Ord Panorama*, April 1, 1960, 8.

26. Clark, "Romeros," 63–64.

27. Shirley Fleming, "The Guitar on the Go," *High Fidelity Magazine*, July 1966, 42–45.

28. Charles Passy, "Guitar Proves Vehicle for Virtuosity," *Palm Beach Post*, November 12, 1993.

29. Ralph Thibodeau, "Romero Guitarists 'Greatest' Quartet," *Corpus Christi Caller*, February 4, 1971, 12G.

30. "Romeros Demolish 'Guitar-Image' Identity of Swivel-Hipped Youths," *The Scrantonian*, March 30, 1969, 6.

31. Nicolas Slonimsky, "Serenade on a Guitar," *Christian Science Monitor*, undated clipping in RA.

32. Lawrence B. Johnson, "Spanish Night Pops Concert 'Successful,'" *Milwaukee Sentinel*, November 15, 1969, part 1, 17.

33. Howard Reich, "As Ambassadors of Classical Guitar, Romeros Are Programmed to Please All," *Chicago Tribune*, May 18, 1986, sec. 13, 16.

34. Harriet Fields, "Audience Captivated by Romero Brothers," *Adrian (MI) Daily Telegram*, February 22, 1972, 18.

35. Marc Donner, "Romeros Concert Entertaining Despite Distractions," *California Tech*, November 16, 1972.

36. Review by Helen Thomsen titled "Beatles Anyone? We Had Romeros," *Fort Bragg (CA) Advocate-News*, November 5, 1964.

37. "Guitarists Score Big Hit at Community Concert," *Scribbles*, March 22, 1968, 1.

38. Marjorie Blaess, "Romeros' Concert Brilliant," *Clinton (Iowa) Herald*, February 7, 1973, 2.

39. For more on this topic, see Walter Aaron Clark, "The *Malagueñas* of Breva, Albéniz, and Lecuona: From Regional Fandango to Global Pop Tune," in *The Global Reach of the Fandango in Music, Song, and Dance: Spaniards, Indians, Africans, and Gypsies*, ed. Meira Goldberg (Newcastle upon Tyne: Cambridge Scholars, 2016), 236–43.

40. Paul Horsley, "Pepe Romero Has Never Known Life without the Guitar," *Kansas City Star*, September 24, 2000.

41. Letter in the RA.

42. The amount was $13,139.36, though it is possible that the Romeros had additional resources.

CHAPTER 6. HOLLYWOOD

1. A receipt documents the purchase of an 1856 Torres on April 22, 1960, for 10,000 pesetas. A letter in the RA dated May 7, 1962, notes that they had sold a Santos Hernández for $1,100.

2. "CR Discovers & Records Unique Family of Spanish Guitarists," *Good Time Jazz & Contemporary Records News*, Summer 1960, 1, 7.

3. Bernstein, "Royal Family of the Guitar," 102. In reference to the *New York Times Magazine* piece, Herb Fox at Columbia Management said in a note to the family, "It is not only rare but almost unprecedented for such a publication to print such an interesting and revealing story about a contemporary musical dynasty." Note in the RA. The Romeros' managers were thrilled with this publicity, and for good reason.

4. Lucas publicity materials in the RA.

5. Mimi Clar, "Romero Family Shows Artistry on Guitars," *Los Angeles Times*, January 22, 1961.

6. Herbert Donaldson, "Family Guitarists Second to None," *Los Angeles Examiner*, January 23, 1961, sec. 2, 6.

7. Letter in the RA.

8. Dale Vincent, "One Man's Family: 3 Sons, Dad Play Classical Guitars," *Chicago Sun-Times*, October 12, 1961, 32.

9. Years later, Celin would remark to Mary McGarry in an interview titled "Romero Family's Virtuosity Transforms 'Humble' Guitar" (*Anchorage Times*, January 15, 1977, 19), on the appreciative and attentive Anchorage audience: "He said they enjoyed presenting a concert in our city."

10. Jack Loughner, untitled review, *San Francisco News-Call Bulletin*, October 30, 1961, in the RA.

11. Alexander Fried, "Four Guitarists," *San Francisco Examiner*, October 30, 1961.

12. Dean Wallace, "Fabulous Romeros: Family Triumph on the Guitar," *San Francisco Chronicle*, October 30, 1961, 38. Wallace was working on a biography of the Romeros in the late 1990s but got only as far as some chapter summaries, now in the RA.

13. Cyrus Durgin, " Guitar-Playing Romeros: Father and Three Sons," *Boston Globe*, December 9, 1961, 10.

14. Judith Robison, "Father, 3 Sons Give Program of Guitar Music," *New York Herald Tribune*, December 15, 1961, and Alan Rich, "4 Romeros on 4 Guitars," *New York Times*, December 15, 1961. Rich said of their Telemann encore, "The noise was prodigious, but perfectly glorious."

15. Louis Biancolli, "4 Romeros Debut at Town Hall," *World Telegram and Sun*, December 15, 1961, 24.

16. "Romero Four Triumph in N.Y. Debut," *Santa Barbara News-Press*, January 7, 1962.

17. On which the Santa Barbara press once more breathlessly reported, in Ronald D. Scofield, "Romeros Score Triumph in N.Y.," *Santa Barbara News-Press*, April 22, 1962, C-10.

18. William Albright, "Music: Guitarist Pepe Romero," *Houston Post*, December 6, 1975, 7F.

19. Ronald D. Scofield, "Romeros Score Triumph in N.Y.," *Santa Barbara News-Press*, April 22, 1962, C-10.

20. "Bach in the Bedroom," *Time*, April 20, 1962, 80. Celin was getting in trouble with the Army reserve because his concert appearances were interfering with his obligations to participate in occasional weekend training sessions. In fact, he was on the verge of a court-martial when this *Time* article appeared. The army decided it did not want the bad publicity that would ensue from putting a crimp in Private Romero's budding career, so it backed off.

21. *Viva Mejor* 4, no. 2 (1980).

22. An unidentified press clipping in the RA, however, does establish that Celedonio gave a recital at the Madrid Ateneo in 1930, when he was seventeen. The critic praised his "clean and secure" technique as well as his interpretations of a diverse repertoire.

NOTES TO CHAPTER 6

23. This quotation is from the transcript of an interview done on National Public Radio's *All Things Considered*, Sunday, September 9, 2001, in connection with the Romero documentary that aired the following Friday, September 14, on the Public Broadcasting System.

24. Donal Henahan, "Talent-Laden Romero Guitar-Playing Family Performs at Tully," *New York Times*, March 29, 1971, 40.

25. Reich, "As Ambassadors of Classical Guitar," 17.

26. Marilyn Tucker, "Romeros' Powerful Guitar Concert," unidentified clipping in the RA.

27. "Entertainers Entertained," *Billings (MT) Gazette*, morning ed., November 10, 1963, 2.

28. Allen Hughes, "Montoya Plays with Eagerness of Youth," *New York Times*, March 29, 1971, 40.

29. Lawrence Cluderay, "Superb Romeros Made Music Fun," *The Province* (Vancouver, British Columbia), October 26, 1968.

30. Bruce Johnson, "Encores Almost the Best Part," *Davenport-Bettendorf Times-Democrat*, March 24, 1974, 9A.

31. Wayne Johnson, "Romeros Exciting with Symphony," *Seattle Times*, April 9, 1974.

32. William J. Nazzaro, "Spanish Royal Family of the Guitar," *Philadelphia Evening Bulletin*, July 22, 1969, 35.

33. Interview by Virginia Lucier, "Auditorium Filled for Concert by Romeros," *Birmingham Massachusetts News*, March 6, 1965.

34. Harry Rolnick, "Guitarist's Playing Draws Comparisons with Cellist," *South China Morning Post*, December 16, 1982.

35. Ayke Agus, *Heifetz As I Knew Him* (Portland, OR: Amadeus Press, 2005), 243.

36. Judith Hunt, "Memory Music," *Anchorage Daily News*, October 20, 1972.

37. Interview by Tully Potter, "Angel Romero: Tully Potter Talks to One of Los Romeros," *Hi-Fi News & Record Review*, August 1983, 57.

38. Hilmar Grondahl, "Trio of Guitarists a Talented, Entertaining Substitute," *The Oregonian*, January 10, 1974, 2M.

39. Lyle Nelson, "Some Hot Music on a Cold Night at the Shell," *Honolulu Star-Bulletin*, July 18, 1966.

40. Bob Woessner, "Romeros Expand Guitar's Potential," *Green Bay Press-Gazette*, February 10, 1973.

41. Valerie Scher, "Guitar's First Family Offers Trills, Thrills," *San Diego Union-Tribune*, May 10, 1995.

42. Marc Donner, "Romeros Concert Entertaining despite Distractions," *California Tech*, November 16, 1972.

43. Kay Potter, "Bird 'Upstages' Romero Concert," *Culpeper Star-Exponent*, March 1, 1971.

44. Robert Finn, "Guitar Virtuoso Shows Precision in Technique," *Cleveland Plain Dealer*, October 23, 1988.

45. Roy Howard Beck, "Romeros Concert Requires Patience," *Grand Rapids Press*, March 10, 1973, 5-B.

46. Albert Goldberg, "Guitarist Stars in 'Musica de Espana,'" *Los Angeles Times*, July 18, 1964, II-7.

47. Earl J. Dias, writing in the *New Bedford (MA) Sunday Standard Times*, said of Celin that "with his well-trimmed beard [he] looks like a Renaissance portrait of a Spanish grandee." Undated clipping in the RA.

48. Allen Hughes, "4 Romero Guitars at Carnegie Hall," *New York Times*, February 18, 1967.

49. In fact, the title of their first quartet album was *The Royal Family of the Spanish Guitar* (Mercury, 1963), which provided the inspiration for the title of this book.

50. Audrey Johnson, "Superb Performance by Romeos [sic]," *Victoria (BC) Daily Times*, December 11, 1970, 26.

CHAPTER 7. DEL MAR

1. Gregory Nelson Joseph, "Area Charms 'Royal Family of Guitar,'" *San Diego Tribune*, January 13, 1986, C1, C3.

2. Joe Saltzman, "Pepe Romero's Guitar: In a World of Its Own," *Los Angeles Times*, September 30, 1982, 6.

3. Donald Rosenberg, "Spanish Guitarist Expresses Music of His Soul," *Akron Beacon Journal*, 1987 but otherwise undated clipping in the RA.

4. Maria C. Hunt, "Beautiful Music, Beautiful Food: Guitar-Playing Romeros Share Traditional Dish of Their Homeland," *San Diego Union-Tribune*, October 31, 2001, E1, E3.

5. Interview by Marilyn Gump, "Family Strums Its Heritage," *Wichita Eagle*, February 23, 1970.

6. Sydney Palmer, "Ole Pepe!" *Everett (WA) Herald*, March 1, 1971.

7. Ana Lilia Cortes-Monzingo, "Este Viernes 10, el esperado concierto del cuarteto de gutiarras de 'Los Romero,'" *El Mexicano*, February 9, 1989, 1.

8. Scher, "Guitar's First Family Offers Trills."

9. "Performance to Aid Soccer Team," *Del Mar Citizen*, May 19–25, 1982.

10. Letter in the RA.

11. Letter in the RA.

12. "Well-Toasted President," *Washington Post*, March 8, 1978, D15.

13. Letter in the RA.

14. The three basic grades of Spanish knighthood are, from lowest to highest: Caballero, Comendador, and Comendador de Número. "Commander of Number" signifies the limited number of such appointments. A *comendador* is entitled to be addressed as *ilustrísimo señor* (most illustrious lord), whereas a *comendador de número* is *exelentísimo señor* (most excellent lord).

15. John Henken, "Romeros Play a Guitar Marathon," *Los Angeles Times*, May 12, 1981, 5.

CHAPTER 8. THE WORLD

1. Press report from Hans J. Schlotzheimer in Salzburg, now in the RA.

2. Interview with Joan Mooney, "Brothers Have Been in Tune since Childhood," *Sunday Telegraph* (Sydney), July 1, 1979, 49.

3. W. Sch., "'Gitarren-Paganinis' im Kammermusiksaal," *Berliner Morgenpost*, November 7, 1987, 7.

4. "Alemania, patria divina de la música." Celedonio wrote this on some stationery provided by the Ponderosa Best Western Motel in Billings, Montana [RA].

5. "Münchner sind wie die Spanier," *Bild* (Munich), February 2, 1970, 13.

6. Unidentified clipping in the RA.

7. Helge Andresen, "Der Sinneswandel kam nach der Pause," unidentified clipping of a review of a concert in Harrislee, Germany in the RA.

8. Michael Scheerer, "Die Kunst der Flügelmänner," *Stadt Kassel*, undated clipping in the RA.

9. Monika Pfützenrueter, "Wenn die Romeros loslegen," *Münsterrsche Zeitung*, October 25, 1989.

10. Elena Jarvis, "Guitar Playing Sacred Art to Romero Family," *Colorado Springs Gazette Telegraph*, March 28, 1980, 8-E.

11. Marisa Guerrero, "Los Romero: 'España ha dado los mejores guitarristas de la historia de la música," *El Correo Español—El pueblo vasco*, June 26, 1986.

12. Maite Baoyna, "Nuestro cuarteto ha conquistado América," unidentified clipping in the RA of a Málaga newspaper, July 21, 1974, 4–5.

13. "El cuarteto Los Romeros," *Sur* (Málaga), June 25, 1989, 8.

CHAPTER 9. CELEDONIO AND ANGELITA, THE POET AND HIS MUSE

1. Florence Brooks, "Father and Three Sons Delight in Outstanding Guitar Concert," *Music of the West Magazine*, 16. Undated clipping in the RA but from early 1961.

2. Walter Aaron Clark, *Enrique Granados: Poet of the Piano* (New York: Oxford University Press, 2006; paperback 2011). Spanish translation by Patricia Caicedo (Barcelona: Boileau, 2016), 9–10.

3. Letter dated November 23, 1981, in RA.

4. Published by Raúl Romero, a cousin of Celedonio's who was living in the United States at that time.

5. "Yo he visto una torre de siglos pasados, convertida en nada. Yo sé de montañas que fueron muy altas y ya no son nada de ciudades grandes y con lindas playas pero el tiempo pasa y pasa y no respeta nada."

6. From an interview with William Hellweg in publicity materials for the *Carmen* recording (Philips).

7. Eduardo Garrigues, "El último adelantado español en California," *ABC*, May 21, 1996, 52.

8. Doria Avila, "Warmth and Verve Shine Forth from Elder Romero," *McAllen (TX) Monitor*, May 5, 1987, 12A.

9. Clark, "Romeros," 62–63.

10. Ana Lilia Cortes-Monzingo, "Este Viernes 10, el esperado concierto del cuarteto de guitarras de 'Los Romero,'" *El Mexicano*, February 9, 1989, 1.

11. Ibid.

12. Undated Lucas publicity materials in the RA.

13. Ibid.

14. Ibid.

15. From an unidentified clipping in the RA. At one of my first lessons with Pepe, he assigned two things for me to do: listen to Mozart's *Don Giovanni* and read *Don Quixote*. It was in this way, he said, that I would gain valuable insights into Spanish culture and the Spanish character.

16. From the written transcript of an interview that Laurel Ornish recorded with Mamá and Papá on September 30, 1991, in Del Mar. I thank Laurel for sharing this material with me.

17. He wrote this on their program from the Charleston Symphony Orchestra's 1979–80 season.

18. From "Las Castañuelas Dichosas (A Angelita)," in *Poemas, Prosas, Pensamientos y Cantares*, 16, in the RA.

19. Susan Yerkes, "Sweet Strings," *San Antonio Light*, March 22, 1989.

20. Marc Shulgold, "The Romeros: A Family Gathering," *Los Angeles Times*, December 10, 1983, V-7.

21. Unidentified clipping in the RA.

22. Joe Saltzman, "Pepe Romero's Guitar: In a World of Its Own," *Los Angeles Times*, September 30, 1982, 6.

23. Reported in Arthur Lightbourn, "Famed Del Mar Family Boasts 'The House of the Guitar,'" *Carmel Valley News/Del Mar Village Voice*, March 8, 2002, 20. She became a citizen of the United States in 1970.

CHAPTER 10. CELIN, THE ROMANTIC

1. Karl Ludwig Nicol, "Ein Romero kommt selten allein: Porträt der Guitarristen-familie 'Los Romeros,'" *Fono Forum*, June 1978, 597.

2. Undated quotation in Lucas publicity materials, in RA.

3. Interview by R. H. Joseph, "For Romero Family, Love of Music, Art Apparent," *Clayton News/Daily* (Jonesboro, GA), January 3, 1996, 8.

4. Clark, "Romeros," 61–62. Pepe insists, "Without his teaching, example, and companionship, I could have never done or accomplished what I have. Celin is a big part of my accomplishments."

5. Ibid., 63.

6. Ibid., 60.

7. An unidentified clipping in the RA features an interview with Celin by Seville journalist Marta Carrasco.

8. Clark, "Romeros," 64.

9. Ibid.

CHAPTER 11. PEPE, THE PHILOSOPHER

1. Frederick Smith, "Coming from Guitarist Family a Pleasant Burden for Pepe Romero," *Lakeland (FL) Ledger*, February 11, 1994, 6.

2. Interview by Jürgen Christ, "Mein Vater und ich, wir sind ein Gitarrist," *Gitarre und Laute*, March 1999, 61.

3. German review from Uhlen. "Kunst is alles, mit den Augen zu hören und mit den Ohren zu sehen." Unidentified clipping in the RA.

4. Unidentified clipping from *Dallas Morning News* in the RA.

5. Daniel Buckley, "Romero Excels As Soloist and Accompanist," *Tucson Citizen*, February 20, 1991, 3B.

6. Fernando Sor, *Method for the Spanish Guitar*, trans. from the original 1830 French edition by Arnold Merrick (New York: Da Capo Press, 1980), 32.

7. Smith, "Coming from Guitarist Family," 6.

8. "The First Family of the Guitar," *Shanghai Daily*, September 9, 2005, 17.

9. Unidentified clipping in the RA.

10. Saltzman, "Pepe Romero's Guitar," 6.

11. Allan Kozinn, "Pepe Romero: Member of Los Romeros Solo Classical Artist," *Guitar Player*, January 1981, 32.

12. Ana María Davila, "Pepe Romero: 'Para hacer arte, has de saber donde estan las raices,'" *El Mundo*, November 4, 1995, 60.

13. Excerpted from publicity materials in the RA, pertaining to an upcoming concert with the Dallas Symphony.

14. John Duarte, "Pepe Romero," *Gramophone*, December 1981, 856.

15. "Rodrigo, Torroba and the Romeros: An Important Triangle," *Virtuoso: Ambassador Performing Arts Newsletter*, March–May 1992, 1, 7.

16. Laurel Ornish, "The Soul of the Land: For Classicist Pepe Romero, It's Feelings, Not Notes," *Dallas Observer*, August 22–28, 1996, 70.

17. Michael Lawson, "World Class Guitarist Pepe Romero Strums to Classical Beat," *San Diego Sun*, February 24, 1994, D&E-1.

18. Charles Baines, "Pepe: Spain's Prince of Strings," *Sunday Morning Post* (Hong Kong), December 13, 1992, 12.

19. Lawson, "World Class Guitarist," D&E-1.

20. Roger Catlin, "'Guitar is a Bridge...,'" *Washington Post*, from late December 2011 but otherwise undated clipping in RA.

21. HHB, "Pepe Romero," *Göppinger Kreisnachrichten*, November 12, 1982. Peter Pfäggen's interview in *Gitarre und Laute*, January 1984, 61, reported the number as two hundred, again half and half.

22. From an unidentified clipping in the RA.

23. Saltzman, "Pepe Romero's Guitar, 6.

24. Horst Hentschel, "Pepe Romero—the Virtuous Stylist," *Classical Guitar*, November/December 1983, 23.

25. Duarte, "Pepe Romero," 856.

26. Interview by George Varga, "Romeros' Strong Family Chords," *San Diego Union*, January 17, 1986, E1.

CHAPTER 12. ANGEL, THE PROTEUS

1. His participation in a horse auction was even reported in the *Los Angeles Times* (February 8, 1981, VII-17): "Periodically, he stands and makes a bid, eventually buying

several mares because 'they struck me right.' No, he doesn't really know anything about horses—but this year, he's decided to 'break in.' 'Not for the tax advantage,' he says vehemently, 'just for the pleasure of it.'"

2. From an interview titled "Angel Romero . . . denn alles ist logisch," in *Konzertgitarre Markt und Musik*, no. 4 (1986): 47.

3. Kathlyn Russell, "Talent: A Gift of God," *Escondido (CA) Times-Advocate*, August 23, 1979, B-1.

4. Thérèse Wassily Saba, "Angel Romero: Guitarist, Conductor and Composer," *Classical Guitar Magazine*, April 2010, 15. The recording dates from the year 1963, when he was actually seventeen, not fourteen.

5. Piano reduction published in Mainz by Schott, 1984. It includes Angel's fingerings.

6. Saba, "Angel Romero," 15.

7. John Henken, "Lalo Schifrin's Guitar Concerto at the Bowl," *Los Angeles Times*, September 19, 1984, VI-7.

8. Jim Woodward, "Guitarist Embellishes Evening of Spanish Melodies, *Central Florida News-Journal*, July 26, 1989, 6A.

9. The quotes here are gleaned from interviews with Angel.

10. "Angel Romero . . . denn alles ist logisch," 51.

11. Interview by Patrick Taggart, "Romero Plays the Family Way," *Austin American-Statesman*, January 21, 1983, F6.

12. Russell, "Talent: A Gift of God," B-5.

13. Ibid.

14. During an interview with Cindy Shubin ("The Romeros: An Interview with Angel," *Guitar Player*, April 1972, 35), he said, "I asked a guitar maker if he would allow me to work in his shop. Julius Gido in Burbank, a fantastic maker, by the way. It took me two months. I have used it for concert work. It amazed me incredibly that it had a fantastic sound when I was finished with it. I'm sure it was by accident! But, the very nice airlines, they have done their job of breaking the top of it on one of my last flights."

15. Evelyn Field, "A Classicist Right to His Fingertips," *The Star* (Johannesburg), September 10, 1981, 6.

16. Mary C. Wickenden, "Romeros Quartet Share Love of Guitar with Concert Audience," *Ridgecrest (CA) Valley Independent*, January 11, 1968. John Huxhold ("Romeros' Guitars Put Crowd on a String, *St. Louis Post-Dispatch*, April 2, 1984) thought that "Angel has the stage presence of a movie star; his dealings with the audience are pure Hollywood."

17. Wickenden, "Romeros Quartet Share Love."

18. R. W. Stiles, "Romeros Bring Sunny Spain into Pasadena," *Pasadena Star-News*, undated clipping in the RA.

19. María Cristina Alarcón, "Una familia unida por la música," *Noticia hispanoamericana* 11, no. 39 (September 26–October 2, 2001), 1.

20. Interview by Bill Fark, "Guitarist Romero Returns to Conducting," *North County Times*, January 21, 2000, 16.

21. Ibid.

22. Bernstein, "Royal Family of the Guitar," 102.

23. Fark, "Guitarist Romero Returns to Conducting," 16.

24. Saba, "Angel Romero," 11.

25. Fark, "Guitarist Romero Returns to Conducting," 16.

26. Bob Barrett, "Angel Romero: Classical Guitarist Has Little Time to Play for Fun," *Knoxville News-Sentinel*, January 11, 1987.

27. Field, "Classicist Right to His Fingertips."

28. Meredith Wynne, "Maestro Angel Romero: At Home on Stage and at the Podium," *Flagstaff Live*, March 14–20, 2002.

29. William Sullivan, "Aspiring Conductor Wants World to Hear Music of Spanish Composers," *Los Angeles Times*, August 12, 1981, II-6.

30. Valerie Scher, "Romero Takes the Podium: As a Conductor, Lauded Guitarist Displays Charisma," *San Diego Union-Tribune*, November [?], 2002, D1–2.

31. Joel D. Amos, "Guitar Virtuoso Romero Conducts SD Symphony," *San Diego Union-Tribune*, November 28, 2002, 12.

32. Valerie Scher, "Conductor Pulls Out All the Stops for 'Ode to Joy!,'" *San Diego Union-Tribune*, February 9, 2005, D1-2.

33. Interview with Mamá and Papá recorded by Laurel Ornish, September 30, 1991, in Del Mar. She went on to say that Celin's temperament was "muy gracioso" (very humorous), while Pepe as a young boy was "serious all the time."

34. Field, "Classicist Right to His Fingertips," 6.

35. Simi Horwitz, "Angel Romero: World Famous Guitarist Plays at Alice Tully Hall on March 7th," *TV Shopper*, March 2–8, 1991, 15. I hasten to point out here something that Angel said to me: "If I have no peer, there's no point to it." Angel includes among his "peers" Celedonio and Pepe, of course, in addition to Segovia, Narciso Yepes, John Williams, and Julian Bream.

36. See Matthew 5:15: "Neither do men light a candle, and put it under a bushel, but on a candlestick; and it giveth light unto all that are in the house."

37. Undated clipping in the RA.

38. Angel found ways to retaliate. In an interview with Keith Marshall ("Strumming Attractions," *New Orleans Times-Picayune*, September 10, 2001, D8), he confided, "I was always trying to steal Celin's girlfriends; that is the job of the younger brother."

39. Saba, "Angel Romero," 12–14.

40. Frank J. Sulloway, *Born to Rebel: Birth Order, Family Dynamics, and Creative Lives* (New York: Vintage Books, 1997), 353.

41. Wilma Salisbury, "PBS Documentary Shows Talent Is in the Blood of Guitar Ensemble," *The Cleveland Plain Dealer*, September 14, 2001.

CHAPTER 13. THE ROMERO TECHNIQUE

1. Quoted in *Desmangue: Revista del Centro Hispanoamericano de Guitarra* 1, no. 1 (October 1996): 14. It is probably not a coincidence that the "strings as princesses" metaphor was earlier used by Lorca in his poem "Adivinanza de la guitarra," from the *Seis caprichos* of the *Poema del cante jondo*.

2. Interview by Virginia Muñoz, "Pepe Romero, el mago que embruja con una guitarra," *Sur* (Málaga), August 25, 1988, 8.

3. Carmen Teresa Roiz, "Los Romeros: Una familia de guitarristas que ha sabido mantener la tradición musical," *Vista Magazine*, September 2001.

4. In Bernstein, "Royal Family of the Guitar," 108, Pepe recalled being filled with pride assisting his father in copying out and adding fingerings to the *25 Melodious Studies* by Matteo Carcassi.

5. Rex Anderson and David Kennedy, "Pepe Romero Masterclass," *Guitar: The Magazine for All Guitarists*, October 1983, 13.

6. Horwitz, "Angel Romero, 15.

7. Interview in *Guitar and Lute*, no. 7 (September 1978): 17.

8. James Wierzbicki, "Romero's Guitar Touch Is One Perfect Gesture," *St. Louis Post-Dispatch*, September 11, 1989.

9. Clark, *Enrique Granados*, 23–24.

10. Smith, "All in the Family," 13.

11. The text of his talk is in the RA, dated May 13, 1996.

12. Donn E. Pohren, *Lives and Legends of Flamenco* (Madrid: Society of Spanish Studies, 1988), 264.

13. Rosenberg, "Spanish Guitarist."

14. Kozinn, "Pepe Romero," 32. In another interview, Pepe says to "'adjust nails to your hand position, not vice versa. Obsession with nail length and shape in the early stages of learning, he says, can adversely affect one's playing position. [As he instructed one student,] You are striking the strings; you are not moving them and letting them go. It is a very common mistake among guitarists that they always think of a note when they pluck it—and then they forget it!'" (Anderson and Kennedy, "Pepe Romero Masterclass," 15).

15. Robert Finn, "Romero Is Bringing Golden Age of Guitar," *Cleveland Plain Dealer*, October 19, 1988.

16. Anderson and Kennedy, "Pepe Romero Masterclass," 14.

17. Buckley ("Romero Excels As Soloist and Accompanist," 3B), noted something similar: "No matter how fast or in what tangled shapes the fingers flew, . . . Romero's tone maintained its unsullied luster, warmth, evenness, balance and appropriate character."

18. According to Celino, in my conversations with him.

19. Shubin, "Romeros," 36.

20. Clark, "Romeros," 61.

21. *The Art of Spanish Guitar: A Method by Celino Romero* (Indianapolis: Amsco, 2006), 13.

22. Roiz, "Los Romeros," 18.

23. Laurel Ornish, "The Romeros: Three Generations of the 'Royal Family of the Guitar,'" *On the Air Magazine*, May 1993, 36.

24. Frank Magiera, "'Royal Family of Guitar' to Play at Mechanics Hall," *Worcester (MA) Telegram and Gazette*, February 23, 1990, A11.

25. Tracie Cone, "Audience for Guitar Growing, Musician Says," *Winston-Salem Journal*, March 14, 1984, 27.

26. Clark, *Enrique Granados*, 204.
27. Kyle MacMillan, "Natural Romero Finds Captivating Sounds," *Omaha World-Herald*, February 9, 1988.
28. Sue Tenorio, "Pepe Romero Conducts Master Class," *El Extra News* (Hartford), October 17, 1997, 14.
29. Clark, *Enrique Granados*, 70.
30. "Angel Romero . . . denn alles ist logisch," 48.
31. Henry Adams, "Interview: The Romeros," *Guitar and Lute*, no. 7 (September 1978): 17.
32. *The Celedonio Romero Method for the Classical Guitar* (Woodmere, N.Y.: Juan Orozco, 1990), 9.
33. Adams, "Interview," 17.
34. Shubin, "Romeros," 36.
35. Diane Windeler, "Pepe Romero: Guitar Was My 1st Language," *San Antonio Light*, November 16, 1984.
36. Kozinn, "Pepe Romero," 32.
37. Ibid., 33.
38. Saltzman, "Pepe Romero's Guitar," 6.
39. Clark, *Enrique Granados*, 69–70.
40. "Angel Romero . . . denn alles ist logisch," 49.
41. Anderson and Kennedy, "Pepe Romero Masterclass," 14.
42. Ibid.
43. Anne Mendelsohn, "Masters Teach Guitar Students," *La Jolla Light*, July 1, 1976.
44. G'anna Hayes, "Romeros Are Teachers of Top Guitar Profs," *Odessa American*, January 24, 1971, 6-D. The interview states that Darryl Saffer, a former Romero student, was a professor of guitar at Southern Methodist University.
45. See Parkening's fascinating self-portrait, written with Kathy Tyers, *Grace like a River: An Autobiography* (Carol Stream, Ill.: Tyndale House, 2006), 26.

CHAPTER 14. THE ROMERO REPERTOIRE

1. Adams, "Interview," 15.
2. Ken Herman, "A Crucible of Contemporary Music: Generating Regional Excitement Even As It Builds an International Reputation, the UCSD School of Music Strives to Make History—Not Retell It," *Ranch and Coast*, September 1988, 30.
3. Joaquín Rodrigo, "Por una música de vanguardia: Pero que no repugne a la sensibilidad de los grandes auditorios actuales," *YA*, January 13, 1971.
4. "Nusquam est qui ubique est." From *Epistulae Morales*, II, 2. See Rose Williams's delightful volume *Latin Quips at Your Fingertips* (New York: Barnes and Noble, 2001), xxviii. Frederick the Great cleverly adapted it as follows: "He who defends everything defends nothing."
5. James Reel, "Romero's Guitar Is Recording-Studio Perfect," *Arizona Daily Star*, February 20, 1991.
6. Unidentified clipping in the RA, titled "Lorimer Gives Esoteric Performance: Romero's Playing Full of Intensity, Emotion."

NOTES TO CHAPTER 14

7. John Duarte, *Gramophone*, 1992, 88.

8. Raymond Ericson, "Music: Romero Guitars," *New York Times*, February 28, 1976.

9. Greg Wager, "The Romeros Quartet: A Family Tradition," *Revue* (Magazine of the Orange County Performing Arts Center), February 1, 1988.

10. Letter in the RA.

11. In an interview by Laurel Ornish ("Guitar's First Family Visits: Romeros, Symphony Made History Together," *San Antonio Express-News*, May 9, 1995, 12B), Celedonio stated that they had already played it hundreds of times around the world, in every city with a major symphony orchestra.

12. "Rodrigo, Torroba and the Romeros: An Important Triangle," *Virtuoso* 3, no. 3 (March–May 1992): 7.

13. Lloyd Stewart, "A Magical Evening Planned for Jewel Charity Ball," from a Texas newspaper at the time of the premiere (name and date of the paper not included in the clipping from the RA), translated by the reviewer from the original German.

14. Ibid.

15. "Unique Festival of Spanish Guitar Music," *Ambassador International Cultural Foundation: News of the Performing Arts and Ambassador Auditorium Calendar of Events*, December 1983–February 1984, 1–2.

16. John Duarte, "Record Reviews," *Gramophone*, 1984, 36.

17. John Duarte, review, *Records and Recording*, December 1975, 48–49.

18. "Unique Festival of Spanish Guitar Music," 2.

19. "Rodrigo, Torroba and the Romeros," 7.

20. For more about this fascinating composer, see Walter Aaron Clark and William Craig Krause, *Federico Moreno Torroba: A Musical Life in Three Acts* (New York: Oxford University Press, 2013; paper 2016).

21. "Rodrigo, Torroba and the Romeros," 7.

22. In his *Gramophone* review of this recording, John Duarte states that he played the recording for Segovia, who was "visibly moved." Undated clipping in the RA, probably from early 1982. Pepe's former student, Vicente Coves, has recently recorded it for Naxos in a series of recordings devoted to Torroba's guitar music, which Pepe and Vicente are making together. See appendix 3 for more information on these CDs.

23. Undated clipping in RA, *Gramophone*, 842.

24. Concerning Torroba's *Concierto en flamenco*, Sabicas said to Pepe, "Man, the way you play my music so well and seeing as how you're a classical guitarist who reads music and has no problem playing with an orchestra, why don't you play Torroba's concerto?" Quoted in the program notes for a performance of the concerto in Málaga in 2007, with the Orquesta Filarmónica de Málaga. Angel Romero conducted on this occasion.

25. Letter in the RA.

26. Antonio Iglesias, "Los Romero y Theo Alcantara, en un estreno de Moreno Torroba," *Informaciones*, November 19, 1979.

27. *Music Week*, December 6, 1980, British publication; untitled clipping in the RA.

28. Ibid.

29. *Classical Topics*, no. 12 (December 1979): 3.
30. Ibid.
31. Ibid.
32. Enrique Franco, "Composiciones de Moreno Torroba y Strawinsky," *El País*, November 20, 1979, 35.
33. Phillip Truckenbrod, "4 Guitarists, Symphony Win Essex Bravos," *Newark Star-Ledger*, February 20, 1973, 30.
34. Marilyn Gump, "Family Strums Its Heritage," *Wichita Eagle*, February 23, 1970.
35. Albert Goldberg, "Romeros in Bowl Program, *Los Angeles Times*, August 2, 1969, II-7.
36. Tom Ineck, "Orchestra to Premiere 'Zareh': Guitarist Pepe Romero Will Play Tjeknavorian Concerto," *Lincoln Journal-Star*, November 20, 1988, 1H.
37. John Henken, "Lalo Schifrin's Guitar Concerto at the Bowl," *Los Angeles Times*, September 19, 1984, VI-7.
38. Mark Swed, "Pop Trumps Polish in Bowl Tango Concert," *Los Angeles Times*, August 4, 2016, E1, E5.
39. This work is available on both CD and DVD. See appendixes 3 and 4 for information about them.
40. Gordon Emerson, "Longtime Friendship Results in an Unusual Composition," *New Haven Register*. Undated clipping in the RA.
41. "Guitarist Who Fuses Jazz, Classical Styles," *Contra Costa Times*, August 15, 1979, 44.
42. Liner notes for the recording (see appendix 3).
43. Ibid.
44. "Poor Sancho. . . . Nobody says anything about you. I give you a present of a cortijo." See Laurel Ornish, "Recuerdos de Celedonio Romero (1913–1996)," *Soundboard* 24, no. 2 (Fall 1997): 24. The quotation is taken from Ornish's radio interview with Celedonio in Galveston, Texas, on March 7, 1993.
45. Potter, "Angel Romero," 57.
46. Gump, "Family Strums Its Heritage."
47. John Hinterberger, "Romeros in Fine Performance," *Seattle Times*, April 2, 1968, 17.
48. Howard Reich, "As Ambassadors of Classical Guitar, Romeros Are Programmed to Please All," *Chicago Tribune*, May 18, 1986, section 13, 17.
49. Press release in the RA.
50. Adams, "Interview," 16.
51. Allan Kozinn, "The Guitar Enters Music's Mainstream," *New York Times*, February 18, 1979, 26.
52. Greg Wager, "Music Is Nonstop for Pepe Romero," *Los Angeles Times*, December 4, 1987, VI-6.
53. Derrick Henry, "Guitar 'Fantasia' by Sor Gets Its Premiere 160 Years Later," *Atlanta Journal-Constitution*, May 3, 1992, N6.
54. M. Sei., "Kammermusik," *Fono Forum*, February 1981, 152.

55. Publicity materials from Philips in connection with recording of *Carmen*, in the RA.
56. Ibid.
57. Carol Sowell, "Symphony's Spanish Accent Slightly Uneven," *Arizona Daily Star*, April 23, 1982.
58. Jann Kelso, "Classical Castanets in Cowtown Benefit," *Dallas Morning News*, February 21, 1985.
59. Claire Eyrich, *Dallas Star-Telegram*, undated clipping in RA.
60. Greg Wager, "Music Is Nonstop for Pepe Romero," *Los Angeles Times*, December 4, 1987, VI-6.
61. Keith Marshall, "Strumming Attractions," *New Orleans Times-Picayune*, September 10, 2001, D8.
62. Hentschel, "Pepe Romero—the Virtuous Stylist," 24.
63. Untitled clipping in the RA, dated February 24, 1994.

CHAPTER 15. BREAKIN' UP IS HARD TO DO

1. Rosenberg, "Spanish Guitarist."
2. Bob Crimeen, "3 of a Kind," *The Sun* (Canberra), on June 27, 1979, 25.
3. Diane Windeler, "The Romeros Have Stayed Close," *San Antonio Light*, March 19, 1989, K3.
4. Interview by Cleora Hughes, "Romeros Have Plenty of Pluck," *St. Louis Post Dispatch*, March 30, 1984.
5. Fede included this anecdote in the foreword he submitted for the present volume. I decided to excerpt and use it here instead.
6. In an otherwise unidentified clipping in the RA, titled "Four Romeros—Talented, Romantic, Hotheaded Family."
7. Hentschel, "Pepe Romero—the Virtuous Stylist," 24.
8. "Documentary on Classical Guitar Masters to Air on PBS," *La Voz*, August 9, 2001, 2.
9. Donal J. Henahan, "Romero Family Is a Lively Show," *Chicago Daily News*, March 21, 1966, emphasis added.
10. Dagmar Zschiesche, "Große Vorfreude auf Los Romeros nicht ganz erfüllt," *Westfalische Rundschau*, October 24, 1987. This *Verspätung* was also criticized by G. v. H., "Von der hohen Kunst des Gitarrenspiels," *Westfalenpost*, October 24, 1987, EG2.
11. John Henken, "The Romeros Will Still Be a Family Affair at the Bowl," *Los Angeles Times*, September 9, 1992, F5.
12. Both the letter from CAMI and the fax from ICM cited here are in the RA.

CHAPTER 16. THE NEXT GENERATIONS

1. Eulogy in the RA.
2. Letter from Bill Clinton dated October 9, 1997, to the Guitar Foundation of America convention, held that year in San Diego and honoring Celedonio. Letter in the RA.
3. From "Cuando yo muera," in *Poemas, Prosas, Pensamientos y Cantares*, 7.

4. Celedonio and Angelita are buried in El Camino Memorial Park, 5600 Carroll Canyon Road, San Diego, Lakeview Mausoleum Bay, crypt 2, tier A.

5. Valerie Scher, "Romero Guitar Dynasty Still Adding to Its Family Albums," *San Diego Union-Tribune*, August 25, 1994, Night and Day section, 31.

6. Ornish, "Romeros,'" 37.

7. Jeffrey Kaliss, "A Family Affair: The Romeros Celebrate 55 Years as a Preeminent Musical Force," *Classical Guitar Magazine*, March 18, 2015, http://classicalguitarmagazine.com/the-romeros-celebrate-55-years/, accessed April 27, 2017. This article originally appeared in the Spring 2017 issue, no. 377.

8. Radio interview with Laurel Ornish, March 6, 1993, in Galveston, Texas.

9. Lawson, "World Class Guitarist," D&E-1.

10. Susan Isaacs Nisbett, "All in the Family: The Romeros Make Music a Sacred and Beautiful Genetic Destiny," *Ann Arbor News*, January 5, 2000, 4.

11. His first serious companion was Virginia Kaechele, whom he met in 1989. They have a daughter named Angelita Natalia (b. 1992), though their union did not last. A subsequent relationship produced twins named Alejandro and Angelito Romero (b. 2000).

12. A brief marriage to Susan Parker ended in annulment after a year, though they also remain close friends. In fact, she was the maid of honor at his wedding with Nefretiri. Susan's subsequent husband was Angel's best man.

13. Lisa Millegan, "Modesto Holds a Place in the Heart of Angel Romero," *Modesto Bee*, March 3, 2006, H-9, H-13.

14. James Wierzbicki, "Romeros' Four Guitars Recall Flamenco Flavor, Fire," *St. Louis Post-Dispatch*, February 14, 1994.

15. Christopher Hume, "Guitar Family Romero in Classical Mode," *Toronto Star*, May 14, 1997.

16. Lightbourn, "Famed Del Mar Family,'" 20.

17. "Sicut erat in principio, et nunc, et semper, et in saecula saeculorum" (usually translated "world without end"). From the Gloria Patri, also known as the Lesser Doxology.

ENCORE

1. Letter in the RA.

2. Reported in Gonzalo Fausto, "La guitarra al Vaticano," *El Sol*, July 26, 1989, 13. Of this concert Pepe later joked: "I play for God, so playing for the Pope was no big deal." See Lawson, "World Class Guitarist," D&E-1. The Romeros had already had an audience with the pope three years earlier, on Wednesday, September 18, 1983.

3. "Inmortalidad," from *Poemas, Prosas, Pensamientos y Cantares*, 2.

4. Doria Avila, "Warmth and Verve Shine Forth from Elder Romero," *McAllen (TX) Monitor*, May 5, 1987, 12A.

5. "Una Gran Señora," from *Poemas, Prosas, Pensamientos y Cantares*, 10.

6. Merton (1915–68) was from the United States and a prolific author of books on comparative religion and spirituality; for example, see his remarkable volume *Mystics and Zen Masters* (New York: Farrar, Straus and Giroux, 1999). Thich Nhat Hanh (1926–)

is Vietnamese, and his writings include *Going Home: Jesus and Buddha as Brothers* (New York: Riverhead Books, 2000).

7. Thomas Hardy (1840–1928) authored a remarkable novel titled *Jude the Obscure* (1895), to which I allude here. His 1912 poem *The Convergence of the Twain*, from which this poetic passage is taken, ponders the chance encounter of an iceberg with the *Titanic*. Hardy's conception of such ironies was fundamentally fatalistic, tragic, and proof of the nonexistence of a benevolent god. In that sense, it is not consistent with Celedonio's view.

8. In the interview with Wilma Salisbury ("PBS Documentary"), Pepe recalled his father's conviction that "every note resonates in the universe forever once it is released from the guitar."

9. "Hoy cantan las estrellas / y nada más." From *De un cancionero apócrifo, Abel Martín: Los complementarios, Recuerdos de sueño, fiebre y duermivela*, XII.

GLOSSARY OF NAMES AND TERMS

NAMES

Aguado y García, Dionisio (1784–1849): celebrated guitarist and composer of numerous concert and pedagogical works for guitar.

Albéniz, Isaac (1860–1909): Virtuoso pianist and composer of works for piano, for voice, chorus, orchestra, and the stage. Best known for his Spanish-style piano works that have been transcribed for guitar and are staples of the guitar repertoire.

Boccherini, Luigi (1743–1805): Italian composer active in Spain. Composed several quintets for guitar and string quartet that often evoke the soundscape of old Madrid.

Bream, Julian (1933–): English guitar virtuoso who played a major role in transforming the instrument's repertoire by commissioning contemporary works beyond the Spanish pale. As a lutenist, he was a leading figure in the performance of Renaissance and Baroque music on original instruments.

Carcassi, Matteo (1792–1853): Italian guitarist and composer best known for his pedagogical work *25 Melodic and Progressive Studies*, op. 60, for the guitar.

Carulli, Ferdinando (1770–1841): Italian guitarist and composer who wrote solos, duets, and concertos for the guitar.

De Visée, Robert (1655–1733): one of the leading Baroque guitarists, whose Suite in D Minor is an evergreen favorite with classical guitarists.

Falla, Manuel de (1876–1946): one of Spain's greatest composers in the modern era, celebrated for his ballets such as *El amor brujo* and *El sombrero de tres picos*, as well as his opera *La vida breve*. All are redolent of flamenco.

GLOSSARY OF NAMES AND TERMS

Fortea, Daniel (1878–1953): a prominent disciple of Francisco Tárrega and friend of Celedonio Romero.

Giuliani, Mauro (1781–1829): Italian guitarist and composer whose solos and concertos are standard repertoire. His enduring pedagogical works include numerous exercises for the right and the left hands.

Granados, Enrique (1867–1916): one of the major figures in the evolution of Spanish musical nationalism, renowned for his piano works evoking Spanish folklore, for example, twelve *Danzas españolas*, and the art of Francisco Goya (1746–1828), for example, *Goyescas*, which he converted into an opera. The *Danzas* are popular in guitar transcription, as is the Intermezzo from the opera *Goyescas*.

Llobet, Miquel (1878–1938): a leading disciple of Francisco Tárrega whose numerous arrangements and transcriptions have found a permanent place in the repertoire.

Lucia, Paco de (1947–2014): the most influential flamenco guitarist after Sabicas and progenitor of Nuevo Flamenco, a fusion of traditional flamenco with elements of popular music from the Americas.

Milán, Luis de (ca. 1500–ca. 1561): vihuelist and composer whose magnum opus is *El Maestro* (1535). His *Pavanas* from this collection are very popular with guitarists.

Molino, Francesco (1775–1847): a prominent guitarist and composer who wrote numerous solos, chamber works, and a concerto for guitar.

Moreno Torroba, Federico (1891–1982): the leading composer of zarzuela during the twentieth century and a major contributor to the guitar repertoire. He composed solos, quartets, and several concertos.

Mudarra, Alonso (ca. 1510–1580): vihuelist and composer of *Tres libros de música en cifras* (1546), which incudes the *Fantasía X*, much beloved by modern guitarists.

Rodrigo, Joaquín (1901–99): the leading composer of concert music in Spain during the second half of the twentieth century. He made major contributions to the guitar repertoire, especially several concertos, the most famous of which is the *Concierto de Aranjuez* (1939).

Sabicas (né Agustín Castellón Campos, 1912–90): one of the greatest guitarists in the history of flamenco, whose style and technique set the standard for many who followed him.

Sáinz de la Maza, Regino (1896–1981): a leading guitar virtuoso in Spain during the middle decades of the twentieth century. He performed the premiere of Joaquín Rodrigo's *Concierto de Aranjuez*, in 1940.

Sanz, Gaspar (1640–1710): Baroque guitarist and composer whose magnum opus is the *Instrucción de música sobre la guitarra española* (1674). Many of the pieces in this collection are favorites with classical guitarists.

Segovia, Andrés (1893–1987): a transformative figure in the history of the guitar, who worked with many composers to create new repertoire for the instrument, which he then championed in numerous recordings and while touring internationally.

Sor, Fernando (1778–1839) (Catalan Josep Ferran Sorts i Muntades): Catalan guitarist, teacher, and composer whose pedagogical studies and solo works form the foundation of the modern guitar's repertoire. Sor resided and taught throughout Europe and was a versatile composer who wrote ballet, opera, and choral music.

Tárrega, Francisco (1852–1909): the father of the modern classical guitar. He made lasting contributions to guitar pedagogy as well as the repertoire, through his many transcriptions and original compositions, especially *Recuerdos de la Alhambra*.

Turina, Joaquín (1882–1949): Spanish composer of a wide variety of concert works, for guitar, piano, voice, orchestra, and chamber ensemble.

Villa-Lobos, Heitor (1887–1959): Brazilian composer who contributed numerous works to the guitar repertoire, especially his *Douze Études*, *Cinq Préludes*, and *Suite populaire bresilienne*.

Williams, John (1941–): Among the leading disciples of Segovia, the Australian-English guitar virtuoso has gained renown not only for his mastery of the traditional repertoire but also for the promotion of music by modern composers, as well as by Barrios and other overlooked masters of the past. He has also collaborated with creative artists in the popular sphere.

Yepes, Narciso (1927–97): one of the leading classical guitarists of the twentieth century, renowned for performing on the ten-string guitar.

TERMS

Albaicín: the historic Roma district in Granada and one of the birthplaces of flamenco.

bailaor/bailaora: Andalusian dialect for *bailador*, a male dancer, or *bailadora*, a female dancer. From *bailar*, to dance.

baile: flamenco dance.

bulerías: a *palo* of flamenco with a fast tempo and complex rhythms, featuring a twelve-beat *compás* with accents on 12, 3, 6, 8, and 10.

café cantante: literally, a "singing café," a locale where flamenco was performed during the nineteenth and early twentieth centuries, a period named after this kind of establishment, now often referred to as a *peña* or *tablao*.

cantaor/cantaora: Andalusian dialect for *cantador*, a male singer, or *cantadora*, a female singer. From *cantar*, to sing.

cante: flamenco singing.

cante jondo: "deep song," a profound, tragic, and intensely emotional style of flamenco singing.

compás: the metric structure of flamenco. Each *palo* (genre) has its characteristic organization of beats into patterns of strong and weak.

copla: a song or song verse, alternating with refrains, *estribillos*.

duende: the profound emotion of flamenco, tantamount to "soul" in the blues. A *duende* is actually a spirit being that possesses or guides an inspired performer.

estribillo: a song refrain, alternating with *coplas*.

falseta: guitar-solo passages in the context of a flamenco performance in which the guitarist can demonstrate his or her technical skill and musical inventiveness.

fandango: a lively type of song and dance in triple meter and existing in regional varieties, for example, *malagueñas, rondeñas, verdiales*, and *fandangos de Huelva*.

flamenco: a complex art form involving poetry, singing, dancing, and instrumental performance, mostly guitar. The origins of the term are not certain, but flamenco as we know it evolved during the 1800s.

flamenquistas: flamenco artists and aficionados.

guajira: a lively type of song and dance that originated in Cuba and made its way to Spain. Characterized by a regular alternation of 6/8 and 3/4, that is, hemiola.

jornalero: day laborer or field hand.

jota: a lively song and dance in triple or compound-duple meter. Though it originated in Aragon, regional variants of it are found throughout Spain, including Valencia, Navarra, and Andalusia.

juerga: a private flamenco party that attracts not only professionals but also aficionados. *Juergas* typically take place in the late evening but may go on for days.

letra: the lyrics of a song.

malagueña: a type of fandango associated with the city of Málaga. Though originally a lively dance, by the early 1900s it had evolved into a type of *cante* accompanied by guitar.

palo: any type or genre of flamenco. Means literally a "suit of cards," indicating that each *palo* offers a wide variety of creative possibilities.

punteo: plucking the strings of the guitar. This includes all manner of scales and arpeggios.

rasgueo: strumming the strings of the guitar. There are dozens of different strumming patterns using all five digits of the right hand.

Roma: a more accurate term for Gypsies, who originally migrated out of northwestern India during the Middle Ages and settled throughout Eurasia and North Africa (hence their Spanish name, *gitanos*, short for *egiptanos*).

sevillanas: a type of song and dance related to the lively, triple-meter Castilian *seguidillas* and associated with Seville, where it is commonly performed during the spring *feria* (festival).

tablature: a system of musical notation for fingerboard instruments commonly used during the sixteenth and seventeenth centuries. Features a series of parallel lines indicating the strings, vertical lines to indicate metrical units, numbers or letters within the lines to indicate frets, and conventional rhythmic symbols above the lines to indicate note durations.

tertulia: a regular but informal gathering of like-minded artists and intellectuals in a café or restaurant to discuss matters of mutual interest, especially culture and politics.

tocaor/tocaora: Andalusian dialect for *tocador*, a male guitarist, or *tocadora*, a female guitarist. From *tocar*, to play.

toque: flamenco guitar playing.

Triana: a district (or *barrio*) of Seville traditionally inhabited by Spanish Roma and considered to be one of the cradles of modern flamenco.

trilleras: works songs associated with threshing wheat.
verdiales: a type of fandango native to the mountainous region north of the city of Málaga.
vihuela: a guitar-like plucked-string instrument popular in Spain during the Renaissance. Had five or six courses, double strings except for the highest, single, string.
zarzuela: a type of Spanish-language musical theater alternating spoken dialogue with set musical numbers. Its golden age was from 1850 to 1950.

SELECTED BIBLIOGRAPHY

Adams, Henry. "Interview: The Romeros," *Guitar and Lute*, September 1978, 15–17.
Anderson, Rex, and David Kennedy. "Pepe Romero Masterclass." *Guitar: The Magazine for All Guitarists*, October 1983, 13–15.
"Angel Romero . . . denn alles ist logisch!" *Konzertgitarre Markt und Musik*, no. 4 (1986): 47–51.
Beevor, Antony. *The Battle for Spain: The Spanish Civil War, 1936–1939*. Rev. ed. London: Penguin Books, 2006.
Bernstein, Paul. "The Royal Family of the Guitar." *New York Times Magazine*, November 29, 1981, 98–110.
Bream, Julian, and Graham Wade. *The Art of Julian Bream*. Blaydon on Tyne, UK: Ashley Mark, 2008.
Christ, Jürgen. "Mein Vater und ich, wir sind ein Gitarrist." *Gitarre und Laute*, March 1999, 61–64.
Clark, Walter Aaron. *Enrique Granados: Poet of the Piano*. New York: Oxford University Press, 2006. Paperback, 2011. Spanish translation by Patricia Caicedo. Barcelona: Boileau, 2016
———. *Isaac Albéniz: Portrait of a Romantic*. Oxford: Oxford University Press, 1999. Paperback, 2002. Spanish translation by Paul Silles. Madrid: Turner, 2002.
———. "The *Malagueñas* of Breva, Albéniz, and Lecuona: From Regional Fandango to Global Pop Tune." In *The Global Reach of the Fandango in Music, Song, and Dance: Spaniards, Indians, Africans, and Gypsies*, edited by Meira Goldberg, 236–43. Newcastle upon Tyne: Cambridge Scholars, 2016. Originally published in *Música oral del sur: Revista internacional*, no. 12 (2015): 325–32.

———. "The Romeros: Living Legacy of the Spanish Guitar; An Interview with Celín Romero." *Soundboard Magazine: The Journal of the Guitar Foundation of America* 36, no. 2 (2010): 60–64.

Clark, Walter Aaron, and William Craig Krause. *Federico Moreno Torroba: A Musical Life in Three Acts*. New York: Oxford University Press, 2013. Paperback, 2016. Spanish translation by Luis Gago. Madrid: Instituto Complutense de Ciencias Musicales, 2018.

Coelho, Victor Anand, ed. *The Cambridge Companion to the Guitar*. New York: Cambridge University Press, 2003.

DeMaria, Rusel. *Paco de Lucia: My Memories of a Flamenco Legend*. N.p.: Waterfront Digital Press, 2014.

Fleming, Shirley. "The Guitar on the Go." *High Fidelity Magazine*, July 1966, 42–45.

García Lorca, Federico. *Collected Poems*. Rev. bilingual ed. Edited by Christopher Maurer. New York: Farrar, Straus and Giroux, 2002.

Garno, Gerard, and Graham Wade. *A New Look at Segovia: His Life, His Music*. 2 vols. Pacific, Mo.: Mel Bay, 1997.

Gibson, Ian. *Federico García Lorca: A Life*. London: Faber, 1989.

———. *Ligero de equipaje: La vida de Antonio Machado*. 4th ed. Madrid: Prisa Ediciones, 2014.

González Mira, Pedro. "O el amor por la guitarra." *Ritmo*, no. 640 (February 1993): 7–10.

Heck, Thomas. *Mauro Giuliani: A Life for the Guitar*. 3rd ed. N.p.: Guitar Foundation of America, 2013.

Hentschel, Horst. "Pepe Romero—the Virtuous Stylist." *Classical Guitar*, November/December 1983, 23–25.

Hess, Carol A. *Sacred Passions: The Life and Music of Manuel de Falla*. New York: Oxford University Press, 2005.

Jeffery, Brian. *Fernando Sor: Composer and Guitarist*. 2nd ed. Soar Chapel, UK: Tecla Editions, 1994.

Kamen, Henry. *The Disinherited: Exile and the Making of Spanish Culture, 1492–1975*. New York: HarperCollins, 2007.

Kozinn, Allan. "Pepe Romero: Member of Los Romeros Solo Classical Artist." *Guitar Player*, January 1981, 32–36.

Laverde, Manuel. "Los Romero y la guitarra." *Temas*, April 30, 1965, 20–25.

Machado, Antonio. *Border of a Dream: Selected Poems*. Translated by Willis Barnstone. Port Townsend, Wash.: Copper Canyon Press, 2004.

May, Janice. "Angel Romero." *Classical Guitar*, September–October 1983, 13–15.

Moser, Wolf. *Francisco Tárrega y la guitarra en España entre 1830 y 1960*. Valencia: Piles, 2009.

Ornish, Laurel. "Recuerdos de Celedonio Romero (1913–1996)." *Soundboard* 24, no. 2 (Fall 1997): 20–26.

———. "The Romeros: Three Generations of the 'Royal Family of the Guitar.'" *On the Air Magazine*, May 1993, 6–7, 36–37.

SELECTED BIBLIOGRAPHY

Orringer, Nelson. *Lorca in Tune with Falla: Literary and Musical Interludes*. Toronto: University of Toronto Press, 2014.

Parkening, Christopher, with Kathy Tyers. *Grace like a River: An Autobiography*. Carol Stream, Ill.: Tyndale House, 2006.

Pohren, Donn E. *The Art of Flamenco*. Shaftesbury, UK: Musical New Services, 1984.

———. *Lives and Legends of Flamenco: A Biographical History*. Madrid: Society of Spanish Studies, 1988.

Rius, Adrián. *Francisco Tárrega (1852–1909): Biography*. Valencia: Piles, 2006.

Roberts, John Storm. *The Latin Tinge: The Impact of Latin American Music on the United States*. 2nd ed. New York: Oxford University Press, 1998.

Romero, José Francisco. *Sueños de luna*. Málaga: Ediciones del Genal, 2014.

Saba, Thérèse Wassily. "Angel Romero: Guitarist, Conductor and Composer." *Classical Guitar Magazine*, April 2010, 11–16.

Sarriá Muñoz, Andrés. *Breve historia de Málaga*. Málaga: Editorial Sarria, 2004.

Shubin, Cindy. "The Romeros: An Interview with Angel." *Guitar Player*, April 1972, 16, 34–36.

Small, Mark. "In the Hands of Angel: Angel Romero Remains a Vital Force in Classical Music." *Classical Guitar*, Spring 2016, 38–43

Smith, Nevada. "All in the Family." KPBS's *On Air Magazine*, June 2001, 12–13.

Starling, William. *Strings Attached: The Life and Music of John Williams*. Hull, UK: Robson Press, 2012.

Thomas, Hugh. *The Spanish Civil War*. New York: Simon and Schuster, 1994.

Tyler, James, and Paul Sparks. *The Guitar and Its Music: From the Renaissance to the Classical Era*. New York: Oxford University Press, 2002.

Wade, Graham. *Joaquín Rodrigo—A Life in Music; Travelling to Aranjuez: 1901–1939*. Withernsea, UK: GRM, 2006.

———. *Mel Bay Concise History of the Classic Guitar*. Pacific, Mo.: Mel Bay, 2001.

INDEX

ABC (newspaper), 59
Academy of St. Martin-in-the-Fields, 184, 226–27, 241–42, 246, 267–68
Academy of the West, 260
Adams, Henry, 196, 239
Adrian (MI) Daily Telegram, 90
Adventures of Ozzie and Harriet, The (TV series), comparison to, 101
Akron (OH) Beacon Journal, 116, 200, 248
Alarcón, Agustín, 34, 50
Albéniz, Isaac: birth, 5; "Cádiz," 166; Cruz del Caballero de la Orden de Isabel la Católica, 120; death, 6; "Granada (Serenata)," 34; "Leyenda," 90; *Rumores de La Caleta*, 4, 99
Albéniz, Luisa, 65
Aleixandre, Vicente, 14
Alessandro, Victor, 220
Alfonso XIII, King of Spain, 36–38
Alice Tully Hall (New York City), 217–18
Allen, Woody, as fan, 181
Almodóvar, Pedro, as fan, 181
Álvarez González, Antonio, 46–47
Amaya, Carmen, 236
Ambassador Auditorium (Los Angeles), 117, 162, 221, 254
Ambassador Foundation (Pasadena), 222–23
Ameling, Elly, 222–23, 247

American Sinfonietta, 235
Anchorage (AK) Daily News, 108–9
Andaluz. See *Concierto andaluz* (Rodrigo)
Angarola, Anisa, 213
Angel. *See* Romero, Angel (son of Celedonio)
Angel/EMI label, 121
Angelita. *See* Romero, Angelita (wife of Celedonio)
Angelita (Quartet no. 1) (Madina), 229
Angel Vals nos. 1 and 2 (Celedonio Romero), 235
Anglada, Aurelio, 42
Ann Arbor (MI) News, 265
Appleson, G. B., 250
Ara, Agustín León, 222–23
Aranjuez. See *Concierto de Aranjuez* (Rodrigo)
Arizona Daily Star, 217, 244
Arnaz, Desi, as friend, 95, 181
Around the World in 80 Days (film), 77
Arrieta, Emilio, *Fantasy on Themes from [Emilio] Arrieta's "Marina"* (Tárrega), 242
Art of the Spanish Guitar, The (Celino Romero), 203, 262
Asilo de los Ángeles, 56

INDEX

Asociación de la Prensa, 59
Asociación Española Contra el Cancer (Spanish Association against Cancer), 118
Asociación Mútuo Benefica del Colegio Oficial de Practicantes de Málaga y su Provincia, 51
Aspen Music Festival, 212
Ateneo de Sevilla, 219–20
Atkins, Chet, 91
Atlanta Journal-Constitution, 241
Austin American-Statesman, 179
Austin Symphony, 119
Australia, 121–22
Ávila, Paco, 66

Bach, Johann Sebastian, 99–100, 209–10, 235; Brandenburg Concerto no. 3, 237; Cantata no. 68, 237; Chaconne from Second Violin Partita in D Minor, 98, 99, 189, 257; Gavotte from Lute Suite no. 4. in E Major, 102; Lute Suite no. 1 in E Minor, 90
Baez, Joan, 87
baile de luis Alonso, El (Giménez), 238
Balada, Leonardo, xi
Ball, Lucille, 181
Banda Municipal (Málaga), 42
Barcelona (steamship), 27
Barcelona Guitar Society, 57
Barili, Ortiz, 34
Barrios, Agustín, 240
baseball, 25
Basilio, Padre, 51
BBC, 67
Beach Boys, 182
Beatles, 91
Beckman Auditorium (California Institute of Technology), 90, 111, 120
Beethoven, Ludwig van, 122, 184, 185, 257
Be Here Now (Watts), 205
Beijing Philharmonic, 184
Bella (album, Angel Romero), 182, 184
Bellingham Festival of Music (Washington state), 235
Belmar, Juan, 33
Beneficent Mutual Association of the Official School of Practitioners of Málaga and Its Province, 51
benefit concerts, 42, 50–51, 98, 118–19, 182, 244–45, 257; organized under false pretenses, 61–62
Benny, Jack, as friend, 181
Bergonzi, Carlo, 242
Berliner Morgenpost (newspaper), 122
Berliner Philharmonie, 172
Berliner Symphoniker, 184
Berlioz, Hector, 183
Biancolli, Louis, 100
Bienvenido-Welcome (film), 182
Billings (MT) Gazette, 106
Blöchinger, Edmund, 264
Bob Jones University (South Carolina), 258
Boccherini, Luigi, 240, 241–42, 258
Bogotá Philharmonic, 184
bohème, La (Puccini), 242
Bohemios (Vives), 238
Bolling, Claude, 182; *Concerto for Classic Guitar and Jazz Piano*, 233
Bonanza (TV series), comparison to, 101
Born to Rebel (Sulloway), 188–89
Boston Conservatory, 212
Boston Globe, 99
Bound by Honor (Blood In, Blood Out) (film), 182
"Bourée" (Tull), 90
Bream, Julian, 217
breathing, 210–11
Brentano, Clemens, 13
Bretón, Tomás, *La verbena de la paloma*, 238
Breva, Juan, 31
Brown, Iona, 246
Brown, Ray, 233
Brubeck, Dave, 233
Bucolic Suite (Madina), 228
Buddhist perspective, 272–73. *See also* Noble Eightfold Path of guitar
bulerías, 30–31, 243–44
By the Sword (film), 182

"Caballos de Media Luna (Fantasía)" (Celedonio Romero), 151
Cabra, Niño de, 31
Cabrillo National Monument (San Diego), 120
"Cádiz" (Albéniz), 166
Cádiz, Spain, 27

INDEX

Caja de Beneficencia, 37
Calhoun, Rory, 96
California Army National Guard, 103
California Institute of Technology (Cal Tech), 90, 111, 120
California State University, Dominguez Hills, 212–13
California State University, Fullerton, 213
California State University, Los Angeles, 193
California State University, Monterey Bay, 83
California State University, Northridge, 212–13
California Tech (campus newspaper), 90
Cal Tech, 90, 111, 120
Canadian Brass, 247
Canberra Sun (newspaper), 248–49
Cantata no. 68 (Bach), 237
Capricho árabe (Tárrega), 195–96
Caracol, Manolo, 65
Carcassi, Matteo, 207
Carlos IV, King of Spain, 51
Carmen (Bizet), 66, 161, 238–39
Carmona, Juan Miguel, 265
Carnegie Hall (New York City), 39, 113–14, 172, 206, 225–26
Carreras, José, 109
Carreras, Sandro, 50
Carter, Jimmy, 119, *143*
Carulli, Ferdinando, 240, 241
Carvalho, Eleazar de, 112–13
Casa de América, 157
Casa del Pueblo (Málaga), 35
Casals, Pablo, 77, 107
Cash, Johnny, 91
castanet playing, of Angelita Romero (wife of Celedonio), 123, *146*, 160, 161–62, 228, 238, 242, 258
Castelnuovo-Tedesco, Mario, Concerto in D Major, 212
Catedral de Colonia, La / The Cathedral of Cologne (Celedonio Romero), 235
Cavestany, Juan Antonio, 34
CBS Calendar, 97
Celedonio. *See* Romero, Celedonio
Celedonius, Saint, 23
Celin. *See* Romero, Celin (son of Celedonio)

Central Florida News-Journal, 178
Central Obrera Nacional-Sindicalista, 45–46
Centro de Estudios Andaluces (Málaga), 49, 51
Cerezo, Atilano, 49
Cervantes, Miguel de, 77, 154
Chacón, Antonio, 31
Chapí, Ruperto, *La revoltosa*, 238
Chet Atkins International Guitar Competition, 91
Chicago Daily News, 252
Chicago Sinfonietta, 184
Chicago Sun-Times, 98
Chicago Tribune, 89–90
Chihara, Paul, *Guitar Concerto*, 233
Christian Science Monitor, 89
Christopher, George, 80
chulapona, La (Moreno Torroba), 223–24
Clark, Ramsey, 80
Clark, Roy, 91
Classical Guitar and Beyond (Kanengiser), 213
Classical Guitar Mastery (Kanengiser), 213
Cleveland Plain Dealer (newspaper), 189
Clinton, Bill, 119–20, 258
Clinton (IA) Herald, 91
Club de Católicos, 85
Cold War, 78, 102
colic nephritis, 59, 104
Columbia Artists Management, Inc. (CAMI), 100, 220, 253–55, 260
Columbus, Christopher, reception for descendant of, 120
Concerto for Classic Guitar and Jazz Piano (Bolling), 233
Concerto in A Minor (Vivaldi), 246
Concerto in D Major (Castelnuovo-Tedesco), 212
Concerto in D Major (Vivaldi), 185, 237, 260
Concerto in D Major for Four Violins (Telemann), 123, 237
Concerto in G Major (Vivaldi), 267–68
Concierto andaluz (Rodrigo), 119, 220–21, 222, 256–57; and *Concierto de Cienfuegos* (Palomo), 230; and *Concierto ibérico* (Moreno Torroba), 226; premiere of, xiii, 220; recording of, 100, 220; at World Expo, xiv, *145*

335

INDEX

Concierto de Aranjuez (Angel Romero painting), 180
Concierto de Aranjuez (Rodrigo), 110, 219, 220; Angel and, 178, 181, 189, 220, 231–32; jazz arrangements of, 91–92; Pepe on, 171–72; recording of, 100, 178, 220; reviews of, 112–13, 162, 178, 231–32; transcribed for harp, 238
Concierto de Cienfuegos (Palomo), 230
Concierto de estío (Rodrigo), xiv
Concierto de la amistad (Schifrin), 232
Concierto de Málaga (Celedonio Romero), 234
Concierto en flamenco (Moreno Torroba), 225
Concierto Festivo (Cordero), 232
Concierto flamenco (Madina), 229
Concierto ibérico (Moreno Torroba), xii, 226–27, 230
Concierto madrigal (Rodrigo), xiv, 112, 222, 228–29, 261
Concierto Mariachi (Zearott), 232–33
Concierto para una fiesta (Rodrigo), xiv, 66, 221–22
Concierto vasco (Basque concerto) (Madina), 228
Confederación Nacional del Trabajo, 45
Constanzo, Irma, 226
Contemporary Records label, 97–98, 100, 245
Conti, Bill, 182
Contra Costa Times, 233
Contreras, Pablo, 264
Cordero, Ernesto, *Concierto Festivo*, 232
Córdoba Guitar Festival, 214
Cordobesa, La, 245–46
Corea, Chick, 91–92
Corey, Jeff, 181
Corpus Christi Caller (newspaper), 88
Correo de Andalucía, El (newspaper), 50
Cortijo de Don Sancho, El (Celedonio Romero), 235
Coves, Manuel, 214
Coves, Vicente, 214
Cranston, Earl, 106
Cruz del Caballero de la Orden de Isabel la Católica, 120, 125, 176
Cuba, Romero family in, 18–19, 21–26, 44, 130
Cugat, Xavier, 6, 104

Culpeper (VA) County High School, 111–12
Curtain, Phyllis, 247

Dallas (TV series), 221
Dallas Morning News (newspaper), 244–45
Danza rapsódica (Madina), 228
Darío, Rubén, 50
Davis, Miles, *Sketches of Spain*, 91–92
Dearman, John, 212
De Cádiz a la Habana (Pepe Romero), 236
Deer Hunter, The (film), 182
DeKeyser music store (Hollywood), 201
Delegación Provincial de Educación Popular, 50
Delegación Provincial del Frente de Juventudes, 49, 61, 62
Delegación Provincial de Sindicatos (Provincial Delegation of Unions), 50, 56–57
Del Mar, Calif., 1–4, 26, 114, 115–20
Del Mar College, 88
de los Ángeles, Victoria, 247
Delos label, 154
Diálogos para guitarra y orquesta (Moreno Torroba), 224–25, 228
Diario de Cádiz, 50
Dochado Díaz, Miguel, 39
Doktor, Paul, 199
Domingo, Plácido, 177, 247
Domínguez, Francisco, 31
Domínguez, Paco, 53
Don Giovanni (Mozart), 65, 242
Don Quixote (Cervantes), 77, 134, 161
Doors, The, 90
Do What You Love, the Money Will Follow (Sinetar), 204
Duarte, John, 172, 217, 222, 224–25
Dudamel, Gustavo, 184
Dunn, Alex, 213–14
Durante, Jimmy, as friend, 181

Ebell-Wilshire Theater (Hollywood), 96–97
Eddy, Kristine, 95
Ed Sullivan Show, The (TV program), 6, 104–5
Effortless Classical Guitar (Kanengiser), 213
Eisenhower, Dwight, 105–6
El Camino College, 212, 213
England, 121

INDEX

Escondido (CA) Times-Advocate, 179
Escudero, Mario, 97, 200, 225–26
Estampas (Moreno Torroba), 227–28
estro harmonico, L', op. 3 (Vivaldi), 246
Étude no. 1 in E Minor (Villa-Lobos), 110
Euro-Asia Philharmonic Orchestra, 184
Evie. See Stoddard, Farrington (Fe) and Evelyn (Evie)

Falange (Phalanx), 45–46, 48–50, 52, 55, 61
Falla, Manuel de, 238
Fantasía (Celedonio Romero), 26, 99, 234, 235
Fantasía flamenca (Moreno Torroba), 225–26
Fantasía in D Minor for guitar solo (Sor), 241, 257
Fantasía XVI (Milán), 257
Farrington F. Stoddard Artists & Management, 81–82
Faust (Gounod), 242
Fazzi, Christopher, *Guitar Concert, Western Suite*, 232
Fe. See Stoddard, Farrington (Fe) and Evelyn (Evie)
Fernández Mata, M., 64
Ferrer, Manuel, *Fantasy on the Quartet of Verdi's "Rigoletto*,*"* 242
Ferrer, Mel, as acquaintance, 95
Festival of Saint James (Málaga), 50–51
Fiedler, Arthur, 183, 228–29
Fiesta Pequeña (Santa Barbara Mission), 82
¡Flamenco fenómeno! (Contemporary Records), 97–98, 245
Fleming, Shirley, 87–88
Fleuret, Adrienne, 59
Fono Forum (magazine), 163
Fort Bragg (CA) Advocate-News, 90–91
Fortea, Daniel, 33, 35
Fort Ord, Calif., 83–85
Fort Worth Chamber Orchestra, 221–22
Fosforito (Antonio Fernández Díaz), 31
Foster, Eric, 213
Fox, Herbert O., 220, 254–55
Franco, Enrique, 227
Franco, Francisco: love of the arts, 54–55, 220–21; Celedonio Romero performs for, 51–52; Romero Quartet performs for, 220–21; Spanish Civil War, xi, 41–48

(see also Spanish Civil War); women and, 64–65, 159
Franco, Vicky, 220–21
Frente de Juventudes (Youth Front), 49, 61, 62
Fritzsche, Carl F., 83–84
Frühbeck de Burgos, Rafael, 178, 229–30
Fundación Esperanza (Hope Foundation), 118

Galán, Juan, 31
Galaxy Ball Saturday (Fort Worth), 244–45
Gallego Molina, Dolores "Loli" (sister-in-law of Celedonio), 39–40
García Lorca, Federico, 43, 154, 156–57, 244, 269
Garrigues, Eduardo, 157
Gashen, Terry, 266
Gastor, Diego del, 196
Germany, 122–24
Gestoría Administrativa (Administrative Agency), 59
Gil de Gálvez, José Manuel, 74, 164
Giménez, Gerónimo, *El baile de Luis Alonso*, 238
Giuliani, Mauro, 171, 207, 216, 240–42, 246–47; *Handel Variations*, 247
Giussani guitars (Italy), 57
Godfrey, Arthur, 87
Goldberg, Albert, 112–13
Goldberg, Whoopi, as fan, 181
Gómez, Guillermo, 82
Góngora, Luis de, 34
Good Time Jazz & Contemporary Records News, 95
Goodwill Gala (Orange County), 182
Gould, Glenn, 178
Gould, Morton, 2–3, 115, 183; *Troubadour Music*, 231–32
Goya guitars (U.S.), 87
Goyescas (Granados), 100, 154
Gramophone (magazine), 172
"Granada (Serenata)" (Albéniz), 34
granadinas, 25
Granados, Enrique: background, 5; death, 6; *Goyescas*, 100, 154; practice and, 206–7; teaching, 197, 210
Gran Teatro Falla (Cádiz), 50

INDEX

Great Hall of the Pillars (Moscow), 172
Greco, José, 77
Green Bay (WI) Press-Gazette, 110
Greif, Matthew, 212–13
Grusin, Dave (composer), 182
guajira, 3, 26
Guernica (Picasso), 43
Guindos, Los, 35–36, 37, 40
guitar builders, 2, 31, 57, 87; Paco Domínguez, 53; Hauser, 63; Santos Hernández, 236; Antonio de Lorca Ramírez, guitar by, *132*; Pepe Jr. and Bernardo, 116, *148–49*, 264–65; Miguel Rodríguez, 109
Guitar Concert, Western Suite (Fazzi), 232
Guitar Concerto (Chihara), 233
Guitar Foundation of America, 213, 217
Guitar Gallery (Houston), 266
Guitar Heroes (LAGQ CD), 212
Guitar Player (magazine), 201, 208–9
"guitarra es mi vida, La" (Celedonio Romero), 1, 157
Guitar Summit (1994), 247
Guthrie, Robert, 212
Gutiérrez Ternero, Josefa (grandmother of Celedonio), 17

Habichuela el Viejo (guitarist), 169
Hackford, Taylor, 182
Handel Variations (Giuliani), 247
Harris, John, 198
Hauser, Hermann, Jr., 57
Hauser guitars (Germany), 57, 63
Hay, Betty Jo, 244–45
Heavin, Hadley, 214
Heck, Thomas, 240
Heifetz, Jascha, 108, 193
Hellweg, Wilhelm, 239, 242
Henahan, Donal, 105
Henken, John, 120, 178, 232, 253
Hepburn, Audrey, as acquaintance, 95
Herald (Everett, WA), 117
Hermanitas de la Cruz (Little Sisters of the Cross), 49, 61, 62
Hernández, Santos, 236
Hi-Fi News, 109
Hitler, Adolf, 34, 45–46
Hollins University, 214

Hollywood Bowl, 96, 112–13, 181, 231–32, 233
Homenaje a la seguidilla (Moreno Torroba), 226
Honolulu Star-Bulletin, 110
Honolulu Symphony, 110, 229
Hootenanny (TV program), 91
Hope, Bob, as friend, 95, 181
Hope, Dolores, as friend, 181
Houston Post, 101
Hoyos, Julio de, 50
Hübscher, Jürgen, 6
Hurok, Sol, 100

Ibérico. See *Concierto ibérico* (Moreno Torroba)
Imperio, Pastora, 30
International Creative Management (ICM), 254–55
"Internationale" (communist hymn), 42–43
Introduction to the Chôros (Villa-Lobos), 243
Iturbi, Amparo, 77
Iturbi, José, 77, 83, 235

J. & J. Lubrano, 241
Jack Paar Show, The (TV program), 97, 99
Jeffery, Brian, 240
Jennings, Captain, 85
Jesus, 205
Jethro Tull, 90
Jobim, Antonio Carlos, 6
John Paul II (pope), 144, 161, *271*
Jones Hall (Houston), 101, 266
Jordan Hall (Boston), 99
Jotrón, Spain, 14, 16–18, *128*
Juan Carlos, King of Spain, 120
Juilliard String Quartet, 99, 101
Juventud Artística (Artistic Youth), 32

Kanengiser, William, 212, 213
Kansas City Guitar Society, 229
Kansas City Star, 92
Kennedy, John Fitzgerald, 96–97, 114
Kennedy, Robert, 114
Kiesgen, Charles, 58–59
Kimball Recital Hall (University of Nebraska, Lincoln), 232

INDEX

King, John, 241
Knight, Goodwin J., 76
Knoxville News-Sentinel, 183
Knoxville Symphony, 183
Koblenz Festival, 269
König Albert (steamer), 21
Kotke, Leo, 247
Kozinn, Allan, 240
Krause, William, 214
Kressin, Angelina (daughter of Pepe), 264
Kressin, Jacob (grandson of Pepe), 264
Kressin, Joseph (son-in-law of Pepe), 264
Kressin, Leah (granddaughter of Pepe), 264

Lady of the Equestrian Order of the Holy Sepulchre of Jerusalem, 162
Lagoya, Alexandre, 222, 239, 261
La Jolla Light (newspaper), 211
Lamborghini, Susan, 266
Lao-tzu, 203–4
Lasuén, Fermín, 76
Lecea, José Rodríguez Díaz de, 62–68, 77
Lecuona, Ernesto, *Malagueña*, 91, 244
Ledger, The (Lakeland, FL), 168
Lehman Collection, Metropolitan Museum of Art (New York City), 169
"Leyenda" (Albéniz), 90
"Libertad" (Celedonio Romero), 71
Lincoln Center (New York City), 186, 217–18
Lincoln Journal-Star, 232
Lisbon, Portugal, 59
Little Sisters of the Cross, 49, 61, 62
Llobet, Miquel, 33
Lobato, Chano, 245
Lobero Theatre (Santa Barbara), 80–82, 97, 138, 270
London Symphony Orchestra, 178, 233
López Alarcón, Enrique, 34
López Cobos, Jesús, xi–xii
López González, María (grandmother of Celedonio), 17–20
Lorca Ramírez, Antonio de, 31; guitar by, 132
Lorimer, Michael, 217, 224, 258
Los Angeles Chamber Orchestra, 233
Los Angeles County Museum of Art, 120
Los Angeles Examiner, 97, 163

Los Angeles Guitar Quartet (LAGQ), 212–13, 258
Los Angeles Guitar Society, 75
Los Angeles Philharmonic, 120, 178, 184, 232
Los Angeles Times: concert reviews, 97, 120, 178, 231–32, 241; on *Concierto de Aranjuez*, 112–13; interviews and news of Romeros, 116, 120, 184–85, 253
Los Romeros (DVDs). See *Romeros, Los*
Louisville Symphony Orchestra, 185
Lucas, James, 86, 92, 96–97, 100, 105, 159–60
Lucia, Paco de, 246
Luisa Fernanda (Moreno Torroba), 223–24

Macaluso, Vincenzo, 212
Machado, Antonio, 14, 28–29, 274
Machado, Manuel, 34
Madina, Francisco de (Aita Madina), commissioned works, 228–29
Madrid Conservatory, 102–3
Madrigal. See *Concierto madrigal* (Rodrigo)
Magdalena, María, 245
Mairena, Antonio, 31
Málaga (Dochado Díaz), 39
Málaga, Spain, 13–20, 26, 129, 133; cultural institutions, 31, 33–34, 41, 50–51, 56–57; Romero family lives in, 27–63, 165, 166; Romero Quartet performs in, 124–25
Málaga Cinema, 56–57
Málaga Conservatory, 31, 33–34, 41, 50–51, 103
Malagueña (Lecuona), 91, 244
Malak (goddess of beauty), 15
Malats, Joaquim, *Serenata española*, 39
Manén, Juan, 30
Manne, Shelly, 95, 233
Manolete (Manuel Santiago Maya, singer), 42
Mariani, E., 50
Marqués de Alcántara, El, 76
Marquina, Pascual, 229
Marriner, Neville, xii, 226–27, 233
Martínez, Juanito, 32–33
Masonic Auditorium (Santa Barbara), 79–80

INDEX

Masonic Evergreen Lodge No. 2569 (Riverside), 100
Masters, Martha, 213
Max, Sabine, 155
McKay, William and Carol, 221–22
Megias, Pedro, 41
Melchor (dog), 106
Mercé, Antonia (La Argentina), 30
Mercury label, 100, 156, 220, 244, 245
Mercury News, 187
Mérimée, Prosper, 239
Merton, Thomas, 272–73
Mertz, Johann Kaspar, 242
Metamorfosi de concert (Montsalvatge), 229
Metropolitan Museum of Art (New York City), 169
Mexicano, El (newspaper), 118, 158–59
Milagro Beanfield War, The (film), 182
Milán, Luis de, 57, 99, 257
Modern Jazz Quartet, 91–92
Modesto Bee (newspaper), 268
Molina Moles, Andrés, 34–35
Molino, Francesco, 240, 241
Monitor (newspaper, McAllen, TX), 157–58
Montalban, Ricardo, as friend, 95, 181
Montana State University, Bozeman, 212
Montoya, Carlos, 6, 67, 87, 107
Montsalvatge, Xavier, 228; *Metamorfosi de concert*, 229
Moore, Dudley, as acquaintance, 181
Moreno Torroba, Federico, xii–xiii, 5, 6, 57, 146, 164, 172–73, 214; *La chulapona*, 223–24; commissioned works, 222–28; *Concierto en flamenco*, 225; *Concierto ibérico*, xii, 226–27, 230; *Diálogos para guitarra y orquesta*, 224–25, 228; *Estampas*, 227–28; *Fantasía flamenca*, 225–26; *Homenaje a la seguidilla*, 226; *Luisa Fernanda*, 223–24; *Ráfagas*, 227, 249–50; *Romance de los pinos*, 224; Segovia and, 55; *Sonata-Fantasía* and *Sonata-Fantasía II*, 228; *Sonatina*, 3, 34, 162, 228, 257; *Sonatina trianera*, 228; *Tonada concertante*, 222–23, 226
Moreno-Torroba Larregla, Federico, xii–xiii, 55, 238, 249–50
Morris, Scott, 213
Mottola, Tony, 87, 95

Mount Baker Theatre (Washington state), 235
Mozarteum (university, Salzburg), 214, 263
Mudarra, Alonso de, 171
Muestra del Cine Film Festival (Guadalajara), 182
Mundo, El (Spain), 171–72
Muñoz Molleda, José, 228; *Tríptico*, 229
Murcia Symphony Orchestra, 118
Music of the West Magazine, 153
Musikverein (Vienna), 172
Mussolini, Benito, 45

National Confederation of Labor, 45
Nationalist Syndicalist Workers Council, 45–46
Navas, José, 33–34, 42, 45, 60
Naxos label, 214, 226
NDR Symphony Orchestra, 184
Newark Star-Ledger, 228–29
New Haven Register, 232–33
New Haven Symphony Orchestra, 232–33
New York Catholic Charities Fund Appeal, 118–19
New York Herald Tribune, 100
New York Times, 100, 107, 113–14, 217–18
New York Times Magazine, 96, 182
News-Call Bulletin (San Francisco), 98–99
Nhat Hanh, Thich, 273
niña de blanco, La (Jiménez Matecón), 230
Niña de los Peines (Pastora Pavón Cruz, singer), 30, 65
Ninety-Second Street Y (New York City), 229
Nixon, Richard, 119
Noad, Frederick, 95, 212, 240
Noble Eightfold Path of guitar, 194–214; right action, 203–4; right concentration, 210–11; right effort, 206–7; right livelihood, 204–6; right mindfulness, 207–10; right sound, 200–202; right thought, 198–200; right understanding, 195–98
Noches de España: Romantic Guitar Classics (Philips), 241
Nocturnos de Andalucía (Palomo), 229–30
Nogales Sevilla, José, 55
Noirot and Company, 18
Norddeutscher Rundfunk (broadcaster), 124

INDEX

Norman, Jessye, 247
Norman, Theodore, 75, 80
North, Alex, 96
North County Times, 181–82, 183
Northeastern University, 214
Noseda, Gianandrea, 229

Odessa American, 211
Oklahoma City University, Wanda L. Bass School of Music, 214
Old Globe Theater (San Diego), 118
Omaha World-Herald, 206
Omega Guitar Quartet, 217–18
On the Air Magazine, 261
Opera Fantasy for Guitar: Pepe Romero (Philips), 242
oración del torero, La (The toreador's prayer) (Turina), 185–86, 238
Orchestra Hall (Chicago), 98, 102
Organización Sindical Española, 46
Oribe, José, 95
Ormandy, Eugene, 183–84
Ornish, Laurel, 161
Orpheus Chamber Orchestra, 172
Orquesta de Baja California, 184, 186
Orquestra de Cadaqués, 229

Palacete de la Moncloa (Málaga), 51
Palacio de La Granja (Spain), 220–21
Palau de la Música Catalana, 258
Palmer, Michael, 232–33
Paloma, La (album), 217
Palomo, Lorenzo, xi, 228, 238; *Concierto de Cienfuegos*, 230; *Nocturnos de Andalucía*, 229–30
Parkening, Christopher, 95, 211–12
Pasadena Star-News, 181
Pass, Joe, 247
Passy, Charles, 88
Pavón, Arturo, 65
Pavón, Tomás, 65
Peña, Paco, 247
Peña Guitarrística Tárrega (Barcelona), 57
Peña Juan Breva museum (Málaga), 31
"Pensamiento" (Celedonio Romero), 11
Pepe. *See* Romero, Pepe (son of Celedonio)
Pepe Romero Plays Flamenco (Mercury), 245

Pepperdine University, Malibu, 212
Pérez Peña, J. M., 59
Performing Arts Center (El Cajon), 118
Performing Arts Center (Escondido), 264
Philips label, 121, 224, 226–27, 239, 241, 242, 245
Phoenix Symphony, 232
Phonogram Inc., 155
Piatigorsky, Gregor, 193
picados, 196–97
Picasso, Pablo, 43, 107
Pile, Randy, 213
Pinazo, Manolito (cousin of Celedonio), 43
Pinazo Gutiérrez, José (grandfather of Celedonio), 17
Pinazo Gutiérrez, Josefa (mother of Celedonio), 18–19, 130; becomes widow in Spain, 37; in Cuba, 18–19, 21–26; in Spain, 18–19, 27–49
Pittsburgh Symphony, 184
Planeta, El (singer), 31
"Plegaria" (Gómez), 82
PM East-West (television program), 97
Poema del cante jondo (García Lorca), 156–57
Poemas, Prosas, Pensamientos y Cantares (Celedonio Romero), 155
Poet of the Guitar, The (Delos CD), 154
Pohren, Donn E., 200
Portugal, Celedonio's guitar performances in, 59
Presti, Ida, 222, 239, 261
Previn, André, 178
Price, Robin, 55
Primo de Rivera, Antonio, 45–46
Primo de Rivera, José Antonio, 45–46
Primo de Rivera, Miguel, 36
Professional Group of Journalists of the Spanish Graphics Federation, 42
prostitution, in Spain, 64–65
Province, The (newspaper, Vancouver, BC), 107
Provincial Delegation of the Youth Front, 49, 61, 62
Puente, Tito, 6
Pujol, Emilio, 95, 240
Pulpón, Antonio, 66
Pumping Nylon (Tennant), 213

INDEX

Quartet in A Major (Vivaldi), 111
Quartet no. 1 (*Angelita*) (Madina), 229
Queen Elizabeth Hall (London), 121
Queipo de Llano y Sierra, Gonzalo, 45

Radiodiffusion et Télévision Françaises, 59
Radio Nacional de España (Málaga), 39, 41, 56, 59–60
Radio Sevilla, 56
Ráfagas (Moreno Torroba), 227, 249–50
Ramírez, Alexander Sergei, 214
Ramón Jiménez, Juan, 230
rasgueados (strumming patterns), 66, 196–97
RCA Records, 82–83, 236, 246
Real Orquesta Sinfónica de Sevilla, 230
Recuerdos de la Alhambra (Tárrega), 34, 96, 111, 119, 123, 195–96
Redondo Union High School (CA), 100
Rehabilitation Institute of Chicago, 98
Reiss, Kristina (granddaughter of Pepe), 264
Reiss, Lane (son-in-law of Pepe), 264
Reiss, Susanna (daughter of Pepe), 264
Rejto, Gabor, 193, 247
Remembering the Future: Angel Romero (RCA Victor Red Seal), 236, 246
Retes, Gabriele, 182
revoltosa, La (Chapí), 238
Ricardo, Niño, 65, 97
Rice University, 266
Ridgecrest (CA) Valley Independent, 181
Rigoletto (Verdi), 242
Rincones de España (Corners of Spain, arr. Angel Romero), 178, 236
rivalry, 251
Rivera Pons, Leandro, 33–34, 39
Robert Schumann Hochschule (Düsseldorf), 214, 263
Rodrigo Festival (London, 1986), xiv
Rodrigo, Cecilia, xiii–xiv
Rodrigo, Joaquín, xiii–xiv, 5, 145, 172–73; commissioned works, 219–23; *Concierto andaluz* (see ; *Concierto andaluz* [Rodrigo]); *Concierto de Aranjuez* (see *Concierto de Aranjuez* [Rodrigo]); *Concierto de estío*, xiv; *Concierto madrigal*, xiv, 112, 222, 228–29, 261; *Concierto para una fiesta*, xiv, 66, 221–22; *Sones en la Giralda* (Sounds in the Giralda), 237–38; themes in *Rincones de España* (Corners of Spain, arr. Angel Romero), 178, 236; "Tonadilla," 261
Rodríguez, Miguel, 264
Rodríguez Cabrillo, Juan, 157
Rodríguez guitars (Spain), 57, 109
Rogers, Ginger, as friend, 181
Roma, 7, 52, 55, 60, 160
Roman, Virgilio, 32
Romance de los pinos (Moreno Torroba), 224
Romanillos, José Luis, 264
romero (pilgrim), 13–14
Romero, Adolfo (brother of Celedonio): in Cuba, 22–23; military service in Spain, 38, 40, 47, 48
Romero, Angel (Miguel Angel, son of Celedonio), *135–36, 138–39*; acting, 181–82; arrangements and transcriptions, 98, 178, 182, 184, 236, 238; artistic talent, 179–80; birth in Spain, 52, 53; breakup of original Romero Quartet, 248–55; compositions, 182; conducting, 183–86; daredevil activities, 186–89; early education, 78, 96, 161; early performances, 56, 78–79, 82–83, 96; exemption from U.S. military service, 103; family members/next generations, *142*, 267–69; guitar studies, 53–56, 165; honors and awards, 126, 176, 182; improvisation and, 246; profile, 176–89; Proteus, comparison to, 177; recordings, 182, 184, 236, 246, 267, 288–89, 294–96; on Romero guitar method, 195, 196, 201–2, 207; solo career, 145, 163, 177, 178–79, 182, 184, 236, 241, 246, 248–55, 267, 288–89, 294–96. *See also* Romero family; Romero Quartet
Romero, Angelita (née Inez de los Ángeles Gallego Molina, wife of Celedonio), *131–32, 135–38, 140*; castanets, 123, *146*, 160, 161–62, 228, 238, 242, 258; cooking skills, 116–17, 160; death in 1999, 258; early history in Spain, 40; family members/next generations, *142*, 256–70; honors and awards, 161, 162; meets and marries Celedonio, 38–41; profile, 159–62. *See also* Romero family
Romero, Bella (daughter of Angel), 4, 182, 184, 269
Romero, Bernardo (grandson of Pepe), 4, 8, 24–25, 116, *149*, 264, 265

342

INDEX

Romero, Carissa Sugg (second wife of Pepe), 4, 107, 160, 172, 187, 251, 265–67

Romero, Celedonio, *132*, *135*, *137–39*, *146*, *150*; arrangements and transcriptions, 237; birth in Cuba, 23, 44, *130*; birth of sons in Spain, 44, 52–53; breakup of original Romero Quartet, 248–55; compositions, 26, 99, 234–36; as daredevil, 189; death in 1996, 199, 256–58; employment in Spain, 36, 37, 45–46; family members/next generations, *142*, 256–70; family origins in Spain, 16–20; guitar performances in Portugal, 59; guitar performances in Spain, 34–35, 38–39, 42, 50–52, 56–57, 59–63; guitar performances in U.S., 80, 81–82, 263; guitar studies, 32–34, 41, 103; guitar teaching, 53–56, 95, 155, 158, 165, 170, 195–96, 199, 201, 203, 207, 211–12 (*see also* Romero guitar method); health issues, 49, 59, 236, 256–58; honors and awards, 120, 125–27, 157, 214; meets and marries Angelita, 38–41; military service in Spain, 41, 44–45, 46–47, 50, *133*; musical compositions, 51, 57, 86; poetry and prose, 1, 11, 32, 71, 151, 154–59, 160–61, 244, 271, 272; profile, 154–59; and Radio Nacional de España, 41, 56, 59–60; recordings, 154, 288, 289; Segovia and, 33, 41, 46, 57, 67, 99, 107, 123; Spanish Civil War and aftermath, 41–52. *See also* Romero family; Romero Quartet

Romero, Celin (Celedonio Gustavo Adolfo, son of Celedonio), *138–39*; arrangements, 85–86, 182; birth in Spain, 44; early education, 161; engineering studies, 67, 79; as family driver, 79, 105–6, 109–10, 115–16; family members/next generations, *142*, 148–49, 259–63; first performances in Spain, 56; guitar studies, 53–56, *134*; guitar teaching, 6, 54, 60, 95, *148*, 213–14, 263 (*see also* Romero guitar method); health issues, 85; home in Del Mar, 3–4; honors and awards, 126, 214; military service in U.S., 83–86, *139*; profile, 163–67; recordings, 289; on Romero guitar method, 202, 204, 205–7; transcriptions, 166; wedding in 1966, 78. *See also* Romero family; Romero Quartet

Romero, Celino (son of Celin), *149*; guitar instruction book, 203, 262; joins Romero Quartet, *147*, 253–55, 256, 260–62; solo career, 260

Romero, Joaquín (grandson of Angel), 268

Romero, Josefita (sister of Celedonio), in Cuba, 22–23, 25

Romero, José Francisco (grandson of Uncle Pepe), 14

Romero, Kimberly Joolingen (daughter-in-law of Pepe), 264–65

Romero, Kristine Meigs Eddy (first wife of Pepe), *142*, 263–65, 266

Romero, Laurie Wanda Barc (first wife of Celin), *142*, 259–62

Romero, Lito (son of Angel), 3, 180, 267–68; guitar teaching, 193–94 (*see also* Romero guitar method); joins Romero Quartet, *147*, 256, 267–68

Romero, Maximino (brother of Celedonio): birth in Cuba, 22; employment in Spain, 49; military service in Spain, 37–38, 47, 48

Romero, Maximino ("Maxi," grandson of Celin), 262

Romero, Michelle Zubia (daughter-in-law of Celin), 262

Romero, Nefretiri Morte ("Nefy," second wife of Angel), 4, 268–69

Romero, Nino (grandson of Celin), *149*, 262

Romero, Owen (grandson of Pepe), 264

Romero, Paco, 245

Romero, Pepe (José Luis, son of Celedonio), *134–35*, *138–40*; arrangements and transcriptions, 237–38; artistic talent, 55, 63, 169, 180, 189, 196; birth in Spain, 52; car accident, 110; compositions, 236; early education, 78, 96, 161; early performances, 56, 66, 82; exemption from U.S. military service, 104; family members/next generations, *142*, *148*, 263–67; guitar studies, 53–56, 165, 208; Guitar Summit (1994), 247; guitar teaching, 5–6, 47, 90, 95, *148*, 202, 206, 208–14, 245, 263, 264, 266, 267 (*see also* Romero guitar method); health issues, 62, 74, 104; honors and awards, 96, 126, 214; profile, 168–75; recordings, 289, 290–94;

343

Romero, Pepe (*continued*): on Romero guitar method, 195–99, 201–4, 206–11, 217; solo career, 122–23, 145, 163, 172, 174, 217, 241–43, 245–46, 253–55, 290–94. *See also* Romero family; Romero Quartet

Romero, Pepe ("Uncle Pepe," brother of Celedonio): birth in Spain, 19; in Cuba, 21–26; employment in Spain, 36, 49; guitar performances, 32; guitar studies, 30; memoirs, 14; military service in Spain, 36–37, 47–48; return to Spain, 27–57; wife, Lola, 37, 41, 48

Romero, Pepe, Jr. ("Little Pepe," son of Pepe), 1, 2, 24–25, 116, 148, 264–65

Romero, Raquelle Angela (granddaughter of Celin), 262

Romero, Ruth María Fernández (daughter-in-law of Angel), 268

Romero, Sophia (granddaughter of Pepe), 264

Romero, Tina (daughter of Pepe), 90

Romero, Valentina Lucia (granddaughter of Angel), 268

Romero, Wendy Winkelman (first wife of Angel), 142, 267–68

Romero Escacena, Baldomero, 46

Romero Falcón, José (grandfather of Celedonio), 17

Romero family: arrival in the United States, 73–75; benefit concerts (*see* benefit concerts); Catholic faith and spirituality, 23–24, 78, 84, 85, 118–19, 161, 162, 257–58, 271–73; chronology, 275–77; deaths of Celedonio and Angelita, 256–58; family dynamics, 248–55, 258–59; family members/next generations, 256–70; gain U.S. citizenship, 80; genealogy, 280–84; guitars used by, 2, 57, 63, 87, 109, 116, 236, 264–65; home in Valencia, Spain, 64; homes in Cuba, 18–19, 21–26; homes in Del Mar, Calif., 1–4, 26, 114–20; homes in Hollywood, 94–114; homes in Málaga, Spain, 27–63, 165, 166; homes in Santa Barbara, Calif., 75–93; homes in Seville, Spain, 64–70, 165, 238–39; lack of racial and class prejudice, 40, 55, 60, 91, 111, 160; leaves Spain for the United States, 67–75; love of literature and reading, 32, 154–59, 160–61; love of soccer, 4, 32, 56, 118, 261, 267; profiles, 153–89; prosperity of, 117–20, 163–64, 180; recordings, 285–96; sponsorship by the Stoddards, 60–61, 67–70, 74–75, 78–82

Romero guitar method, 193–214; antidotes to nervousness, 197–98, 210–11; breathing, 210–11; concentration, 210–11; conscious awareness/informed intuition, 207–10; focus on present moment, 204–6; hand position, 196–97, 201–2, 203; humility and love of the music, 203–4; love as foundation, 38, 158, 167, 170, 174–75, 203–4, 217; past students, 211–14; positive outlook, 198–200; repertoire and (*see* Romero repertoire); technique vs. repertoire, 195–98; tone production and color, 200–202; velocity, 196–97, 202; visualization, 209–10, 211

Romero guitars, 2, 24–25, 116, 264–65

Romero López, José (father of Celedonio), 17–26, 29–37, 273–74, 130; birth in Spain, 18; as builder in Cuba, 19–20, 24–26, 28; as builder in Spain, 18–19, 29–30; daredevil activities, 273; death in Spain, 37

Romero Quartet, 285–88, 140–42; breakup of original group, 248–55; Celino replaces Angel, 147, 253–55, 256, 260–62; compositions for, 2–3, 219–33; as cultural ambassadors, 118–25; current status, 269–70; death of Celedonio Romero, 199, 256–58; early performances and reception, 82–83, 86, 87–92, 96–108, 113–14; family appeal of, 101–3; formation of, 86; Grammy President's Merit Award, 147; guitar method (*see* Romero guitar method); head of state appearances, 119–20, 143, 220–21; international tours, 121–25, 144; Lito replaces Celedonio, 147, 256, 267–68; managed by Columbia Artists Management, Inc. (CAMI), 100, 220, 253–55, 260; managed by Jim Lucas, 86, 92, 96–97, 100, 105, 159–60; Melchor (dog) travels with, 106; personal diplomacy, 106–8; profiles, 153–89; recordings, 82–83, 100, 121, 154, 156, 244, 285–88; repertoire (*see* Romero repertoire); as Royal Family of the Guitar, 113–14, 120; spelling of

INDEX

names, 7, 112; television appearances, 6, 97, 99, 104–5, *141*; tour mishaps and disruptions, 108–13; U.S. tours, 96–114, 140–41

Romero repertoire, 215–47; arrangements/transcriptions, 85–86, 98, 166, 182, 184, 236–39; collaborations, 247; commissions, 2–3, 219–33; compositions by Romeros, 2–3, 26, 51, 57, 86, 99, 182, 234–36; consistency of, 215–19, 269; improvisations and unnotated music, 243–47; recordings, 285–96; revivals, 239–43

Romeros, Los: Die Gitarren-Dynastie (Norddeutscher Rundfunk broadcast/DVD), 124

Romeros, Los: The Royal Family of the Guitar (PBS documentary/DVD), 124

Romero Studio of Guitar (Hollywood), 95
Ross, Celina (daughter of Angel), 267
Rossini, Gioachino, 241, 242
Rossiniana, La (Giuliani), 242
Royal Philharmonic Orchestra (London), 184
Royal Theatre (British Columbia), 114
Royce Hall (UCLA), 186
Rozsnyai, Zoltán, 183
Rubin, David, 63
Rubinstein, Arthur, 206
Rubinstein, Erna, 95
Rubinstein Medal, 214
Rumores de La Caleta (Albéniz), 4, 99
Rundfunk Sinfonieorchester Berlin, 229–30

Sabicas (Agustín Castellón Campos), 6, 67, 97, 225; on American enthusiasm, 87; arrangements of, 268; compositions, 112, 171; as inspiration, 225, 236; super-virtuosity, 200
Saborit, Ernesto, 21
Saddleback College (California), 213
Sagi-Barba, Emilio, 30
Saint Francis Hotel (San Francisco), 119
Saint James Catholic Church (Solana Beach, CA), 118, 257–58
Sáinz de la Maza, Regino, 41, 171, 219
Salk Institute, benefit for, 118
Salle Chopin-Pleyel (Paris), 58–59
Salzburg Mozarteum (university), 214, 263

Salzburg Summer Academy, 214
San Antonio Light (newspaper), 249
San Antonio Symphony, 178, 220
Sanchez, Angela Romero (daughter of Celin), 260
Sanchez, Carl Robert (son-in-law of Celin), 260
San Diego Chamber Orchestra, 184, 185–86
San Diego Community College District, 213, 263, 264
San Diego Mesa College, 260
San Diego State University (SDSU), 118, 193, 263, 267
San Diego Symphony, 115, 183, 184–85, 231–32
San Diego Tribune, 115–16, 120
San Diego Union-Tribune, 111, 116–17, 118, 185
San Dieguito Surf Soccer Club, 118
San Francisco Chronicle, 79–80, 99
San Francisco Conservatory of Music, 96
San Francisco Examiner, 99
San Francisco Symphony Orchestra, 228–29
Sanlúcar, Manolo, 258
Santa Barbara, Calif., 75–93, *136–38*
Santa Barbara City College, 263
Santa Barbara County Bowl, 229
Santa Barbara News-Press, 81, 101
Santa Barbara Symphony, 118, 184
Santa Mercedes (steamship), 68
Sanz, Gaspar, 99, 171
Saura, Carlos, as fan, 181
Scarlatti, Domenico, 99–100
Schifrin, Lalo, *Concierto de la amistad*, 232
Schleswig-Holstein Festival, 214
Schlote, Joachim, 122, 271
Scrantonian (newspaper), 88–89
Seattle Times, 238
Second (Spanish) Republic, 37–38
Seeger, Peter, 87
Segovia, Andrés, xi, xii, 77, 91, 211–12; guitar teaching, 6; hand position, 196, 203; in later years, 199, 226; Moreno Torroba and, 55; repertoire choices, 55, 57, 89, 216–18, 240; Celedonio Romero and, 33, 41, 46, 57, 67, 99, 107, 123; tone production, 201; works commissioned for, 223–25

345

INDEX

Segura y Saénz, Pedro, 43
Seneca the Younger, 217
Serenata al alba del día (Rodrigo), xiv
Serenata española (Malats), 39
Serrano, Juan, 200
sevillanas, 6
Seville, Spain, 57, 59, 61–70, 135; World Expo in, 145
Seville Royal Symphony Orchestra, 258
Shadows and Light: Joaquín Rodrigo at 90 (documentary film), xiv
Shanghai Daily, 170
Shanghai Symphony, 184
Shearing, George, 233
Sherwood Auditorium (La Jolla), 185–86
Shirer, Greg (son-in-law of Pepe), 213, 264
Shirer, Tina (daughter of Pepe), 264
Shubin, Cindy, 207
Siete canciones populares españolas (Falla), 238
Silvestri, Alan, 182
Simón Bolívar Youth Orchestra, 184
Sinatra, Frank, as friend, 181
Sinatra, Nancy, 104
Singapore Symphony Orchestra, 184
Sketches of Spain (Davis), 91–92
Slate, Pepi (daughter of Angel), 267
Slonimsky, Nicolas, 89
"Sloop John B," 182
soccer, 4, 32, 56, 118, 261, 267
sombrero de tres picos, El (Falla), 238
Somewhere in Time (film), 182
Sonata-Fantasía (Moreno Torroba), 228
Sonata-Fantasía II (Moreno Torroba), 228
Sonatina (Moreno Torroba), 3, 34, 162, 228, 257
Sonatina trianera (Moreno Torroba), 228
Sones en la Giralda (Sounds in the Giralda) (Rodrigo), 237–38
Song of Myself (Whitman), 2
Sopranos, The (TV series), 96
Sor, Fernando, 169–70, 171, 207, 240, 246–47; *Fantasía* in D Minor for guitar solo, 241, 257
Sotheby's, 241
South China Morning Post, 108
Southern Methodist University, 212
Spain: birth of Romero Quartet members in, 44, 52–53; Celedonio guitar performances in, 34–35, 38–39, 42, 50–52, 56–57, 59–63; Civil War (*see* Spanish Civil War); images of, in United States, 77–78; military service of Romeros, 36–38, 40, 41, 44–48, 50; Romero family leaves for the U.S., 67–75; Romero family origins in, 16–20; Romeros return from Cuba to, 27–57; Second Republic, 37–38. *See also* Málaga, Spain
Spanish-American War (1898), 21–22
"Spanish Caravan" (The Doors), 90
Spanish Civil War, xi, 41–48; Falange (Phalanx), 45–46, 48–50, 51, 52, 55, 61; Gran Olvido (Great Forgetting), 54, 223; military service of Romero brothers, 41, 44–48, 133; postwar period, 48–52, 54, 223
Spanish flu, 26
Spanish Guitar Music (Contemporary Records), 97–98
Spellman, Cardinal Francis, 118–19
Spivey Hall (Atlanta), 241
Stamos, John, 182
Stern, Isaac, 181
Stern magazine, 221
Stevenson, Robert, 6
Stewart, Patrick, as fan, 181
St. Louis Post-Dispatch, 196, 269
Stoddard, Farrington (Fe) and Evelyn (Evie): financial difficulties, 92–93; guitar studies, 60, 95; sponsorship of Romero family, 60–61, 67–70, 74–75, 78–82
"Stormy Weather" (arr. Celin Romero), 85–86, 182
Stover, Richard, 240
Suite andaluza (Celedonio Romero), 234, 235
Suite madrileña no. 1 (Celedonio Romero), 236
Sullivan, Ed, 6, 104–5
Sullivan, Father, 84
Sulloway, Frank J., 188–89
Sur (Málaga newspaper), 31, 79, 81, 125
Swed, Mark, 232

Tao Te Ching (Lao-tzu), 203–4
Tárrega, Francisco, 33, 165, 166, 171, 235; *Capricho árabe*, 195–96; *Fantasy on Themes from [Emilio] Arrieta's "Marina,"* 242; *Recuerdos de la Alhambra*, 34, 96, 111, 119, 123, 195–96

INDEX

Tchaikovsky Conservatory (Moscow), 214
Teatro Campos Eliseos (Bilbao), 50
Teatro de la Maestranza de Sevilla, 230
Teatro Lope de Vega (Seville), 35, 66
Teatro Miguel de Cervantes (Málaga), 14, 31, 34–35, 38, 42, 102
Teatro Real (Madrid), 226
Tebaldi, Renata, 242
Tedesco, Tommy, 95
Telemann, Georg Philipp, arrangements of, 123, 237
Téllez, Gabriel (Tirso de Molina), 65, 154
Temple University Music Festival (Philadelphia), 107–8
Tennant, Scott, 212, 213
Tenorio, Juan, 65
Ternero, Antonio, 29
tertulias, 31, 160, 165
Texas Mental Health Association, benefit for, 244–45
Thibodeau, Ralph, 88
Thomas Aquinas, Saint, 272
Thornton Chamber Orchestra (University of Southern California), 184
Time magazine, 101–2
Titanic (ship), 23, 27
Tito, Josip Broz, 119, *143*
Tjeknavorian, Loris, *Zareh*, 232
Tolstoy, Leo, 258–59
Tomatito (José Fernández Torres), 31
Tonada concertante (Moreno Torroba), 222–23, 226
"Tonadilla" (Rodrigo), 261
Tonight Show, The (TV program), 6, 105
Tornsäufer, Claudia (partner of Celin), 4, 164, 262–63, 266
Toronto Star, 269
Torroba. *See* Moreno Torroba, Federico
Touch of Class, A (Telarc), 267
Town Hall (New York City), 100, 179
Traphagen, Drake, 264
traviata, La (Verdi), 242
Tríptico (Muñoz Molleda), 229
Troubadour Music (Gould), 231–32
trovatore, Il (Verdi), 242
Tucson Citizen, 169
Turina, Joaquín, 35, 214; *La oración del torero* (The toreador's prayer), 185–86, 238

typhus, 49, 236

Unión Cristiana de Jóvenes (Málaga), 34
University of Arizona, 259–60
University of California, Los Angeles (UCLA), 186
University of California, Riverside (UCR), 6, 188
University of California, San Diego (UCSD), 6, 193, 213–14, 216–17
University of Granada, 265
University of Kansas, 6
University of Nebraska, Lincoln, 232
University of Nebraska, Omaha, 214
University of North Carolina School of the Performing Arts, 5–6
University of Puerto Rico, 232
University of San Diego, 213
University of Southern California (USC), 184, 193–95, 212; Thornton School of Music, 213
University of Victoria (British Columbia), 96, 157, 213
U.S. Army, 80, 83–86
U.S. Foreign Service (USFS), 63

Valencia, Spain, 64
Vélez, Alberto, 200
verbena de la paloma, La (Bréton), 238
Veterans' Auditorium (San Francisco), 98–99
Victoria (BC) Daily Times, 114
vida breve, La (Falla), 238
Vida Gráfica (newspaper), 34
Villa-Lobos, Heitor, 99; Étude no. 1 in E Minor, 110; *Introduction to the Chôros*, 243
Virgen de la Victoria, 15
Visée, Robert de, 99
visualization: in concentration process, 211; as guide for playing guitar, 209–10
Vivaldi, Antonio, 55; Concerto in A Minor, 246; Concerto in D Major, 185, 237, 260; Concerto in G Major, 267–68; *L'estro harmonico*, op. 3, 246; Lute Concerto in D Major, 260; Quartet in A Major, 111
Vives, Amadeo, *Bohemios*, 238

Waikiki Shell (HI), 110

INDEX

Wallace, Dean, 99
Ward, Robert, 214
Washington Post, 119
Wayne, Chuck, 87
Weizäcker, Richard von, 263
West Los Angeles Symphony Orchestra, 186
West Side Story (musical), 238
Wichita Eagle, 237
Williams, John (guitarist), 182, 240
World Expo (Seville, 1992), xiv
World of Flamenco (Mercury), 156, 244–45
World Telegram and Sun, 100
World War I, 26, 29
Wyman, Jane, 96

Yale University, 212
Yepes, Narciso, 54, 229
York, Andrew, 213
Young Guns II (film), 182
Young Musicians Federation competition, 212
Youth Front (Frente de Juventudes), 49, 61, 62

Zabaleta, Nicanor, 238
Zarate Guitar Quartet, 217–18
Zareh (Tjeknavorian), 232
zarzuela (Spanish operetta), 30, 223–24, 238–39
Zearott, Michael, *Concierto Mariachi*, 232–33

WALTER AARON CLARK is Distinguished Professor of Musicology and the founder/director of the Center for Iberian and Latin American Music at the University of California, Riverside. His books include *Isaac Albéniz: Portrait of a Romantic* and *Enrique Granados: Poet of the Piano*. In 2016, King Felipe VI of Spain made him a Knight Commander of the Order of Isabel the Catholic.

MUSIC IN AMERICAN LIFE

Only a Miner: Studies in Recorded Coal-Mining Songs   *Archie Green*
Great Day Coming: Folk Music and the American Left   *R. Serge Denisoff*
John Philip Sousa: A Descriptive Catalog of His Works   *Paul E. Bierley*
The Hell-Bound Train: A Cowboy Songbook   *Glenn Ohrlin*
Oh, Didn't He Ramble: The Life Story of Lee Collins, as Told to Mary Collins
   Edited by Frank J. Gillis and John W. Miner
American Labor Songs of the Nineteenth Century   *Philip S. Foner*
Stars of Country Music: Uncle Dave Macon to Johnny Rodriguez
   Edited by Bill C. Malone and Judith McCulloh
Git Along, Little Dogies: Songs and Songmakers of the American West   *John I. White*
A Texas-Mexican *Cancionero*: Folksongs of the Lower Border   *Américo Paredes*
San Antonio Rose: The Life and Music of Bob Wills   *Charles R. Townsend*
Early Downhome Blues: A Musical and Cultural Analysis   *Jeff Todd Titon*
An Ives Celebration: Papers and Panels of the Charles Ives Centennial Festival-
   Conference   *Edited by H. Wiley Hitchcock and Vivian Perlis*
Sinful Tunes and Spirituals: Black Folk Music to the Civil War   *Dena J. Epstein*
Joe Scott, the Woodsman-Songmaker   *Edward D. Ives*
Jimmie Rodgers: The Life and Times of America's Blue Yodeler   *Nolan Porterfield*
Early American Music Engraving and Printing: A History of Music Publishing
   in America from 1787 to 1825, with Commentary on Earlier and Later
   Practices   *Richard J. Wolfe*
Sing a Sad Song: The Life of Hank Williams   *Roger M. Williams*
Long Steel Rail: The Railroad in American Folksong   *Norm Cohen*
Resources of American Music History: A Directory of Source Materials from Colonial
   Times to World War II   *D. W. Krummel, Jean Geil, Doris J. Dyen, and Deane L. Root*
Tenement Songs: The Popular Music of the Jewish Immigrants   *Mark Slobin*
Ozark Folksongs   *Vance Randolph; edited and abridged by Norm Cohen*
Oscar Sonneck and American Music   *Edited by William Lichtenwanger*
Bluegrass Breakdown: The Making of the Old Southern Sound   *Robert Cantwell*
Bluegrass: A History   *Neil V. Rosenberg*
Music at the White House: A History of the American Spirit   *Elise K. Kirk*
Red River Blues: The Blues Tradition in the Southeast   *Bruce Bastin*
Good Friends and Bad Enemies: Robert Winslow Gordon and the Study of American
   Folksong   *Debora Kodish*
Fiddlin' Georgia Crazy: Fiddlin' John Carson, His Real World, and the World of His
   Songs   *Gene Wiggins*
America's Music: From the Pilgrims to the Present (rev. 3d ed.)   *Gilbert Chase*
Secular Music in Colonial Annapolis: The Tuesday Club, 1745–56   *John Barry Talley*
Bibliographical Handbook of American Music   *D. W. Krummel*
Goin' to Kansas City   *Nathan W. Pearson Jr.*
"Susanna," "Jeanie," and "The Old Folks at Home": The Songs of Stephen C. Foster
   from His Time to Ours (2d ed.)   *William W. Austin*
Songprints: The Musical Experience of Five Shoshone Women   *Judith Vander*

"Happy in the Service of the Lord": Afro-American Gospel Quartets in Memphis
    Kip Lornell
Paul Hindemith in the United States   *Luther Noss*
"My Song Is My Weapon": People's Songs, American Communism, and the Politics
    of Culture, 1930–50   *Robbie Lieberman*
Chosen Voices: The Story of the American Cantorate   *Mark Slobin*
Theodore Thomas: America's Conductor and Builder of Orchestras, 1835–1905
    Ezra Schabas
"The Whorehouse Bells Were Ringing" and Other Songs Cowboys Sing
    Collected and Edited by Guy Logsdon
Crazeology: The Autobiography of a Chicago Jazzman   *Bud Freeman,
    as Told to Robert Wolf*
Discoursing Sweet Music: Brass Bands and Community Life in Turn-of-the-Century
    Pennsylvania   *Kenneth Kreitner*
Mormonism and Music: A History   *Michael Hicks*
Voices of the Jazz Age: Profiles of Eight Vintage Jazzmen   *Chip Deffaa*
Pickin' on Peachtree: A History of Country Music in Atlanta, Georgia
    Wayne W. Daniel
Bitter Music: Collected Journals, Essays, Introductions, and Librettos   *Harry Partch;
    edited by Thomas McGeary*
Ethnic Music on Records: A Discography of Ethnic Recordings Produced in the United
    States, 1893 to 1942   *Richard K. Spottswood*
Downhome Blues Lyrics: An Anthology from the Post–World War II Era
    Jeff Todd Titon
Ellington: The Early Years   *Mark Tucker*
Chicago Soul   *Robert Pruter*
That Half-Barbaric Twang: The Banjo in American Popular Culture   *Karen Linn*
Hot Man: The Life of Art Hodes   *Art Hodes and Chadwick Hansen*
The Erotic Muse: American Bawdy Songs (2d ed.)   *Ed Cray*
Barrio Rhythm: Mexican American Music in Los Angeles   *Steven Loza*
The Creation of Jazz: Music, Race, and Culture in Urban America   *Burton W. Peretti*
Charles Martin Loeffler: A Life Apart in Music   *Ellen Knight*
Club Date Musicians: Playing the New York Party Circuit   *Bruce A. MacLeod*
Opera on the Road: Traveling Opera Troupes in the United States, 1825–
    60   *Katherine K. Preston*
The Stonemans: An Appalachian Family and the Music That Shaped Their Lives
    Ivan M. Tribe
Transforming Tradition: Folk Music Revivals Examined   *Edited by Neil V. Rosenberg*
The Crooked Stovepipe: Athapaskan Fiddle Music and Square Dancing in Northeast
    Alaska and Northwest Canada   *Craig Mishler*
Traveling the High Way Home: Ralph Stanley and the World of Traditional Bluegrass
    Music   *John Wright*
Carl Ruggles: Composer, Painter, and Storyteller   *Marilyn Ziffrin*
Never without a Song: The Years and Songs of Jennie Devlin, 1865–1952
    Katharine D. Newman

The Hank Snow Story   *Hank Snow, with Jack Ownbey and Bob Burris*
Milton Brown and the Founding of Western Swing   *Cary Ginell,
   with special assistance from Roy Lee Brown*
Santiago de Murcia's "Códice Saldívar No. 4": A Treasury of Secular Guitar Music from
   Baroque Mexico   *Craig H. Russell*
The Sound of the Dove: Singing in Appalachian Primitive Baptist Churches
   Beverly Bush Patterson
Heartland Excursions: Ethnomusicological Reflections on Schools of Music
   Bruno Nettl
Doowop: The Chicago Scene   *Robert Pruter*
Blue Rhythms: Six Lives in Rhythm and Blues   *Chip Deffaa*
Shoshone Ghost Dance Religion: Poetry Songs and Great Basin Context
   Judith Vander
Go Cat Go! Rockabilly Music and Its Makers   *Craig Morrison*
'Twas Only an Irishman's Dream: The Image of Ireland and the Irish in American
   Popular Song Lyrics, 1800–1920   *William H. A. Williams*
Democracy at the Opera: Music, Theater, and Culture in New York City,
   1815–60   *Karen Ahlquist*
Fred Waring and the Pennsylvanians   *Virginia Waring*
Woody, Cisco, and Me: Seamen Three in the Merchant Marine   *Jim Longhi*
Behind the Burnt Cork Mask: Early Blackface Minstrelsy and Antebellum American
   Popular Culture   *William J. Mahar*
Going to Cincinnati: A History of the Blues in the Queen City   *Steven C. Tracy*
Pistol Packin' Mama: Aunt Molly Jackson and the Politics of Folksong   *Shelly Romalis*
Sixties Rock: Garage, Psychedelic, and Other Satisfactions   *Michael Hicks*
The Late Great Johnny Ace and the Transition from R&B to Rock 'n' Roll
   James M. Salem
Tito Puente and the Making of Latin Music   *Steven Loza*
Juilliard: A History   *Andrea Olmstead*
Understanding Charles Seeger, Pioneer in American Musicology
   Edited by Bell Yung and Helen Rees
Mountains of Music: West Virginia Traditional Music from *Goldenseal*
   Edited by John Lilly
Alice Tully: An Intimate Portrait   *Albert Fuller*
A Blues Life   *Henry Townsend, as told to Bill Greensmith*
Long Steel Rail: The Railroad in American Folksong (2d ed.)   *Norm Cohen*
The Golden Age of Gospel   *Text by Horace Clarence Boyer;
   photography by Lloyd Yearwood*
Aaron Copland: The Life and Work of an Uncommon Man   *Howard Pollack*
Louis Moreau Gottschalk   *S. Frederick Starr*
Race, Rock, and Elvis   *Michael T. Bertrand*
Theremin: Ether Music and Espionage   *Albert Glinsky*
Poetry and Violence: The Ballad Tradition of Mexico's Costa Chica   *John H. McDowell*
The Bill Monroe Reader   *Edited by Tom Ewing*
Music in Lubavitcher Life   *Ellen Koskoff*

Zarzuela: Spanish Operetta, American Stage   *Janet L. Sturman*
Bluegrass Odyssey: A Documentary in Pictures and Words, 1966–86
    Carl Fleischhauer and Neil V. Rosenberg
That Old-Time Rock & Roll: A Chronicle of an Era, 1954–63   *Richard Aquila*
Labor's Troubadour   *Joe Glazer*
American Opera   *Elise K. Kirk*
Don't Get above Your Raisin': Country Music and the Southern Working Class
    Bill C. Malone
John Alden Carpenter: A Chicago Composer   *Howard Pollack*
Heartbeat of the People: Music and Dance of the Northern Pow-wow   *Tara Browner*
My Lord, What a Morning: An Autobiography   *Marian Anderson*
Marian Anderson: A Singer's Journey   *Allan Keiler*
Charles Ives Remembered: An Oral History   *Vivian Perlis*
Henry Cowell, Bohemian   *Michael Hicks*
Rap Music and Street Consciousness   *Cheryl L. Keyes*
Louis Prima   *Garry Boulard*
Marian McPartland's Jazz World: All in Good Time   *Marian McPartland*
Robert Johnson: Lost and Found   *Barry Lee Pearson and Bill McCulloch*
Bound for America: Three British Composers   *Nicholas Temperley*
Lost Sounds: Blacks and the Birth of the Recording Industry, 1890–1919   *Tim Brooks*
Burn, Baby! BURN! The Autobiography of Magnificent Montague
    Magnificent Montague with Bob Baker
Way Up North in Dixie: A Black Family's Claim to the Confederate Anthem
    Howard L. Sacks and Judith Rose Sacks
The Bluegrass Reader   *Edited by Thomas Goldsmith*
Colin McPhee: Composer in Two Worlds   *Carol J. Oja*
Robert Johnson, Mythmaking, and Contemporary American Culture
    Patricia R. Schroeder
Composing a World: Lou Harrison, Musical Wayfarer   *Leta E. Miller*
    and Fredric Lieberman
Fritz Reiner, Maestro and Martinet   *Kenneth Morgan*
That Toddlin' Town: Chicago's White Dance Bands and Orchestras,
    1900–1950   *Charles A. Sengstock Jr.*
Dewey and Elvis: The Life and Times of a Rock 'n' Roll Deejay   *Louis Cantor*
Come Hither to Go Yonder: Playing Bluegrass with Bill Monroe   *Bob Black*
Chicago Blues: Portraits and Stories   *David Whiteis*
The Incredible Band of John Philip Sousa   *Paul E. Bierley*
"Maximum Clarity" and Other Writings on Music   *Ben Johnston,*
    edited by Bob Gilmore
Staging Tradition: John Lair and Sarah Gertrude Knott   *Michael Ann Williams*
Homegrown Music: Discovering Bluegrass   *Stephanie P. Ledgin*
Tales of a Theatrical Guru   *Danny Newman*
The Music of Bill Monroe   *Neil V. Rosenberg and Charles K. Wolfe*
Pressing On: The Roni Stoneman Story   *Roni Stoneman, as told to Ellen Wright*

Together Let Us Sweetly Live   *Jonathan C. David, with photographs by Richard Holloway*
Live Fast, Love Hard: The Faron Young Story   *Diane Diekman*
Air Castle of the South: WSM Radio and the Making of Music City   *Craig P. Havighurst*
Traveling Home: Sacred Harp Singing and American Pluralism   *Kiri Miller*
Where Did Our Love Go? The Rise and Fall of the Motown Sound   *Nelson George*
Lonesome Cowgirls and Honky-Tonk Angels: The Women of Barn Dance Radio   *Kristine M. McCusker*
California Polyphony: Ethnic Voices, Musical Crossroads   *Mina Yang*
The Never-Ending Revival: Rounder Records and the Folk Alliance   *Michael F. Scully*
Sing It Pretty: A Memoir   *Bess Lomax Hawes*
Working Girl Blues: The Life and Music of Hazel Dickens   *Hazel Dickens and Bill C. Malone*
Charles Ives Reconsidered   *Gayle Sherwood Magee*
The Hayloft Gang: The Story of the National Barn Dance   *Edited by Chad Berry*
Country Music Humorists and Comedians   *Loyal Jones*
Record Makers and Breakers: Voices of the Independent Rock 'n' Roll Pioneers   *John Broven*
Music of the First Nations: Tradition and Innovation in Native North America   *Edited by Tara Browner*
Cafe Society: The Wrong Place for the Right People   *Barney Josephson, with Terry Trilling-Josephson*
George Gershwin: An Intimate Portrait   *Walter Rimler*
Life Flows On in Endless Song: Folk Songs and American History   *Robert V. Wells*
I Feel a Song Coming On: The Life of Jimmy McHugh   *Alyn Shipton*
King of the Queen City: The Story of King Records   *Jon Hartley Fox*
Long Lost Blues: Popular Blues in America, 1850–1920   *Peter C. Muir*
Hard Luck Blues: Roots Music Photographs from the Great Depression   *Rich Remsberg*
Restless Giant: The Life and Times of Jean Aberbach and Hill and Range Songs   *Bar Biszick-Lockwood*
Champagne Charlie and Pretty Jemima: Variety Theater in the Nineteenth Century   *Gillian M. Rodger*
Sacred Steel: Inside an African American Steel Guitar Tradition   *Robert L. Stone*
Gone to the Country: The New Lost City Ramblers and the Folk Music Revival   *Ray Allen*
The Makers of the Sacred Harp   *David Warren Steel with Richard H. Hulan*
Woody Guthrie, American Radical   *Will Kaufman*
George Szell: A Life of Music   *Michael Charry*
Bean Blossom: The Brown County Jamboree and Bill Monroe's Bluegrass Festivals   *Thomas A. Adler*
Crowe on the Banjo: The Music Life of J. D. Crowe   *Marty Godbey*
Twentieth Century Drifter: The Life of Marty Robbins   *Diane Diekman*
Henry Mancini: Reinventing Film Music   *John Caps*

The Beautiful Music All Around Us: Field Recordings and the American
    Experience   *Stephen Wade*
Then Sings My Soul: The Culture of Southern Gospel Music   *Douglas Harrison*
The Accordion in the Americas: Klezmer, Polka, Tango, Zydeco, and More!
    Edited by Helena Simonett
Bluegrass Bluesman: A Memoir   *Josh Graves, edited by Fred Bartenstein*
One Woman in a Hundred: Edna Phillips and the Philadelphia Orchestra
    Mary Sue Welsh
The Great Orchestrator: Arthur Judson and American Arts Management
    James M. Doering
Charles Ives in the Mirror: American Histories of an Iconic Composer   *David C. Paul*
Southern Soul-Blues   *David Whiteis*
Sweet Air: Modernism, Regionalism, and American Popular Song
    Edward P. Comentale
Pretty Good for a Girl: Women in Bluegrass   *Murphy Hicks Henry*
Sweet Dreams: The World of Patsy Cline   *Warren R. Hofstra*
William Sidney Mount and the Creolization of American Culture
    Christopher J. Smith
Bird: The Life and Music of Charlie Parker   *Chuck Haddix*
Making the March King: John Philip Sousa's Washington Years, 1854–1893
    Patrick Warfield
In It for the Long Run   *Jim Rooney*
Pioneers of the Blues Revival   *Steve Cushing*
Roots of the Revival: American and British Folk Music in the 1950s   *Ronald D. Cohen
    and Rachel Clare Donaldson*
Blues All Day Long: The Jimmy Rogers Story   *Wayne Everett Goins*
Yankee Twang: Country and Western Music in New England   *Clifford R. Murphy*
The Music of the Stanley Brothers   *Gary B. Reid*
Hawaiian Music in Motion: Mariners, Missionaries, and Minstrels   *James Revell Carr*
Sounds of the New Deal: The Federal Music Project in the West   *Peter Gough*
The Mormon Tabernacle Choir: A Biography   *Michael Hicks*
The Man That Got Away: The Life and Songs of Harold Arlen   *Walter Rimler*
A City Called Heaven: Chicago and the Birth of Gospel Music   *Robert M. Marovich*
Blues Unlimited: Essential Interviews from the Original Blues Magazine
    Edited by Bill Greensmith, Mike Rowe, and Mark Camarigg
Hoedowns, Reels, and Frolics: Roots and Branches of Southern Appalachian
    Dance   *Phil Jamison*
Fannie Bloomfield-Zeisler: The Life and Times of a Piano Virtuoso
    Beth Abelson Macleod
Cybersonic Arts: Adventures in American New Music   *Gordon Mumma,
    edited with commentary by Michelle Fillion*
The Magic of Beverly Sills   *Nancy Guy*
Waiting for Buddy Guy   *Alan Harper*
Harry T. Burleigh: From the Spiritual to the Harlem Renaissance   *Jean E. Snyder*
Music in the Age of Anxiety: American Music in the Fifties   *James Wierzbicki*

Jazzing: New York City's Unseen Scene   *Thomas H. Greenland*
A Cole Porter Companion   *Edited by Don M. Randel, Matthew Shaftel,
   and Susan Forscher Weiss*
Foggy Mountain Troubadour: The Life and Music of Curly Seckler   *Penny Parsons*
Blue Rhythm Fantasy: Big Band Jazz Arranging in the Swing Era   *John Wriggle*
Bill Clifton: America's Bluegrass Ambassador to the World   *Bill C. Malone*
Chinatown Opera Theater in North America   *Nancy Yunhwa Rao*
The Elocutionists: Women, Music, and the Spoken Word   *Marian Wilson Kimber*
May Irwin: Singing, Shouting, and the Shadow of Minstrelsy   *Sharon Ammen*
Peggy Seeger: A Life of Music, Love, and Politics   *Jean R. Freedman*
Charles Ives's *Concord*: Essays after a Sonata   *Kyle Gann*
Don't Give Your Heart to a Rambler: My Life with Jimmy Martin, the King of
   Bluegrass   *Barbara Martin Stephens*
Libby Larsen: Composing an American Life   *Denise Von Glahn*
George Szell's Reign: Behind the Scenes with the Cleveland Orchestra
   Marcia Hansen Kraus
Just One of the Boys: Female-to-Male Cross-Dressing on the American Variety
   Stage   *Gillian M. Rodger*
Spirituals and the Birth of a Black Entertainment Industry   *Sandra Jean Graham*
Right to the Juke Joint: A Personal History of American Music   *Patrick B. Mullen*
Bluegrass Generation: A Memoir   *Neil V. Rosenberg*
Pioneers of the Blues Revival, Expanded Second Edition   *Steve Cushing*
Banjo Roots and Branches   *Edited by Robert Winans*
Bill Monroe: The Life and Music of the Blue Grass Man   *Tom Ewing*
Dixie Dewdrop: The Uncle Dave Macon Story   *Michael D. Doubler*
Los Romeros: Royal Family of the Spanish Guitar   *Walter Aaron Clark*

The University of Illinois Press
is a founding member of the
Association of American University Presses.

———————————————————

Composed in 10.5/14.5 Chaparral Pro
with Cyclone Layers display
by Lisa Connery
at the University of Illinois Press
Cover designed by Dustin J. Hubbart
Cover illustration: During the 2011–12 concert season, Angel (center) occasionally rejoined Los Romeros (from left to right, Lito, Celino, Pepe, Celin) to form a quintet. The Romero Quartet is still going strong, as is Angel. (Courtesy of Los Romeros)
Manufactured by Sheridan Books, Inc.

University of Illinois Press
1325 South Oak Street
Champaign, IL 61820-6903
www.press.uillinois.edu